Day by Day With God's

Enduring Words

By David Guzik

with Ruth Gordon

*The grass withers, the flower fades,
but the word of our God stands forever.*
Isaiah 40:8

Enduring Words

Copyright ©2020 by David Guzik

Edited and Compiled by Ruth Gordon

Printed in the United States of America or in the United Kingdom

Hardcover Print Edition ISBN: 978-1-939466-59-4

Enduring Word

5662 Calle Real #184

Goleta, CA 93117

Electronic Mail: ewm@enduringword.com

Internet Home Page: www.enduringword.com

All rights reserved. No portion of this book may be reproduced in any form (except for quotations in reviews) without the written permission of the publisher.

Scripture references, unless noted, are from the New King James Version of the Bible, copyright ©1979, 1980, 1982, Thomas Nelson, Inc., Publisher.

Editor's Preface

This 365-Day Devotional is a culmination of 25 years of Pastor David Guzik's Weekly Inspiration by E-Mail. This format is unique in that, rather than a verse and a brief anecdote, Guzik intends to build up the Church of Jesus Christ by teaching the Word, to increase Christian faithfulness, and to encourage Christians and empower them for service.

Guzik believes "that all people are sinners by nature and choice and therefore, are under condemnation; that God regenerates by the Holy Spirit those who repent of their sins and confess Jesus Christ as Lord; that Jesus Christ baptizes the seeking believer with the Holy Spirit." (Excerpt from Pastor Guzik's Statement of Faith)

During the editing process, I was perpetually challenged, inspired, encouraged, exhorted, repentant, as well as filled with joy, hope, and strength. Our prayer is that in these pages, through the transformative power of God's enduring words, that you will be uplifted, instructed, and better prepared to face any difficulties that lay ahead in your life.

The scope of this devotional includes a vast list of subjects ranging from Adam to Worship. There is a Topical Index in the back that can be used instead of the Daily Calendar format. At the end of each day's devotion, there is a positive takeaway or call-to-action to focus on and encourage you throughout the day.

Get ready for a daily exploration into the profound sanctuary of the Word of God. Prepare yourself to better know Him, and the power of His love.

Ruth Gordon, Editor

rjoygordon@gmail.com

January 1

Themes for a New Year

I am the vine, you are the branches. He who abides in Me, and I in him, bears much fruit; for without Me you can do nothing. (John 15:5)

I can do all things through Christ who strengthens me. (Philippians 4:13)

For many of us, the New Year is a strategic time – a time when we are more willing than ever to change our outlook and approach to life.

Why not use the beginning of a new year to re-establish a proper focus in your Christian life? I can't think of two more important principles to keep in mind than John 15:5 and Philippians 4:13. Let's consider them "bookends" for this year and all our life.

Jesus said, **without Me you can do nothing**. Jesus is the vine, and we are the branches. He is our source of life and nourishment. What other things do you gain strength from? Here, the secret is abiding: a close, intimate walk with Jesus; living with Him. Such a walk is forever built on the basics of the Christian life: prayer, Bible reading and study, fellowship with believers, and service to God's church and a needy world. When we do this, we naturally bear **much fruit** for God.

Many sense they have borne little fruit for God – but this comes naturally as we abide. This can be a year when you bear **much fruit** for God – leading others to Jesus Christ; serving God's people in new capacities; seeing the work of God's kingdom grow.

It is an important principle: **without Me you can do nothing**. But the truth of Philippians 4:13 is just as important to remember for the New Year: **I can do all things through Christ who strengthens me**. This is the other side of the coin of John 15:5 – without Jesus, we can do nothing; with Him, we can do all things. **All things** is pretty big – yet the promise of Philippians 4:13 is even more powerful than we might first think.

If we look at the context of Philippians 4:13 we understand the power of some of the **all things** Paul could do through the strength of Jesus. It was the strength to be abased, to be hungry, to suffer need, to be in distress – and through it all to have a joy and contentment that rises above every difficult circumstance. Through Jesus, Paul had the strength to abound, to be full, and to accomplish big things.

Your peace and joy throughout the past year were directly tied to the proportion that you lived within these two principles. When you find people thoroughly dependent on Jesus and receiving His strength for the trials and work of life, you will find them full of peace and joy.

No matter how great last year was in these areas, there is no reason why it can't be even better as you depend more and more on these two great themes for the coming New Year.

January 2

All Things New

Then He who sat on the throne said, "Behold, I make all things new." And He said to me, "Write, for these words are true and faithful." (Revelation 21:5)

The start of a new year is a good time to pause and think about what new things God may have for us. I'm firmly convinced that God likes doing new things, but not because He is easily bored. Many today need a constant rush new things or they can't pay attention, but God isn't like that.

The triumphant declaration **Behold, I make all things new** comes at the *end* of the Book of Revelation. It comes after God's people have been gathered to heaven, after the rise and fall of the Antichrist, after Armageddon, after the glorious return of Jesus Christ, and after the judgment of the nations. After all that, *God is not finished making things new.*

New things will be part of heaven. All through time, we see that God loves new things. In Leviticus God asked for a new grain offering. In Numbers God gave Israel new wine and new grain. In the Psalms God speaks of a new song. Isaiah God declares new things for His people. In Jeremiah God announced a new covenant. In Lamentations God's mercies are new every morning. In Ezekiel God gives believers a new heart and a new spirit. In Matthew Jesus looks for new wineskins, and in John Jesus gave a new commandment. 2 Corinthians says that God makes His people a new creation and that He makes things new, and Revelation promises a New Jerusalem. God even made sure Jesus was buried in a new tomb.

So, hear God say it to you today: **Behold, I make all things new.** Something about the new year speaks to our God-given love of new things. It is true that we can take that love for new things and make it an idol; but the basic desire a new thing is in us because we are made in the image of God.

It's worth it to be happy and excited about a new year, to receive it with faith, happiness, and celebration. Think of what God wants to make new this year. In this new year, God has new mercies and new grace for you. He has new blessings, new opportunities, and new victories for you over stubborn sins. God has new faith to replace your old fears, and new life for many who will repent and believe upon Jesus Christ this year.

I don't doubt that God also has new challenges and new responsibilities for you this year – but whatever new that comes to you from the hand of Jesus will be a blessing.

Jesus is an expert at doing new things. What He did on the cross, in dying for our rescue, in being buried, and in rising again from the dead was all completely new.

Be blessed as the year begins and let Jesus the carpenter build some new things in your life in the coming months.

January 3

Commitment Declared and Enjoyed

With my lips I have declared all the judgments of Your mouth. I have rejoiced in the way of Your testimonies, as much as in all riches. I will meditate on Your precepts, and contemplate Your ways. I will delight myself in Your statutes; I will not forget Your word. (Psalm 119:13-16)

Psalm 119 is like a love song – a love song to God and to His written Word, the clearest way He reveals Himself to humanity.

Here, the psalmist said, **with my lips I have declared all the judgments of Your mouth.** He understood the importance of not only silently reading or hearing the Word of God but also in saying it. To declare God's Word (**all the judgments of Your mouth**) with his lips was another part of his relationship with and love for God.

We may confidently conclude that there is not enough – never enough – of this among the people of God. God's people should have His Word not only in their minds and hearts but also on their lips. Saying it is powerful and must not be neglected. When we talk about God's Word, we glorify God, we make others stronger in faith, and we make ourselves better.

The psalmist was so taken by the words of God that he wrote, **I have rejoiced in the way of Your testimonies, as much as in all riches**. He knew the true value of God's Word; it gave him as much joy as all riches might.

It could be reasonably asked of every Christian: "For what amount would you deny yourself to ever hear or read God's Word again?" It is to be feared that like Esau, many would sell this birthright treasure for the equivalent of a bowl of stew.

This treasuring of the Bible led him to proclaim the course of his life: **I will meditate…and contemplate…. I will delight…I will not forget Your word**. The greatness of God's Word led the psalmist to a great resolution of life. His life would be filled with God's Word, in his mind (**meditate** and **contemplate**), heart (**delight**), and habits (**not forget**).

This giving of the fullness of life to God's Word – in mind, heart, and habits – is a good description of what the psalmist meant by *taking heed* in Psalm 119:9. This will see the young man cleanse his way and enjoy the fullness of such a God-honoring life.

In it all, he would find great happiness – saying, **I will delight myself in Your statutes**. According to Adam Clarke, the sense of this ancient Hebrew phrase is strong, meaning "I will skip about and jump for joy."

We can almost hear a challenge from the psalmist: "You live your compromising, impure life that thinks it knows pleasure and satisfaction; I will cleanse my way and give the fullness of my life to God and His Word, and we will see who will be more blessed, happier, and more filled with life."

Take the challenge and live the more blessed and happy life.

January 4

Beginning with Truth

Stand therefore, having girded your waist with truth, having put on the breastplate of righteousness, and having shod your feet with the preparation of the gospel of peace. (Ephesians 6:14-15)

This great section of Paul's letter to the Ephesians is meant to equip and help the Christian win in the spiritual battles common to the disciples of Jesus Christ. The idea is that if we take the spiritual armor that God gives to us, we can stand strong in our spiritual battles.

That is why verse 14 begins with the phrase, **stand therefore**. By the Holy Spirit's inspiration, Paul knew that we could only stand when we are equipped with the spiritual protection (armor) God gives us in Jesus Christ. Each part of this symbolic armor matches a specific aspect of the Christian life that enables us to stand against spiritual attacks.

Remember that Paul wrote this while he was in the custody of Roman soldiers. It was easy for him to look at the equipment that his guards wore and connect it to how God has equipped the believer. As he describes this spiritual armor, the order in which the pieces of armor are described is the order in which the soldier would have to put them on.

He began with the idea of a belt: **Having girded your waist with truth**. Truth is represented as a **belt** that protected the mid-section and was also used to gather up the garments so the soldier could fight effectively.

Strictly speaking, the belt is not part of the armor; but the clothing underneath must be gathered up before the armor can be put on. Remember, in those days, men often wore long, robe-like clothes. It would have been hard to fight and maneuver in hand-to-hand combat wearing a robe. The bottom part of a man's robe would be tucked into the belt to make the man more prepared to fight. It kept the other pieces of armor in place and made it possible for the soldier to use the rest of the armor effectively.

When a soldier sat down and was relaxed, he often took off his belt. Putting on the belt meant that the soldier was prepared for action. It made him have freedom of movement, and it put him in a frame of mind ready for battle. Spiritually speaking, the same idea was communicated by Jesus in Luke 12:35-36.

The belt of truth puts on the biblical beliefs of the Christian as a whole – what other passages call "the faith." Many people believe that the church will never go forward until it takes *off* this belt of truth, but that is entirely wrong. This is the armor we need to *have* – it is a foundation that Christians live on all the time, our understanding of and confidence in the fundamental doctrines of the faith.

Whatever you do – do not let go of the truth, biblical truth. That keeps everything else together and ready to use.

January 5

Taking Care of First Things First

Therefore if you bring your gift to the altar, and there remember that your brother has something against you, leave your gift there before the altar, and go your way. First be reconciled to your brother, and then come and offer your gift. Agree with your adversary quickly, while you are on the way with him, lest your adversary deliver you to the judge, the judge hand you over to the officer, and you be thrown into prison. Assuredly, I say to you, you will by no means get out of there till you have paid the last penny. (Matthew 5:23-26)

One purpose of the Sermon on the Mount is to expose the contrast between true and false religion, but not only in a theological sense. In that great sermon, Jesus emphasized how our ideas about God are lived out in life.

Jesus has in mind someone doing something good in a religious sense – bringing a **gift to the altar** of sacrifice at the temple in Jerusalem. That was a good and honorable thing to do. Yet Jesus told us that if, on the way to the altar, we remembered that something was wrong in our relationship to a brother (or sister) in the faith. we should then stop.

Jesus continued: **Leave your gift there before the altar, and go your way** and make reconciliation with your brother in the faith. Jesus considered it more important to be reconciled to a brother than to perform a religious duty. Jesus says we must **first be reconciled to your brother**. We can't think that our service towards the Lord justifies bad relationships with others.

Instead of going on in our intended service to God, you should **agree with your adversary quickly**. When we ignore it or pass it off, it genuinely imprisons us – Jesus described it like being **thrown into prison**. Jesus said that one would remain in prison until they had **paid the last penny**.

Even if one were to allow for a certain amount of passionate over-stating, these are sobering words from Jesus. The implication is that chronic neglect of relationships shows something is fundamentally wrong in our relationship with God.

Jesus pressed on us an urgency to get it right with people. The truth is that when we don't get along with our brothers and sisters in the faith, it reflects on something disturbing in our relationship with God.

Paul expressed the same idea in Ephesians 4:26-27 (*do not let the sun go down on your wrath*). When we hold on to our anger against another we then sin – and we *give place to the devil* as Paul said in Ephesians 4. We should do what Paul commanded in Romans 12:18: *If it is possible, as much as depends on you, live peaceably with all men.*

Take care of these first things first – get relationships right before bringing your service or sacrifice to God.

January 6
Putting It Into Action

Praying always with all prayer and supplication in the Spirit, being watchful to this end with all perseverance and supplication for all the saints; and for me, that utterance may be given to me, that I may open my mouth boldly to make known the mystery of the gospel, for which I am an ambassador in chains; that in it I may speak boldly, as I ought to speak. (Ephesians 6:18-20)

The apostle Paul related what we need to live the Christian life to the armor that a Roman soldier used and wore. Following that section, Paul tells us what we should do with that spiritual armor; how we put it into action.

Primarily, it is done through prayer: **Praying always with all prayer**. The idea is all kinds of prayer, or prayer on prayer. We should use every kind of prayer: group prayer, individual prayer, silent prayer, shouting prayer, walking prayer, kneeling prayer, eloquent prayer, groaning prayer, constant prayer, fervent prayer – just pray.

It is through prayer that spiritual strength and the armor of God go to work. In theory, the prayerless Christian can be strong and wearing all the armor – but goes into battle through prayer.

Often, we do not pray because we are overconfident in our abilities. Winston Churchill said to Britain in the early days of World War II: "I must drop one word of caution, for next to cowardice and treachery, overconfidence leading to neglect and slothfulness, is the worst of wartime crimes." It is especially true in the spiritual war we fight.

Paul reminded us that we could pray **for all the saints**. We can battle spiritually not only on our behalf but also on behalf of others. The soldier isn't only concerned for his or her safety. They feel the instinct to protect and battle on behalf of others.

After bringing up the idea that spiritual warfare can be waged on behalf of others, Paul asked his readers to pray for him, asking for **utterance**, the ability to speak and **boldly make known the mystery of the gospel**. Paul could have asked prayer for many things, but he wanted them to pray for this.

We could imagine Paul asking for many things, such as relief from his imprisonment or other comforts. But his heart and mind were fixed on his responsibility as an ambassador of the gospel. He probably has in mind his upcoming defense before Caesar.

Specifically, Paul asked, **that utterance may be given to me**. The idea behind **utterance** is *clear speaking*. Added to **boldly**, Paul asked for prayer that he might proclaim the gospel both clearly and with a fearless power. It is easy to neglect one or the other.

It all comes back to the idea of spiritual battle. When Paul preached under challenging circumstances, he knew the spiritual struggle firsthand and knew the prayers of others would help.

If you want to do something with the armor of God, pray!

January 7

The Choice Between Two Masters

No one can serve two masters; for either he will hate the one and love the other, or else he will be loyal to the one and despise the other. You cannot serve God and mammon. (Matthew 6:24)

In this section of the Sermon on the Mount, Jesus emphasized the idea that His followers must make choices – choosing between two treasures, between two visions, and now between two masters. To follow Jesus means that one must decide not to follow anything or anyone contrary to Jesus.

No one can serve two masters. Having two masters is not like working two jobs. Jesus had the master and slave relationship in mind, and no slave could **serve two masters**.

Jesus told us that serving two masters is a simple impossibility. If you think that you are successfully serving two masters, you're deceiving yourself. It can't be done. As ancient Israel struggled with idolatry, they thought they could worship the Lord God and Baal. God continually reminded them that to worship Baal was to forsake the Lord. To be **loyal to the one** is to **despise the other**.

This is true in many areas of life, but Jesus brought the point to the subject of money and material things, when He said, **you cannot serve God and mammon**. Among Bible experts, there are different opinions regarding the origin of the word **mammon**. Some think it was the name of a pagan god. Others believe the name comes from the Hebrew word, which means, "to trust" because we are often tempted to trust in material things. Whatever its origin, the meaning is clear: **mammon** is materialism, or wealth personified.

According to one commentator (R.T. France), the idea of mammon itself was morally neutral. The word was used in some ancient Jewish writings that showed this, translating Proverbs 3:9 as "Honor God with your mammon" and Deuteronomy 6:5 as "You shall love the Lord your God with…all your mammon." Therefore, it could be said that mammon itself represents material things that we possess or want. Those things can be used for God's kingdom and glory, or they can be destructive idols in our life.

Jesus is addressing the heart. Many people would say they love God, but the way they serve the god of money shows that they do not. How can we tell which master we serve? One way is by remembering this principle: you will sacrifice for your God. If you will sacrifice for the sake of money, but will not sacrifice for the sake of Jesus, don't deceive yourself: money or mammon is your God.

We must remember that we don't have to be rich to serve mammon (money and material things). The poor can be just as greedy and covetous as the rich can be.

Don't serve your money. Let your money serve the Lord, and it will serve you, even increasing your reward in heaven.

Mammon is a good servant but a terrible master.

January 8

The Sacrifice That Pleases God

Then Samuel said: "Has the Lord as great delight in burnt offerings and sacrifices, as in obeying the voice of the Lord? Behold, to obey is better than sacrifice, and to heed than the fat of rams. For rebellion is as the sin of witchcraft, and stubbornness is as iniquity and idolatry. Because you have rejected the word of the Lord, He also has rejected you from being king." (1 Samuel 15:22-23)

King Saul had directly disobeyed God's command, and then he made excuses when the prophet Samuel confronted him. Samuel explained why the king's disobedience was so serious to God: **Has the Lord as great delight in burnt offerings and sacrifices, as in obeying the voice of the Lord? Behold, to obey is better than sacrifice, and to heed than the fat of rams.**

Samuel meant that religious observance without obedience is empty before God. Someone could make a thousand sacrifices to God, work a thousand hours for God's service, or give millions of dollars to His work. But all these sacrifices mean little if there isn't a surrendered heart to God, shown by simple obedience.

When King Saul offered a sacrifice, it was the flesh of another creature. What God wanted was the sacrifice of obedience, offering his own will to God.

Samuel said that **rebellion** was like **the sin of witchcraft** and that **stubbornness** was like **iniquity and idolatry**. A rebellious, stubborn heart rejects God just as someone rejects God by occult practices or idolatry.

Saul's problem wasn't just that he neglected some ceremony. That was how Saul thought of obedience to God. But religious observance was not Saul's problem; the problem was that his heart became rebellious and stubborn against God. Real worship begins with the surrender of the will.

Then the word came to Saul, who had **rejected the word of the Lord**. God declared Saul as **rejected from being king**. In his empty religious practice, rebellion, and stubbornness against God, Saul rejected God's Word. God rightly rejected him as king over Israel.

God rejected Saul as king, yet it would be more than 15 years before there was another king crowned in Israel. Saul's rejection was final, but it wasn't immediate. God used more than 15 years to train up the right replacement for Saul.

It would be easy to ask, "Why was Saul rejected as king because he didn't kill a king and a few sheep and oxen?" Later kings of Israel would do far worse, and not be rejected as king. Why was God so tough on Saul? But God saw Saul's heart and saw how rebellious and stubborn it was. Saul's condition was like an iceberg: what was visible might be a manageable size, but there was far more under the surface that couldn't be seen. God could see it.

Today, pray that God moves in you to give Him a surrendered will – which is far better than any sacrifice you could make.

January 9

Go

And He said, "Go, and tell this people: 'Keep on hearing, but do not understand; keep on seeing, but do not perceive.' Make the heart of this people dull, and their ears heavy, and shut their eyes; lest they see with their eyes, and hear with their ears, and understand with their heart, and return and be healed." (Isaiah 6:9-10)

The prophet Isaiah described a dramatic experience in chapter 6. He saw the throne room of God, the worshipping angels surrounding the throne, and the Lord Himself enthroned majestically with the train of His robe filling the heavenly temple. Isaiah heard the Lord ask, "Who shall I send? Who will go for us?" and Isaiah responded by making himself available.

The prophet heard a simple but challenging word: **Go**. It wasn't enough for Isaiah to have a spectacular experience; it had to work out in real life. Isaiah might have been content to enjoy his experience or even to tell others about it. Though Isaiah's experience was glorious, he wasn't stuck there. He had to **go**. And the "going" wouldn't be easy – God told Isaiah to bring this message to the people: **Keep on hearing, but do not understand; keep on seeing but do not perceive**. It's a crazy job description. We wonder if Isaiah would have volunteered if he'd known what it was ahead of time. God told Isaiah to go and preach to a people who wouldn't respond, so their guilt would be certain.

What preacher could be satisfied with a ministry that made the heart of these people dull, and their ears heavy, and shut their eyes? Isaiah might not be satisfied with it. The people might not be satisfied with it. But God would be satisfied with it.

Yet if some did respond to Isaiah's message, they would **understand with their heart**, and **return and be healed**. This shows what the Word of God can accomplish when it is received with open eyes, ears, and hearts. It brings understanding to our hearts, it makes us return, and it brings healing to our lives. If you are under the Word of God and these things aren't happening to you, ask God to work with your eyes, ears, and heart.

We can't hear the charge to Isaiah without remembering Jesus' command to us: *Go therefore and make disciples of all the nations, baptizing them in the name of the Father and of the Son and of the Holy Spirit* (Matthew 28:19). The **go** for Isaiah is also a "go" to you and me from the mouth of Jesus. When we say, "Here am I! Send me" to the Lord, we should expect Him to say, "Go." He may say, "Go and serve Me here" or "Go and serve me there" or "Go and be prepared for future service."

We can go with our presence, go with our prayers, or go with our provision for the work, but God always has a "Go" for us.

Are you going?

January 10

How to Give Your Life Away

By this we know love, because He laid down His life for us. And we also ought to lay down our lives for the brethren. (1 John 3:16)

For whoever desires to save his life will lose it, but whoever loses his life for My sake and the gospel's will save it. (Mark 8:35)

Many years ago, a truck driver named Reginald Denny was beaten severely during some riots in Los Angeles. About the same time another man named Wallace Tope was also beaten – and murdered – during the same riots. Denny got more attention because his beating was broadcast live on television. But Tope died because he loved Jesus Christ.

Wallace Tope was beaten as he preached the gospel to looters in Hollywood. After Tope was attacked, police wondered why a white evangelist would venture into a riot and preach to looters, but Tope wanted to be where the action was. Before the Berlin Wall fell, he smuggled Bibles into East Germany and was arrested while preaching to some soldiers.

When the riots started, Tope wanted to get on the streets and preach but none of his friends at seminary would go with him. He went alone to the corner of Sunset and Western, one of his regular corners for preaching. After handing one looter a tract, Tope was threatened and punched. Wallace Tope began walking back to his car to leave when another looter ran across the parking lot and attacked Tope, beating him for several minutes.

When Tope lay there bloody and beaten, he still held onto his gospel tracts, and began witnessing to the ambulance attendant, saying, "Believe in Jesus for your salvation." He softly added, "God bless you," then fell into a coma. For quite a while, he remained in a "persistent vegetative state" from head injuries, but never recovered and went to be with Jesus.

Many of us are afraid to tell others about Jesus because we are afraid of social rejection. Thank God for examples like Wallace Tope, who ended up giving his life so he could tell people about Jesus. We can easily be fooled into thinking that we can follow Jesus and give up absolutely nothing. We may not be called to offer our lives in the dramatic way Wallace Tope did, but we must lay down our lives nonetheless.

We don't lay down our lives to earn God's love or salvation. We do it out of a grateful response because Jesus gave absolutely everything for us. We love Him because He first loved us. We lay down our lives for Him because He first laid down His life for us.

Imagine that your life is worth $1,000. You could lay down your life by shelling out $1,000 at once. Or you could get 20,000 nickels and give them away one by one. Either way, you are laying down your life – actually giving something up for Jesus. What will you give Him today?

January 11

Impulse, Circumstances, or God?

But Jonah arose to flee to Tarshish from the presence of the Lord. He went down to Joppa, and found a ship going to Tarshish; so he paid the fare, and went down into it, to go with them to Tarshish from the presence of the Lord. (Jonah 1:3)

God gave Jonah a job to do, but Jonah did not want any part of it. It is not a stretch to think that Jonah knew the job would be difficult and was intimidated. Nahum 3:1-4 tells us how wicked the people of Nineveh were. Jonah had good reason to expect that if he went to Nineveh at the best he would be mocked and treated as a fool. He might even be attacked and killed if he did what the Lord told him to do.

Nevertheless, for Jonah, it was more than an issue of a difficult job. It was also because Jonah did not want the Assyrians in Nineveh to escape God's judgment.

We don't doubt that Jonah felt like going to Tarshish – exactly the opposite direction as Nineveh. An impulse drove him there, but it was a dangerous impulse. Jonah is an example of how dangerous it is to do things under mere impulse instead of doing things by the guidance of the Holy Spirit.

- An impulse may be very brave yet be wrong (Jonah was brave to set out on such a long sea-journey).
- An impulse may appear to be self-denying yet be wrong (it cost Jonah a lot of money and comfort to go on this long sea-journey).
- An impulse may lay claim to freedom yet be wrong (wasn't Jonah "free" to go to Nineveh?).
- An impulse may lead someone to do something that they would condemn in others (what would Jonah say to another prophet disobeying God?).
- An impulse can make us do to God or others what we would never want to be done to ourselves.

Jonah might have even thought that the Lord was guiding him through circumstances. After all, he got the money and was able to pay the fare. This shows the danger of being guided by circumstances. Whether circumstances are for us or against us, we must let God's Word be our guide. It is very easy to interpret circumstances in any way we want to. If we are set on a wrong course, it is no problem for the devil and our deceitful heart to work together and interpret circumstances so that they say whatever we want to hear.

Nevertheless, Jonah paid the fare. When you run away from the Lord, you never get to where you intend to go, and you always pay your own fare. When you go the Lord's way, you not only get to where you are going, but He pays the fare.

Let God's Word map out your itinerary, not only impulses or circumstances – and let Him pay the fare!

January 12

Good Start, Bad Finish

Then Samuel explained to the people the behavior of royalty, and wrote it in a book and laid it up before the Lord. And Samuel sent all the people away, every man to his house. And Saul also went home to Gibeah; and valiant men went with him, whose hearts God had touched. But some rebels said, "How can this man save us?" So they despised him, and brought him no presents. But he held his peace. (1 Samuel 10:25-27)

Now was the time – Israel was about to recognize their first human king. God had reigned as king over the 12 tribes up to this point, but because the people insisted, God relented and gave them the kind of king they wanted – a man named Saul.

God warned them. Before they crowned Saul, Samuel explained to Israel the **behavior of royalty**. The prophet Samuel taught them God's guidelines for rulers and subjects, probably using Deuteronomy 17:14-20. The people still agreed to receive a king, and then they went home, **every man to his house**.

That included the new king Saul. We read that **Saul also went home to Gibeah**. At the time, there was no palace or capital city. So, Saul walked home with his future leaders, the **valiant men** who went with him.

We notice something important. God called Saul to be king and to lead the nation. Yet, this was not something he could do himself. He needed brave men around him, men **whose hearts God had touched**.

Every leader wants those kinds of people around him. Yet not everyone was so supportive of King Saul. There were some rebels, and **so they despised him**. But notice Saul's reaction to the rebels: **But he held his peace**. Saul reacted to this wisely (**he held his peace**). An insecure or unwise leader might feel the need to crush any opposition or regard them as enemies. Saul did neither, understanding that it might take him some time to win over the doubters.

F.B. Meyer says that the more literal translation of the original Hebrew would be, "He was as though he had been deaf." He heard their despising words, but he chose not to hear or regard those words.

Saul started with great promise. He was chosen and anointed by God and filled with the Holy Spirit. Saul was supported by a great man of God and by almost all Israel. He was surrounded by valiant men, men whose hearts God had touched. In the beginning, Saul was wise enough to not regard every doubter or critic as an enemy.

Despite all these significant advantages, Saul still ended badly. He had to choose to walk in the advantages God gave him, and he had to decide not to go his own way. Saul chose poorly and finished as a ruined man. Saul's good start wasn't enough; he had to keep making the right choices to end well.

So do we – choose wisely today!

January 13
Combining Love with Discernment

Do not give what is holy to the dogs; nor cast your pearls before swine, lest they trample them under their feet, and turn and tear you in pieces. (Matthew 7:6)

In the previous section of the Sermon on the Mount, Jesus warned us against judgmental attitudes and criticism that is often blind to oneself. Yet following on that, Jesus then said, **do not give what is holy to the dogs, nor cast your pearls before swine**.

After the warning against the harsh condemnation of others, Jesus then reminded us that He did not mean to imply that the people of His Kingdom should suspend all discernment. They must discern that some good, precious things should not be given to those who will receive them with contempt. We might say that Jesus meant, "Don't be judgmental, but don't throw out all discernment either."

The **dogs** and **swine** mentioned here are often understood as those who are hostile to the kingdom of God and the message that announces it. Our love for others must not blind us to their hardened rejection of the Good News of the kingdom.

Yet we may also see this in the context of the previous words against hypocrites. It may be that in Jesus' mind, the dogs and swine represent hypocritical, judgmental believers. These sinning hypocrites should not be offered the costly pearls that belong to the community of the saints.

The commentator William Barclay said that the ancient Christian writing known as the Didache said this: "Let no one eat or drink of your Eucharist except those baptized into the name of the Lord; for as regards this, the Lord has said, 'Give not that which is holy unto dogs.'"

We can also say that Jesus spoke in the context of correcting another brother or sister. Godly correction is a valuable pearl (though it may sting for a moment) that must not be cast before swine (those who are determined not to receive it).

Our pearls of the precious gospel may only confuse those who do not believe, who are blinded to the truth by the god of this age (2 Corinthians 4:4) and may only expose the gospel to their ridicule. Jesus indeed told us to take the gospel all over the world (Mark 16:15). Yet the apostle Paul and his associates, when they saw that certain people were "hardened and did not believe" and that they "spoke evil of the Way before the multitude" then Paul no longer preached to them (Acts 19:9). He refused to continue to cast those pearls before those who rejected them.

Jesus didn't say this to discourage us from sharing the gospel. Jesus told us to let our lights shine before the world (Matthew 5:13-16). Jesus said this to call us to discernment, and to encourage us to look for prepared hearts that are ready to receive.

When we find such open hearts, we can trust that God has already been working on them. Today, pray for the discernment Jesus wanted us to have.

January 14
God's Answer to the Prayer of Faith

And the prayer of faith will save the sick, and the Lord will raise him up. And if he has committed sins, he will be forgiven. Confess your trespasses to one another, and pray for one another, that you may be healed. The effective, fervent prayer of a righteous man avails much. (James 5:15-16)

In the previous verses, James wrote how the sick should ask for prayer. Many have wondered if James here guaranteed healing for the sick who are prayed for in faith. Some have interpreted the idea behind **save the sick** as not explicitly being healing and **raise him up** as being a reference to ultimate resurrection. The reference to **sins being forgiven** adds to the idea that James here considered this a spiritual work and healing, not necessarily physical healing.

The context of the statement demands that James does not exclude physical healing as an answer to prayer, though he does seem to mean something broader than only physical healing. We should pray for others in faith, expecting that God will heal them, then leave the matter in God's hands.

God does not grant immediate healing for every prayer of faith, and the reasons are hidden in the heart and mind of God. Still, many are not healed simply because there is no prayer of faith offered. The best approach in praying for the sick is to pray with humble confidence that they will be healed unless God clearly and powerfully makes it clear that this is not His will. Having prayed, we leave the matter to God.

Often, we do not pray the **prayer of faith** out of concern for God's reputation if there should be no healing. We should remember that God is big enough to handle His reputation.

James reminds us of what we should receive: **The effective, fervent prayer of a righteous man avails much**. In writing about the need to pray for the suffering, for the sick, and the sinning, James points to the effective nature of prayer – when it is **fervent** and offered by a **righteous man**.

The idea of **fervent** in this context is strong. Much of our prayer is not effective simply because it is not fervent. It is offered with a lukewarm attitude that almost asks God to care about something that we care little about. Effective prayer must be fervent, not because we must emotionally persuade a reluctant God, but because we must gain God's heart by being fervent for the things He is.

A **righteous man** offers the effective prayer. This is someone who recognizes the grounds of his righteousness reside in Jesus, and whose personal walk is generally consistent with the righteousness that he has in Jesus. That kind of prayer **avails much**.

The answer it brings will be in the wisdom and plan of man, not necessarily over every expectation of man, but it will also **avail**.

Today, you can trust that God has promised it so.

January 15

The Reasons for Judgment

The earth mourns and fades away, the world languishes and fades away; the haughty people of the earth languish. The earth is also defiled under its inhabitants, because they have transgressed the laws, changed the ordinance, broken the everlasting covenant. Therefore the curse has devoured the earth, and those who dwell in it are desolate. Therefore the inhabitants of the earth are burned, and few men are left. (Isaiah 24:4-6)

Many Bible scholars think that Isaiah 24 speaks of an ultimate season of judgment that God brings on the earth, sometimes called the "great tribulation" because of what Jesus said in Matthew 24:21. However, the principles explained here go beyond just one season of judgment. In this season of judgment, even the earth suffers: **The earth mourns and fades away**. Revelation 8:7-13 describes the terrible effect of God's judgments on the earth.

God is not punishing the earth. This isn't God's fault. Instead, this is man's fault because the **inhabitants** of the **earth** make her **defiled**. Man pollutes the earth with his sin and great wickedness, so the earth must also endure some of the righteous judgment of God. In this sense, the most ecologically responsible thing anyone could do is to honor God, walk right with Him, and live in obedience to Him!

God is greater than His creation. The Bible never teaches that God is bound up together with what He has created. God is separate from His creation, and when the earth fades away the Lord God will remain unchanged.

Israel sinned as they **transgressed** God's **laws**. Transgression is to step over the line God has established. Transgression is the spirit of our age. Old advertising slogans told us, "Nothing is taboo" and "Break all the rules" and "Just do it." These ideas come at us constantly: you don't have to respect God's boundaries; you can make your own. "Follow your heart" becomes "Do whatever you want."

Israel sinned as they **changed** God's **ordinance**. The Hebrew word for **ordinance** here is *Torah*, which often means the law of God and the Word of God. Mankind is ripe for judgment because we have changed God's Word into something "lighter," into something more acceptable to us.

When once it was universally recognized that it was wrong to lie, wrong to cheat, wrong to be sexually immoral, today much of that is approved and celebrated!

Every time a preacher soft-peddles the gospel, a politician twists the Scriptures to rise in the polls, or a counselor twists the context of God's Word to make it fit a crazy psychological theory, they have **changed the ordinance**.

Because of man's sin, the **curse has devoured the earth**. Humanity's hardened, repeated rejection of God brings both near correction and ultimate judgment.

Thank God that for all who put their trust in Him, Jesus bore the judgment they deserve. This gives even more reason for us to be faithful in an age that is ripe – perhaps over-ripe – for judgment.

January 16

Justice and Mercy

Now it happened, when David and his men came to Ziklag, on the third day, that the Amalekites had invaded the South and Ziklag, attacked Ziklag and burned it with fire, and had taken captive the women and those who were there, from small to great; they did not kill anyone, but carried them away and went their way. (1 Samuel 30:1-2)

David offered himself to fight for the Philistines against the Israelites, but the Philistine leaders didn't accept the offer. David and his men went back to Ziklag, the Philistine city where they lived.

They marched about 25 miles (40 km) a day over three days – a reasonably fast pace for a group that size. As they came close to Ziklag, they were tired, hungry, and ready to return to the families.

As they came within sight of their city, the hearts of David and his men must have brightened. As soldiers, they were discouraged that they hadn't been allowed to fight with the Philistines. But they knew they were coming home, and home meant family and familiar surroundings. Those bright thoughts turned dark.

They saw smoke rising from their city in the distance, but it wasn't the smoke of cooking fires. It was too black and too much smoke. They wondered why no one had come to greet them.

What they saw when they came closer horrified them. Ziklag was a burned ruin. While David and his mighty men were busy fighting against their people, the Amalekites attacked the defenseless city. They kidnapped the women and children and stole everything of value. Ziklag was a ghost town, a pile of burned rubble with no survivors; it seemed all was lost.

There was a touch of both justice and mercy in all this. The justice was that the Amalekites did to David what he had done to them because he had brought this same calamity to other cities. 1 Samuel 27:8-11 says during his time among the Philistines, David made his living as a bandit, robbing cities and *whenever David attacked the land, he left neither man nor woman alive.*

The mercy was that the Amalekites were more merciful than David was – where David killed all in the cities he attacked, at least the Amalekites took the people captive instead of killing them.

God, who is great in mercy, does not discipline us as much as we deserve. Like a compassionate father, He tempers His discipline with kindness and love.

If we think about what we deserve, it might be easy to despair. David and his men probably deserved to have all their women and children killed, because that's what they did to others. Yet God showed mercy to David.

God still shows mercy: *He saved us, not because of the good things we did, but because of His mercy* (Titus 3:5, NLT).

Find time today to thank God for His great mercy to you.

January 17

Do the Work Right at Our House

Next to them Jedaiah the son of Harumaph made repairs in front of his house. (Nehemiah 3:10)

Nehemiah 3 is all about getting God's work done. Nehemiah was a man moved by God to get the walls and gates surrounding Jerusalem rebuilt. The city was in a bad state of disrepair, discouragement, and defeat because of their lack of security and safety.

Through Nehemiah 3, different people do different kinds of work. Verse 10 tells us of **Jedaiah**, a man who repaired the portion of the wall right **in front of his house**. Many times, when God calls us to His work, the most important place to work is right in front us – at our own homes. Five times in the chapter, it speaks of those who worked on the section right in front of their house.

The names of the men who are said to have **made repairs in front of his house** have something to teach us.

The name **Jedaiah** (3:10) means "he who calls to God"; our homes must be places of prayer where the family calls to God. What is the state of prayer in your home? Is God glorified through prayer? The name "he who calls to God" reminds us of the need to make our homes places of prayer.

Benjamin (3:23) means "son of my right hand." The "son of my right hand" was a protector; someone always on hand, ready to help and protect. When we give attention to the work of God at our homes, it must be with a heart to make our homes places of protection and peace. We need refuge from the pressures and influences of the world. Ask God to make your home just such a place.

The name *Zadok* (3:29) means "justice"; our homes must be places of justice and integrity. The most important place where fairness and integrity need to be shown in our homes is with the promises we make to each other. Marriages are essentially based on a promise – vows made between a man and a woman before their God, regarding their commitment to one another. When promises are made and kept there is a sense of peace in the home. When promises are not kept, there is a sad sense of injustice and lack of integrity.

Meshullam (3:30) means "devoted"; our homes must be places of devotion and separation to God. What is the level of spiritual devotion in your home? When God calls you to give attention to the "repairs in front of your house," how much of it has to do with cultivating an atmosphere of devotion and love to God? Each of us, no matter what our station in life, knows there are places where God wants to work in our homes.

When we endeavor to do the work of the LORD, we should start right where we are – right in front of our homes, especially the work of prayer, protection, integrity, and devotion.

January 18

Living in the Freedom

Stand fast therefore in the liberty by which Christ has made us free, and do not be entangled again with a yoke of bondage. (Galatians 5:1)

Paul makes it clear – Jesus sets us free but need to take care we do not become entangled in bondage again. How can we be brought under bondage?

Long ago, two brothers fought for piece of land in what is now Belgium. The older brother's name was Raynald, but everyone called him "Crassus," a Latin nickname meaning "fat," for he was terribly overweight. After a tough battle, Raynald's younger brother Edward took his lands. But Edward didn't kill Raynald. Instead, he had a room in the castle built around "Crassus," a room with only one skinny door. The door wasn't locked, the windows weren't barred, and Edward promised Raynald he could regain his land and title anytime he wanted. All he had to do was leave the room. The obstacle to freedom wasn't the door or the windows, but Raynald himself. He was so overweight that he couldn't fit through the door. All Raynald needed to do was diet down to a smaller size and walk out a free man.

However, his younger brother kept sending him tasty foods, and Raynald's desire to be free never won out over his desire to eat. Some accused Edward of being cruel to his brother, but he simply replied: "My brother is not a prisoner. He may leave when he wants to." But Raynald stayed in that room for ten years, until Edward himself was killed in battle.

This is a dramatic picture of how many Christians live. Jesus has set them forever free legally, and they may walk in that freedom from sin whenever they choose. But since they keep yielding their bodily desires to the service of sin, they live a life of defeat, discouragement, and imprisonment. Because of unbelief, self-reliance, or ignorance, many Christians never live in the freedom Christ paid for on the cross.

D. L. Moody used to speak of an old black woman in the South following the Civil War. Being a former slave, she was confused about her status and asked: "Now is I free, or been I not? When I go to my old master, he says I ain't free, and when I go to my own people they say I is, and I don't know whether I'm free or not. Some people told me that Abraham Lincoln signed a proclamation, but master says he didn't; he didn't have any right to."

That is exactly the place many Christians are. They are, and have been, legally set free from their slavery to sin, yet they are unsure of that truth. And of course, our "old master" is always trying to convince us that we are not free from his dominion.

Today, don't listen to your old master. Do all you can to walk in the liberty for which Jesus has set you free.

January 19

Free from Bitterness

Therefore David took hold of his own clothes and tore them, and so did all the men who were with him. And they mourned and wept and fasted until evening for Saul and for Jonathan his son, for the people of the LORD and for the house of Israel, because they had fallen by the sword. (2 Samuel 1:11-12)

For more than 15 years, David endured tremendous difficulty because of Saul the Son of Kish, the King of Israel. Saul never had a close relationship with God. After a good start Saul became proud and hardened against God. When God said He would replace Saul, the king viewed every potential replacement with fear and dread. As David rose to prominence after killing Goliath, he became the focus of Saul's murderous jealousy. The paranoia of the powerful made David live as a fugitive his entire young adult life.

Now David heard that Saul was dead. His tormentor could touch him no more, and David could return to Israel, his city, his family, and his career – life as a fugitive was over. How did David react? He **wept** – tears of sorrow, not tears of joy.

Out of pure jealousy, hatred, spite, and ungodliness Saul took away David's family, home, career, security, and the best years of David's life – and Saul was unrepentant to the end. Yet David **mourned** and **wept** and **fasted** when he learned of Saul's death.

David had many reasons to be bitter and full of hatred. Some would say that the circumstances *demanded* that David hate Saul – but he didn't. This powerfully demonstrates that our hatred, bitterness, and lack of forgiveness are chosen, not imposed on us. David chose to become better instead of bitter.

And so did all the men who were with him. David's men had their own reasons to hate Saul, but they followed the example of their leader and responded to Saul's hatred and venom with love.

David's sorrow was first for Saul, but it was also for his close friend Jonathan. Even more, it was for the people of God who were in a dangerous and desperate position considering the death of the king and the defeat by the Philistines.

David heard the throne of Israel was now vacant, and it seemed that the royal anointing he received some 20 years before might finally be fulfilled with the crown set on his head. Nevertheless, David expressed little thought for himself. He thought of Saul, Saul's family, and Israel as a whole.

That's the nature of Jesus – others-centered, not self-centered. We see others-centeredness shine brightly every time we let go of bitterness and soften our heart towards those who hurt us.

Today, in Jesus' name let go and find freedom from the prison of bitter resentment.

January 20

Favor Like a Shield

But let all those rejoice who put their trust in You;
Let them ever shout for joy, because You defend them;
Let those also who love Your name be joyful in You.
For You, O Lord, will bless the righteous;
With favor You will surround him as with a shield. (Psalm 5:11-12)

Psalm 5 contrasts the righteous and the wicked, and these closing lines of Psalm 5 show how one is made righteous – by trusting God: **Let all those rejoice who put their trust in You**. The righteous trust the Lord and love His name. Their righteousness is evident in their words. They rejoice, they shout for joy, and they are joyful in the Lord.

We can take this line – **let all those rejoice who put their trust in You** – in four ways. We can take it as a permit, a precept, a prayer, and a promise.

First, you have *permission for joy*. God permits you to be as happy as you want to be. He doesn't set a limit on your joy or your happiness. You have divine permission to shout for joy.

Second, you have *a precept, a command, for joy*. It is as if God calls us out of prisons of depression and sadness and tells us to enter the King's palace. That sadness makes sense in jail, but it doesn't fit for those who are free.

Third, you have *a prayer for joy*. You should pray for joy, both in yourself and others – especially praying for servants of the Lord. When joy is lost in serving God, it is a powerfully bad example to others. Remember, the joy of the Lord is our strength – especially in serving God.

Finally, you have *a promise for joy*. When we put our trust in the Lord, we can confidently expect to receive joy. God will turn our night seasons into dawns of daytime. Our darkest times are temporary.

At the end of this psalm, David declared: **You, O Lord, will bless the righteous; with favor You will surround him as with a shield**. This is the greatest blessing of all – the favor of God. Knowing that God looks on us with favor and pleasure is the most excellent knowledge in the world. This is our standing in grace.

A shield does not protect any one area of the body. It is large and mobile enough to cover any and every area of the body. It is armor over armor. This is how fully the favor of God, our standing in grace, protects us.

When Martin Luther was on his way to face a Cardinal of the Roman Catholic Church to answer for what they called his heretical teachings, one of the Cardinal's servants taunted him saying, "Where will you find shelter if your protector should desert you?" Luther answered, "Under the shelter of heaven." Luther was confident in the shield of God's favor.

Today, you also can be confident in that shield.

January 21

Where to Live

Therefore let that abide in you which you heard from the beginning. If what you heard from the beginning abides in you, you also will abide in the Son and in the Father. (1 John 2:24)

By nature, we are attracted to things just because they are new. We almost always think of new as being better. But when it comes to truth, new is not better as John tells us: **that what you heard from the beginning** is better. Paul had the same thought in Galatians 1, where he told us that even if an angel from heaven should bring a new and different gospel to us, we must reject the angel and their message. It isn't easy to do this, because we are tempted to be *tossed to and fro and carried about with every wind of doctrine, by the trickery of men, in the cunning craftiness of deceitful plotting* (Ephesians 4:14). Sometimes people itch for something "new" and "exciting," even if it leads them away from what they **heard from the beginning**.

But **what you heard from the beginning** doesn't describe whatever teaching any Christian happened to receive when they first followed Jesus. For these believers, **the beginning** described that time when they were under the teaching of the apostles, which is recorded in the New Testament. It is the message of the Bible in general and the New Testament specifically.

To say it clearly, believers abide in **what you heard from the beginning** when they stay close to our Bible. Suppose that was your environment when you were a young Christian – then, wonderful. But if it was not, then put yourself in that environment now. This is John's point when he wrote, **let that abide in you**. It doesn't mean just knowing it, but also living in it. When we live in the simplicity of the truth of Jesus Christ, we **will abide in the Son and the Father**. Our world is filled with people searching for God, some sincerely and some insincerely. But if someone wants to live in God, John tells us how: let the message of the apostles (**what you heard from the beginning**) live in you.

John didn't say, "If you know God's Word, you know God," because someone can have a basic, intellectual knowledge of the Bible and not know God. But he did say, "If God's Word lives in you, God lives in you." We can come to a living, growing relationship with God through His Word.

Living in Jesus is not a passive thing; it is active. We must mentally and spiritually give ourselves to living in Jesus. Charles Spurgeon said, "We abide in him, not by a physical law, as a mass of iron abides on the earth; but by a mental and spiritual law, by which the greatness of divine love and goodness holds us fast to the Lord Jesus."

Where are you living today? Live in His Word, and you will live in Him.

January 22
Example of a Living Faith

But do you want to know, O foolish man, that faith without works is dead? Was not Abraham our father justified by works when he offered Isaac his son on the altar? Do you see that faith was working together with his works, and by works faith was made perfect? And the Scripture was fulfilled which says, "Abraham believed God, and it was accounted to him for righteousness." And he was called the friend of God. You see then that a man is justified by works, and not by faith only. (James 2:20-24)

In his letter to Christians, James painted the contrast between a living faith (that indeed saves) and a dead faith that accomplishes nothing for eternity. James used the Old Testament to demonstrate what he already said about the character of a living faith, showing that a faith that is not accompanied by works is a dead faith that cannot rescue.

Here is an example from the life of Abraham, that he was **justified by works when he offered Isaac his son on the altar**. Abraham was justified by faith long before he offered Isaac (according to Genesis 15:6). But his obedience in offering Isaac demonstrated that he did trust God.

James correctly estimates that Abraham did offer **Isaac his son on the altar**, even though the angel stopped him from actually killing his son. Yet he had offered Isaac his son in his firm resolution and intention and undoubtedly would have completed the act had not God stopped him. Abraham was so complete in his obedience that he counted Isaac as dead and set him on the altar.

James tells us **faith was working together with his works**. Faith and works cooperated perfectly together in Abraham. If he had never believed God, he could have never done the good work of obedience when asked to offer Isaac. As well, his faith was proven true – was completed, was made perfect – by his obedient works.

James applied the principle: **You see then that a man is justified by works, and not by faith only**. The faith only that will not justify a man is a faith that is without works, a dead faith. But true faith, living faith, shown to be true by good works, will alone justify.

Works must accompany a genuine faith, because genuine faith is always connected with regeneration – being born again, becoming a new creation in Jesus (2 Corinthians 5:17). If there is no evidence of a new life, then there is no genuine, saving faith.

The great preacher of Victorian England, Charles Spurgeon, is reported to have said: "The grace that does not change my life will not save my soul." I've read a lot of Spurgeon and have never come across that exact quote. Yet even if Spurgeon never did say it, the idea is valid: real faith, real grace, will show itself in real life.

Does it show in yours?

January 23

Crying Out and Hoping in His Word

I cry out with my whole heart; Hear me, O LORD! I will keep Your statutes. I cry out to You; save me, and I will keep Your testimonies. I rise before the dawning of the morning, and cry for help; I hope in Your word. (Psalm 119:145-147)

The psalms resonate with the believer's heart because they so powerfully and eloquently express the feelings and emotions the God-follower experiences. Psalm 119:145 is an excellent example of this: **I cry out with my whole heart.... I will keep Your statutes**. The psalmist pleaded with God, crying out before Him. In his pleading, he wanted to **keep** the Word of God. This was not merely a cry for help or deliverance or forgiveness; this was a cry for obedience.

In Psalm 119:85-86, the author prayed for help against his enemies. Here he prayed for help against himself. He knew that prayer could help bring the strength necessary to honor God's Word, so his whole heart cried out for this help.

When the whole heart cries out to God, the prayers don't need to be either elegant or eloquent.

We could say God doesn't look at the *elegance* of your prayers, to see how neat they are. He doesn't examine the *geometry* of your prayers, to see how long they are. God isn't counting the *arithmetic* of your prayers, to see how many they are. God doesn't look at the *music* of your prayers, to see how melodic they are. Nor does God study the *logic* of your prayers, to see how smart they are.

In truth, God looks at the *sincerity* of prayers to see how heart-filled they are.

The psalmist repeated it: **I cry out to You; save me, and I will keep Your testimonies**. The psalmist passionately cried out to God for the wisdom and strength and ability to obey God. **I cry out to You**, means that his prayer was not merely mental, but also vocal. This is prayer that pleases God.

His prayer's expectant faith is shown in these words: **I rise before the dawning of the morning, and cry for help; I hope in Your word**. The psalmist passionately depended on God and His Word, but that did not eliminate the participation of the psalmist in any way. He still woke early to seek God in prayer (**cry for help**) and was helped by God's Word (**I hope in Your word**).

It is essential to use prayer in our study of the Word of God; We also use the Word in our prayers, which shows us:

- The nature and heart of the God we pray to.
- What we have received from God and should thank Him for.
- His greatness, informing and expanding our praise.
- His moral will, directing us to pray that we can do it.
- His promises to His people, which we claim by faith.
- Substance for our prayers, as we read the Scriptures.

Today, cry out to God and hope in His Word.

January 24

Hard Hearts Made Soft

And the LORD said to Moses, "When you go back to Egypt, see that you do all those wonders before Pharaoh which I have put in your hand. But I will harden his heart, so that he will not let the people go." (Exodus 4:21)

Moses was almost ready to go back to Egypt, as God told him to. But before he left, God wanted him to know something important. God wanted Moses to know that he would show signs to Pharaoh and make these requests to him, but Pharaoh would not listen. In fact, the LORD said, **I will harden his heart, so that he will not let the people go**.

It brings up a good question: Is it fair for God to harden a man's heart?

Let's look at the whole picture. Sometimes it says that God hardened the heart of Pharaoh (Exodus 4:21). Sometimes it says that Pharaoh hardened his own heart (Exodus 8:15). Sometimes it simply states that Pharaoh's heart was hardened, without saying who did it (Exodus 7:13).

So which description is accurate? How did it really happen? All three were correct. But when we consider the occasions where God hardened Pharaoh's heart, we must never think that God did it *against* Pharaoh's will. It was never a case of Pharaoh saying, "Oh, I want to do what is good and right and I want to bless the people of Israel" and God saying back, "No, for I will harden your heart against them!" When God hardened Pharaoh's heart, He allowed Pharaoh's heart to do what Pharaoh wanted to do – God gave Pharaoh over to his sin (as in Romans 1:18-32).

However, it never says that God hardened Pharaoh's heart until Exodus 9:12. Before that, God announced that he would harden Pharaoh's heart (Exodus 4:21 and 7:3), and this was the fulfillment of it. Yet it is said at least six times before Exodus 9:12 that Pharaoh hardened *his own* heart (Exodus 7:13, 7:22, 8:15, 8:19, 8:32, 9:7). We see that God's hardening of Pharaoh's heart was the strengthening of what he already had set himself towards.

All God must do to harden hearts is give the sinful heart what it wants. What we need is a new heart. Ezekiel 36:26 makes a precious promise: *I will give you a new heart and put a new spirit within you; I will take the heart of stone out of your flesh and give you a heart of flesh*. What is the condition of your heart before God? If you are tired of your hard heart, you can ask God to change it. No one ever came to God looking for a soft heart and received a hard heart instead.

God showed His mercy to Moses by telling him about Pharaoh's hardened heart so that Moses would not be surprised that Pharaoh rejected him.

Today, let God show you that He is in control, and submit your heart to Him.

January 25

The Highway of Holiness

A highway shall be there, and a road, and it shall be called the Highway of Holiness. The unclean shall not pass over it, but it shall be for others. Whoever walks the road, although a fool, shall not go astray. (Isaiah 35:8)

Most of us today take good roads for granted. We may have to live with the frustrations of endless road construction, detours, and delays; but it is all for the purpose of giving us good, safe roads. We travel today over distances and at speeds beyond the imagination of people in the ancient world, and we rarely think it is something special.

In the ancient world, it was different; a good road was a remarkable technological achievement. A good road meant trade, progress, and security. A good road cost a lot of money to make and to maintain, and most people traveled on rough paths better suited for donkeys than for people.

The prophet Isaiah spoke and wrote some 2,500 years ago – and in a part of the world that was not as advanced as some others. At that time and place, Isaiah announced the greatest road construction project of all time: the building of **a Highway of Holiness**.

Isaiah announced that in the ministry of the Messiah, there would be a wonderful highway, a road, known as the **Highway of Holiness**. The ancient Hebrew word for **highway** indicates what the English word says: "a high-way." It speaks of a raised road, lifted above the ground. It is a glorious road to travel on!

The construction of this **Highway of Holiness** was the greatest engineering feat ever accomplished. One may drive through long tunnels that seem to extend forever through Alpine mountains. One may travel over amazing bridges, lifted high over deep valleys, carrying constant traffic. Many people look at these tunnels and bridges and wonder, "How did they make that?"

Charles Spurgeon said, "Engineering has done much to tunnel mountains, and bridge abysses; but the greatest triumph of engineering is that which made a way from sin to holiness, from death to life, from condemnation to perfection."

At the same time, this highway isn't for everyone: **The unclean shall not pass over it**. You can't make it on this highway by paying your way. You are only allowed on this highway if you are cleansed by the great work of the Messiah.

Furthermore, **whoever walks the road, although a fool, shall not go astray**. When we stay on God's **Highway of Holiness**, even though His work in us isn't complete (we may still in some ways be foolish), yet we are safe because we are on His highway. There are guardrails on the dangerous curves, and He keeps us from falling off as He develops the wisdom and maturity in us that will also keep us on the highway.

Today, get on God's **Highway of Holiness**; make progress on it, invite others to join you – and remember to enjoy the journey.

January 26

Not by Might

So he answered and said to me: "This is the word of the LORD to Zerubbabel: 'Not by might nor by power, but by My Spirit,' says the LORD of hosts." (Zechariah 4:6)

Building a new temple 70 years after the Babylonians destroyed Solomon's temple, had stalled. Zerubbabel was the civic leader of Jerusalem and had the responsibility to finish rebuilding the temple, and he needed encouragement to do the work. God's Word came to him simply and powerfully: **Not by might nor by power, but by My Spirit**, said the LORD. In the vision of Zechariah 3, God spoke to Zerubbabel about the issue of purity. But purity alone isn't enough to accomplish the work of God. The work of God needs God's resources and not those of human **might** or **power**.

The word **might** focuses on collective strength, the resources of a group or an army. The word **power** focuses on individual strength. God says, "not by the resources of many or by one, but by My Spirit. It will not be by your cleverness, your ability, or your physical strength that the temple will be rebuilt, but by the Spirit of God." The necessary resource for God's work is the Holy Spirit and God promised Zerubbabel a rich resource in the Spirit of God. When we trust in our own resources – whether they are small or great in man's eyes – then we don't enjoy the full supply of the Spirit.

This great statement is connected to an earlier vision in the chapter – the vision of the olive trees and the lampstands supplied by oil coming right from the olive trees. We see that God wanted Zerubbabel to know that the Holy Spirit would continually supply his need, just as the olive trees in the vision continually supplied oil to the lamps on the lampstand. God wants His supply and our reliance on the Holy Spirit to be continual.

Oil is a good representation of the Holy Spirit:
- Oil lubricates – making for less friction among those filled with the Spirit.
- Oil heals – the Spirit of God brings healing and restoration.
- Oil lights when burned in a lamp – where the Spirit of God is there is light.
- Oil warms – where the Spirit of God is there are warmth and comfort.
- Oil invigorates – the Holy Spirit invigorates us for His service.
- Oil adorns as perfume – the Holy Spirit adorns us and makes us more pleasant to be around.
- Oil polishes – the Holy Spirit smoothens our rough edges.

The Holy Spirit works with and through human energy and initiative, but it's possible to have all the energy and initiative, but none of the Spirit. Is that what you want more of?

Today, ask for an outpouring of the Spirit in and through your life, and determine that it will not be by might, nor by power, but by His Spirit.

January 27

A Good Mourning

Blessed are those who mourn, for they shall be comforted. (Matthew 5:4)

Jesus, at the beginning of His great Sermon on the Mount, says that there is a particular blessing set aside for **those who mourn**.

These words challenge us as they are translated into our language, but in the vocabulary of the ancient Greek text, they are even a greater challenge. There were several different words one might use to describe mourning in that ancient Greek language, but the one used here is especially intense. According to the well-known historical and grammatical scholar William Barclay, "The Greek word for to mourn, used here, is the strongest word for mourning in the Greek language. It is the word which is used for mourning for the dead, for the passionate lament for one who was loved."

What is it that Jesus expects us to mourn over? The answer is found in noticing the progression of these Beatitudes. First one recognizes their poverty of spirit: *Blessed are the poor in spirit, for theirs in the kingdom of heaven* (Matthew 5:3). Having recognized our poverty of spirit we are expected to mourn over it.

Jesus did not speak of a casual sorrow for the consequences of our sin, but deep grief before God over our fallen condition. The weeping is for the needy condition of both the individual and society; but with the awareness that they are low and needy *because of sin*. **Those who mourn** essentially mourn over sin and its effects.

The apostle Paul spoke with the same idea, describing this mourning as the godly sorrow that produces repentance to salvation (2 Corinthians 7:10). It isn't that the mourning itself is so good; rather, the result of it is good. It leads to repentance and salvation.

As Jesus promised: **For they shall be comforted**. Those who mourn over their sin and their sinful condition are promised comfort. God allows this grief into our lives as a path, not as a destination. He never wanted us to be stuck on mourning, but to use it as the pathway to receive His comfort.

We have two pearls on a beautiful necklace: first poverty of spirit, and then the right reaction to that poverty – genuine mourning over our condition. This is the attitude within man that contradicts the dispassionate coolness attractive to many in the modern age; this is an attitude that knows how important it is to be right and reconciled with God. It is another way to express the feeling, "God, I want you."

Those who mourn can know something special of God. They can experience what Paul calls the *fellowship of His sufferings* (Philippians 3:10). They can also experience closeness to the *Man of Sorrows* who was acquainted with grief (Isaiah 53:3). And they can look for others who also mourn and point them to Jesus — thereby finding blessing and comfort, even amid mourning.

It can be a mourning leading to good instead of despair.

January 28

The Kind of Prayer God Hears

Now this is the confidence that we have in Him, that if we ask anything according to His will, He hears us. (1 John 5:14)

In this passage, we see the purpose of prayer, and the secret of power in prayer: to ask; to ask anything; to ask anything according to His will; and once having so asked, to have the assurance that He hears us.

First, God would have us **ask** in prayer. Much prayer fails because it never asks for anything. God is a loving God; He a generous giver and He wants us to ask Him.

Second, God would have us **ask anything** in prayer. This is not to say that anything we ask for will be granted, but that we can and should pray about everything. God cares about our whole life, and nothing is too small or too big to pray about. *And whatever we ask we receive from Him, because we keep His commandments and do those things that are pleasing in His sight.* (I John 3:22)

Next, God would have us ask **according to His will**. It is easy for us to only be concerned with our will before God and to have a fatalistic view regarding His will ("He will accomplish His will with or without my prayers anyway, won't He?"). But God wants us to see and discern His will through His Word, and then to pray His will into action.

If it's God's will, why doesn't He just do it, apart from our prayers? Why would He wait to accomplish His will until His people pray? Because God has appointed us to work with Him, as 2 Corinthians 6:1 says. God wants us to work with Him, and that means bringing our will and agenda into alignment with His. He wants us to care about the things He cares about, and He wants us to care about them enough to pray passionately! *Be anxious for nothing, but in everything by prayer and supplication, with thanksgiving, let your requests be made known to God.* (Philippians 4:6)

When we ask **according to His will** – when we are praying the promises of God – we can know that we have the petitions that we asked of God, and so we pray with real and definite faith.

The most powerful prayers in the Bible are those that understand the will of God and ask Him to perform it. We may be annoyed when one of our children says, "Daddy, this is what you promised, now please do it," but God is delighted. It shows our will is aligned with His, our dependence is on Him, and that we take His Word seriously.

We pray, "Your will be done on earth as it is in heaven." Through the kind of prayer John writes about in 1 John 5:14, we can partner with God in the accomplishing of His will on this earth.

Have you planned anything more important than that today?

January 29

You Can't Save Yourself

And she will bring forth a Son, and you shall call His name Jesus, for He will save His people from their sins. (Matthew 1:21)

The angel Gabriel brought this dramatic announcement to Mary and told her that she would bear a son miraculously – and that the son would **save His people from their sins**. The people could not save themselves from their sin. They needed a Savior to come and save them.

Some things you should not do for yourself. I read of a woman named Heather who lived in England. When she was 29 years old, doctors said she had an illness called myalgic encephalomyelitis, which leaves sufferers permanently exhausted. Heather felt she had the cure for her illness, but doctors wouldn't do it for her. She flew to the United States but could not find a doctor to do it. So, she did it herself. Heather drilled a hole in her head in front of a mirror, a headache treatment from the Middle Ages known as trepanation. Despite drilling too deeply and nearly puncturing her brain, she said "I have no regrets. I generally feel better and there's definitely more mental clarity." If she had more mental clarity, to begin with, she would never have tried such a foolish thing.

But the matter of our salvation is more than something that we *should not* do for ourselves. It is something that we simply *cannot* do for ourselves. Sometimes we think we can save ourselves when we compare our lives to those around us. "I'm not nearly as bad as him," we think. "Surely God must approve of me, while He must disapprove of him." On a human level, it is all very logical.

Salvation is not accomplished on a human level. It happens on a divine level as we receive what Jesus did for us on the cross. It is as if three men were in a boat, in the middle of the ocean. Their boat develops a leak, and they decide their only chance is to swim for land. The first man splashes for a short distance, but he can't swim – so he drowns. The next man is a fair swimmer, so he swims for a good distance before he drowns. The third man is an Olympic swimmer and swims a far distance – but he also drowns never seeing land. One made it much farther than the others, but they all perished.

It's the same way with trying to save yourself. You may do much better than someone else, but you can't do it good enough to succeed. You need to trust in what Jesus did to save you, because God promised that Jesus **will save His people from their sins**.

We are not right with God because of what we do for Him. We are made right with God because of what Jesus did for us.

Today, thank Him for the promise: **He will save His people from their sins**.

January 30

Not Against Flesh and Blood

For we do not wrestle against flesh and blood, but against principalities, against powers, against the rulers of the darkness of this age, against spiritual hosts of wickedness in the heavenly places. (Ephesians 6:12)

The fact that our real battle is not **against flesh and blood** is lost on many followers of Jesus, who put all their efforts in that direction. Paul's idea here is much the same as in 2 Corinthians 10:3-4: *For though we walk in the flesh, we do not war according to the flesh. For the weapons of our warfare are not carnal but mighty in God for pulling down strongholds.*

Then Paul described just whom we do battle against: **principalities, against powers, against the rulers of the darkness of this age, against spiritual hosts of wickedness in the heavenly places.** Paul used a variety of terms to refer to our spiritual adversaries. We should regard them as being on many different levels and of many different ranks, yet they all have one goal: to knock the Christian down from their place of standing.

It is doesn't matter if the particular opponent we face is a principality, a power, or a ruler of the darkness of this age. Collectively, they are all members of **spiritual hosts of wickedness in the heavenly places**. They are all part of a spiritual army that is organized and established into ranks – and under the headship of Satan, the devil, who comes against us with his strategies. We learn more about these principalities and powers from other passages in the New Testament.

- Romans 8:38 tells us that principalities cannot keep us from God's love. Therefore, there is a limit to their power.
- Ephesians 1:20-21 tells us that Jesus is in enthroned in heaven, far above all principalities and powers. Colossians 1:16 tells us that Jesus created principalities and powers. Colossians 2:10 tells us that Jesus is head over all principality and power. Therefore, Jesus is not the opposite of Satan or principalities.
- Ephesians 3:10-11 explains the church makes known the wisdom of God to principalities and powers. 1 Corinthians 15:24 tells us that principalities and powers have an end; one day, their purpose will be fulfilled, and God will no longer let them work. Therefore, God has a purpose in allowing their work.
- Colossians 2:15 tells us that Jesus disarmed principalities and powers at the cross. Therefore, our victory is rooted in what Jesus did, not in what we do. It isn't that there is no doing on our part – but our doing is the appropriation and application of what Jesus did.

Understanding our spiritual adversaries – what they can and can't do – is an essential part of success in our struggle against them.

Remember today that our adversaries in this struggle are not human, but spiritual – and Jesus has defeated them.

January 31

Stand

Therefore take up the whole armor of God, that you may be able to withstand in the evil day, and having done all, to stand. (Ephesians 6:13)

Paul introduced the idea of "the whole armor of God" in Ephesians 6:11. Now, he details the specific items and the primary purpose of spiritual warfare and the armor of God.

We are given this spiritual armor so **that you may be able to withstand in the evil day, and having done all, to stand**. This describes how we use the strength of God and the armor of God.

The main picture in Paul's mind is not that the Christian goes out attacking spiritual enemies. That concept may have its place in the Christian life, but that isn't Paul's thinking.

Instead of picturing an "army" of God's people seeking out and attacking some demonic fortress, we are to have the idea that Jesus illustrated in His ministry. Jesus didn't patrol around, looking for demons to conquer. Jesus knew what God the Father wanted Him to do, He set about doing it, and He dealt with satanic opposition when it arose. When satanic opposition raised itself, Jesus stood against it and was not moved.

God has given us a call, a mission, a course to fulfill. Satan will do his best to stop it. When he attacks and intimidates, we are to stand. This is Paul's emphasis in Ephesians 6:11 and 6:13. We love an energetic church that advances God's Kingdom so vigorously that it shakes the councils of hell, but we don't let principalities and powers set our agenda. We do the Lord's work and stand against every hint of spiritual opposition.

When we look through the New Testament, we see that God gives the Christian a glorious standing to maintain by faith and spiritual warfare:

- We stand in grace (Romans 5:2).
- We stand in the gospel (1 Corinthians 15:1).
- We stand in courage and strength (1 Corinthians 16:13).
- We stand in faith (2 Corinthians 1:24).
- We stand in Christian liberty (Galatians 5:1).
- We stand in Christian unity (Philippians 1:27).
- We stand in the Lord (Philippians 4:1).
- We should stand perfect and complete in the will of God (Colossians 4:12).

Each of these is a place to stand. We should expect that from time to time, spiritual attack will attempt to shake us from this standing.

God helping you, stand today.

February 1

How to Be a Doer of the Word

If anyone among you thinks he is religious, and does not bridle his tongue but deceives his own heart, this one's religion is useless. Pure and undefiled religion before God and the Father is this: to visit orphans and widows in their trouble, and to keep oneself unspotted from the world. (James 1:26-27)

James begins: **If anyone among you thinks he is religious**. Real religion is not shown by merely hearing the Word, but by doing it. One way to do God's Word is to control the tongue. The New Testament never uses this ancient Greek word for **religious** in a positive sense (Acts 17:22, 25:19, 26:5; Colossians 2:23). James used it here of someone religious, but not right with God, and it is evident because he **does not bridle his tongue**.

There is a warning that one's **religion** may be truly useless. A believer's walk with God is **useless** if it does not translate into the way they live and treat others. Many are deceived in their own heart regarding the reality of their walk with God.

James here seems to echo the ideas and words of Jesus, especially in passages such as Matthew 23. There Jesus rebuked the hypocritical religious men of His day who gave much attention to the ceremonial aspects of the law but gave little attention to the more essential elements of the law.

It wasn't that James saw no value in the public display of religion. He speaks of the assembly of believers in James 2:2. And James understood the need for leaders and elders in the church in James 5:14. So James wasn't against displays of religion and religious leaders – just hollow, empty religion. A faithful religious life is true **before God** and **pure and undefiled** in His sight.

In addition, a real walk with God shows itself in simple, practical ways. Those who **visit orphans and widows in their trouble** display some of the marks of true religion. Another mark is to keep oneself unstained by the world's corruption.

James thought that real religion was shown in charity and purity. The charity is of the kind that cares enough to visit the needy. The purity is of the sort that recognizes that there should be some separation from life as the culture commonly lives it.

That is in the idea of the phrase **unspotted from the world**. A Christian should not retreat from the world. They should interact with **orphans and widows in their trouble** and others in need. The Christian is in the world; they are not of it and should remain **unspotted from the world**.

In these two ways, James expresses a life that does God's Word. Of course, being a doer of the Word is broader than only those – but the areas of charity and purity still challenge our lives today.

Today, be more than a hearer of the Word – be a doer.

February 2

Partial Obedience

And Saul attacked the Amalekites, from Havilah all the way to Shur, which is east of Egypt. He also took Agag king of the Amalekites alive, and utterly destroyed all the people with the edge of the sword. But Saul and the people spared Agag and the best of the sheep, the oxen, the fatlings, the lambs, and all that was good, and were unwilling to utterly destroy them. But everything despised and worthless, that they utterly destroyed. (1 Samuel 15:7-9)

God commanded King Saul and the Israelites to carry out a unique war of judgment against the Amalekites. Saul's initial response was right; we read **Saul attacked the Amalekites.** This was in obedience to the LORD, but it was selective incomplete obedience. First, Saul **took Agag king of the Amalekites alive**, while he also **utterly destroyed all the people with the edge of the sword**. This was partial obedience, because God commanded Saul to bring His judgment on all the people, including the king.

No matter what the reason, when the people saw that Saul kept Agag alive, they also disobeyed and saved the best of the livestock for themselves. God commanded in 1 Samuel 15:3 that every ox and sheep, camel, and donkey be destroyed, and Saul and the people of Israel did not do this.

In a typical war in the ancient world, armies were freely permitted to plunder their conquered foes. This was often how the army was paid. But it was wrong for anyone in Israel to benefit from the war against the Amalekites because it was an appointed judgment from God. This was just as wrong as a hangman emptying the pockets of the man he just executed for murder.

Nevertheless, **everything despised and worthless, that they utterly destroyed**. They were careful to keep only the best for themselves. We can imagine they were all pleased with what they gained after the battle.

This perhaps was worst of all because Israel did not show God's heart in judgment. When they came home happy and excited because of what they gained from the battle, it implied something joyful about God's judgment. This dishonored God, who brings His judgment reluctantly and without pleasure, longing that men and women would instead repent.

The Scottish preacher Alexander Maclaren wisely observed: "Partial obedience is complete disobedience. Saul and his men obeyed as far as suited them; that is to say, they did not obey God at all, but their own inclinations, both in sparing the good and destroying the worthless. What was not worth carrying off was destroyed, not because of the command, but to save trouble."

Sometimes partial obedience is better than total disobedience; but there are other times when it is complete disobedience. This was one of those times, and we must always be on guard against the tendency to obey God only as far as it suits us. That isn't obedience at all; it is self-love with a thin spiritual covering.

God help us all to give Him better obedience than that.

February 3

Worse Before Better

So the same day Pharaoh commanded the taskmasters of the people and their officers, saying, "You shall no longer give the people straw to make brick as before. Let them go and gather straw for themselves. And you shall lay on them the quota of bricks that they made before. You shall not reduce it. For they are idle; therefore they cry out, saying, 'Let us go and sacrifice to our God.' Let more work be laid on the men, that they may labor in it, and let them not regard false words." (Exodus 5:6-9)

The people of Israel had been slaves in Egypt for about 400 years. After 400 years, a people get used to their condition. Over time, people tend to adjust to their slave conditions. Now, at the appointed time, God sent a man named Moses. Moses used to be a prince in Egypt, perhaps even heir to the throne.

But when Moses murdered an Egyptian slave master, he fled Egypt and lived in the wilderness for 40 years. At God's calling, Moses came back and brought a message to the millions of Israelite slaves in Egypt: "God has sent me to be your deliverer. God will free you and take you out of Egypt to your own country where you will never be slaves again."

The Israelite slaves were excited – deliverance sounded wonderful! But when they showed up for work the next day, things were worse, not better. Moses told Pharaoh to let the people of Israel go. First, Moses only asked for three days off so they could go and worship God in the wilderness. But Pharaoh not only denied the three days off work; he saw the request itself as a waste of good working time.

Pharaoh then punished Israel because Moses made the request. Pharaoh must have thought, "The Israelites seem to have enough time to make these crazy requests – then they must have enough time for more work." Pharaoh commanded the Israelites now must gather their own straw for making bricks. Straw was an important ingredient in brick because its acidic content made the bricks stronger.

So, when Moses began his work as the deliverer of Israel, the children of Israel were in a worse place than before. At the start, Moses' leadership didn't make anything better. Their hopes were raised, but things got worse and not better.

It isn't surprising that when people first get right with God, sometimes things in their life seem to get worse before they get better. If this is you, don't be discouraged. God has just begun to work, and the danger is giving up because of discouragement.

Don't give up. God's work for Israel was bigger than just bringing them out of Egypt. God wanted to transform them from a slave people to a truly free people.

If God's work in our life means that it must get a little worse before it gets better, then so be it.

February 4

Believing What God Tells You

For by grace you have been saved through faith, and that not of yourselves; it is the gift of God, not of works, lest anyone should boast. (Ephesians 2:8-9)

Many people want to be right with God only if they can earn and deserve that status. But we can't earn the right to be right with God. It's a gift we receive by faith. We must remember that faith is not a good work by which we earn salvation. Although good works accompany true faith, faith in and of itself is not a "work." Faith merely sees the offer God makes and believes it to be true. It looks at God's promises and says, "I believe they are for me."

Faith is refusing to call God a liar. It is taking God's Word at face value and trusting that He and His Word are reliable. When we do not have faith, we deny God's Word is true, and we call Him a liar. What merit is there in not calling God a liar? That is only common sense.

There is a story about a man who was teaching a Sunday school class full of small boys. One day he offered a boy in the class a brand-new watch. The boy thought that it was just a trick. Fearing his classmates would laugh at him when the trick was revealed, he refused the watch. The teacher then offered it to the next boy, but he followed the example of the first boy. One by one, each boy refused the watch because the offer seemed too good to be true; certainly, the teacher just wanted to trick them. But the last boy was bold enough to accept the watch when the teacher offered it to him. When the teacher actually gave it to him, the other boys were amazed and angry.

The teacher used the example situation to show them that no matter how good a gift was offered to them, they must believe the word of the giver and receive the gift before it could do them any good.

In 1829, a Pennsylvania man named George Wilson was sentenced by the United States Court to be hanged for robbery and murder. President Andrew Jackson pardoned him, but the prisoner refused the pardon. Wilson insisted that he was not pardoned unless he accepted it. That was a point of law never raised before, and President Jackson called on the Supreme Court to decide. Chief Justice John Marshall gave the following decision. "A pardon is a paper, the value of which depends on its acceptance by the person implicated. If it is refused, it is no pardon. George Wilson must be hanged." And he was.

Even so, God's offer of pardon and salvation in Christ Jesus is offered to many, but only those who trust in God and His Word will gain the benefits of that pardon.

Under grace, the key principles of life with God are believing Him and receiving from Him. Today, why not simply believe what God says?

February 5

Angels Watching Over You

Are they not all ministering spirits sent forth to minister for those who will inherit salvation? (Hebrews 1:14)

This verse speaks of angels and the role they play in serving on behalf of **those who will inherit salvation** – God's people. It is true that angels often fascinate us – sometimes too much so!

The Bible teaches that angels are real, and they are present among us. We are not to pay them too much attention, lest we fall into the danger of *taking delight in false humility and worship of angels, intruding into those things which he has not seen* (Colossians 2:18). It is good to consider that we relate to angels in a way that many do not understand.

The Bible tells us angels are captivated by the outworking of God's eternal purpose and plan among humanity. We have a constant angelic audience, and God's dealings with humans are instructive to the angels, both good and bad. Several Bible passages show this:

- *Now the manifold wisdom of God might be made known by the church to the principalities and powers in the heavenly places* (Ephesians 3:10). "Principalities and powers" refer to angelic beings.
- *...we have been made a spectacle to the world, both to angels and to men.* (1 Corinthians 4:9)
- *...through those who have preached the gospel to you by the Holy Spirit sent from heaven; things which angels desire to look into.* (1 Peter 1:12)
- *I charge you before God and the Lord Jesus Christ and the elect angels that you observe these things...* (1 Timothy 5:21)
- *For this reason the woman ought to have a symbol of authority on her head, because of the angels.* (1 Corinthians 11:10)

This is one reason why the conduct of the church is so important.

Angelic and demonic beings are looking on, and God intends to teach them through us. We have a constant angelic audience, and God's dealings with humans are a lesson to both good and bad angels. If this communicates anything to us, it should remind us that we are important in God's plan. You may see yourself as an insignificant part in God's eternal plan, but the angels and demons surrounding us disagree with that low estimation. They consider you important enough to put their attention on you. Your life before God matters. God knows it, the angels know it, and even every demon knows it, but you may not be aware of it.

Today, thank God for the important place He has for you in His plan – and live in consideration of His purpose for you.

February 6

Unintentional Danger

And if a person sins unintentionally, then he shall bring a female goat in its first year as a sin offering. So the priest shall make atonement for the person who sins unintentionally, when he sins unintentionally before the LORD, to make atonement for him; and it shall be forgiven him. (Numbers 15:27-28)

It's an old saying: "the road to hell is paved with good intentions." But the truth of this saying is often ignored. Today, we tend to excuse all sorts of things if there might be a good intention behind evil or sinful actions. But the Bible speaks of some sins that are unintentionally committed. Many today live as though if something is unintentional, it cannot be a sin. But many of the worst sins are committed with good intentions. Intentions don't always matter when the result is sin. We can sin in terrible (and stupid) ways even when we don't intend to.

Especially in the 20th century, those dedicated to honorable causes have committed all sorts of terrible atrocities. Communism sought to establish a fair economy, yet it became the instrument of murder for tens of millions of people. Nazism intended to rebuild war-torn Germany and lift national pride – and it ended in the death of millions. Just because we have good intentions doesn't mean that we haven't sinned and perhaps sinned terribly.

In the church, many a gossip, many a talebearer, many a divisive person will claim to have good intentions. The same applies to numberless other sins we are often ready to ignore or think lightly of. We excuse a lot based on the idea, "after all, they meant well."

It isn't that intentional or presumptuous sin isn't also bad – God deals with that in Numbers 15:30-31. Literally, presumptuous sin means to sin "with a high hand." It speaks of a flagrant rebellion against God, the Law of Moses, and God's people as a whole. That kind of sin was not to be tolerated in Israel, and God told them how to deal with presumptuous sin. But just because intentional sin is worse, it doesn't mean that unintentional sin is nothing.

Unintentional sins required blood atonement. A bull had to be sacrificed when the nation was guilty (Numbers 15:24), and a female goat had to be sacrificed when an individual was guilty of unintentional sins. There was no exception. Sin is sin and must be dealt with as such, even if the motive seemed to be good.

It is even more serious when we realize that sin – intentional or unintentional – hinders our fellowship with God. Is there unintentional sin in your life that you excuse because you think you mean well? Even if you mean well, it hinders your fellowship with God.

Today, deal with it the way Moses said to – confess your sin, cover it with the atoning blood (of Jesus Christ), and do whatever you must to stay close to Jesus and away from your sin – intentional or unintentional.

February 7

Stopping Flaming Arrows

Above all, taking the shield of faith with which you will be able to quench all the fiery darts of the wicked one. And take the helmet of salvation, and the sword of the Spirit, which is the word of God. (Ephesians 6:16-18)

One by one, Paul described spiritual truths and principles that help the Christian live for God in this world by comparing those truths and principles to a Roman soldier's armor. Paul recognized that the Christian's struggle was spiritual and not against flesh-and-blood people (Ephesians 6:12). Still, the soldier's armor could describe what a Christian needed to win in his or her spiritual conflict. That armor helped the Roman Legions effectively fight for their empire, and the spiritual armor given to believers helps them to live for God's kingdom successfully.

In Ephesians, the apostle divided this armor of God into two groups: the armor to *have* and the armor to *take*. In Ephesians 6:16, he described the first aspect of the armor to take: **taking the shield of faith with which you will be able to quench all the fiery darts of the wicked one**.

In this, faith is represented as a **shield**, protecting us from all the fiery darts of the wicked one. Those flaming arrows are the persistent efforts of demonic foes to weaken us through fear and unbelief.

The shield Paul described was not a small round one, but a large, oblong shield that could protect the whole body. In ancient warfare, these **fiery darts** were launched in large numbers at the beginning of a battle. The idea was not only to injure the enemy, but also to shoot at him from all possible sides with a massive number of arrows, and thus create confusion and panic.

Consider all the harmful and destructive things that fly through your mind, as if they were flaming arrows meant to strike you down, or cause confusion and panic.

We battle against angry, vengeful, bitter thoughts. We face desperate, downcast, dark feelings. Proud, vain, selfish imaginations come against us. Strong, irrational, unprofitable fears flood on us. We deal with destructive, hateful, jealous lies and foolish, hurtful, debasing lusts.

The wicked one – our spiritual adversary – throws these against us at every opportunity, and they come at us as if they were flaming arrows. Used effectively, the **shield of faith** makes them ineffective.

Do you feel as if you are losing faith? Regard that feeling as a flaming arrow and block it with the shield of faith. Stop *trying* to trust God and *simply* trust Him.

God honors and blesses this humble dependence of faith – and those flaming arrows will not only be stopped before they can injure, but they will also be quenched of all their ability to cause confusion and panic.

Say: "I put my trust in You, O Lord; help me for the sake of Jesus. I choose to not trust in myself, but in who Jesus is, and in what He did for me on the cross. Show Your strength in my weakness."

February 8

Sustained by His Word

Unless Your law had been my delight, I would then have perished in my affliction. I will never forget Your precepts, for by them You have given me life. (Psalm 119:92-93)

Most people find something to delight in – a hobby, interest, entertainment, relationship, or whatever. We don't know what else might have been delightful to the author of Psalm 119, but one thing was clear – the Word of God was his delight.

The psalmist plainly said that God's Word (**Your law**) had been his **delight**. This made the psalmist happy. Reading, studying, and thinking deeply on God's Word was not a burdensome chore; it was a delight.

God met the psalmist in His Word – it was a place of relationship. When we have fellowship with God in His Word, it makes our time in His law delightful. When the Bible seems like an ancient academic work, it may feel like a burden; but it is a delight as the meeting ground with the living God.

This delight had a real result. His relationship with God sustained him so much he said that, without it, he would have **perished** in his **affliction**. The psalmist knew that he would not have been sustained in his season of affliction without his strong, meaningful relationship with God and His Word.

This delight goes beyond mere Bible knowledge. It's a relationship with God in and through His Word that gives strength and spiritual nourishment. His long practice of reading, learning, considering, digesting, and doing God's Word got him through seasons of affliction.

The great preacher of Victorian England, Charles Spurgeon, quoted the story of a man named Alexander Wallace. One day Wallace stood in a grocery shop in a factory town, and an old frail widow came to buy food. Times were hard, and the factories had little work. Many people lived on charity. The poor widow received a small amount of money and used it to buy food. Yet she saved her last bit of money to buy oil for her lamp. Wallace remembered her words: "Now I must buy oil with this, that I may see to read my Bible during these long dark nights, for it is my only comfort now when every other comfort has gone away." She found true delight and life in God's Word.

The psalmist understood, and would never **forget** God's Word, because by that Word God had **given** him **life**. Like the old Scottish widow, he remembered the life-giving power and character of God's Word. It was this life that strengthened him and brought him comfort in the season of affliction. God's Word brings life because it is alive. Even the most gifted preacher doesn't bring life to the Bible or "make the Bible come alive" – it has life in itself.

The Bible will bring life to you, and to all who will give it the honor, attention, and obedience it deserves.

February 9

The Source of Strength

You will keep him in perfect peace, whose mind is stayed on You, because he trusts in You. Trust in the LORD forever, for in YAH, the LORD, is everlasting strength. (Isaiah 26:3-4)

Some have this **perfect peace**, but it is fleeting, and they are not kept there. Others can be kept in peace, but it is not a perfect peace; it is the peace of the wicked, the peace of spiritual sleep, and ultimate destruction.

Who are the people who enjoy this **perfect peace**? Isaiah tells us: **Whose mind is stayed on You**. When we keep our minds stayed – settled on, established on – the LORD Himself, then we can be kept in this perfect peace. This isn't so much a matter of our *spirit* or of our *soul* or of our *heart* – it is a matter of our **mind**.

- Believers are to love the Lord our God with their mind (Matthew 22:37).
- Believers are transformed by the renewing of the mind (Romans 12:2).
- Believers can have the mind of Christ (1 Corinthians 2:16, Philippians 2:5).
- Believers are not to set the mind on earthly things (Philippians 3:19), but on things above (Colossians 3:2).

To be kept in this perfect peace, our mind must be **stayed**. Where does your mind stay, or remain? What do you lay your mind on? To have this perfect peace, your mind cannot occasionally come to the LORD; it must be **stayed** on Him.

If our mind is stayed on ourselves, or our problems, or the problem people in our lives, or on anything else, we can't have this perfect peace. This is the heart that says with the apostle Paul, *that I may know Him* (Philippians 3:10). Satan loves to get our minds on anything except God and His love for us!

To emphasize the point, Isaiah wrote: **Because he trusts in You**. This is another way of expressing the idea of keeping our minds stayed on Him. Almost always, you keep your mind stayed on whatever you are trusting. When we trust the LORD, we keep our minds stayed on Him. It all means that the battle for trust in our lives begins in our minds. If we trust the LORD, it will show in our actions, but it will begin in our minds.

Isaiah continued in verse four: **Trust in the LORD forever**. Because of the promise of Isaiah 26:3, we are exhorted to trust in the LORD forever – and therefore to receive the blessing of His promise, perfect peace!

These two wonderful verses end like this: **For in YAH, the LORD, is everlasting strength**. If the LORD calls us to rely on Him completely with our mind, He appeals to our mind with a rational reason why we should trust the LORD: because He **is everlasting strength**. It isn't that the LORD *has* everlasting strength; He **is everlasting strength**.

Today, that should put your mind at peace – perfect peace indeed!

February 10

Patient Endurance

My brethren, count it all joy when you fall into various trials, knowing that the testing of your faith produces patience. But let patience have its perfect work, that you may be perfect and complete, lacking nothing. (James 1:2-4)

God never intended for trials to work in us a passive resignation; rather, He intends that trials produce in us an active endurance – a true perseverance.

If the Greek language was good enough for Paul, it should be good enough for us! This doesn't mean we must become Greek scholars (though that isn't a bad pursuit), but each of us can become familiar with a few important Greek words in the New Testament.

The ancient Greek word *hupomone* has the sense of a cheerful or hopeful endurance. Common English translations of this word are patience, perseverance, and endurance. You will find this word in passages such as Romans 5:3-4, 2 Corinthians 12:12, Colossians 1:11, and Hebrews 10:36, 12:1.

Hupomone is one of the great words of the New Testament. God's plan for our lives is to work patience in us – but not the kind of patience we usually think of. When we think of patience, we usually have the idea of something passive – as if patience were the kind of thing that would enable a person to wait for two hours in the doctor's waiting room without complaining.

But *hupomone* isn't a passive word at all. It has the idea of an *active endurance*. It isn't the quality that will enable a person to wait passively, but to actively endure to the end until the mission is completed. *Hupomone* is the kind of dogged determination a marathon runner needs to cross the finish line. The Greek scholar William Barclay calls *hupomone* "one of the noblest of New Testament words."

In one ancient writing, *hupomone* is used to describe the ability of a plant to thrive under hard and unfavorable circumstances. Some define *hupomone* as "spiritual staying power." *Hupomone* can transform the hardest trial into real joy because it looks beyond the present difficulty to the victory ahead.

God wants to strengthen us with His might (as in Colossians 1:11), not to make us passive, but to make us the kind of people who will endure to the end, seeing His will done in our lives.

Sometimes people say, "don't pray for patience, because God will send things in your life to produce it." Truthfully, we should all be praying for *hupomone* – active endurance because we need to be conditioned and trained so we can endure to the end. A marathon runner goes through months of conditioning so he can finish the race. Perhaps God has you on His "spiritual conditioning program" right now. If so, don't resent it – but today give thanks that He cares enough about you to train you to make it to the very end.

February 11

Continually Cleansed

But if we walk in the light as He is in the light, we have fellowship with one another, and the blood of Jesus Christ His Son cleanses us from all sin. (1 John 1:7)

One of the valuable assurances for those who come to Jesus is the promise of cleansing from sin. Here in 1 John 1:7, we read the simple declaration: the **blood of Jesus Christ His Son cleanses us from all sin**. John wrote that as believers walk in the light, they will also enjoy the continual cleansing of Jesus. We need a constant cleansing because the Bible says we continually sin and fall short of God's glory (Romans 3:23).

While washing the feet of the disciples, Jesus came to Peter. Hoping to show how spiritual he was, Peter refused this humble act of service from Jesus. Jesus told Peter that if he refused to let Him wash his feet, Peter would have no part in Jesus. After that, Peter told Jesus to wash his whole body! The reply of Jesus was profound: *He who is bathed needs only to wash his feet, but is completely clean; and you are clean, but not all of you* (John 13:10). The continual cleansing mentioned in 1 John 1:7 is the washing of dusty feet that have come in contact with a world that has a lot of dirt.

This continual cleansing is ours by the **blood of Jesus**. Not His literal blood, but His literal death in our place, and the wrath of God that Jesus endured on behalf of His people. That death of Jesus – His blood – paid for all the sins of His people: past, present, and future. The work of Jesus on the cross doesn't only deal with the *guilt* of sin that might send us to hell; it also deals with the *stain* of sin that would hinder our continual relationship with God. We need to come to God frequently with the simple plea, "cleanse me with the blood of Jesus." Not because we haven't been cleansed before, but because we need to be continually cleansed to enjoy a continual relationship.

The blood of Jesus can cleanse us **from all sin**. This includes the sin we inherited from Adam, the sin we committed as children, and the sins of our growing up. Sins like lying, stealing, cheating, adultery, swearing, drugs, drunkenness, promiscuity, and murder. The blood of Jesus can cleanse us from sins that haunt us every day, and from sins we didn't even know we committed.

The blood of Jesus **cleanses us from all sin**. The word **cleanses** was written in the present tense, not the future tense. We do not have to hope we will one day be cleansed. Because of what Jesus did on the cross for us, we can be cleansed today!

God promised that though your sins were as red as scarlet, He would make you as white as snow.

Do you feel guilty or disqualified before God today? Accept the work of Jesus on the cross as full cleansing for your sins.

February 12

Lavishing Love on All

You have heard that it was said, "An eye for an eye and a tooth for a tooth." But I tell you not to resist an evil person. But whoever slaps you on your right cheek, turn the other to him also. If anyone wants to sue you and take away your tunic, let him have your cloak also. And whoever compels you to go one mile, go with him two. Give to him who asks you, and from him who wants to borrow from you do not turn away. (Matthew 5:38-42)

As Jesus helped His followers better understand the Law of Moses, He came to a law that had been often abused. Jesus began by reminding them they had been taught, **an eye for an eye and a tooth for a tooth.** The Law of Moses does teach this (Exodus 21:24), but over time religious teachers moved this command out of its proper place as a principle that *limited* punishment from the civil government to being an *obligation* in personal relationships.

Jesus demonstrated with His life that evil should and must be resisted. Jesus here spoke of the evil that is done against us in personal relationships. Jesus Himself was viciously insulted and spoken against and He responded with strength and love.

Jesus explained a better way than **eye for an eye** in personal relationships – to instead **turn the other** cheek. In this, Jesus did not mean that a disciple of His can never resist or defend against a physical attack. When Jesus spoke of a slap **on your right cheek**, it was culturally understood as a deep insult, not a physical attack (2 Corinthians 11:20). Jesus spoke to personal relationships, and not to the proper work of government in restraining evil (Romans 13:1-4).

In the same thought, Jesus also said that if one **wants to sue you and take away your tunic, let him have your cloak also**. Under the Law of Moses, the outer cloak was something that could not be taken from someone (Exodus 22:26, Deuteronomy 24:13). Jesus wanted His disciples to gladly let go of what the law says they might legally keep.

Then Jesus told His disciples to go the second **mile**. At that time Judea was under Roman military occupation. Any Roman soldier might command a Jew to carry his backpack for one mile. Jesus says, "Go beyond what's required by law and give another mile out of love." This is how the disciples of Jesus transform an attempt to control us into an act of love.

Jesus also told His people, **give to him who asks of you**. The only limit to this kind of sacrifice is the limit that love itself will set. It isn't loving to give in to someone's manipulation without our transforming it into a free act of love. It isn't loving to give someone what they ask for when giving it does more harm than good to them.

Today, pursue the heart of a true disciple of Jesus: lavishing love on all. As Paul said in Romans 12:21, *Do not be overcome by evil, but overcome evil with good.*

February 13

Say What You Mean, Mean What You Say

Again you have heard that it was said to those of old, "You shall not swear falsely, but shall perform your oaths to the Lord." But I say to you, do not swear at all: neither by heaven, for it is God's throne; nor by the earth, for it is His footstool; nor by Jerusalem, for it is the city of the great King. Nor shall you swear by your head, because you cannot make one hair white or black. But let your "Yes" be "Yes," and your "No," "No." For whatever is more than these is from the evil one. (Matthew 5:33-37)

This section of the Sermon on the Mount shows that the great respect the Jewish people had for God's law was often more based on tradition than on a correct understanding of God's Word. In this passage, Jesus dealt with their incorrect understanding of the law against swearing oaths.

Jesus began, by relating the commandment they had heard: **You shall not swear falsely.** It is clear enough in the Hebrew Scriptures; one of the Ten Commandments says, *you shall not take the name of the LORD your God in vain* (Exodus 20:7). Yet by the time of Jesus, the religious leaders (often referred to as the scribes and Pharisees) had twisted this law. It was meant to prevent taking the name of God in vain, but they used it to allow taking virtually any other name in a false oath.

Therefore, in those days it was accepted and common to swear all the time – yet to avoid swearing by the name of God. Jesus mentioned that some would swear by heaven, or by the earth, by Jerusalem, or by one's own head. As Jesus explained later in the Gospel of Matthew, it was also common to swear by the temple, or to swear by the gold in the temple; to swear by the altar, or to swear by the offering on the altar (Matthew 23:16-22). In this, they perhaps kept the letter of the law, but not the intent or spirit of the law.

Correcting this misunderstanding, Jesus said, **do not swear at all**. Jesus reminded us that God is always part of every oath; if you swear by heaven, earth, Jerusalem, or even your head, you swear by God – and your oath must be honored.

Jesus told us that instead of swearing any kind of oath to establish that you are telling the truth, we should simply **let your "Yes" be "Yes."** Having to swear or make oaths shows the weakness of our word. It demonstrates that there is not enough weight in our own character to confirm what we say.

Sometimes a person is entirely truthful, yet not believed – Jesus is the prime example of this. We should make sure that there is nothing in what we say or in our approach to the truth that gives others valid reasons to doubt us.

We should say what we mean and mean what we say.

February 14

Choosing a Difficult Kind of Love

Then the Lord said to me, "Go again, love a woman who is loved by a lover and is committing adultery, just like the love of the Lord for the children of Israel, who look to other gods and love the raisin cakes of the pagans." (Hosea 3:1)

God loves you. Perhaps you have heard or read those words a thousand or more times, and after a while, they begin to lose their impact. They become just three words on a page that no longer amaze you. God knows all about this tendency in us; He knows our frame; He remembers that we are only dust (Psalm 103:14). So, God sends prophets to present the message in new and powerful ways.

When God told Hosea, **go again, love a woman who is loved by a lover and is committing adultery**. He directed Hosea to go back to his wife, even though she was still committing adultery. It wasn't in the past; it was in the present. Yet he was still commanded to go back to her and love her. We learn two important principles from this.

First, Hosea stayed true to his marriage and did not divorce his wife even though she was clearly guilty of adultery. This shows us that though Deuteronomy 24:1 and Matthew 19:7-8 permit divorce when adultery breaks the marriage union, it by no means commands divorce.

Second, it shows us an important principle about love: Hosea was directed to love, even when it must have been hard. One of the illusions is that love has very little to do with our will but in principle, the Scriptures show us love is largely a matter of the will, and when we direct ourselves to love someone God tells us to love, it can and will happen.

Your feelings don't justify a lack of love towards God. When the Bible says, *You shall love the Lord your God with all your heart, with all your soul, and with all your strength* (Deuteronomy 6:5), it directs the command towards our will. No matter what your feelings are, you can choose to love God today.

That's why He told Hosea, **just like the love of the Lord for the children of Israel**. This explains why God commanded Hosea to go back to his still-unfaithful wife. It was not only for the sake of Hosea and his wife Gomer but also so that they would become a living lesson of the Lord's relationship with His people. Israel was still steeped in spiritual adultery, yet God still loved them.

Choice is the missing element in the way many love God and others. They wait to be swept away by feelings; instead, we are responsible to make the choice and then expect that the feelings will follow.

If it seems like too much, think of the greatness of God's love and compassion towards you – that should make you much more loving, compassionate, and forgiving towards others.

February 15
Inward and Outward Repentance

Then Samuel spoke to all the house of Israel, saying, "If you return to the LORD with all your hearts, then put away the foreign gods and the Ashtoreths from among you, and prepare your hearts for the LORD, and serve Him only; and He will deliver you from the hand of the Philistines." So the children of Israel put away the Baals and the Ashtoreths, and served the LORD only. (1 Samuel 7:3-4)

Israel had just been through a season of crisis – the loss of the ark of the covenant. Then the ark came back to them, but many people at Beth Shemesh died because they disobediently looked inside the sacred ark.

After that, **Samuel spoke to all the house of Israel**. Samuel was strangely absent from the whole ark of the covenant disaster. 1 Samuel 4:1 was the last place Samuel was mentioned, right before Israel schemed to use the ark as a good luck charm in battle.

When Samuel spoke, he called the nation to repentance. He said, **if you return with all your hearts, then put away the foreign gods**. The repentance had to be inward (**with all your hearts**) and outward (**put away the foreign gods**).

The inward aspect of repentance was more important and had to come first. That is why Samuel first called Israel to return **with all your hearts**, and then he told them to **put away the foreign gods**.

However, inward repentance is a secret thing. No one can really see the heart of another person. Yet the inward was proved by the outward. We can know if Israel did return **with all your hearts** by seeing if they **put away the foreign gods**. No one could see their heart, but they could see if they put away the foreign gods.

Samuel told Israel that when it came to Yahweh, the covenant God of Israel, they must **serve Him only**. For the most part, Israel did not feel they rejected Yahweh; they thought they only *added* the worship of other gods to their worship of Yahweh. Samuel called on Israel to turn their backs on these other gods and to **serve Him only**.

Thankfully, the children of Israel obeyed. It says, **the children of Israel put away the Baals and the Ashtoreths, and served the LORD only**. The local gods of Baal and Ashtoreth were popular idols among the people of Israel. Baal was attractive because he was thought to be the god of weather, bringing good crops and financial success. Ashtoreth was attractive because she was considered the goddess of fertility, thus connecting her to love and sex.

Today, people still love to make idols of financial success and idols of romantic love and sex. Money and romantic love have their place, but never as idols in our lives.

Make today a day of both inward and outward repentance.

The Right Foundation

February 16

Therefore thus says the Lord God: "Behold, I lay in Zion a stone for a foundation, a tried stone, a precious cornerstone, a sure foundation; whoever believes will not act hastily. Also I will make justice the measuring line, and righteousness the plummet; the hail will sweep away the refuge of lies, and the waters will overflow the hiding place." (Isaiah 28:16-17)

Isaiah 28 begins as a rebuke to the drunkards of Israel, the northern kingdom, especially confronting their lack of self-control. Then it confronted the drunken priests of that same kingdom, painting a bleak picture of their degraded lives. They mocked Isaiah for his simple, clear message. They mockingly said that it was "precept on precept, line on line" – so simple that a child could understand it. Yet God and His prophet Isaiah received that mocking word as a compliment and knew that it made those mockers even more guilty for rejecting such a clear and understandable word.

Instead, the leaders of Israel hid in their "covenant of death" and their "refuge of lies." In response to such wickedness, particularly on the part of Israel's leaders, God laid out a different plan – His plan. Therefore, God said, **Behold, I lay in Zion a stone for a foundation**. In contrast to the weak, narrow foundation of the wicked (*we have made lies our refuge, and under falsehood we have hidden ourselves*, Isaiah 28:15). God has a solid foundation for our life – **a stone for a foundation**.

1 Peter 2:6 applied this passage directly to the Messiah, Jesus Christ. He is the foundation for our lives, and only with a secure, stable foundation can anything lasting be built.

The phrase **Behold, I lay in Zion** shows this is God's work. We are unable to provide the right kind of foundation for our lives, but God can lay a foundation for us.

It is truly **a tried stone**. Our Messiah was **tried**, tested, and proven to be the glorious, obedient Son of God. It is truly **a precious cornerstone**. Our Messiah is **precious**, and a **cornerstone**. The cornerstone provides the lines, the pattern for all the rest of the construction. Our Messiah is a **sure foundation**, and we can build everything on Him without fear.

God made **justice the measuring line, and righteousness the plummet**. In God's building work, it isn't as if He establishes the cornerstone and then walks away and allows the construction to be carried out any old way. He keeps the building straight with justice and righteousness.

Isaiah said, **the hail will sweep away the refuge of lies, and the waters will overflow the hiding place**. The ungodly leaders of Jerusalem *made lies their refuge* and found a hiding place *under falsehood* (Isaiah 28:15). But the storms of life and God's judgment would sweep away their refuge of lies and their hiding place. They had built on the wrong foundation and would therefore see destruction.

Don't be like the ungodly leaders; build your life on the sure foundation.

February 17

Taking Heed

How can a young man cleanse his way?
By taking heed according to Your word. (Psalm 119:9)

Look closely at the answer to the question: **By taking heed according to Your word**.

A morally clean life begins **by taking heed**. A life of moral purity doesn't happen accidentally. If one doesn't take heed, the natural path is towards impurity and degeneration. One must take heed to be pure.

Attention must be given in the right place – a devotion and attention to the Word of God, **by taking heed according to Your word**. This is how one takes heed. The foundation for a morally pure life is found in God's Word, the Bible.

God's Word shows us the *standard* of purity, so we know what is right and wrong

God's Word shows us the *reasons* for purity, so we understand God's commands

God's Word shows us the *difficulty* of purity and reminds us to be on guard.

God's Word shows us the *blessings* of purity, giving the incentive to sacrifice.

God's Word shows us how to be *born again* – converted, so the inner man may be transformed after the pattern of ultimate purity, Jesus Christ.

God's Word shows us how to be *empowered by the Holy Spirit* for a spiritual resource.

God's Word is a *refuge* against temptation, giving a way of escape.

God's Word gives a *protection* against condemnation, showing how to repent after impurity.

God's Word wisely and simply warns, *flee youthful lusts* (2 Timothy 2:22).

God's Word *washes* us from impurity and cleanses our lives spiritually (Ephesians 5:26, John 15:3).

God's Word is a *light* that clears away the deceptive fog of seduction and temptation.

God's Word is a *mirror* that helps one see their spiritual and moral condition and walk in purity.

God's Word is the key to the *renewing of our mind*, which leads to personal, moral, and spiritual transformation (Romans 12:1-2).

Jesus spoke specifically of the power of His Word to cleanse and keep pure: *You are already clean because of the word which I have spoken to you* (John 5:3). *Sanctify them by Your truth. Your word is truth* (John 17:17).

If one is concerned to cleanse his way, he must also be concerned to take heed according to God's Word. We can let the Bible be like our map – showing us our Savior, our rescue from judgment, and the pathway to a God-honoring life. Yet even the best map is useless if you don't pay heed to it.

Today, take heed according to God's Word.

February 18

A Refuge from the Storm

O LORD, You are my God. I will exalt You, I will praise Your name, for You have done wonderful things; Your counsels of old are faithfulness and truth.... For You have been a strength to the poor, a strength to the needy in his distress, a refuge from the storm, a shade from the heat; for the blast of the terrible ones is as a storm against the wall. You will reduce the noise of aliens, as heat in a dry place; as heat in the shadow of a cloud, the song of the terrible ones will be diminished. (Isaiah 25:1, 4-5)

Isaiah 24 spoke of the judgment to come on the world, especially in a coming time of great suffering. During that time, those who have come to trust in the LORD will praise Him, even amid His righteous judgment (Isaiah 24:14). This song shows the kind of heart that praises God during tribulation, even during the great tribulation. Phrase by phrase, this song exalts God.

The singer exalted the LORD, declaring **You are my God**. Knowing that the LORD – the God of Abraham, Isaac, and Jacob, the God revealed in and by Jesus Christ – is our God, makes us want to praise Him.

The singer decided to **exalt** and **praise** the LORD. Worship is never to be only a feeling; God's people are to worship Him with a decision.

He praised God for His **wonderful things**. When we think about all the wonderful things the LORD has done, we easily decide to worship Him. God wants our worship to be filled with thought and remembrance of His great works, not only an emotional response.

The singer declared the **faithfulness and truth** of God. When we remember the greatness and permanence of God's Word, it makes us want to praise Him. There is nothing more reliable, more everlasting, or more enduring than the Word of God.

The worshipper understood that God was a **strength to the poor** and to the **needy**. God is worthy of our praise because He brings strength to those whom the world often overlooks.

We can praise God because He is a **refuge from the storm, a shade from the heat**, and even the strangers (**aliens**) are blessed by His goodness. God will even quiet the song of the **terrible ones**.

We should praise God because these all things are true about Him and His character.

- Do you need God to do some wonderful things?
- Do you need some of God's faithfulness and truth?
- Are you poor and need strength?
- Do you need a refuge from the storm?
- Do you need shade from the heat?

Talk to God about it today.

February 19

Keys to Becoming an Overcomer

And they overcame him by the blood of the Lamb and by the word of their testimony, and they did not love their lives to the death. (Revelation 12:11)

Revelation 12:11 presents three keys to the saints' victory over the enemy of our souls. The first key is that **they overcame** by the **blood of the Lamb**. The second key is that **they overcame** by the **word of their testimony**.

The third key from Revelation 12:11 is that they **overcame** because **they did not love their lives to the death**. The first key overcame Satan's accusations. The second key overcame Satan's deception. This third key overcomes Satan's violence. When we do **not love our lives to the death**, it means that we do not cling to our earthly lives as if that was all that mattered. It shows that we believe in and live for eternity.

In many parts of the world today, the threat of martyrdom hangs like a dark cloud over every day. When those believers live with the heart of the apostle Paul, who believed *to live is Christ, and to die is gain* (Philippians 1:21), then how could Satan's violence against them be effective? Their hearts are set. "Go ahead and afflict or even kill this body. I will not welcome it, but neither will I not offend Jesus and my conscience to avoid it."

However, this idea is also relevant to Christians who are never directly threatened by persecution. Even in the Western world, we can live with an obsessive fear for our physical safety. We can allow the fear of violence, or second-hand smoke, or environmental concerns, or any number of other fears to so dominate our lives that we make our physical life an idol that everything else is sacrificed to. While simple wisdom and prudence tell us to not be careless with our health and safety, neither are we always to consider our own health and safety the highest good. We must not **love our lives to the death**.

The ancient Greek word for **love** here is *agape*, which speaks of a self-sacrificing, decision-based love. It is up to each one of us to choose: will we **love our lives to the death**? Will our physical life be the most precious thing to us, or will we find our life by losing it for Jesus? Jesus said, *for whoever desires to save his life will lose it, but whoever loses his life for My sake and the gospel's will save it* (Mark 8:35). Ultimately, in eternity, we save our life by losing it in Jesus.

Take these three keys:

- **The blood of the Lamb** (the death of Jesus on the cross, as our substitute).
- **The word of their testimony** (the personal experience of Jesus' work).
- Loving not our **lives to the death** (setting Jesus and His Word above even our physical life).

Today, let these keys unlock the door to you becoming an overcomer in Christ.

February 20
Adam's Sin and Our Sin

Therefore, just as through one man sin entered the world, and death through sin, and thus death spread to all men, because all sinned. (Romans 5:12)

Among many educated people today, a literal belief in Adam and Eve is not popular. Yet, if we are to agree with the apostle Paul, we should believe in a literal Adam (see Romans 5:14). If we are to agree with Jesus Himself, we should believe in a literal Adam (see Matthew 19:4-6).

If we believe what the Bible tells us about Adam, we see that he was created perfectly innocent of all sin. When God said that all things were good, He said it *after* He created Adam. But Adam didn't stay perfectly innocent. When he rebelled against God's command to not eat from the tree of the knowledge of good and evil, he took evil advantage of the one thing God told not to do. Every day, we are confronted with a wide selection of sins; but Adam could only sin in one way – and he found it.

Do you remember the last time you felt that you had disappointed God? What was your first reaction as soon as it was over? Probably, you were filled with a new resolve to never do such a terrible thing again. You likely felt that though you had done something bad, you could make a new start of things from this point on. Can you imagine that Adam and Eve felt the same thing? They probably said to each other, "We've done something terrible. But we never have to do it again. Let's make a clean start from this point on and never disobey God again." Obviously, if they ever made such a promise, they failed. And so do we.

Unfortunately, the history of man from Adam's sin onward is a downhill slope. Things go from bad to worse. We advance in technology, and in cultural sophistication. But all it seems to do is provide us with better and more complex ways to sin. Adam and Eve must have been stunned to find not only had they sinned once but also now they were in the grip of sin. Since we are all born sons of Adam or daughters of Eve, we are caught in the same grip.

No matter what powerful things humanity accomplishes such as putting a man on the moon or destroying a world with nuclear weapons, we just can't stop sinning. When Adam and Eve fell, they unleashed the second most powerful force that is ever-present in the universe: the sin and rebellion of man.

The only thing more powerful than the sin of man is the love of God. Romans 5:20 tells us, *where sin abounds, grace abounds much more*. We can't stop sinning, but we can't out-sin the grace of God. No one is rejected before God because they are too great a sinner; they will be rejected because they have not believed on Jesus and received His grace – God's provision for sinners like Adam and like us.

Are you believing Jesus now? Have you thanked Him for His grace today?

February 21

Sinning Without Shame

For Jerusalem stumbled, and Judah is fallen, because their tongue and their doings are against the Lord, to provoke the eyes of His glory. The look on their countenance witnesses against them, and they declare their sin as Sodom; they do not hide it. Woe to their soul! For they have brought evil upon themselves. (Isaiah 3:8-9)

Isaiah was a remarkable prophet. The book of his prophecies has some of the most glorious announcements of blessing and redemption, and some of the harshest words of judgment found in the Bible. Isaiah wrote: **their tongues and their doings are against the Lord**. What they said and what they did **provoked the eyes of His glory**.

It is much easier to think that what we do is offensive to God than to think that what we *say* can provoke the eyes of His glory. But we are commanded to glorify God by what we say just as much as by what we do. Jesus said, *for every idle word men may speak, they will give account of it in the day of judgment. For by your words you will be justified, and by your words you will be condemned* (Matthew 12:36-37).

They knew they were sinful with their tongues and with their doings. Isaiah 3:9: *The look on their countenance witnesses against them*. They had either the smirk of the reprobate or the downcast gaze of those under conviction.

Isaiah also noted that the wicked men of Judah proclaimed **their sin as Sodom**, and they did **not hide it**. Their sin was openly displayed, and they had no sense of shame. The cultural dynamic in Isaiah's day was probably much the same as in our time. In the name of "authenticity" and "honesty" and "let's not be hypocrites," all kinds of sin were approved, and no one was allowed to proclaim a standard unless they lived up to it perfectly.

Isaiah tells us that in some regard, there is something good necessary in hiding sin, in the sense that outward decency is important. It is important to not talk about many sins, even though they certainly exist and sometimes touch the church. It is through these means that God's people declare a standard, even though they or the world do not perfectly measure up to the standard. Ephesians 5:12 matters here: *For it is shameful even to speak of those things which are done by them in secret*.

Isaiah described the sad result in verse 9: **Woe to their soul! For they have brought evil upon themselves**. God did not have to do anything unique or special to bring this judgment on Jerusalem and Judah. All He had to do was leave them alone and allow them to have the evil they brought on themselves. Their sinning without shame bore its own bitter fruit, and God would simply allow them to reap what they had sown.

We can keep from the same bitter fruit by truly committing what we say and what we do to our God.

February 22

Setting the Right Track

**How can a young man cleanse his way?
By taking heed according to Your word.** (Psalm 119:9)

We may think it's a modern question, but some 3,000 years ago, the psalmist asked, **how can a young man cleanse his way?** It was a difficult question then and now. The **young man** has his own challenges in living a pure life.

This is a question that some – even some of God's people – never seem to ask. Sadly, some people never have a life concern for moral purity. They echo the prayer of Augustine before his conversion: "Lord, make me pure – but not yet."

The world tells us, "Have your good time when you are young. When you are older you can settle down." God knows the value and wisdom of living life for God at the earliest time possible – the younger, the better. God always has a claim on the first and best of everything, including the life of a young man or woman.

Even when one has the desire for moral purity, there are many things that may make it difficult for a young person to cleanse their way. The young man has youthful energy and a sense of carelessness – along with a lack of life wisdom.

The young man has the desire for independence, and he gains some measure of independence. They often have a physical and sexual maturity that may run ahead of spiritual and moral maturity.

Sometimes young men must deal with young women who may – knowingly or unknowingly – encourage moral impurity. They must also resist the spirit of the age that both expects and promotes moral uncleanness. In addition, there is the desire to be accepted by peers who face the same challenges. It's not only the young man who has these challenges; older men and women of every age have their own challenges to pure living. But these are often more severely felt in the life of the young man.

God speaks to us about these things because He wants to spare the young man (and the older man) the bondage of sin. This reflects the power of experience to shape our habits. Surrender to any temptation; transfer it from the realm of mental contemplation to life experience, and that temptation instantly becomes much more difficult to resist in the future. Each successive experience of surrender to temptation builds a habit, reinforced not only spiritually, but also by brain chemistry. Such ingrained habits are more difficult to break the more they are experienced, and it's almost impossible to break such habits without replacing them with others.

The words **his way** comes from the Hebrew word connected to the idea of a track or a rut. Youth sets the tracks for the rest of their life. Many older men wish they had cared about such things in their youth.

Today, every one of us can take heed according to God's Word – and grow in purity.

February 23
Make Your Confession

If we confess our sins, He is faithful and just to forgive us our sins and to cleanse us from all unrighteousness. (1 John 1:9)

When you've sinned, do you feel like a crime suspect and think God is watching you, waiting for you to make your confession? If so, you don't understand what confession is all about. God doesn't want us to confess our sins to condemn us or to put us in prison. God wants us to **confess our sins** so that relationship with Him can be restored, and so sin doesn't get in the way. **If we confess our sins, He is faithful and just to forgive**. Though sin is present, it doesn't need to be a hindrance to our relationship with God – we may find complete cleansing (**from all unrighteousness**) as we confess our sins.

To confess means "to say the same as." When we confess our sin, we are willing to say (and believe) the same thing about our sin that God says about it. Jesus' story illustrated this: The Pharisee bragged about how righteous he was, while the sinner just asked, *God be merciful to me a sinner* (Luke 18:10-14).

In 1 John 1:9, **confess** is a present-tense verb. This means we should keep on confessing our sins. It is not speaking of a "once-for-all" confession of sin at our conversion. When you are baptized, you acknowledge your sin by saying you needed to be cleansed and reborn. When you receive communion, you confess your sin by saying you need the work of Jesus on the cross to take your sin away. We need to confess our sin by admitting to God that what we have done is sin, and asking for His divine forgiveness, based on what Jesus did on the cross for us.

It is important to understand that our sins are not forgiven *because* we confess. If this were the case – if forgiveness for a sin could only come when there was a specific confession for that sin – then we would all be under God's judgment, because it would be impossible for us to confess *every* sin we ever commit. We are forgiven because our punishment was put on Jesus. We are cleansed by His blood and not by our confession.

However, confession is still vital to maintaining a relationship with God, which is the context from which John speaks. As God convicts us of sin hindering our fellowship with Him, we must confess it and receive forgiveness and cleansing.

Because of Jesus' work, the righteousness of God is our friend, making sure that we will be forgiven because Jesus paid the penalty of our sin. God **is faithful and just to forgive us** considering what Jesus did for us on the cross.

So, keep your relationship with God as unhindered as possible. Take Him up on His promise to complete forgive when we genuinely confess.

February 24

Think About Your Ways

I thought about my ways, and turned my feet to Your testimonies. I made haste, and did not delay to keep Your commandments. (Psalm 119:59-60)

Psalm 119 is the longest psalm and the longest chapter in the Bible (containing 176 verses). Some great people have memorized this whole psalm, and they found great blessing in doing so. Among these are John Ruskin (19th-century British writer), William Wilberforce (19th-century British politician who led the movement to abolish the British slave trade), Henry Martyn (19th-century pioneer missionary to India), and David Livingstone (19th-century missionary to Africa).

One other man to memorize all of Psalm 119 was Blaise Pascal, the French philosopher and committed Christian. He loved this psalm, and he called verse 59, "the turning point of man's character and destiny." He meant that it was important for every person to consider their ways, understand where danger lies, and then make the necessary change of direction towards God and His wisdom.

It is a simple idea to understand, but it is not so simple to do what the psalmist said: **I thought about my ways and turned my feet to Your testimonies**. Time spent in God's Word gave the psalmist sober reflection about his ways. This led to the insight necessary to turn in the right direction. We can't do these things without God working in us in some way.

First, he studied the Bible, and then he studied his own life. Comparing the two, he realized that he needed to change his direction. Many people never come this far; they never even think about their ways. They pass from this life into eternity with very little serious thought about their life and how they have lived it, and to Whom they must give account.

The author of Psalm 119 was different. He did think about his ways and used that thinking to put his feet in the right direction. Once they were in that correct direction, then he said: **I made haste, and did not delay to keep Your commandments**. Once on the right path (**turned my feet**), now the psalmist could rightly speed his way in the course of obedience.

It is dangerous to make haste on the wrong path; it is glorious to make haste on the right way. We can also say that making haste to God is a sign of revival. When God is moving in power, people make haste to get right with him. When he says he **did not delay**, he meant that indecision was gone. He was determined on his way, and he pursued it.

Spurgeon said it well: "Speed in repentance and speed in obedience are two excellent things. We are too often in haste to sin; O that we may be in a greater hurry to obey."

It all makes sense. First, think about your ways. Then turn your feet in the right direction. Next, move in that direction with speed and purpose.

Today, God helping you, you will.

February 25

Earnest Prayer

Peter was therefore kept in prison, but constant prayer was offered to God for him by the church. (Acts 12:5)

It was a critical time for the church. The first of the apostles had just been martyred. James – one of the closest companions of Jesus – one of the three: Peter, James, and John. Herod was not satisfied. He saw his opinion ratings rise, and figured they would rise even more if he also killed Peter. So, Peter was kept in prison.

Herod trusted in his prisons, guards, and violence. Peter trusted in Jesus' promise that he would not die until he was old (John 21:18). In Acts 12:5 we see that the church trusted in the God who answers prayer. God miraculously freed Peter from prison and then Peter visited the prayer meeting being held on his behalf. Such a glorious answer to prayer is a direct result of the church praying "constantly" to God for Peter.

The ancient Greek word translated **constant** also has the idea of "earnest." Literally, the word pictures someone stretching out all they can to reach or lay hold of something. First, you stand as straight as you can, then you reach as high as possible. Next, you stand on your tiptoes. You angle your shoulder and extend your fingers to reach the object. The idea of that kind of methodical, earnest "stretching out" is what lies behind the word **constant**.

This ancient word was also used in the world of medicine, for the stretching of a muscle to its limits. Luke used this same word for the agonizing prayer of Jesus in the Garden of Gethsemane (Luke 22:44). It means wanting something bad enough that you will stretch for it, reach for it, even agonize for it.

Often our prayer is powerless because it is not earnest. There is no "stretching out" at all in prayer. Earnest prayer has power, not because it persuades a reluctant God, but because it demonstrates that our heart cares passionately about the things God cares about. This fulfills Jesus' promise: *If you abide in Me and My words abide in you, you will ask what you desire and it shall be done for you.* (John 15:7)

How earnest was their prayer? We see from the rest of Acts 12 that they gathered for prayer when most everyone else was asleep. When we are so serious about seeing God's will done that we are willing to give up some normal comforts of life, it shows we are truly earnest. It isn't that we twist the arm of a reluctant God; instead, we simply set our heart in alignment with His. That is prayer's real place of power.

We learn God's will and priorities from His Word, the Bible. But it isn't enough for us to just know them.

We must have an "earnest" desire to see His will done, and that "earnest" desire will show itself in prayer –earnest, "stretched-out" prayer. Pray that way today.

February 26

How to Trust God's Promises

For thus says the LORD **God, the Holy One of Israel: "In returning and rest you shall be saved; in quietness and confidence shall be your strength." But you would not, and you said, "No, for we will flee on horses"; therefore you shall flee! And, "We will ride on swift horses"; therefore those who pursue you shall be swift! One thousand shall flee at the threat of one, at the threat of five you shall flee, till you are left as a pole on top of a mountain and as a banner on a hill.** (Isaiah 30:15-17)

Isaiah 30 was written during a terrible invasion by the cruel Assyrian Empire. They threatened to lay the Kingdom of Judah waste, even as they had other kingdoms stronger than Judah. In the shadow of this threat, Judah chose to not trust God and instead they trusted in an alliance with Egypt.

God offered to Judah the promise of protection from Assyria. They did not need to look to Egypt for help at all. They could have trusted God for His promise. If they did truly return and **rest** in Him, they would be saved, and enjoy God's **strength** in **quietness and confidence**.

Trusting God's promise means **returning**. If there is obvious disobedience in our lives, we must return to the LORD's ways. Disobedience is never consistent with trust in God's promises. Returning is drawing close to the LORD.

Trusting God's promise means **rest**. When we trust in God, we don't have to strive to run all about trying to protect or guard ourselves. When we rest in Him, it shows that we are trusting in God's promises.

Trusting God's promise means **quietness**. You don't need to argue for your side when God is on your side. Be quiet before Him and before others. It shows that you truly trust Him.

Trusting God's promise means profound confidence in the God who loves you. You aren't given to despair or fear because you trust in God's promises. You know He can and will come through. It means that we shall be saved and find strength.

Because Judah rejected God's promise and trusted in horses and other things, they would have to run for their lives. If they had trusted God's promise, they would have seen the LORD's salvation and strength. Instead, they wanted to escape the coming trouble on fast **horses**.

In a tragic reversal of the promise of Leviticus 26:8, **one thousand** would **flee at the threat of one**. This was a fulfillment of the curse promised in Leviticus 26:17: *I will set My face against you, and you shall be defeated by your enemies. Those who hate you shall reign over you, and you shall flee when no one pursues you.*

Today, believe God and His promises to you; to know that **in returning and rest you shall be saved; in quietness and confidence shall be your strength.**

February 27

Resisting and Receiving

So then, my beloved brethren, let every man be swift to hear, slow to speak, slow to wrath; for the wrath of man does not produce the righteousness of God. Therefore lay aside all filthiness and overflow of wickedness, and receive with meekness the implanted word, which is able to save your souls. (James 1:19-21)

James presented the idea of God's perfection (James 1:17: *Every good gift and every perfect gift is from above, and comes down from the Father of lights…*). Considering that truth, he had some guidance for the believer: **Let every man be swift to hear, slow to speak, slow to wrath**. We can learn to be **slow to wrath** by first learning to be **swift to hear** and **slow to speak**. So much of our anger and wrath come from being self-centered, not others centered. **Swift to hear** is a way to be others centered. **Slow to speak** is a way to be others centered.

After all, everyone is given two ears and one tongue – and that tongue is hidden behind teeth and lips. It is good to hear and listen twice as much as we speak and to guard what we say with our tongue.

James continues with the kind of attitude that the perfection of God should prompt us to have: **Slow to wrath; for the wrath of man does not produce the righteousness of God**. Considering the nature of temptation and the goodness of God, we must take special care to be slow to wrath because our wrath does not accomplish the righteousness of God. Our wrath almost always defends or promotes our agenda.

Sadly, the history of religion – sometimes Christianity – includes too much of **the wrath of man**. When religious people go beyond advocating their faith to the place of violence against others in the name of their beliefs, it is a tragic example of the truth that **the wrath of man does not produce the righteousness of God**.

Instead of attacking others with outbursts of wrath, we are much better turning our focus on the sinful impulses within us, to **lay aside all filthiness** and **wickedness**. This has in mind an impure manner of living. Bearing in mind the nature of temptation and the goodness of God, we are to lay aside all impurity, putting them far from us.

Having resisted the evil, we make sure to receive the good: **Receive with meekness the implanted word**. In contrast to an impure manner of living, we should accept God's **implanted word** (doing it with meekness, a teachable heart). This can save us, both in our current situation and eternally. The purity of God's Word can preserve us even in an impure age.

Here James alluded to the spiritual power of the Word of God. When it is implanted in the human heart, it can save your soul. The Word of God carries the power of God.

Let God's Word carry the power of God to you today.

February 28

Repented – and Still Repenting

Those who regard worthless idols forsake their own Mercy. But I will sacrifice to You with the voice of thanksgiving; I will pay what I have vowed. Salvation is of the LORD. (Jonah 2:8-9)

We don't exactly know what it was like for Jonah in the belly of the fish, but it probably wasn't pleasant. It was deep in the fish that Jonah prayed this great prayer and received deliverance from the LORD.

In his prayer, Jonah finally realized that resisting God or running from Him was like being an idolater. He said in his prayer, **those who regard worthless idols forsake their own Mercy**. In the belly of the fish, he finally came to his senses and stopped forsaking the **Lord** who was his Mercy. Now he said, **But I will sacrifice to You**. Jonah repented from running away from God, and he turned to God with both sacrifice and thanksgiving. He would pay his vows to God and do whatever God told him to do. At one time or another, Jonah had probably said what many believers say in their walk with God: "LORD, I'll do whatever You want me to do." Now Jonah realized that he must stop resisting God and he should keep his vows to Him.

In the conclusion of his prayer, Jonah cried out: **Salvation is of the LORD**. This was more than a statement of fact; it was Jonah's triumphant declaration. God has saved and will save, and Jonah meant this personally. Jonah's own salvation was of the LORD; he knew this and declared it. Jonah also now knew this was true in a broader sense; that salvation is not of a nation or a race or a language, and not of man at all. No, **salvation is of the LORD**.

At the end of Jonah's prayer while still in the belly of the fish, Jonah unmistakably repented, but it is not clear *when* he repented. It is hard to say exactly, but there were indications of repentance when...

- Jonah said he feared the LORD and was honest about his story (Jonah 1:9) – this was an indication of repentance.
- Jonah allowed himself to be cast into the sea (Jonah 1:12) – this was an indication of repentance, throwing himself totally on the LORD.
- Jonah called out to God during the three days and three nights in the belly of the fish (Jonah 2:2, 2:4, and 2:7) – this was an indication of repentance.
- Jonah renewed his commitment to the vow he made (Jonah 2:9), another indication of repentance.

So, when did Jonah repent? The answer is found in seeing repentance as more than just a one-time event. Though repentance begins at one point in time, it must continue and mature. It is an event, but it is also a continuing process.

Where are you in repentance? If you have turned to the LORD, keep turning and stay turned to Him.

March 1

Look to Me

Look to Me, and be saved, all you ends of the earth! For I am God, and there is no other. (Isaiah 45:22)

This simple but powerful statement shows God's plan of salvation. All we must do is **look**. It is possible to read many theological books that explain many things – often-good things. Yet the core of bringing man close to God is explained by a simple word with four letters: **look**.

God could simply allow lost man to wander in his lost way; but in love, God begs man, **Look to Me**. This also shows the assurance of salvation: **and be saved** is a certain promise. This wonderful verse also shows the extent of God's saving love: **all you ends of the earth**. Not just a few nations or races, but all **the ends of the earth**.

In Numbers 21, the people of Israel were stricken by deadly snakebites, and Moses used a pole to lift the image of a bronze serpent, and the people who looked to the raised image lived. The people were saved not by doing anything, but by simply looking at the bronze serpent. They had to trust that something as seemingly foolish as looking at a snake raised on a pole would be enough to save them, and surely, some perished because they thought it too foolish to do such a thing.

The promise is simple and clear: **Look to Me, and be saved, all you ends of the earth!** We might be willing to do a hundred things to earn our salvation, but God commands us to only trust in Him – to look to Him!

Charles Spurgeon, the great preacher of Victorian England, how the truth of Isaiah 45:22 had a role in his salvation:

> I had been wandering about, seeking rest, and finding none, till a plain, unlettered, lay preacher among the Primitive Methodists stood up in the pulpit, and gave out this passage as his text: "Look unto me, and be ye saved, all the ends of the earth." I remember how he said, "It is Christ that speaks. 'I am in the garden in an agony, pouring out my soul unto death; I am on the tree, dying for sinners; look unto me! Look unto me!' That is all you have to do. A child can look. One who is almost an idiot can look. However weak, or however poor, a man may be, he can look; and if he looks, the promise is that he shall live." Then, stopping, he pointed to where I was sitting under the gallery, and he said, "Look! Look, young man! Look now!"

Spurgeon explained this "was in accord with that blessed deliverance from sin which I had found in a single moment by looking to Jesus Christ." He was born again by looking to Jesus Christ.

Jesus Christ hasn't stopped saying this to humanity: **Look to Me, and be saved.** Today, look away from sin and self, and look to Him!

March 2

Hope and Salvation on Your Head

Above all, taking the shield of faith with which you will be able to quench all the fiery darts of the wicked one. And take the helmet of salvation, and the sword of the Spirit, which is the word of God. (Ephesians 6:16-18)

God often uses material things to communicate spiritual truths to us. God will take something that we are familiar with – a door, a grapevine, a piece of bread – and He will use those things as illustrations of spiritual principles and truths. God speaks to us in these familiar pictures because it makes it easier to understand spiritual things.

Inspired by the Holy Spirit, the apostle Paul did the same thing. He used the armor of an ancient Roman soldier to explain aspects of the Christian life, especially relating to the spiritual struggle that each follower of Jesus experiences. We all face these spiritual battles; that is why every believer needs to be equipped to fight these battles.

In Ephesians 6:17, Paul told believers to take the **helmet of salvation**. For soldiers in the ancient world, this was usually a leather cap that was studded with metal for extra strength. Often some feather or decoration was added, perhaps to identify the regiment that the soldier belonged to. Therefore, in Ephesians 6:17, the believer's salvation is pictured as this kind of helmet, providing essential protection. The head needs protection, and a soldier would be foolish to go into battle without his helmet.

Paul wrote about this same idea in another passage, 1 Thessalonians 5:8: *But let us who are of the day be sober, putting on the breastplate of faith and love, and as a helmet the hope of salvation.*

1 Thessalonians 5:8 speaks of the helmet of salvation in connection to the hope of salvation. The idea of salvation has a vital link to hope. The helmet of salvation protects us against discouragement and against the desire to give up. This helmet of salvation gives us hope, not only in knowing that we are saved, but also that we will be saved – God will be with us even if the future seems uncertain. The helmet of salvation gives the believer the assurance that God and His people will triumph.

We need the helmet of salvation and all the hope that it brings to us. One of Satan's most effective weapons against God's people is discouragement. The dagger of discouragement has attacked the believer countless times. Satan knows how to use it well!

But when we are adequately equipped with the helmet of salvation, it is hard to stay discouraged. Though wearing the helmet of salvation, our hope is not in ourselves, or even our ability to stay close to Jesus. Our hope is in Jesus Himself, and in the rescue, He brings to us. To put our hope, our confidence in anything else would be as foolish as a soldier going into battle without a helmet.

Today, do not make that mistake.

March 3

Grace Sufficient for You

And He said to me, "My grace is sufficient for you, for My strength is made perfect in weakness." Therefore most gladly I will rather boast in my infirmities, that the power of Christ may rest upon me. (2 Corinthians 12:9)

Paul was troubled by an affliction – a thorn in the flesh – that was not removed by prayer. Yet God had a response for Paul. God told Paul, **My grace is sufficient for you**. Instead of removing the thorn from Paul's life, God gave and would keep giving His **grace** to Paul. The **grace** God gave Paul was **sufficient** to meet his every need.

To receive this, Paul had to believe that God's **grace is sufficient**. We usually don't believe God's grace is sufficient until we believe we are *insufficient*. For many of us, especially in American culture, this is a huge obstacle. We are the people who idolize the "self-made man" and want to rely on ourselves. But we can't receive God's strength until we know our weakness. We can't live in the truth that God's grace is enough until we know that we, in ourselves, are not enough.

My grace is sufficient for you is a great declaration, and you may emphasize any aspect of this sentence.

"My **grace** is sufficient for you." Grace is the favor and love of God in action. It means He loves us and is pleased by us. Can you hear it from God? "My love is enough for you." Isn't it true?

"**My** grace is sufficient for you." Whose grace is it? It is the grace of Jesus. Isn't His love, His favor, enough? What will Jesus fail at? Remember too that Jesus also suffered thorns; He cares, and He knows.

"My grace **is** sufficient for you." It **is** right now. Not that it will be some day, but right now, at this moment, His grace is sufficient. You thought something had to change before His grace would be enough. You thought, "His grace *was* sufficient once, His grace *might be* sufficient again, but not now, not with what I am going through." Despite that feeling, God's word stands. "My grace **is** sufficient for you."

"My grace is **sufficient** for you." It is rather modest of God to describe His grace as **sufficient**. That word can be used of something that barely meets the need, but God's supply is far more than sufficient. The grace of the triumphant, resurrected Jesus is enough – and more than enough!

"My grace is sufficient **for you**." I'm so glad God didn't say, "My grace is sufficient for Paul the apostle." I might have felt left out. But God made it broad enough for all of us. God's grace is sufficient **for you**! Are you beyond it? Are you so different? Is your thorn worse than Paul's or worse than many others who have known the triumph of Jesus? Of course not.

Brother, sister: this sufficient grace is **for you**. By faith, receive it in Jesus' name.

March 4

A Lamp and a Light

**Your word is a lamp to my feet
And a light to my path.** (Psalm 119:105)

In saying, **Your word is a lamp to my feet**, the psalmist felt that as he walked the road of life, God's Word made his steps clear. It is possible to walk the path of life, not knowing if our steps will fall on good ground or dangerous ground. God's Word will be **a lamp to our feet**.

The Bible should help us walk the way God wants us to walk. There are many ways to walk, and each of them says something. Christians are to walk worthy (Ephesians 4:1), uprightly (Isaiah 57:2), in the light (1 John 1:7), and humbly (Micah 6:8). None of these are possible without the Word of God lighting our way.

A lamp must be lighted, and in the days this psalm was written, a lamp was usually fueled by oil – a picture of the Holy Spirit. If the Holy Spirit's teaching does not come with the written word, there will be little light at all. When the Spirit fuels the word, the lamp burns brightly.

He also wrote, **a light to my path**. The Word of God not only showed him where his feet stepped but also the path he should remain on and the next few steps to take.

We need the Bible to teach us right from wrong. We have some inner sense of this in our conscience, but our conscience can be weak, ignorant, or damaged. The Word of God is higher even than our conscience, and it instructs our conscience.

The psalm says, **Your word is a lamp…and a light**. God's Word is light and brings light; it doesn't make things darker or harder to understand. It is a *light book*, not a *dark book*. The Scriptures have a clarity to them and can be understood by open-minded people who prayerfully read.

Not all parts are equally clear and easy to understand, and it is helpful to have wisdom from others in what they have seen in the Scriptures. The Bible can be understood, and Christians do understand it. Think of all the common ground Christians from vastly different denominations have. In common, Christians believe in the truth of a Triune God, the truth of the full deity and full humanity of Jesus, and the truth of our sin. They believe in the truth of Jesus' death for us to save us from sin and death, the work of the Holy Spirit in leading us to faith, and the establishment of the church, the community of believers. We believe in the return of Jesus Christ and the resurrection of the dead.

This doesn't mean that everyone's opinion on the meaning of a Bible passage is just as good as another. It is just the opposite. The Bible is clear enough to be understood, and this means that some so-called understandings are wrong.

Today, thank God for the lamp to our feet and the light to our path!

March 5

Where Faith Comes From

So then, faith comes by hearing, and hearing by the word of God. (Romans 10:17)

We often want to think faith or unbelief has to do with the circumstances or environment we find ourselves in. When faith is weak or unbelief is strong, it is easy to think, "Of course I'm having a hard time trusting God. Look at the mess I'm in." Yet the link between our situation and our trust in God isn't what we might think.

We find an example of this from the Book of Numbers. In Numbers 13, Moses sent twelve spies into the Promised Land. They each saw the same things as they surveyed the land, and all twelve spies came back to report to Moses and the nation of Israel. Ten of the twelve spies said the land was indeed good, just as God had said – yet they said that the enemies of the land were too strong and taking the land would be a suicide mission.

Among those twelve spies, two objected. They presented the minority report. They also agreed the land was good, just as God promised, but they believed God would work through them to conquer even the strongest enemies in the land of Canaan. Those two faithful spies knew if God's Word was right about the land – the LORD said the land was good and it was – then God's Word would also be proven right about the promise to give them the land despite the strong enemies. Seeing God's Word fulfilled gave them the faith to believe God's promise for the future.

The ten unfaithful spies and the two faithful spies saw the same things – they saw the same grapes, the same men, the same land, and the same cities. Yet two of the spies came back singing in faith, and the other ten were filled with a sense of certain doom. It wasn't their experiences that made the difference – all twelve spies had the same experiences. It was something more profound than what they had experienced.

Ultimately, faith does not come from circumstances or environment, but from our heart – specifically, from the work of God's Word in our heart. We often want to blame our unbelief on the difficult times in life, but faith or unbelief are not connected to our circumstances.

A story illustrates this principle. There were two sons who had a terrible, alcoholic father, but the sons were different from each other as adults. One was a responsible, godly man, successful in family, business, and life. The other became an abusive alcoholic just as his father was. When asked why they turned out the way they did, each had the same answer: "With a father like mine, how could I have turned out any differently?"

It stands true: **Faith comes by hearing and hearing by the word of God**.

Today, bring yourself to God and His Word, with their faith-building power, and don't wait for an environment or circumstance to build faith in you.

March 6

All I Know

And I, brethren, when I came to you, did not come with excellence of speech or of wisdom declaring to you the testimony of God. For I determined not to know anything among you except Jesus Christ and Him crucified. (1 Corinthians 2:1-2)

Paul's arrival to Corinth is described in Acts 18. He came and met a Christian couple named Aquila and Priscilla, who were tentmakers (leatherworkers) by trade, like Paul. He served in Corinth for more than a year and a half, supporting himself (Acts 18:3).

In Paul's day, Corinth was already an old city. Because of its busy economy and many visitors, Corinth had a remarkable reputation for loose living, especially sexual immorality. In classical Greek, to *act like a Corinthian* meant to be sexually immoral, and a *Corinthian companion* was a prostitute. This immorality was permitted (even encouraged) under the widely popular worship of Aphrodite (also known as Venus, the goddess of fertility and sexuality).

When Paul came to such a challenging field of ministry, he did the only thing he could: preach **Jesus Christ and Him crucified**. Only Jesus could be the answer for such an immoral place. Preaching to entertain wouldn't work. Preaching the gospel of self-help couldn't help. The messages of salvation by good works or noble intentions wouldn't change lives.

That's why Paul didn't come to Corinth as a philosopher or a salesman, worried about the **excellence** of his **speech**. Paul came as a *witness* (**declaring to you the testimony of God**). Paul was a smart man who could reason and debate persuasively, but he didn't use that approach in preaching the gospel. He made a conscious decision (**I determined**) to put the emphasis on **Jesus Christ and Him crucified**. Paul was an ambassador, not a salesman.

In taking this approach, Paul understood he didn't cater to what his audience *wanted*. He already knew *the Jews request a sign, and Greeks seek after wisdom* (1 Corinthians 1:22), but he didn't care. He was **determined** to preach **Jesus Christ and Him crucified**. If a preacher is not careful, he will get in the way of the gospel instead of being a servant of the gospel. Paul could say, "All I know is Jesus Christ, and Him crucified for me."

There's a story of a little girl who went to a traditional church with her family every week. The church had stained glass windows, and there were beautiful images of different Bible characters in the window behind the preacher. One day a very short man was the guest preacher, and because he was much shorter, the girl could see the stained-glass window with Jesus behind the guest. She wanted to know where the regular pastor ways, so she asked: "Where's the man who usually stands in the pulpit so we can't see Jesus?"

Whether you're a preacher or not, make sure you don't get in the way of Jesus. Proclaim **Jesus Christ and Him crucified**.

March 7

I Can See Clearly Now

Beloved, now we are children of God; and it has not yet been revealed what we shall be, but we know that when He is revealed, we shall be like Him, for we shall see Him as He is. (1 John 3:2)

In this passage, the Bible makes a remarkable promise: one day, not only shall we **be like Him**, but one day, **we shall see Him as He is**. Perhaps this is the greatest glory of heaven: not to be personally glorified, but to be in the unhindered and unrestricted presence of our Lord.

The apostle Paul said of our present life, *now we see in a mirror, dimly, but then face to face. Now I know in part, but then I shall know just as I also am known* (1 Corinthians 13:12). Today, when we look into a good mirror, the image is clear. But in the ancient world, mirrors were made from polished metal, and the image was always unclear and somewhat distorted. We see Jesus now only in a dim, obscure way, but one day we will see Him with perfect clarity.

Heaven is very precious to us for many reasons. We long to be with our loved ones who have passed before us, and whom we miss dearly. We long to be with the great men and women of God who have passed before us in centuries past. We want to walk the streets of gold, see the pearly gates, and see the angels around the throne of God worshiping Him day and night. However, none of those things, precious as they are, make heaven truly "heaven." What makes heaven truly heaven is the completely unhindered and unrestricted presence of our Lord. To **see Him as He is** will be the most wonderfully significant experience of your eternal existence.

In heaven, Jesus will still bear all the scars of His earthly suffering. After Jesus rose from the dead in His glorified body, His body uniquely retained the nail prints in His hands and the scar on his side (John 20:24-29).

We know this because in Zechariah 12:10, Jesus speaks prophetically of the day when the Jewish people will turn to Him and see Him in glory: *then they will look on Me whom they pierced. Yes, they will mourn for Him as one mourns for his only son, and grieve for Him as one grieves for a firstborn*. Zechariah 13:6, continues the thought: *and one will say to him, "What are these wounds between your arms?" Then He will answer, "Those with which I was wounded in the house of My friends."*

In writing **for we shall**, John connects seeing **Him as He is** and our becoming like Jesus. Could it not be said that the same principle works right now? To the degree that you see Jesus **as He is**, is the same degree you are like Him in your life.

Today, how clearly do you see Jesus? It will be evident in what you are becoming.

March 8

Just Passing Through

To the pilgrims of the dispersion. (1 Peter 1:1)

Peter clearly wrote to Christians, and in the opening of his first letter he gave them a descriptive title: **pilgrims**. When you say the word "pilgrim" to most of us, we think either of a cowboy like John Wayne addressing his fellow cowboys, or strict men with tall black hats.

When the Bible addresses Christians as **pilgrims**, the idea is of someone who lives as a temporary resident in a foreign land. Pilgrims have a homeland, but that isn't where they presently live. A pilgrim isn't the same thing as an immigrant because pilgrims are sojourners and travelers. They are just passing through their present place, so the great danger for them is to set roots down too deeply in the here and now.

Pilgrims are always outnumbered. They live among those who are "natives" and "permanent residents," but pilgrims live in constant awareness of their true home. They are homesick for heaven, because they know that as good as it may be in the land they presently live, it still isn't "home."

In the early Christian writing, *The Epistle to Diognetus*, we get the idea of what pilgrims are.

> They inhabit the lands of their birth, but as temporary residents of it; they take their share of all responsibilities as citizens and endure all disabilities as aliens. Every foreign land is their native land, and every native land a foreign land...they pass their days on earth, but their citizenship is in heaven.

In reference to heaven as the native country, a pilgrim is one who sojourns on earth. When we love this world too much, we aren't living as pilgrims. When we can't be distinguished from the "natives" and "permanent residents," we aren't living as pilgrims. When we no longer yearn for our heavenly home, we aren't living as pilgrims. When we feel too at home in this "country," we aren't living as pilgrims.

God doesn't want us to be miserable here, but He also doesn't want us to feel too settled. It's possible for one to feel that he is finally finding his place in this world, when really the world is finding its place in him.

An old hymn reflects the heart of a pilgrim:

This world is not my home; I'm just passing through
My treasures are laid up somewhere beyond the blue
The angels beckon me from heaven's open door
And I can't feel at home in this world anymore.

Perhaps you have recently felt "out of sorts," and like you don't really belong. Instead of taking it as something bad why not take it as a blessing?

Today, God may be reminding you that your citizenship is in heaven.

March 9

Who Can Stand Before the Holy God?

And the men of Beth Shemesh said, "Who is able to stand before this holy Lord God? And to whom shall it go up from us?" (1 Samuel 6:20)

The Philistines captured Israel's ark of the covenant, but then they sent it back on a cart pulled by two cows to the Israeli village of Beth Shemesh.

The men of Beth Shemesh were happy to have the ark of the covenant back in Israel, but they did something strictly forbidden – they looked in the ark of the covenant. Because they pried into things that they should not have, there came on them some plague or slaughter.

In response, the men of Beth Shemesh said: **Who is able to stand before this holy Lord God?** In their disrespect for God, the men of Beth Shemesh offended the holiness of the Lord. They knew the Lord was holy, but it did not make them want to be closer to God. Instead, it made them want to distance themselves from God.

The basic idea behind holiness is not moral purity (though it includes moral purity). Holiness is the idea of apartness – that God is separate, different from His creation, both in His essential nature and in the perfection of His attributes.

When Peter saw the holy power of Jesus, he said, *Depart from me, for I am a sinful man, O Lord!* (Luke 5:8). When the disciples saw the holy Jesus shining forth at the transfiguration, they were greatly afraid (Matthew 17:6). When we meet the holy God, we will be excited and terrified all at once. Many of our modern world's thrill-seeking pleasures are weak attempts to imitate the fulfillment we can only find by meeting the holy God.

Who is able to stand before this holy Lord God? In one sense, the men of Beth Shemesh showed a bad heart in asking this question. Their question made it seem that God was too harsh instead of understanding that they were too disobedient.

Who is able to stand before this holy Lord God? In another sense, the men of Beth Shemesh asked a good question. God is, in fact, holy, and who is able indeed to stand before Him?

Though God is holy, though He is apart from us, instead of building a wall around His apartness, God calls us to come to Him and share His apartness. As it says in 1 Peter 1:16, God calls us to *be holy, for I am holy*. Holiness is not so much something we have, as much as it is something that has us.

Holiness is not achieved through our own efforts, but it is received, as we are now new men and women in Jesus. Holiness is part of the new man that we are in Jesus (Ephesians 4:24), and we are invited to be partakers – sharers of Jesus' holiness (Hebrews 12:10).

In Jesus, today you can **stand before this holy Lord God**.

March 10

Honor Him with What He Gives

For she did not know that I gave her grain, new wine, and oil, and multiplied her silver and gold; which they prepared for Baal. (Hosea 2:8)

Hosea prophesied to Israel in a time of political and economic success – but spiritual and moral failure. What did people do with all that political security and material abundance? In Hosea 2:8, we learn that Israel took the material abundance God gave them and they wasted it in sacrifices to Baal and other pagan gods.

Even when Israel went after other gods, the Lord still provided for her – He **gave her grain**, but **she did not know** it. This showed His great, unselfish love to Israel. Even though Israel took what God provided and prepared it for Baal.

The way God provided for Israel when **she did not know** was illustrated by what God told Hosea to do with his adulterous wife, named Gomer. When Hosea provided for Gomer, she spent it on her adulterous lovers. It's as if Hosea went to the house of Gomer's lover, where she lived in adultery. He knew that this scoundrel couldn't provide for Gomer and that she lived in poverty. Hosea knocked at the door. He spoke to the man who answered and asked him, "Are you the man living with Gomer?" The man wondered what business it was of Hosea's; then he revealed: "I'm Hosea, her husband. I've brought these groceries and money so she can be provided for." When Hosea left, Gomer and her lover must have thought he was a fool. What a great dinner they had together with the food Hosea brought! But this is how the Lord loves us, lavishing blessing on us even when we are worshipping idols, providing us with blessings we waste on other gods.

The other striking line in Hosea 2:8 comes at the end of the verse: **which they prepared for Baal**. This principle shows how offensive idolatry really is to God. It offends Him for many reasons, but one of them is because whatever we give to an idol, we have received from God.

Think of it like this. God gave to man the trees of the forest and the iron in the ground. He gave man the brains to make an ax and nails from the iron, the energy to cut down the tree, and the skill to fashion the wood into beams. God gave man the cleverness to make a handle from the wood, and to make a head from the iron, and to combine them into an effective hammer. Then man took the beams, the nails, and the hammer and he nailed God to the cross – where God willingly stretched out His arms, dying to take the guilt and penalty man's sin deserved. God did this to make a new, restored relationship between God and man possible.

God has given you great gifts – time, talents, and resources. Do you give them in sacrifice to Him or to idols?

March 11

When You Need a Good Lawyer

My little children, these things I write to you, so that you may not sin. And if anyone sins, we have an Advocate with the Father, Jesus Christ the righteous. (1 John 2:1)

John wrote so that we **may not sin**, yet we do. Those words might only bring discouragement because we do sin. Still, if we do sin, there is provision made – **an Advocate**, a defense lawyer on our side, Jesus Christ Himself. This word for **Advocate** speaks of an attorney (specifically, a defense lawyer). One ancient writer used the term to describe the friends of an accused man, who voluntarily step in and personally urge the judge to decide in his favor.

Thankfully, **we have an Advocate**. Jesus is our defender, even when we sin now. God is not shocked by human behavior; He saw it all in advance, yet His forgiveness is available to us now in Jesus.

It is as if we stand as the accused in the heavenly court, before our righteous Judge, God the Father. Our Advocate stands up to answer the charges against us: "He is completely guilty your Honor. In fact, he has even done worse than what he is accused of at this moment, and he now makes full and complete confession before You." The gavel slams, and the Judge asks, "What should his sentence be?" Our Advocate answers, "His sentence shall be death; he deserves the full wrath of this righteous court."

Throughout this, our accuser Satan is having great fun. We are guilty! We admit our guilt! Our punishment is clear! But then, our Advocate asks to approach the Judge's bench. As he draws close, He says: "Father, this one belongs to Me. I paid his price. I took the wrath and punishment that he deserves from this court." The gavel pounds again, and the Judge cries out, "Guilty as charged! Penalty satisfied!" Our accuser makes a strong protest. "Aren't you even going to put him on probation?" "No!" the Judge shouts. "The penalty has been completely paid by My Son. There is nothing to put him on probation for." Then the Judge turns to our Advocate, and says, "Son, you said this one belongs to You. I release him into Your care. Case closed!"

A human defense lawyer usually argues for the innocence of his client. But our Advocate, Jesus Christ, admits our guilt – and then enters His plea on our behalf, as the One who made an atoning sacrifice for our sinful guilt. When John says, **Jesus Christ the righteous**, he means that Jesus is fully qualified to serve as our Advocate, because He is without sin and is perfect. He has passed heaven's bar exam and is entirely qualified to represent clients in heaven's court of law.

The next time you feel "arrested" by the conviction of sin, call your Advocate in Heaven, plead guilty, and throw yourself on the mercy of the court.

March 12

Hold Me Up

Uphold me according to Your word, that I may live; and do not let me be ashamed of my hope. Hold me up, and I shall be safe, and I shall observe Your statutes continually. (Psalm 119:116-117)

One aspect of the beauty of Psalm 119 is how the psalmist comes back again and again to the benefits of God's Word. Here, in these two verses, the psalmist wrote of how the Word of God supported him in daily living.

He stated clearly: **Uphold me according to Your word, that I may live**. The psalmist knew that he could not stand before his enemies without God holding him up. Without this continual support from God, he could not live – either physically or spiritually.

In writing, **uphold me**, his idea was that this support would come according to God's Word. It would be both consistent with God's Word and find its source in God's Word. Through God's Word, the Lord's promises, hope, guidance, instruction, and actual spiritual strength came to him. Without all that, he could not stand.

With it, he could confidently pray, **do not let me be ashamed of my hope**. The psalmist could pray this because he had his hope correctly set. It was established on God and His Word (Psalm 119:43, 49, 74, 81, 114). When our hope is correctly set, we can ask God to protect and vindicate us.

This brief section contains a second request: **Hold me up, and I shall be safe, and I shall observe Your statutes continually**. Again, he asked to be supported by the strength that comes from God and primarily through His Word. In receiving this support and security, the psalmist would use it for further obedience to God.

This constant dependence on God – the constant prayer, **hold me up, and I shall be safe** – will keep one safe. If you are worried about holding up, then consciously ask God to hold on to you, and trust Him to do it.

In his commentary on Psalms, James Boice wrote of the Benedictines' monastic order, back in the Middle Ages. Among those monks, a man who hoped to join their order had a preparation period. If he still wanted to become a monk and commit himself to the monastery for the rest of his life after the end of the preparation time, they had a special ceremony.

In the ceremony to receive a man into their monastic order, the Benedictines required the man to stretch out his arms and repeat Psalm 119:116 three times: **Uphold me according to Your word, that I may live; and do not let me be ashamed of my hope.**

When he did this, all the other monks repeated the words and sang "Glory Be to the Father." It was their way of recognizing that a monk's vows could only be fulfilled when God upheld the monk and that all the glory should go to God.

Let Him hold you up today.

March 13

A Better Refuge

You shall appoint cities to be cities of refuge for you, that the manslayer who kills any person accidentally may flee there. They shall be cities of refuge for you from the avenger, that the manslayer may not die until he stands before the congregation in judgment. (Numbers 35:11-12)

In ancient Israel, it was not left entirely up to the government to bring a murderer to justice. Each extended family had a recognized avenger who made sure that one who murdered a family member would likewise be killed. This practice was based on a correct understanding of Genesis 9:6: *Whoever sheds man's blood, by man his blood shall be shed; for in the image of God, God made man.* This system was an effective deterrent to murder and not a bad institution – yet the system had a fatal weakness: What if a death were accidental, yet difficult to prove it was an accident?

For this reason, God commanded that Israel appoint six cities of refuge, with three on each side of the Jordan River. Roads were built and maintained to these cities of refuge (Deuteronomy 19:3). The city was no good to the slayer if they could not get there quickly. This meant that the cities were close to all; no one was very far from a city of refuge – which meant a lot when the avenger of blood chased you.

The Scriptures also tell us that anyone – stranger or citizen of Israel – who needed to find protection in the cities of refuge could – protection was not limited to the children of Israel.

The Bible applies this picture of the city of refuge to the believer finding refuge in God on more than one occasion. Psalm 46:1 says *God is our refuge and strength, a very present help in trouble.* More than 15 other times, the psalms speak of God as being our refuge. In addition, Hebrews 6:18 says, *that by two immutable things, in which it is impossible for God to lie, we might have strong consolation, who have fled for refuge to lay hold of the hope set before us.* We can flee to Jesus for refuge.

Both Jesus and the cities of refuge are within easy reach of the needy person.

Both Jesus and the cities of refuge are open to all, not just the Israelite.

Both Jesus and the cities of refuge became a place where the one in need could live.

Both Jesus and the cities of refuge are the only alternative for the one in need.

Both Jesus and the cities of refuge provide protection only within their boundaries; to go outside meant death.

With both Jesus and the cities of refuge, full freedom comes with the death of the High Priest.

There remains one crucial difference between Jesus and the cities of refuge. The cities of refuge only helped the innocent; but the *guilty* can come to Jesus and find refuge.

Aren't you glad Jesus is a better refuge?

March 14

Two Ways to Repent

Unless you repent you will all likewise perish.... but unless you repent you will all likewise perish. (Luke 13:3, 5)

This Lord of love, who played with children and blessed them, who received sinners gladly – does the same Jesus command us to repent? Look at the context to understand what Jesus meant with this strong statement.

On that day, accusers approached Jesus with a political question. Soldiers under the command of Pontius Pilate, the Roman Governor of Judea, had massacred several Galilean Jews who came to the temple to sacrifice. It was an appalling crime, and Jesus' accusers wanted Him to express His outrage against Pilate. The attackers thought Jesus was in a lose-lose situation. If Jesus criticized Pilate, He would be an enemy of Rome. If Jesus agreed with Pilate, He would then seem to betray His own people.

Jesus' answer didn't deal with the political issue. Luke says, *Jesus answered and said to them, "Do you suppose that these Galileans were worse sinners than all other Galileans because they suffered such things? I tell you, no; but unless you repent you will all likewise perish."* (Luke 13:2-3) With this call to repentance, Jesus essentially said: "These Galileans died unexpectedly and tragically. Are you ready for such an unexpected death?"

Jesus spoke of another tragedy that seemed to happen by accident. Luke records Jesus' words: *Or those eighteen on whom the tower in Siloam fell and killed them, do you think that they were worse sinners than all other men who dwelt in Jerusalem? I tell you, no; but unless you repent you will all likewise perish.* (Luke 13:4-5)

Jesus cited these two instances of disaster. One was an evil done by the hand of man, and the other a natural disaster. Sometimes we think that those who suffer under such tragedies must have been worse-than-average sinners. We normally think of some people as "good," and some people as "bad," and believe that God should allow good things to happen to good people and bad things to bad people. Jesus dismisses this idea. Jesus' point was not that the Galileans in question were innocent; they were simply not any more guilty than the others. We're all guilty.

Jesus changed the question from "why did this happen?" to "what does this mean to you?" It means that unless you repent, you can face the same fate. It means that we all may die at any time, so repentance must be a top priority. In both cases, those who died did not think they would die soon, but they did, and we can suppose that most of them were not ready.

In the grammar of the ancient Greek, Jesus mentioned two kinds of repentance. Verse five (**unless you repent**) describes "once and for all" repentance; the verb tense in verse three (**unless you repent**) describes continuing repentance.

Have you made the "once for all" turn away from sin and self, and to Jesus? Then move on to continuing repentance, and every day turn your heart and mind toward Him.

March 15

It's Not Enough to Be Smart

We are of God. He who knows God hears us; he who is not of God does not hear us. By this we know the spirit of truth and the spirit of error. (1 John 4:6)

The words **we are of God** sound comforting to some people and terrifying to some others. Those are true and special words to those who are indeed God's people and who display the love, power, and character of Jesus.

However, through the centuries, almost every tyrant, every cruel general, and every wicked leader has used the words **we are of God**. They wanted the added prestige and power that comes when other people think, "God is on their side." Almost everybody wants to believe that God is on their side, and their cause is blessed because they say **we are of God.**

So, when John says **we are of God**, how do we know he is right to say it?

John is right because the **we** he wrote of were the apostles who saw and heard Jesus first-hand. They had a special authority and remarkable confidence because they had a special calling from Jesus. They were His specially authorized representatives. If this was just an individual talking, then his claim to be **of God** might be overconfident. But John spoke as one of God's apostles, and he called forth the gathered testimony of all the apostles, thereby making that testimony the measure of truth and sound doctrine. We know this truth by using the New Testament as our measure, which is the inspired record of the apostles' teaching.

When someone agrees with what God says in the New Testament, they show they know God. When someone contradicts the New Testament, they reveal something is wrong in their knowledge of God. This certainly is not to exclude the Old Testament; since the New has all confidence in the Old, it includes it.

This helps us to know **the spirit of truth and the spirit of error**. If someone hears what God has said in the Bible, we know they have **the spirit of truth**. If they do not hear it, they have the spirit of error. This phrase clarifies that error has a spiritual dynamic to it; it is not just about being educated or smart. The **spirit of error** can powerfully influence some very educated and intelligent people. Since error has a spiritual dynamic, keeping in the **spirit of truth** is mostly a spiritual issue.

Many times, we think the difference between truth and error is all about how smart someone is. It's been said that people often asked Albert Einstein what he thought about God. Einstein's brilliance as a scientist was unquestioned, but he didn't have any more insight into spiritual truth than anyone else. We keep in the spirit of truth not by brainpower, but by clinging to Jesus, the One who said, *I am the truth* (John 14:6).

Are you in the spirit of truth today?

March 16

Being an Overcomer

And they overcame him by the blood of the Lamb and by the word of their testimony, and they did not love their lives to the death. (Revelation 12:11)

The 1960s folk song, "We Shall Overcome," expressed the confidence of victory when facing great opposition. Revelation 12:11 presents three keys to the saints' victory over our opponent, the enemy of our souls. We know the first key: **they overcame him by the blood of the Lamb.**

The second key is in the phrase, **they overcame him…by the word of their testimony**. If the **blood of the Lamb** overcomes Satan's accusations, then the **word of their testimony** overcomes Satan's deception. Knowing and remembering the work of God in their life protects against Satan's deceiving work.

It is very important that each one of us has a word of our testimony. We give testimony about something that we have experienced first-hand. In a court of law, the witness is called to give testimony about what they have personally seen or heard or know. If the lawyer asks them a question about what someone else experienced, that is hearsay and is not admissible. On this same principle, we can't live "hearsay" Christian lives. We need to have a personal encounter with Jesus and have a personal testimony of what we have experienced from Him.

When we are grounded in the word of our testimony, it is a lot harder for Satan to deceive us. He is an expert at spinning a foggy web in our head, making us wonder if all this "God stuff" is real at all. But when we can stand on the remembrance of specific things we have seen God do in our lives, we know He is for real and His work in our life is real.

In John 9, we have the account of when Jesus healed a man who was born blind. Jesus performed this miracle as a simple act of mercy, but the religious leaders of the day wanted to use it as an excuse to attack Jesus. They fired all sorts of confusing theological questions at the man who was healed, trying to get him to say something bad about Jesus. Finally, the blind man said: *One thing I know: that though I was blind, now I see.* (John 9:25) That was the word of his testimony, and no one could argue against it.

You may know many theological facts about Jesus, but never have had a word of testimony, knowing you have experienced His forgiveness, His love, His healing, His comfort, His strength, His miraculous power, or any number of other ways He works in our life. If you do not have a word of testimony regarding His work in your life, make it the passion of your life to compile one.

If you do have this word of your testimony, let Jesus increase it – and most of all, then you must use it to be an overcomer.

March 17

Grace to the Humble

But He gives more grace. Therefore He says: "God resists the proud, but gives grace to the humble." (James 4:6)

It is helpful to look at this beautiful verse in some depth. First, **He gives more grace**. Then **God resists the proud**. Third, notice the blessed contrast: it is true that **God resists the proud**, but He **gives grace to the humble**.

To be in God's grace means to be in a place of favor and acceptance before Him. How can we stand in this place of favor? As we grow up, we learn how to gain favor and acceptance from people. We learn how to be people pleasers. All this can work in making others like us, but it doesn't work to obtain favor from God. We can't gain God's grace by trying to be good children, nor can we give enough money to His work so that God's approval is earned.

Instead, we come into a place of grace, favor, and acceptance by faith. When we come to Jesus in faith, He directly gives us the grace of God. It is that simple. Just like Paul said, *I thank my God always concerning you for the grace of God which was given to you by Christ Jesus.* (1 Corinthians 1:4)

With this kind of direct access to God's favor, we might wonder why people aren't always lining up to receive this grace from God.

The proud man or woman rejects grace because under grace, God won't consider any goodness or worth they think they have. Grace is undeserved favor, given apart from any consideration of goodness or worth in the receiver. The proud person doesn't want to have anything to do with a system that will not consider what a marvelous person they are, so the proud person rejects grace and is resisted by God. Grace and pride are irreconcilable enemies because pride demands to have it's worth glorified, and grace refuses to consider it.

On the other hand, the humble realize their unworthiness and their complete inability to be worthy. Yet, they find themselves blessed, on another principle outside of themselves. They are the ones who say, "God, be merciful to me a sinner," recognizing God owes them nothing but judgment. When they come to God with such humility, they find His favor and approval are there waiting for them, and for all who will come to God with an honest recognition of their unworthiness.

It isn't that we earn grace by our remarkable humility. Instead, the humble are naturally open to God's grace given freely in Christ. Pride proves we disagree with God's plan of grace because it isn't based on earning and deserving. Humility demonstrates that we agree with His plan, recognizing both our unworthiness and God's greatness.

So, what do we do? We put away our pride and, in humility, enjoy the grace of God. Humbly, receive God's grace today!

March 18

Tried and Proven

**Trouble and anguish have overtaken me,
Yet Your commandments are my delights.
The righteousness of Your testimonies is everlasting;
Give me understanding, and I shall live.** (Psalm 119:143-144)

There is a lot of trouble in this world, and everyone has some share in it. There are troubles that we experience and the problems we observe. Some of these troubles come from evil men; some come from natural calamity. It sometimes drives us to despair, wondering where God is amid all the trouble.

In such seasons, it's good to read what the psalmist wrote: **Trouble and anguish have overtaken me, yet Your commandments are my delights**. Despite the difficulties of his life, the psalmist still found delight in God's Word. His appreciation of God and His Word was not only valid in good times, but also in **trouble and anguish**.

This is one of the great qualities of the Christian faith. It's true in the darkest of days, even in times of trouble and anguish. Christianity was born into a world that knew evil, tragedy, and sorrow on a scale far beyond what most of us know.

When Jesus was about 11 years old, there was a Jewish revolt against the Romans in the Galilee region. The rebels took over a city about 4 miles (6.5 km) from Nazareth. When the Romans crushed the rebellion, they leveled the city, sold the surviving women and children into slavery, and crucified 2,000 men along the roads all around Nazareth. From His youngest days, Jesus looked at the horror and brutality of this world and was determined to not only pay the price to forgive and redeem the penalty of it all, but also to transform men and women to make such things far less common.

The psalmist knew what Jesus also knew – **trouble and anguish have overtaken me, yet Your commandments are my delights**. For them, the truth and promises of God's Word were not just helpful hints or theoretical statements. They were the reason for delight, even in the most challenging seasons.

He continued, **the righteousness of Your testimonies is everlasting; give me understanding, and I shall live**. We might think that what the psalmist needed to live was deliverance from his trouble and anguish. He found that understanding the Word of God was even more important.

One reason he found this to be so was that he understood that the righteousness of God's Word is **everlasting**. He knew the eternal character of the Word of God, and it made that word even more important and relevant to him.

I've read that there used to be a habit among some Christians to write the letters T and P in the margin of the Bible, next to specific promises of God.

The letters stood for "Tried and Proven," because they discovered for themselves precisely what the psalmist found – that we could test the promises of God and prove them to be true. You can prove it for yourself.

March 19
Asking Without Doubting

If any of you lacks wisdom, let him ask of God, who gives to all liberally and without reproach, and it will be given to him. But let him ask in faith, with no doubting, for he who doubts is like a wave of the sea driven and tossed by the wind. For let not that man suppose that he will receive anything from the Lord; he is a double-minded man, unstable in all his ways. (James 1:5-8)

James told the followers of Jesus to take a joy-filled attitude in their trials, allowing endurance to have its perfect work. James tells us about wisdom in the following lines because trials bring a necessary season to seek wisdom from God. We often did not know we needed wisdom until our time of difficulty. Once in a stressful and testing time, we need to know if a particular trial is something God wants us to *eliminate* by faith or *endure* through faith. This requires wisdom.

In trials, we need wisdom more than we need knowledge. Knowledge is raw information, but wisdom knows how to use it. Someone once said that knowledge is the ability to take things apart, but wisdom is the ability to put things together.

To receive wisdom, we **ask of God** – who gives wisdom generously (**liberally**), and without despising our request (**without reproach**). We are often ready to go anywhere but God when we need wisdom – we go to books, ceremonies, institutions, human analysis – but shouldn't we begin by simply asking God? He may use all sorts of ways to bring us wisdom, but we should start by asking Him.

When we want wisdom, the place to begin is in the Bible. The place to end is in the Bible. True wisdom will always be consistent with God's Word.

He gives generously and without reproach. Knowing God's generosity – that He never despises or resents us for asking for wisdom – should encourage us to ask Him often. We understand that He is the God of the open hand, not the God of the clenched fist.

Our request for wisdom must be made like any other request. We must **ask in faith**, without doubting God's ability or desire to give us His wisdom. To emphasize the point, James adds: **With no doubting.... let not that man suppose that he will receive anything from the Lord**. The one who doubts and lacks faith should not expect to receive anything from the Lord. This lack of faith and trust in God also shows that we have no foundation, being unstable in all our ways.

The one who fails to ask this way is **like a wave of the sea driven and tossed by the wind**. A wave of the sea is a fitting description of one who is hindered by unbelief and unnecessary doubts.

Today, let us come to the God of the open hand – and come in faith, believing that He is who He says He is.

March 20

Rise and Shine

Arise, shine; for your light has come! And the glory of the Lord is risen upon you. For behold, the darkness shall cover the earth, and deep darkness the people; but the Lord will arise over you, and His glory will be seen upon you. The Gentiles shall come to your light, and kings to the brightness of your rising. (Isaiah 60:1-3)

After the thick and desperate darkness described in Isaiah 59, the prophet gave a wonderful announcement: **light has come!** The Redeemer of Isaiah 59:20 brings glorious, shining redemption – so God tells His people to respond to it, and to arise and shine.

First, we receive God's light (**your light has come**), and then we have a service to put forth (**arise, shine**). It all begins with the shining of God's light. You can't shine until **your light has come**, but once it has come, there is something wrong if you don't arise and shine. It's a call to live like you are in the light instead of in the darkness.

This is no earthly light; it is the **glory of the Lord** that rises over God's people, light that emanates from His presence. This is like the light of Jesus in the Transfiguration, when *His face shone like the sun, and His clothes became as white as the light* (Matthew 17:2).

The shining of this light and the effect that it has on the people of God also impacts those who are far from God (**Gentiles shall come to your light**). When the Lord lifts His glorious light over Israel, the Gentile nations shall see it and are attracted. Even kings will be drawn **to the brightness of** Israel's rising.

The promise of the Gentile world coming to the Messiah's light and even **kings to the brightness** of His **rising** has an ultimate fulfillment in what some call the Millennial Kingdom of Jesus Christ. This will be a time when Jesus reigns over the world in a way not yet seen, when swords are beaten into plowshares and when the lamb lies down with the wolf. The Old Testament tells us that another aspect of this special era of God's work will be the exaltation of Israel among the nations. Yet when God lifts Israel during those coming days of His Great Kingdom, it isn't merely for Israel's sake; it is so that through Israel, and especially through Israel's Messiah, blessing can come to all nations.

God will do that ultimate work in a time of His choosing. Yet we, who have also received this glorious light, can also see the same kind of work happen in us. We can let God shine His light on us; we can rise in response to that light, and we can live lives that draw others to the light of God shining in us.

God has some glory to shine out through you; so rise and shine!

March 21

A Good Reminder

But I want to remind you, though you once knew this, that the Lord, having saved the people out of the land of Egypt, afterward destroyed those who did not believe. (Jude v. 5)

The apostle Jude wanted to warn Christians about the danger of false teaching and false living in the Church. Jude didn't want his readers to react in the wrong way, so he assured them of the certain judgment of these dangerous people by using three Old Testament examples.

Jude knew he wasn't telling them anything new, but they needed to hear these things again and apply them to their present situation. If we don't know what Jude wrote about, it shows we need to deepen our understanding of the Bible.

First, Jude reminded them of Israel in the days of the Exodus: **The Lord, having saved the people out of the land of Egypt**. Jude wrote of what happened in Numbers 14. God delivered the people of Israel out of slavery in Egypt to a place called Kadesh Barnea on the threshold of the Promised Land. But the people refused to trust God and go into the Promised Land of Canaan. Therefore, almost none of the adult generation who left Egypt entered the Promised Land.

Think of what God did for the people of Israel in this situation, and then how they responded to Him. They experienced God's miraculous deliverance at the Red Sea. They heard the very voice of God at Mount Sinai. They received His daily care and provision in the wilderness. Yet they lapsed into unbelief and were never permitted to enter the place of blessing and rest God had for them.

The result was tragic: the Lord **afterward destroyed those who did not believe**. Those who doubted and rejected God at Kadesh Barnea paid a bigger price than just not entering the Promised Land. They also received the judgment of God. Psalm 95 describes how God's response: *For forty years I was grieved with that generation, and said, 'It is a people who go astray in their hearts, and they do not know My ways. "So I swore in My wrath, they shall not enter My rest."* (Psalm 95:10-11)

The people of Israel started out from Egypt well enough. They had plenty of blessings from God along the way. But they did not endure to the end, because they did not believe God's promise of power and protection.

Jude thought seems to be, "These people causing trouble among believers might have started out well. But so did the children of Israel, and God **afterward destroyed those who did not believe**." It warns us that we also must follow Jesus to the end, and never be among those who did not believe. The final test of our Christianity is endurance. Some start the race but never finish it.

Determine for yourself that, in Jesus, there's no turning back – by His grace you will be a finisher, not only a starter.

March 22

How Temptation Comes, How It Works

Let no one say when he is tempted, "I am tempted by God"; for God cannot be tempted by evil, nor does He Himself tempt anyone. But each one is tempted when he is drawn away by his own desires and enticed. Then, when desire has conceived, it gives birth to sin; and sin, when it is full-grown, brings forth death. Do not be deceived, my beloved brethren. (James 1:13-16)

Temptation does not come from God, though He allows it. God does not draw us to evil, though He may test our faith without drawing us to evil. James made it clear that God does not **tempt anyone**.

James spoke of how we should act in hard times. He knew that many of us find it easy to blame God when we are in a trial. Yet, by His very nature, God is unable to either be tempted, **nor does He Himself tempt anyone**.

We see that God sometimes allows difficult tests to come to His people, even some who might be thought of as His "favorites." We think of the hard command God gave to Abraham (Genesis 22:1), and the affliction He allowed to come to Job (Job 1-2). Other times God may send tests as a form of judgment on those who have rejected Him, such as sending a spirit to bring deception (1 Kings 22:19-23) or in the departing from a man and refusing to answer him (1 Samuel 28:15-16). But in no case does God work to draw a person to perform evil.

If temptation does not come from God, where does it come from? Many of us like to always blame temptation on the devil but isn't always true. God doesn't tempt us. Instead, temptation comes when we are **drawn away** by our fleshly desires and enticed – with the world and the devil providing the enticement.

Satan certainly tempts us, but temptation has a hook in us because of our fallen nature, which corrupts our God-given desires. We often give Satan too much credit for his tempting powers and fail to recognize that we are **drawn away** by our **own desires**. Some people practically beg Satan to tempt them.

Then James reminded us of where temptation leads: **When desire has conceived, it gives birth to sin**. Springing forth from corrupt desire is sin. Springing forth from sin is death. This progression to death is an inevitable result that the tempter always tries to hide from us, but that should never deceive us.

That's why James wrote this: **Do not be deceived, my beloved brethren**. The tempter's grand strategy is to convince us that following our corrupt desires will somehow produce life and goodness for us.

If we remembered that Satan only comes *to steal, and to kill, and to destroy* (John 10:10), we could more effectively resist the deceptions and destructions of temptation.

March 23

Dead Faith or Living Faith?

If a brother or sister is naked and destitute of daily food, and one of you says to them, "Depart in peace, be warmed and filled," but you do not give them the things which are needed for the body, what does it profit? Thus also faith by itself, if it does not have works, is dead. (James 2:15-17)

James had in mind a **brother or sister** who lacked food and clothing, and they came to other believers for help – yet the professed believers did not help those in need. To fail in the simplest good work towards a brother or sister in need demonstrates a lack of living faith, and only a living faith in Jesus saves.

The cold heart of dead faith says, **be warmed and filled** – knowing the needy person needs clothing and food. The need is known, but nothing was done to help them beyond saying a few religious words.

This kind of dead faith does not **profit** anything. Real faith, and the works that accompany it, aren't made up of only "spiritual" things, but also of a concern for the most basic needs – such as the need for comfort, covering, and food. When needs arise, we should sometimes pray less, and do more to help the person in need. Sometimes prayer can be a substitute for action.

James observed that this faith, without any **works** that prove it is a living faith, can be called **dead** faith, and it won't save anyone. Faith alone saves us, but it must be a living faith. We can tell if faith is alive by seeing if works accompany it. If faith is claimed by works are absent, it may be dead faith.

Living faith is real faith. If we believe something, we'll follow through and act on it. If we put our trust and faith in Jesus, we will care for the naked and destitute as He told us to do.

Some signs of living and saving faith are:
- Looks not to self, but Jesus Christ.
- It agrees with God's Word, both inwardly and with words.
- Grounded in what Jesus did on the cross and by the empty tomb.
- Will naturally be expressed in repentance and good works.
- May sometimes doubt, yet the doubts aren't bigger than the faith, or more permanent than the faith. "Lord, I believe; help my unbelief." (Mark 9:24)
- Wants others to come to the same faith.
- Says more than the mere words "Lord, Lord," as in Matthew 7:21-23.
- Not only hears the Word of God but does it, as in Matthew 7:24-27.

It is vital for each person to look at his or her life and judge: "Do I have a living faith, or am I supposing that I can be saved by a dead faith"?

Ask yourself this today because everything rests on this fundamental question.

March 24

God's Wonderful Custom

Look upon me and be merciful to me,
As Your custom is toward those who love Your name.
Direct my steps by Your word,
And let no iniquity have dominion over me. (Psalm 119:132-133)

Psalm 119 is the great song about the goodness and glory of God's Word, and almost every one of its 176 verses mentions the Word of God in some way. Verse 132 may be one of the few verses (perhaps five in the entire psalm) that does not mention God's Word. Instead, Psalm 119:132 is a prayer made up of two requests and one reason.

We read, **look upon me, and be merciful to me**. Those are two requests, the first asking God to **look**, and the second asking God to **be merciful**. The second line of verse 132 gives a reason to believe why God would answer such a prayer: because the psalmist knew that this was God's **custom...toward those who love His name**. Remember that in the culture of the Old Testament world, a name meant more than a person's title – it was a reflection and a declaration of their character. Loving God's name describes loving His character, Who He is.

It is wonderful to think that God has a custom, a pattern of action, towards those who love His name. That custom is to look on them (giving them His attention) and to be merciful. Knowing this is God's custom, we should learn all we can about God's nature and character, so we will love Him more and stand on this wonderful promise.

Yet God's look – the turning of His attention – would be a curse and not a blessing unless His mercy came with it. If we have the first, we must have the second.

Notice that this custom of mercy is **toward those who love Your name**. To love the name of God means to love the person of God, the character of God, the revelation of God, and to love the glory of God.

In verse 133, the psalmist explained what he wanted to do with the mercy that he received from God. He said to God, **direct my steps by Your word**. He tried to take that mercy and use it to walk rightly before God. One part of this was to let no iniquity **have dominion over** his life.

Many people today want to direct their steps by something else, anything else, other than the word of God. The way many people live today, they say, "Direct my steps by my feelings." Or, they say "Direct my steps by my lusts." Instead of God's word, people will direct their steps by their friends, their parents, their circumstances, their comforts, or even by "fate."

Is it much better to say to God, **direct my steps by Your word**. The sense of the Hebrew here is "Make my steps firm in Your Word."

Today, walk forward in life with great confidence as you find direction in God's Word.

March 25

Against the Pride of Success

The LORD of hosts has purposed it, to bring to dishonor the pride of all glory, to bring into contempt all the honorable of the earth. (Isaiah 23:9)

The LORD God spoke these words through the prophet Isaiah, and He spoke the words against the great city of Tyre.

In biblical times, Tyre was the leading city of Phoenicia, the great sea power of the ancient world. Because it was such an important harbor and shipping center, Tyre was synonymous with commerce and materialism.

Tyre was an inland city and an island city. The Assyrians and the Babylonians conquered the inland city, just as Isaiah prophesied. In 332 B.C., Alexander the Great conquered the island city.

In Isaiah's word against Tyre, God mainly spoke against the city's great pride. Isaiah 23 tells how the merchants of the world will mourn when judgment comes against the city (Isaiah 23:5-7). It also tells us something interesting about Tyre in Isaiah 23:8: *Who has taken this counsel against Tyre, the crowning city, whose merchants are princes, whose traders are the honorable of the earth?*

This means that Tyre was a city where money and success ruled. In ancient Tyre, the *merchants are princes*, and the *traders are the honorable of the earth*. To be a leader or honorable in ancient Tyre, one didn't need to be of royal heritage, or be a good or honest person. The only thing needed was success in business!

Yet all their success just made them proud. So, as it says in Isaiah 23:9, **The LORD of hosts has purposed it, to bring dishonor the pride of all glory**. Tyre had become proud and full of self-glory. But **the LORD of hosts has purposed** to judge and humble Tyre, and Isaiah announced it.

Thinking about ancient Tyre and the judgment God brought against them should make us soberly consider our own standing with God. Are you successful? Has God graciously granted fruit to your work? Take care that you aren't proud and self-reliant. Give special opportunity for the self-searching that the Holy Spirit does in the heart of those who ask Him.

There are many people who stand strong against the trials of adversity who ultimately fail when confronted with the trials of success. We must remind ourselves that success has its own set of temptations and trials. One of the greatest tests of success is dealing with the tendency of pride.

As always, we can look to Jesus: was there anyone more successful, or anyone who had ever achieved more? Yet we rightly honor our humble Savior, who even knowing that all things had been given to Him washed feet (John 13:3-5).

Therefore, learn from Tyre. If God has granted you success, thank Him for it and enjoy it in every right and proper way. But determine to ruthlessly deal with the tendency to pride, so that God doesn't determine to **bring dishonor the pride of all glory** in your life.

March 26

According to Your Word

Then the LORD **said: "I have pardoned, according to your word."** (Numbers 14:20)

There are 73 verses in the New King James Bible where "according" and "word" are used in the same verse. The exact phrase "according to your word" is used 18 times in the Bible, and most of the time man says it to God. Psalm 119:58, is a good example: *Be merciful to me according to Your word.*

Numbers 14:20 is the only place where God said to man, **according to your word**. Moses was the man, and the **word** was the anguished, passionate prayer by Moses on behalf of Israel when God intended to destroy the nation. Numbers 14:19 says: *Pardon the iniquity of this people, I pray, according to the greatness of Your mercy, just as You have forgiven this people, from Egypt even until now.*

It wasn't that Israel hadn't sinned badly – they had. On the threshold of the Promised Land, they refused to trust God and enter in. The men hid behind supposed concern for their wives and children, and they wouldn't trust God to fulfill His promise. For this great sin, God asked Moses to step aside so He could destroy the nation and start over again with Moses. But Moses wouldn't get out of the way – he boldly appealed to God. Moses knew God's power and he appealed to it. Moses knew God's promise and he appealed to it. Moses knew God's glory and he appealed to it. When Moses cried out to God, he gave us a spectacular example of intercessory prayer.

What made this intercession spectacular was not primarily Moses' method (appealing to God's glory, power, and promise), but Moses' *heart*. Moses was totally others-centered, not concerned for his own glory, but only for Israel. It was God's intention to develop in Moses this kind of heart, transforming him into the image of His Son (Romans 8:29), long before the time of Jesus!

The words **I have pardoned** proves that Moses' heart and method of intercession were successful. But God did not finish with pronouncing a pardon – the full statement is **I have pardoned, according to your word**.

The phrase **according to your word** means that Moses' prayer *mattered*. We don't understand the relationship between the eternal, sovereign plan of God and our prayers. God wanted Moses and all of us to understand that his prayers directly affected the outcome. We should pray as if our prayers will decide life and death or heaven and hell.

How could life or death for Israel depend on the prayers of one man? God wants us to pray with this kind of passion, believing that eternity may depend on our prayer. It can be difficult to reconcile this with knowing God has a pre-ordained plan, but God didn't want Moses to concern himself with that – he was to pray as if it really mattered.

If we believe that, we will truly pray.

March 27

On Eagles' Wings

You have seen what I did to the Egyptians, and how I bore you on eagles' wings and brought you to Myself. (Exodus 19:4)

The people of Israel had finished the first part of their journey out of Egypt towards Mount Sinai where they would stay a year as God gave them His law. As they arrived at the same mountain where the LORD spoke to Moses out of the burning bush, God had something extraordinary to say to them.

First, He reminded them of His triumph over the Egyptians (**You have seen what I did to the Egyptians**). Israel needed to be reminded over and over that the LORD their God was greater than any of Egypt's pretend deities. There should never be a competition in our life between God and anything else; we need to remember that He is greater than anyone and anything else.

Next, He spoke to them about His loving care. In saying, **How I bore you on eagle's wings**, the LORD used a precious – and powerful – picture. It is said that an eagle does not carry her young in her claws like other birds. Instead, the young eagles attach themselves to the back of the mother eagle and are protected from any attack from the ground as they are carried. An arrow from a hunter must pass through the mother eagle before it could touch the young eagle.

The LORD has the same loving care for you. Whatever arrows or attacks come your way have first come through the LORD Himself. First, Jesus endured all temptation while He walked this earth as a man. The Bible says that Jesus *was in all points tempted as we are, yet without sin* (Hebrews 4:15). Enthroned in heaven, at the right hand of God the Father, Jesus understands perfectly every arrow shot at you, because in some way the same arrow was shot at Him.

Second, whatever comes our way comes by the allowance of God. God is never the source of evil or temptation, but it is entirely within God's power to stop any trial or temptation. The fact that God allows it means He has a purpose for it in your life – and the purpose isn't to kill you. The death-arrow would have to go through Him before it ever comes to His child.

He spoke to Israel about the purpose of His deliverance. He rescued Israel so they could have a relationship with Him. When He brought them out of Egypt, God said He **brought you to Myself**.

God works the same way in our lives. Jesus does not rescue us so we can live to ourselves, but so we live to Him. As 2 Corinthians 5:15 says, *He died for all, that those who live should live no longer for themselves, but for Him who died for them and rose again.* His purpose is to bring us to Himself.

Today, enjoy the relationship God rescued you to have with Him.

March 28

When I See the Blood

Now the blood shall be a sign for you on the houses where you are. And when I see the blood, I will pass over you; and the plague shall not be on you to destroy you when I strike the land of Egypt. (Exodus 12:13)

Pharaoh resisted God's call to let the people of Israel go. The LORD sent plague after plague to make the message understood, but Pharaoh didn't listen. God then declared one final plague: the Angel of the LORD would go through the land of Egypt and kill the firstborn of every family – every family that was not protected by the sacrificial blood of a lamb.

For Israel to be spared the judgment on the firstborn, they had to apply the blood just as God said to do. The blood of the lamb was essential to what God required. If an Israelite home didn't do what God said to do with the blood of the lamb, they could sacrifice the lamb and eat it, but God's judgment would still visit them. By the same token, if an Egyptian home believed in the power of the blood of the lamb, and they made a proper Passover sacrifice, they were spared the judgment. The only thing that held back God's hand of judgment was the blood of the lamb.

When the ministry of Jesus first began, John the Baptist looked at Jesus and said, *Behold, the Lamb of God who takes away the sin of the world* (John 1:29). Jesus is the Passover Lamb for all who put their trust in Him. He was without blemish. His death – represented by His blood – was on our behalf. This points to the fact that we must do more than know that Jesus died for us. We must do more than embrace Jesus in a superficial way. We must do what He said to do with His blood – trust that it pays the penalty for our sin.

It was a bloody mess to take the blood of a lamb and use it to mark the sides and top of a doorway. It was a bloody mess for a man to die on a cross, especially the sinless Son of God. But God can do something extraordinary even through a bloody mess. It isn't that God likes the gore, but He does insist that our sin be paid for, and since the God we have sinned against is a great God, the price to be paid is a great price. It's not that God likes to look at blood – but He does like to look at the price that has been paid and the restoration with man that comes from that price paid.

At the end of it all, there are only two ways people try to be right with God. Some vainly hope to be right based on what they can do for God, and some are right based on what God did for them in Jesus.

Are you trusting in what you can do for God or what Jesus did for you, expressed by that blood?

March 29

He Has Shown You

He has shown you, O man, what is good; and what does the LORD **require of you but to do justly, to love mercy, and to walk humbly with your God?** (Micah 6:8)

This famous verse expresses in one sentence what God looks for from man, especially as it relates to the way we treat one another.

In Micah 6, the prophet pictured a court of law, with Israel "on trial" before the LORD. In the presence of unshakable witnesses (such as "the mountains" and "the hills" and the "strong foundations of the earth") God said to Israel, "Arise, plead your case" – and God brought His case, His complaint against Israel.

As Israel stepped up, God asked them, "What have I done to you?" The LORD had done nothing but good to Israel, yet He was repaid with rejection and rebellion. God reminded Israel, "I redeemed you from the house of bondage." God did them an enormous amount of good. He redeemed them and gave them godly leaders.

It was time for Israel to answer these charges from God. They protested: "With what shall I come before the LORD? Just what do You want from me?" They continued, "Will the LORD be pleased with thousands of rams, ten thousand rivers of oil? You are being unreasonable."

God stopped the shouting of the angry defendant: "You act as if it is some mystery what I require of you. It is no mystery at all. I have shown you clearly what is good and what I require of you." Micah 6:8: **He has shown you, O man, what is good; and what does the L**ORD **require of you but to do justly, to love mercy, and to walk humbly with your God.** We can think of God explaining it like this:

- **Do justly**: "Act in a just, fair way towards others. Treat them the way you want to be treated."
- **Love mercy**: "Don't just show mercy but also love to show it. Give others the same measure of mercy you want to receive from the Me."
- **To walk humbly**: "This is a key to justice and mercy. If you truly walk humbly with Me, then doing justly and loving mercy come naturally."
- **With your God**: "Remember who I am – your God. If you keep that in mind, you will walk humbly before Me."

So, walk humbly when you are spiritually strong. Do it when you have much work to do. Be humble in all your motives. Walk humbly when studying God's word, when under trials, and in your devotions. Be humble when dealing with sinners and before your brothers and sisters in Christ.

The point is clear. When God exposed Israel's rebellion and ingratitude, they protested that He asked too much. God does not ask too much of man. Do justly, love mercy, and walk humbly with your God.

Informed by God's Word, motivated by your relationship with Him, and empowered by the Holy Spirit, you can do it.

March 30

The Real Jesus

By this you know the Spirit of God: Every spirit that confesses that Jesus Christ has come in the flesh is of God. (1 John 4:2)

True biblical prophecy and true biblical teaching will present a true Jesus Christ. In the apostle John's day, the critical issue was if Jesus had indeed come in a real body of flesh and blood. Some teachers back then said that Jesus, being God, could not have actually become a flesh and blood human, because God could have no partnership with "impure" material things.

Today, some deny that Jesus is really God (such as the Jehovah's Witnesses, Mormons, and Muslims). But way back in John's time, in that time closest to the actual life and ministry of Jesus on this earth, people did not have a hard time believing Jesus was God; they had a hard time believing that He was also a real man. This false teaching said Jesus was truly God (which is correct), but really a make-believe man.

Today, we are passionate about saying, "Jesus is God," and we should be. But it is no less important to say, "Jesus is a man," because both the deity and humanity of Jesus are essential truths.

Some think that the only test of false doctrine is to see if a person **confesses that Jesus Christ has come in the flesh**. This is not the only test, but it was the most important issue challenging the church in John's immediate time. But today, a person might **confess that Jesus Christ has come in the flesh** yet deny that Jesus is God as the Bible teaches that He is God. The principle of presenting a true Jesus is essential to true spiritual evaluation. No one who presents a false Jesus or one untrue to the Scriptures can be regarded as a true prophet.

There is always a lot of curiosity about the "true Jesus." Some academics say that they want to discover the true Jesus, and when they say this, they often assume that the true Jesus is not the Jesus of the Bible. They think that the Jesus of the Bible is a make-believe Jesus, and they need to discover the true Jesus behind the myths of the Bible.

Not only is this position uninformed (because it ignores the remarkable, historical validity of the New Testament), but it is also arrogant, because once they throw out the record of the New Testament, those academics are left with little more than their personal opinions. They present their baseless views as if they were scholarly facts.

The devil does not care at all if you know Jesus, or love Jesus, or pray to Jesus – if it is all directed towards someone other than the biblical Jesus, the Jesus who exists. Some imagine a false Jesus, a make-believe Jesus, a Jesus who is not there, and who cannot rescue us.

Do you know the Jesus of the Bible? He is the only real Jesus.

March 31

It Had to Happen

Whom God raised up, having loosed the pains of death, because it was not possible that He should be held by it. (Acts 2:24)

When Peter preached his sermon on Pentecost, he could have stopped after quoting the prophet Joel. But Peter hadn't yet spoken about the saving work of Jesus on our behalf. Then came this essential message.

In bringing the core message to his audience, he first confronted them with their sin. Peter did not flinch at saying, **you crucified this Man who was sent by God** – his first concern was not to please his audience but to tell them the truth. But Peter couldn't stop there, as if his point was only to make them feel bad about their sin. He had to show that there were facts *greater* than man's guilt in executing the Son of God.

The greater facts were God's power and the greatness of Jesus, both demonstrated by the resurrection. **It was not possible** for Jesus to remain bound by death, as explained by Peter's following quotation from Psalm 16. Jesus couldn't remain a victim of the sin and hatred of man. He had to come out ahead, glorious in triumph over it. To demonstrate this, notice that Peter used the term **pains of death**. The word **pains** is the word for "birth pains." The idea is that the tomb was a womb for Jesus! As one commentator wrote, "It was not possible that the chosen one of God should remain in the grip of death; the abyss can no more hold the Redeemer than a pregnant woman can hold the child in her body."

As a baby must come out of the womb, the resurrection of Jesus was a "must". There was no way the Holy One – the sinless Son of God – could remain bound by the chains of death.

When Jesus died on the cross, He bore the full judgment of God as if He were a guilty sinner, guilty of all our sin, even being made sin for us (2 Corinthians 5:21). Yet even that was an act of holy, giving love for us. Therefore, Jesus Himself did not become a sinner, even though He bore our sin's full guilt. This is the good news – that Jesus took our punishment for sin on the cross and remained a perfect Savior through the whole ordeal – proved by His resurrection.

For this reason, He remained the Holy One, even in His death; and it was not possible that God's Holy One could remain bound by death – the resurrection had to happen. We don't see many things in life that *must* happen. In almost everything, we can think of another way things could turn out. But it was not this way with the resurrection of Jesus – it had to happen. It could be no other way.

And it proves that God's love and power are greater than the worst of man's sin and rebellion.

April 1
Terms of the Contract

And Moses wrote all the words of the LORD.... [they] offered burnt offerings and sacrificed peace offerings of oxen to the LORD .... Then he took the Book of the Covenant and read in the hearing of the people. And they said, "All that the LORD has said we will do, and be obedient." And Moses took the blood, sprinkled it on the people, and said, "This is the blood of the covenant which the LORD has made with you according to all these words." (Exodus 24:4-8)

In the book of Exodus, God made a covenant with the people of Israel, and Exodus 24 was the signing ceremony for the contract. In Exodus 24:3, Israel verbally agreed to a covenant relationship with God; but there was a sense in which that was not good enough. They had to do specific things to confirm their covenant with God. Then and now, a contract might be valid even if it is only a verbal contract. To make it more than a verbal contract, God commanded a signing ceremony to emphasize the covenant's importance.

First, God's Word must be written: **Moses wrote all the words of the LORD**. God's Word was too important to be left up to human memory.

Second, a covenant is only made with a sacrifice. They **offered burnt offerings and sacrificed peace offerings of oxen to the LORD**. Sacrifice admits our sin and failing before God and addresses our debt and guilt to God through the death of a substitute.

Third, a covenant is made when God's Word is heard and responded to: **he took the Book of the Covenant and read in the hearing of the people**. Our covenant with God is based on His words and His terms, not our words and terms. There must be a response to God's Word. The people answered, **all that the LORD has said we will do, and be obedient**. Just as much as God didn't negotiate His covenant with Israel, neither did He force it – they had to receive it freely.

Fourth, a covenant is made with the application of blood: **Moses took the blood, sprinkled it on the people**. As the nation received the blood of the covenant, it was sealed. The blood represented the life of a being according to Leviticus 17:11: *For the life of the flesh is in the blood*. Blood represents one life being given for another.

The only way we can have a relationship with God is through covenant. He makes the terms of a new contract available to us in Jesus. The night before Jesus died on the cross, He explained how the blood of His covenant saves us: *This is My blood of the new covenant, which is shed for many for the remission of sins*. (Matthew 26:28)

Today, choose to enjoy a new covenant relationship with God, based on who Jesus is and what He did for us, especially at the cross.

April 2

Knowing What Love Is

By this we know love, because He laid down His life for us. (1 John 3:16)

What is love? Everybody wants to know, and many people think they know. Since God is love, and love is of God, it's best to let Him tell us what love is. John tells us we can know what love is because Jesus **laid down His life for us**.

Real love isn't only felt as an inward feeling; it's also shown by demonstration. The ultimate demonstration of love was the giving of Jesus on the cross. Paul, in Romans 5:8, expressed the same idea: *But God demonstrates His own love toward us, in that while we were still sinners, Christ died for us.*

Why is the death of Jesus, the ultimate demonstration of love? It isn't because Jesus died a more horrible death than anyone else, though His death was horrible. It isn't because Jesus was the only one ever to die for someone else. Throughout history, many have died for another.

It's not the death of Jesus by itself that is the ultimate demonstration of love; it is the death of Jesus, and *what it does for us* that shows the highest point of love. Imagine that you are on a pier and see a man jump in the water. He can't swim and is drowning with no one to help him. He cries out with his last breath, "I'm giving my life for you!" This cannot be understood as an act of love. It just seems strange. But if that same man jumps in the water to save me from drowning, and gives his own life that I may survive, I can understand how the giving of his life was a great act of love. The death of Jesus saves us from something more powerful than physical death, so it stands as the ultimate demonstration of love.

There is a real sense in which we would not know what love is all about if it was not for the work of Jesus on the cross. We have an inborn ability to twist the true meaning of love and pursue all kinds of things under the appearance of looking for love. Nature can teach us many things about God. It can show us His wisdom, His intelligence, and His mighty power. But nature, in and of itself, does not teach us that God is a God of love. We needed the death of God the Son, Jesus Christ, to ultimately demonstrate it.

I read in the newspaper of a man who knowingly infected his partner with a deadly disease, and she pressed charges against him. The woman said: "This… is murder. All I wanted is someone to love me, and now I'm going to die for that…"

We all have a craving for love, but we look for it in the wrong ways and the wrong places. We'll never find love anywhere unless we find it first at the cross.

April 3
Bearing Our Sorrows

Surely He has borne our griefs and carried our sorrows; yet we esteemed Him stricken, smitten by God, and afflicted. But He was wounded for our transgressions, He was bruised for our iniquities; the chastisement for our peace was upon Him, and by His stripes we are healed. All we like sheep have gone astray; we have turned, every one, to his own way; and the Lord has laid on Him the iniquity of us all. (Isaiah 53:4-6)

In these verses from the great prophecy of Isaiah 52, The prophet did not have in mind the way the Messiah took our *guilt* and God's *wrath* on Himself. Here, he had in view how the Messiah took our *pain* on Himself. He made our **griefs** and our **sorrows** His own so we wouldn't have to. He took them from us, but for it to do us any good, we must release them.

In His Sacrifice, the Messiah did a holy and loving work, **yet we esteemed Him stricken, smitten by God, and afflicted**. The problem was not in seeing these things, but *only* seeing these things. Men saw the suffering Jesus but didn't understand the reasons why. All of this was for us, for the people of God, **for our transgressions...for our iniquities**. It was in our place that the Messiah suffered.

The prophet also saw through the centuries to know that the Messiah would be beaten with many **stripes** (Mark 15:15). The prophet announced that provision for healing is found in the suffering of Jesus, so **by His stripes we are healed**. In this, did Isaiah have in mind spiritual or physical healing? In Matthew 8:16-17, the view seems to be of physical healing. In 1 Peter 2:24-25, the view seems to be of spiritual healing. God has both our physical and spiritual healing provided for by the suffering of Jesus.

Humanity desperately needed the what the Messiah did, having **gone astray** having **turned** having gone **every one, to his own way**. We are like **sheep**, and sheep can be stupid, headstrong animals.

We are thankful that in His grace, the Lord **has laid on Him the iniquity of us all**. Here we see the partnership between the Father and the Son in the work on the cross. If the Messiah was wounded for our transgressions, then it was also God the Father who laid on Him the iniquity of us all. The Father judged our iniquity as it was laid on the Son.

We see the comprehensive provision of God for human need, made by Jesus on the cross. He bore our **griefs** and **sorrows**; He provided for human healing, and He bore the guilt and penalty of sin that we deserved. Such a remarkable description of the work of Jesus was made hundreds of years before He walked the earth; it's even more amazing God did this for us.

Today, you need to believe this and receive it.

April 4

Witnesses to the Resurrection

And that He was seen by Cephas, then by the twelve. After that He was seen by over five hundred brethren at once, of whom the greater part remain to the present, but some have fallen asleep. After that He was seen by James, then by all the apostles. Then last of all He was seen by me also, as by one born out of due time. (1 Corinthians 15:5-8)

No one saw the actual resurrection of Jesus. No one was present in the tomb with Him when His body transformed into a resurrection body. If someone were there, perhaps in a brilliant flash of light, they would have seen the dead body of Jesus transformed. We know that Jesus could miraculously appear in a room with all the doors locked and the windows shut (John 20:19, 26). Yet the resurrected Jesus was not a phantom; He had a real flesh and bone body.

Though no one saw the actual resurrection of Jesus, many people did see the resurrected Jesus. Paul presented these witnesses to the resurrection, to establish beyond all controversy that Jesus was raised in a resurrection body.

The first witness presented was **Cephas**. Jesus made a special resurrection appearance to Peter (**Cephas**) in Luke 24:34. We can assume that Jesus spoke to some special need for comfort and restoration in Peter.

Paul presents **the twelve** as witnesses. This probably refers to the first meeting Jesus had with His assembled disciples (Mark 16:14, Luke 24:36-43, John 20:19-25). This was the meeting where Jesus appeared in the room with the doors and windows shut and breathed on the disciples, giving them the Holy Spirit.

The meeting of Jesus with **over five hundred brethren at once** is suggested by Matthew 28:10, 16-17. Paul is saying, "Go ask these people who saw the resurrected Jesus. These are not a handful of self-deluded souls; there are literally hundreds who saw the resurrected Jesus with their own eyes."

The **James** mentioned here would be James, the brother of Jesus, who was a prominent leader in the early church (Acts 15:13-21). In the gospels, Jesus' brothers were hostile to Him and His mission (John 7:3-5). But after His resurrection, Jesus' brothers were among the followers of Jesus (Acts 1:14).

All the **apostles** refers to a few different meetings, such as in John 20:26-31, 21:1-25, Matthew 28:16-20, and Luke 24:44-49. Jesus ate with them, comforted them, commanded them to preach the gospel, and told them to wait in Jerusalem for the outpouring of the Holy Spirit.

Finally, Paul could add his testimony (**last of all He was seen by me**), and his encounter with the resurrected Savior was after Jesus ascended to heaven.

The changed character of the apostles and their willingness to die for the testimony of the resurrection, decisively eliminate fraud as an explanation of the empty tomb.

Understand and appreciate all these, but add a final piece of evidence – your own experience of the resurrected Jesus.

April 5

Believe the Creed

The Apostles' Creed reads:

I believe in God the Father Almighty, maker of heaven and earth:

And in Jesus Christ His only Son, our Lord; Who was conceived by the Holy Spirit, born of the Virgin Mary, suffered under Pontius Pilate, was crucified, dead, and buried; He descended into Hades; the third day, He rose again from the dead; He ascended into heaven, and sitteth on the right hand of God, the Father Almighty; from thence He shall come to judge the quick and the dead.

I believe in the Holy Spirit, the holy Christian church, the communion of the saints, the forgiveness of sins, the resurrection of the body, and the life everlasting. Amen.

Every person who walks this earth is a theologian. Whenever a person thinks about God or chooses not to think about God, they show they are theologians. "Theology" means "the science or study of God," and everyone thinks something about God. So, is a theologian – but not everyone is a good theologian. Can you explain what you believe about God to someone else? Does it make sense, and is it truly consistent with what the Bible says?

One way basic theology has been defined, taught, and defended through the centuries is through creeds. A creed is a statement of faith. The most ancient and honored creed among Christians is "The Apostles' Creed." The apostles of the early church didn't write it, but it wonderfully expresses the essence of what they believed, taught, and died for in the days of the New Testament.

The first line of the Apostles' Creed is simple: *I believe in God the Father Almighty.* Can you say it, and believe it? Most people believe God exists, but far fewer actually think and live as though God exists. You may not be a theological atheist, but you may be a practical atheist.

It isn't enough to just say we believe in "God." Those three letters – G, O, and D, can mean something different to every person. That's why the creed is more specific, declaring belief not only in God but in *God the Father Almighty.*

God the Father is the first revealed person of the Trinity. God has fatherly care and concern for us. For many, there is great power and healing in understanding what a wonderful and loving Father God is. Even if you weren't as blessed as I was to have a great father, you still instinctively know how a loving father should care for his children. That's how God cares for you.

God is more than a Father. He is the *Father Almighty.* God has all power and ability. I like the literal meaning of the word translated *Almighty* in the New Testament: "The One who has His hand on everything." That's the God we serve – He has His hand on everything.

Will you let this encourage you today? Knowing that a loving Father has His hand on everything in your life? But it can't encourage you if you don't believe it.

In your heart, agree with the creed: *I believe in God the Father Almighty.*

April 6

The Main Message

For thus says the High and Lofty One who inhabits eternity, whose name is Holy: "I dwell in the high and holy place, with him who has a contrite and humble spirit, to revive the spirit of the humble, and to revive the heart of the contrite ones. For I will not contend forever, nor will I always be angry; for the spirit would fail before Me, and the souls which I have made." (Isaiah 57:15-16)

It is wrong to think that judgment is the great theme of a prophet like Isaiah; the message of God's great love is much greater than the message of judgment.

Isaiah's strong statement against the sin of Judah was not made to leave the people of Judah in their sin and depravity, but to bring them out of it, back into a real relationship of love and commitment to the living and real God. Here Isaiah told Judah – and us – three ways to get right with God, even if our sin has been as black as Judah's.

To be right with God, the first thing to do is to understand His great majesty. He is the **High and Lofty One who inhabits eternity, whose name is Holy.** These titles reflecting God's great majesty, and He expected His people to respond to Him as that kind of a glorious God.

Isn't so much of our neglect and turning away from God simply forgetting how great, how wonderful He is? If we kept that in the proper place in our mind and our heart, we would never turn away from Him to put our hope or trust in something or someone else.

A second aspect in getting right with God is to be contrite and **humble** before the God of great majesty. Isaiah never lost sight of God's glory; he understood that God is the **High and Lofty One**, and He lives in the **high and holy place**. Yet, at the same time, He will live with men – with **him who has a contrite and humble spirit**.

The third thing to understand in getting right with God is His great love. He **will not contend forever** and will not **always be angry**. The Lord shows His mercy to His people and promises to relent and not be angry forever. Though God disciplined His people, He promised to **heal**, to **lead him,** to and to **restore comforts** to His people.

God always wants to bring us back into right relationship with Him. The words and warnings of judgment are like sharp sticks that push a wandering cow. Sometimes we need that, but we never lose sight of the great love of God that promises to not be angry forever but promises to always restore and bless the one **who has a contrite and humble spirit**.

Today, you can be that blessed person.

April 7

A Gospel Worth Dying For

But none of these things move me; nor do I count my life dear to myself, so that I may finish my race with joy, and the ministry which I received from the Lord Jesus, to testify to the gospel of the grace of God. (Acts 20:24)

This comes from an amazingly rich portion of the Book of Acts – Paul's heartfelt words to the leaders of the Christian community in Ephesus. He spent about two years among them and had left several months before. On his way to Jerusalem, Paul spoke with these leaders. What he had to say was so important that he asked them to walk some 30 miles (50 km) to meet him – and they did.

In this one sentence, Paul described his determination, estimation, exertion, and reception.

Paul's *determination*: **None of these things move me**. Despite the uncertainty of his present circumstance and the shadow of suffering on his horizon – Paul refused to be moved. Rooted deeply in Jesus Christ, he was well past the decision to continue with Jesus, determined to be unmoved.

Paul's *estimation*: **Nor do I count my life dear to myself**. Paul did not estimate his earthly life of greater worth than faithfulness to God's call on his life. Like an accountant, he weighed the credits and expenses carefully and decided that he would gladly sacrifice his life for his Lord.

Paul's *exertion*: **So that I may finish my race with joy**. Like a runner pushing himself when he sees the finish line in the distance, Paul fully exerted himself. God helping him, he would finish his race, and do it with joy. Though he relied on God's strength, he didn't expect God to do it for him as he sat by passively.

Paul's *reception*: **The ministry which I received from the Lord**. Though he was aware of his need to put forth his effort, Paul always knew that his ministry was something received from the Lord. In a sense, it was Paul's ministry, his race to run, but it was a received work that he did.

The words **nor do I count my life dear to myself** or **that I may finish my race** show that Paul had his death in mind even at this point. It would be many years until he died, but he considered that what he did with his life *now* was worth dying for.

Is the gospel you preach worth dying for? The gospel of mere moral reform is not really worth dying for. The gospel of "save yourself through good works" also is not. Few people would really die for the gospel of social action and improvement. The gospels of religious traditions, mysticism, self-esteem, ecological salvation, or political correctness are not worth that sacrifice.

Yet there remains a gospel that is worth dying for and living for – it is the gospel of God's grace.

Today, make sure you are living for Jesus Christ and His gospel worth dying for.

April 8

Settled in Heaven

**Forever, O Lord,
Your word is settled in heaven.** (Psalm 119:89)

The poetic genius that wrote Psalm 119 had tremendous confidence in God's Word. He wrote, **Forever, O Lord, Your word is settled in heaven.** He meditated on the unchanging nature of God's Word. Because it **is settled in heaven**, it will not change on earth.

Notice how big his thoughts were. God's Word **is settled in heaven**, not merely in the psalmist's heart or mind. It is objectively settled in heaven, whether the psalmist or anyone else believed it to be or not to be. If someone were to say to the psalmist, "That's your opinion; that is good for you," he would object most strongly that God's Word is settled in heaven quite apart from man's opinion.

Many smart, gifted people have no confidence in the Bible. We care not for any of that when we know, **forever, O Lord, Your word is settled in heaven.**

The writer of Psalm 119 was well acquainted with trouble, but after tossing back and forth on an ocean of difficulty, he now stood on solid ground. He knew that God's Word was certain and reliable. Man's word changes yearly, daily, even hourly. Yet the word of the Lord **is settled in heaven.**

The word is **settled in heaven**. He believed that God's Word was precisely that – not the words of man, but the very words of God. He believed that the Scriptures come from heaven and not earth, from the Lord and not man. He believed what 2 Timothy 3:16 would later say, that *all Scripture is given by inspiration of God, and is profitable for doctrine, for reproof, for correction, for instruction in righteousness.*

This means more than saying that God inspired the men who wrote it, though we believe that He did. God also inspired the very words they wrote. We notice it doesn't say, "All Scripture writers are inspired by God," even though that is true. But that statement doesn't go far enough. God breathed the words they wrote so **Your word is settled in heaven.**

Jesus said in Matthew 5:18, that *one jot or one tittle will by no means pass from the law till all is fulfilled.* The jot refers to yod, the smallest letter in the Hebrew alphabet; it looks like half a letter. The tittle is a small mark in a Hebrew letter, somewhat like crossing a "t" or the tail on a "y."

Jesus said that even these smallest of marks would not pass away from God's Word. He said that heaven and earth would sooner pass away than a yod or a tittle from God's Word. Truly, **Your word is settled in heaven.**

This is confidence for every believer, that God's Word is a settled place to stand. Especially every Bible preacher and teacher should be able to say, **Your word is settled in heaven.**

Today, let God's settled word settle your heart.

April 9

As Secure as You Know How

On the next day, which followed the Day of Preparation, the chief priests and Pharisees gathered together to Pilate, saying, "Sir, we remember, while He was still alive, how that deceiver said, 'After three days I will rise.'" Therefore command that the tomb be made secure until the third day, lest His disciples come by night and steal Him away, and say to the people, 'He has risen from the dead.' So the last deception will be worse than the first." Pilate said to them, "You have a guard; go your way, make it as secure as you know how." So they went and made the tomb secure, sealing the stone and setting the guard. (Matthew 27:62-66)

The disciples were utterly surprised at the resurrection, but the enemies of Jesus remembered that He had promised to rise again, and they took steps to prevent any report of resurrection.

The enemies of Jesus came to Pilate, and he granted their request saying, **you have a guard**. But Pilate added, **make it as secure as you know how**. Pilate knew that if this Man was going to rise from the dead, they could not stop it.

The tomb was secured by a stone, which was a *material obstacle*.

Such stones were large and set in slanted channels with an incline. The stone could not be rolled away from the inside. If enough of the disciples worked together, they could roll away the stone – but not quietly.

The tomb was secured by a seal, which was an *obstacle of human authority*.

The seal was a rope, overlapping the width of the stone covering the entrance to the tomb. On either side of the doorway, there was a glob of wax securing the rope over the stone. You could not move the rock without breaking the seal. The guards watched carefully as the stone was sealed because their careers and perhaps their lives were at stake.

The tomb was secured by a guard, which was an *obstacle of human strength*.

A typical Roman guard detail had four soldiers: two watched while two rested. The soldiers had swords, shields, spears, daggers, and armor. To them, the only sacred thing at this tomb was the Roman seal. These soldiers were not going to be tricked by trembling disciples, and they would not jeopardize their lives by sleeping at their post.

Material obstacles, human authority, and human strength couldn't stand before the resurrected Jesus. Each of these fell away before His power and glory. Think about your life: what are you trying to make secure against the power of Jesus? Perhaps there is an area of your life that you are unwilling to yield to Jesus. Do you see the futility of trying to make anything secure against the power of Jesus?

Whatever you are keeping from Jesus, go ahead and make it as secure as you know how. My prayer is that it will be broken open before the power of our resurrected Jesus.

April 10

They Will Not Find Him

With their flocks and herds they shall go to seek the LORD, but they will not find Him; He has withdrawn Himself from them. (Hosea 5:6)

In the days of Hosea, ancient Israel knew what to do. They knew that they were expected to bring animal sacrifices to the LORD, both for atonement of sin and for fellowship with God. Yet it was possible to perform the action of sacrifice without a heart or life surrendered to God – to make sacrifice an empty ritual. At the time Hosea spoke to Israel, their worship was mainly empty rituals.

We see this in the words, **they shall go to seek the LORD, but they will not find Him**. Earlier, God promised through Hosea that He would leave rebellious Israel alone (Hosea 4:17). That meant that if they made superficial gestures of repentance, they would not find Him. God described their superficial repentance: *they do not direct their deeds toward turning to their God* (Hosea 5:4).

It's important to understand that there is a big difference between superficial religious gestures and a genuine turning of the heart towards God. In a moment of crisis, someone may turn to God for relief but have no intention of surrendering their life to Him.

In many ways, people think they are seeking God when they really aren't. It's just superficial. Our sinful, fleshly nature doesn't mind religion and religious ritual – but it does whatever it can to keep us from really drawing close to God.

God does not reward this kind of superficial seeking. It might fool everyone else, but it doesn't fool God. Therefore, Hosea announced the sad verdict: **He has withdrawn Himself from them**. It can happen. We can be so set in our sin and rebellion that God just leaves us to ourselves. Usually, we don't even notice at first, but when we call on the LORD and do not find Him then we start to see the result of pushing God away.

Martin Luther on his life before coming to rest in faith on Jesus and His work:

> I crucified Christ daily in my cloistered life, and blasphemed God by my wrong faith. Outwardly I kept myself chaste, poor, and obedient. I was much given to fasting, watching, praying, saying of masses, and the like. Yet under the cloak of my outward respectability, I continually mistrusted, doubted, feared, hated, and blasphemed God. My righteousness was a filthy puddle. Satan loves such saints. They are his darlings, for they quickly destroy their body and soul by depriving them of the blessings of God's generous gifts.

Apart from a real relationship with God based on faith, religious traditions and works can't make us right with God. You may be frustrated because you seem to do so much for God, yet it seems that you cannot find Him.

Today, stop relying on empty rituals and come in faith. Let the promise of Jeremiah 29:14 be true for you: *I will be found by you, says the LORD*.

April 11

Still Chosen

For the LORD will have mercy on Jacob, and will still choose Israel, and settle them in their own land. The strangers will be joined with them, and they will cling to the house of Jacob. (Isaiah 14:1)

Many of the Old Testament prophets worked in gloomy times, and Isaiah was no exception. God told him to tell the tribes of Israel that the mighty Babylonian Empire would crush them as an act of God's judgment. Nevertheless, God gave hope amid gloom – so Isaiah 13 ends with the desolation and judgment that will come on Babylon. Since Babylon was Judah's great enemy, any judgment on Babylon was an expression of mercy toward God's people. So, Isaiah follows the pronouncement of judgment on Babylon with the comforting words, **the LORD will have mercy on Jacob, and will still choose Israel**.

Sometimes we feel that we know God chose us, but if He had to choose again, He would change His mind! Often, sin, defeat, and discouragement make us think that God is "stuck" with us now. That isn't the case. His love towards you remains the same all along, even knowing how you would fail Him. God's love to you is based on who He is, not who you are.

That's the most important aspect of God's promise of restoration. It isn't that God must restore His love to us, but we must be restored to receive and respond to His love. We must do what Jude told us to do: *keep yourselves in the love of God* (Jude v. 21). The Babylonians had carried away most of the population of Judah, so the promise of return was precious.

The second aspect of God's work of restoration in His people wasn't just in spiritual things – He promised that there would be tangible evidence of it. It isn't that land is more real than love, but it is more "material" – and God wants to restore us in both ways, regarding the things we see and things we can't see.

The third aspect to the work of restoration had to do with people. Isaiah 14:1: **The strangers will be joined with them**. This is a wonderful and surprising invitation to the Gentiles. The gathered and restored Israel would invite Gentiles to receive the goodness of God with them. Of course, this is the best evidence that we truly have received God's love. When we open our arms to His love, our arms are also open to other people. You can't say that you love God and hate your brother.

In receiving God's work of restoration, Israel practices the very best defense policy – they completely wipe out their enemies. By inviting the strangers to come and be joined with them, Israel eliminates their enemies. The ultimate way to conquer an enemy is to make them your friend.

Have you received God's work of restoration? Do you know that you are still chosen?

April 12

Seasoned With Salt

And every offering of your grain offering you shall season with salt; you shall not allow the salt of the covenant of your God to be lacking from your grain offering. With all your offerings you shall offer salt. (Leviticus 2:13)

Under the old covenant, every offering – including the **grain offering** – had to include **salt**. Salt was so important that here it is connected to the idea of **covenant** (Numbers 18:19, 2 Chronicles 13:5). Why did God command this?

Salt Speaks of Purity. As a chemical compound, salt can't change. It has an inherent purity. God wanted every sacrifice brought before Him to come from a pure heart. Some of what we do for God is from impure motives. We should ask God to give us the purest of motives: to show our gratitude and to honor His glory. I've also heard that salt itself cannot change, but it can be corrupted by what it added to it. When our motives are impure, it is often because we add concern about our own glory and prestige. Ask God to build in you the purity of salt.

Salt Speaks of Preservation. As a preservative, salt stops the normal operations of flesh. It is the nature of flesh to spoil, but salt-cured meat will stay good. Long before we used refrigeration and freezing to keep things, people preserved meats by salting them. When we come before God, we don't come in our own "spoiled flesh." We come in the name of Jesus, based on His merits, not ours. We can only be "preserved" by the constant work of God in us.

Salt Speaks of Value. Salt was an expensive, valued commodity in the ancient world. Roman soldiers were sometimes paid in salt. Adding salt to every sacrifice was a way to make each offering to God a little more costly, a little more precious. We need to put our best into everything and give everything unto God.

Previously, God commanded that sacrifices should not contain honey (Leviticus 2:11). The command to include salt and exclude honey means God wants the sincerity of our service, not things made artificially sweet.

If you go to the marketplace, you can see some foods that are "salt free" or "reduced salt." That might be just what someone needs in their diet, but when we think of what salt symbolized for ancient Israel, we understand that we should never life a "salt free" or "reduced salt" life.

Every day is a gift we can and should give to God. It's proper that we "season" or "sprinkle" our day with the understanding of:

- The purity God wants us to live out: Jesus is the purity of His people.
- The preserving work God wants to do in His people: Jesus preserves believers to the end.
- The value of each moment we give to God: Everything given to Jesus has value and importance.

Even a small sacrifice can be precious before God if it is seasoned with salt!

April 13

People Who Love Too Much

Do not love the world or the things in the world. If anyone loves the world, the love of the Father is not in him. (1 John 2:15)

The Bible speaks to us about those people who love too much and their tragic end. These people do love God – but they also love the ways, thinking, and the attitude of this world. They love too much.

The **world**, in the sense John meant it here, is not the global earth, nor is it the mass of humanity (which God Himself loves, as in John 3:16). Instead, it is the community of sinful humanity that is united in rebellion against God. Not just humanity itself, but the collective mindset and attitude that unites man against God.

There are some attractive things about this world. The world's progress, technology, government, and organization can make man better off, but not better. Because we like being better off, it is always easy to fall in love with the world. But we are warned that we must not **love the world**. There is an anti-God or ignoring-God way of doing things that characterize human society, and it is easy to **love the world** in this sense.

If you love the world, there are rewards to be gained. You may find a place of prestige, of status, of honor, of comfort. The world system knows how to reward its lovers! The rewards that come from this world – even at their best – last only as long as we live. The problem is that though we gain prestige, status, honor, and comfort in this world, we lose the prestige, status, honor, and comfort of heaven.

What that world wants from us is our love, as expressed in time, attention, and expense. We are encouraged and persuaded to give our time, attention, and money to the things of this world instead of the things of God. Love for the world is incompatible with a love for God: **if anyone loves the world, the love of the Father is not in him**. So, if we claim to love God, and yet love the world, there is something wrong with our claim to love God.

Through the centuries, Christians have dealt with the magnetic pull of the world in different ways. At one time, it was thought that if you were a committed Christian and wanted to love God instead of the world, you should leave human society and live as a monk or a nun out in a desolate monastery. But this has never really worked.

First, we bring the world with us into the monastery! The other problem is that Jesus intended us to be in the world, but not of the world. Our challenge is to be in it, without giving it our love. Are you one of those people who love too much?

Today, ask God to help you to love the world less – and especially, to love Him more.

April 14

Being Fair to All

For if there should come into your assembly a man with gold rings, in fine apparel, and there should also come in a poor man in filthy clothes, and you pay attention to the one wearing the fine clothes and say to him, "You sit here in a good place," and say to the poor man, "You stand there," or, "Sit here at my footstool," have you not shown partiality among yourselves, and become judges with evil thoughts? (James 2:2-4)

James pictured a man coming into a Christian meeting, an **assembly**. In the ancient Greek, **assembly** is literally "synagogue," the name for the Jewish meeting place. James calling a Christian meeting place a synagogue shows that he wrote before Gentiles were widely received into the church. At the time James wrote, most Christians came from a Jewish heritage. This is the only place in the New Testament where an assembly of Christians is called a synagogue.

When Christians met, there was to be nothing marking the difference between those "higher" and "lower." That is why James described the situation with **a man with gold rings**. This showed the man was rich. According to some in the Roman world, the rich marked their wealth by wearing many rings, especially on their left hand. There were even shops in ancient Rome where you could rent rings for special occasions to give the impression that you were richer than you really were.

Imagine a Christian meeting with a rich man showing off his wealth with gold rings. Then, **there should also come in a poor man**. When James wrote **a poor man**, he used a word that meant "very poor." When the rich man entered, everyone took care of him and made a fuss over him. When the poor man entered, no one cared – or worse, they mistreated him.

To favor the rich man over the poor man shows a deep carnality among Christians. Such people **become judges** and have **evil thoughts**. Their evil thoughts are evident through unfair actions.

To show partiality proves that we care more for the outward appearance than we do the heart. *For the Lord does not see as man sees; for man looks at the outward appearance, but the Lord looks at the heart.* (1 Samuel 16:7)

To show **partiality** means that we misunderstand who is important and blessed in the sight of God. When we assume that the rich man is more important or more blessed by God, we put too much value in material riches.

To show **partiality** also is evidence of a selfish streak in us. We favor the rich man over the poor man because we can get more from him. He can do favors for us that the poor man can't.

That is why – in our daily life and meetings together – we should do all we can to be fair to everyone, not favoring one over another.

Today, do your best to see things from God's view, not just from what comes naturally.

April 15

Forget-Him-Not

Because you have forgotten the God of your salvation, and have not been mindful of the Rock of your stronghold, therefore you will plant pleasant plants and set out foreign seedlings; in the day you will make your plant to grow, and in the morning you will make your seed to flourish; but the harvest will be a heap of ruins in the day of grief and desperate sorrow. (Isaiah 17:10-11)

A comedian had a joke where he recommended a way to get out of any problem – just say, "I forgot." Didn't obey the speed limit? Tell the police, "I forgot." Late for work? Tell your boss, "I forgot." Didn't pay your taxes? Tell the tax man, "I forgot." The humor was in the absurdity of it all. Everyone knows that saying "I forgot" isn't a good excuse.

In the case of Israel, there was nothing funny about it. Look at what God promised: **You will plant pleasant plants…you will make your seed to flourish; but the harvest will be a heap of ruins**. One aspect of the LORD's judgment against Israel would be to bring their hard work to nothing.

This can be one of the most devastating aspects of God's judgment. Haggai 1:6 speaks of this work of the LORD: *You have sown much, and bring in little; you eat, but do not have enough; you drink, but you are not filled with drink; you clothe yourselves, but no one is warm; and he who earns wages, earns wages to put into a bag with holes*. Few things are more frustrating than working hard and having it come to nothing. Sometimes God brings us severe mercy and allows us little progress so we will see the futility of our rebellion and turn to Him. How much better it is to listen to Jesus and to have our service directed and blessed by Him (Luke 5:1-10).

God brought this severe mercy on Israel: **Because you have forgotten the God of your salvation**. Why does God need us to remember Him? It is a sin to forget the God of your salvation because He created you, and He is the God of your salvation. If you forget Him, you can forget about your salvation.

We can forget because of sleepiness; we can forget because we are distracted. Satan does not care about how he does it, but he does want us to forget the God of our salvation. He will use whatever he can – prosperity, pain, pleasure, plenty, or privation – whatever might make us forget what we should remember and remember what we should forget.

Has God put you in a place of difficulty, where you must remember and rely on Him? It is one way of making sure that you don't forget. Instead of becoming cranky and impatient in this time, why not thank God for sending you a "forget-Him-not"?

That flower coming from God's garden often has a few thorns, but it always has a beautiful fragrance.

April 16

What God Wants

For I desire mercy and not sacrifice, and the knowledge of God more than burnt offerings. (Hosea 6:6)

The prophet Hosea told Israel what God wanted instead of empty sacrifices. He put it powerfully and eloquently: **For I desire mercy and not sacrifice, and the knowledge of God more than burnt offerings.**

At this time the people of Israel were still good at bringing sacrifice, but they had forsaken mercy, and they abandoned mercy because they gave up the knowledge of God and truth (Hosea 4:1). Sacrifice was a valued part of the covenant God made with Israel on Mount Sinai. Yet compared to mercy and the knowledge of God, sacrifice was far less important.

As a faithful prophet, Hosea made known the same nature of God that was perfectly revealed in Jesus Christ. Jesus twice quoted this passage of Hosea to the religious leaders of His day because they also missed the heart of God, focusing on the misguided and superficial things.

First, Jesus quoted this passage in Matthew 9:13. He sat down to dinner with many notorious sinners, reaching out to these spiritually needy and hungry people. When the Pharisees criticized Him, Jesus answered: *But go and learn what this means: "I desire mercy and not sacrifice."*

The second time is found in Matthew 12:7. The Pharisees criticized the disciples of Jesus. The Pharisees were hung up on traditional religious interpretations of the Sabbath. Jesus jumped to their defense and told the Pharisees: *But if you had known what this means, "I desire mercy and not sacrifice," you would not have condemned the guiltless.*

Jesus taught: *Therefore if you bring your gift to the altar, and there remember that your brother has something against you, leave your gift there before the altar, and go your way. First be reconciled to your brother, and then come and offer your gift* (Matthew 5:23-24). Are you fulfilling the command of Romans 12:18? It says, *If it is possible, as much as depends on you, live peaceably with all men.* Sometimes it isn't possible – even Jesus had enemies, but He treated even them with the mercy of Hosea 6:6.

Hosea also told us that God values **the knowledge of God more than burnt offerings**. Israel brought animals for sacrifice, but they never brought themselves as a living sacrifice (Romans 12:1). They missed what God really wants: a deep, close relationship with Him – expressed by the phrase, **the knowledge of God**.

I suppose that many who read this find some way to do things for God that others don't do. Good for you and God bless you. But are you doing something for God when He would rather you *first* get something right with another person? Are you doing something for God when He would rather you first draw closer to Him in "the knowledge of God?"

Today, remember God's priorities – and make them your priorities.

April 17

Planting Seeds

But someone will say, "How are the dead raised up? And with what body do they come?" Foolish one, what you sow is not made alive unless it dies. And what you sow, you do not sow that body that shall be, but mere grain; perhaps wheat or some other grain. But God gives it a body as He pleases, and to each seed its own body. (1 Corinthians 15:35-38)

The Corinthian Christians wanted to know, **how are the dead raised up?** The answer is obvious: God raises the dead. As the apostle Paul said to Agrippa in Acts 26:8, *Why should it be thought incredible by you that God raises the dead?*

They also wanted to know, **and with what body do they come?** Paul answered this question with the analogy of the seed, explaining that our bodies are like "seeds" that "grow" into resurrection bodies. When you bury the body of a believer, you are sowing a seed that will come out of the earth as a resurrection body. This means that the Christian looks at death in an entirely different way.

No one likes the sound of the coffin lid closing, and the farmer does not like the act of scattering seed on the cold, dry earth just for its own sake. Nevertheless, no farmer weeps when he sows his seed because he sows in genuine confidence of a future harvest. At the open grave, the Christian should have the same confidence when the "seed" is "planted." Our loved ones in the Lord are not lost; they are sown.

The seed analogy gives us more than hope; it also helps us understand the nature of our resurrection body. Paul describes it like this: **You do not sow that body that shall be.... But God gives it a body as He pleases, and to each seed its own body**. When you plant a wheat seed, a big wheat seed does not come up. Instead, a stalk of wheat grows. So, even though our resurrection bodies come from our present bodies, we should not expect that they will be the same bodies as before or even just improved bodies. They will be truly connected to our present bodies, yet in a more glorious form than ever.

The resurrection body of Jesus was connected to His previous body in appearance and general material nature – He was no phantom or ghost. Yet His resurrection body was more than just a better version of His previous body. Something had fundamentally changed in its nature because it was described as a flesh and bone body instead of the far more typical phrase flesh and blood body (Luke 24:39). Jesus remains in His resurrected glory without aging or diminishing in strength – and that is something completely out of the realm of these bodies we know.

God has saved, is saving, and will save those who trust in Jesus and He will save them completely – body, soul, and spirit.

April 18

What He Heard in Heaven

And one cried to another and said: "Holy, holy, holy is the LORD of hosts; the whole earth is full of His glory!" And the posts of the door were shaken by the voice of him who cried out, and the house was filled with smoke. (Isaiah 6:3-4)

Isaiah had a unique privilege – to be carried away up to heaven and to see the presence of the LORD. Almost certainly he saw this in a vision, but it was no less real to him than if he had been there bodily. Nevertheless, this was more than a vision; Isaiah had a "multi-sensory" experience as he recorded it in Isaiah 6, far beyond any experience one could have on earth.

Isaiah heard: **One cried to another and said....** The seraphim do not directly address the LORD. They proclaim His glorious nature and character to one another in the presence of the LORD. When they do, they cry out **Holy, holy, holy is the LORD of hosts**. They say it three times because there are Three Persons in the One God. To say, **Holy, holy, holy is the LORD** declares His holiness in the highest possible degree.

Holiness, at its root, has the idea of apartness. It describes someone, or something, which is set apart from other people or things. An object can be holy if it is set apart for sacred service. A person is holy if they are set apart for God's will and purpose. What is the LORD set apart from?

He is set apart from creation, in that the LORD God is not a creature, and He exists outside of all creation. If all creation were to dissolve, the LORD God would remain.

He is set apart from humanity, in that His "nature" or "essence" is Divine, not human. Yet, because man is made in the image of God (Genesis 1:26-27), humanity is compatible with Divinity. They are different, but they do not automatically oppose each other. This is how Jesus, the Second Person of the Trinity, could add humanity to His deity when He became a man. Unfallen humanity is not deity, but it is compatible with it.

God's holiness is a part of everything He is and does. God's power is holy. God's love is holy. God's wisdom is holy. Holiness is not an aspect of God's personality; it is one characteristic of His entire Being.

Isaiah felt **the posts of the door were shaken by the voice of him who cried out**. The seraphim are majestic beings, and their voices carry weight. When they speak, the doorposts of God's throne room shake. They sang so powerfully that the doorposts were shaken! Shouldn't we sing with the same passion, the same heart, and the same intensity? Do those angels have more to thank and praise God for than we do? Of course not!

Even so, we should not hold back in declaring our appreciation and praise. Instead, we should shake some doorposts!

What We Say and Who We Are

A good man out of the good treasure of his heart brings forth good; and an evil man out of the evil treasure of his heart brings forth evil. For out of the abundance of the heart his mouth speaks. (Luke 6:45)

People speak according to their character. When there is good in our hearts, it will show in the words we choose to speak. When there is evil in our hearts, it is certain to show itself the way we talk, sooner or later. Whatever is most abundant in our hearts will show itself in our speech.

Many years ago, a woman named Ann Landers gave advice to people in a daily newspaper column, often with a touch of humor. Ann Landers was at a fancy reception in Washington and was introduced to a pompous senator. "So, you're Ann Landers," he drawled, "say something funny." Without missing a beat, she replied: "So you're a politician. Tell me a lie." Both the senator and the newspaper columnist believed that people usually speak according to their character. According to Jesus, that is a true principle.

It's amazing how much sin has to do with the words we say. Slander, gossip, envy, jealousy, hatred, anger, and immorality all usually express themselves in the words we choose to speak. But in a way, the words are just a symptom. The real problem is a heart that isn't where it should be with God. We can't imagine Jesus sinning with His words – that just isn't what would flow from His heart. But what do your words say about the condition of your heart? Looking at our words is a great diagnostic tool to see the condition of our heart and character.

In the early part of the 20th century, there were some amazing times of revival in the coal mining regions of Wales. They noticed that when so many hearts were turning to Jesus, life improved everywhere – crime was down, family discord was down, violence was down, and even worker productivity was up – except in the coal mines. For several weeks after the revival began, production in the coal mines slowed. Some people thought many of the miners were reading their Bibles or going to prayer meetings instead of working, but that wasn't the case. Instead, the problem was the mules that worked in the coal mines. The mules had become accustomed to only moving at the sound of terrible cursing and profanity. When many coal miners started living for Jesus, they just couldn't talk that way anymore, and production slowed until the mules got used to a more Christian vocabulary!

The point is clear – words changed when the heart changed. We need to seek God, asking Him to help us draw near to Him. As we are transformed into the likeness of Jesus, it will show in the way we speak to each other. Who you are is on display when people hear what you say.

That's why we should pray, *Let the words of my mouth and the meditation of my heart be acceptable in Your sight, O Lord, my strength and my Redeemer.* (Psalm 19:14)

April 20

Who Are You Calling a Liar?

He who believes in the Son of God has the witness in himself; he who does not believe God has made Him a liar, because he has not believed the testimony that God has given of His Son. (1 John 5:10)

These inspired words from the apostle John are easy to understand, but hard to receive. When we refuse to believe in Jesus, we reject the testimony God gave to us about His Son. Therefore, if we refuse to believe in Jesus, we call God a liar. Not many people think they would call God a liar to His face, but John says this is what they are doing.

John exposed the great sin of unbelief. The word used for **believe** here has the sense of "to trust in, rely on, and cling to." Most people who refuse to believe God (in the full understanding of the word) don't intend to call God a liar, but they still do it.

The great English preacher Charles Spurgeon said something striking about unbelief. In a sermon, Spurgeon said: "The great sin of not believing in the Lord Jesus Christ is often spoken of very lightly and in a very trifling spirit, as though it were scarcely any sin at all; yet, according to my text, and, indeed, according to the whole tenor of the Scriptures, unbelief is calling God a liar, and what can be worse?"

It is common for someone to say, "Well, I want to believe, but I can't." It would be more accurate for that person to say, "I will not believe." Unbelief is our fault, not our misfortune. It is a disease, but also a crime. Your unbelief may make you miserable, but rightly so because you are calling the God of truth a liar.

Other people may say, "Well, I will try to believe, and I will keep on trying." But it's a terrible thing to *try to believe*. If I made a statement and someone answered, "I don't believe you. I would like to, but I can't. I'm really trying to believe you, but I am not there yet." What would he mean by that? He must mean that I am so untrustworthy, such a confirmed liar, that even though he *wants* to believe me, he can't. Even with all the effort he can make in my favor, it is still beyond his ability to believe me. When someone says, "I'm trying to believe God," isn't that saying the same thing?

There is no passage in the Bible that says, "Try and believe." It merely says, "Believe in the Lord Jesus Christ." He is the Son of God; He has proved it by His miracles. He died to save sinners – therefore, trust Jesus. Jesus Christ deserves your total trust and child-like confidence. Will you refuse Him these? Don't be guilty of calling God a liar. None of us want to do that, so trust God today.

Let God speak to you through His Word, and then believe what He says.

April 21

Your Cross to Bear

Whoever desires to come after Me, let him deny himself, and take up his cross, and follow Me. (Mark 8:34)

It was like a "good news-bad news" joke. This was the good news: the disciples understood that Jesus was the Messiah, the Son of the Living God. The bad news was that this Messiah would be rejected by the religious and political leaders of His day and be executed in a degrading, tortured manner.

Then came more good news and more bad news. The good news was after His death, Jesus would rise again the third day. The bad news was that His disciples had to deny themselves, take up their cross, and follow Him. That last part must have really troubled the disciples. It was bad enough for them to hear that Jesus would suffer, be rejected, and die on a cross. Then Jesus told them that they must do the same thing!

When Jesus said any follower of His must **take up his cross** everybody knew what He meant. Everyone knew that the cross was a relentless instrument of death. The cross wasn't about religious ceremonies, traditions, or spiritual feelings. The cross was a method of execution.

In these twenty centuries after Jesus, we have done a pretty good job in sanitizing and ritualizing the cross. How would we receive it if Jesus said, "Walk down death row daily and follow Me"? Taking up your cross wasn't a journey; it was a one-way trip.

When you take up your cross, it doesn't mean that you bear some irritation in life. Some people have a physical problem, and they say, "This is my cross to bear." Others have a financial or a social problem, and they say, "This is my cross to bear." But cross-bearing doesn't refer to some irritation in life. Instead, it means to walk the way of the cross. The picture is of a man, already condemned, and required to carry his cross on the way to the place of execution, just as Jesus did. Martin Luther said that every Christian must be a cross-man.

Jesus didn't only say that we must take up our cross. He said that a man must **deny himself** and **take up his cross**. This means that **deny himself** and **take up his cross** express the same idea. The cross wasn't about self-promotion or self-affirmation. The person carrying a cross knew they couldn't save themselves. Denying self is not the same as self-denial. We practice self-denial when, for a good purpose, we occasionally give up things or activities. But we deny self when we surrender ourselves to Christ and determine to obey His will. Denying self means to live as an others-centered person. Jesus was the only person to do this perfectly, but we are to follow in His steps (**and follow Me**).

This is following Jesus at its simplest: He carried a cross; He walked down death row; so must those who will follow Him.

April 22

What's the Use?

What does it profit, my brethren, if someone says he has faith but does not have works? Can faith save him? (James 2:14)

The letter the apostle James wrote to early Christians is practical. Here he demonstrates that by asking, **what does it profit, my brethren?** That is another way to ask, "What good is it? What good is this faith you claim to have?"

James thought it impossible that someone could genuinely have saving faith, but no practical evidence of that faith in daily life (works). The idea is that someone can say he has faith, but that faith never shows itself in good works. So, the question is valid: Can that kind of **faith save him**?

James had in mind this kind of person: someone says he has faith but does not have works. James wrote to Christians from a Jewish background that had discovered the glory of salvation by faith. They knew how exciting it was to be free from the mindset of works-righteousness. But it seems that some of them then went to the other extreme and began to think that works didn't matter at all.

Therefore, James asked the very relevant question: **Can faith save him?** It is important to say that James did not contradict the apostle Paul, who insisted that we are saved by faith and not of works (Ephesians 2:9). James clarified the kind of faith that receives salvation. We are saved by grace through faith, not by works, but saving faith will have works that accompany it. As the saying goes: faith alone saves, but the faith that saves is not alone; it has good works with it.

On these points, James and Paul wouldn't argue; they would agree. Paul also understood the necessity of works in demonstrating the character of true faith. Paul wrote: *For we are His workmanship, created in Christ Jesus for good works, which God prepared beforehand that we should walk in them* (Ephesians 2:10). He also wrote: *This is a faithful saying, and these things I want you to affirm constantly, that those who have believed in God should be careful to maintain good works* (Titus 3:8). Paul and James agreed!

When James asks, **can faith save him?** We understand the sense as "can *this kind* of faith save him? This so-called faith that is bare, and not accompanied by good works?"

It's not hard to understand. It's one thing to talk the talk of faith; it's another thing to walk the walk of faith. Faith that exists only in words, only in the sense of intellectual agreement separated from daily life, this kind of faith cannot save. Faith alone saves, but saving faith is a living, working thing.

One claims to have faith, but what is the use of that faith? If the use of that faith translates into works, one may have confidence that their faith is indeed the faith that saves.

Is your faith in Jesus a real and living faith?

April 23

Falling Down

Without Me they shall bow down among the prisoners, and they shall fall among the slain. (Isaiah 10:4)

The mighty Assyrian Empire threatened the Kingdom of Israel and Israel wasn't ready to face the threat. They were not ready politically, militarily, or most of all spiritually. Their only hope was to utterly rely on the Lord God, but they wouldn't do that. Sadly, Israel wanted to be independent of their God, and their "declaration of independence" would be their ruin.

The ruin didn't have to come directly from the hand of an avenging God. In declaring their independence from God, Israel sowed the seeds of their own destruction. When the Assyrian threat came, all God had to do was let Israel stand on their own two feet. They couldn't stand at all and would soon fall down.

That's why God said, **without Me they shall bow down among the prisoners, and they shall fall among the slain**. All God had to do to bring extreme judgment on Israel was to withdraw His protection. The Lord declared, **"Without Me** you have no hope before your enemies." For a long time, Israel lived without God in their worship and obedience. Soon they would stand before their enemies without God. It's a painful truth – when we reject God long enough, He will give us exactly what we want. We don't realize how much we need God until we stand where the Israelites stood and find ourselves without God.

Tragically, they could not stand at all. Instead, they would **bow down**. When the Assyrians conquered other nations, it wasn't enough for them to just win a military victory. They had a perverse pleasure in humiliating and subjugating their conquered foes. They did everything they could to bring them low. Here, God says, "You rejected Me so without Me you **shall bow down** in humiliation and degradation before your enemies."

Bowing down isn't always a bad thing. One of the Hebrew words commonly translated worship in the Old Testament is *shachah*. It means to bow down, to reverently bow or stoop, or to pay homage. But Isaiah 10:4 uses another word for **bow down**, the Hebrew word *kara*. It isn't a good word; it means to sink, to drop, to bring low, or to subdue. Israel had a choice – bow down in a good way before their loving God, or bow down in a humiliated, low way before their enemies. Which would it be?

This reminds us of Philippians 2:10-11, where the apostle Paul said *at the name of Jesus every knee should bow, of those in heaven, and of those on earth, and of those under the earth, and that every tongue should confess that Jesus Christ is Lord, to the glory of God the Father*.

We might say that we will either bow down to the Lord in worship, or it will be said of us, **without Me they shall bow down** in suffering and humiliation.

Today, set your course – which will it be?

April 24

This Might of Yours

Then the LORD turned to him and said, "Go in this might of yours, and you shall save Israel from the hand of the Midianites. Have I not sent you?" (Judges 6:14)

In the days of the Judges, God called an unexpected man named Gideon to deliver Israel. Gideon was a man who didn't want the job and didn't think he was worthy of the job. Gideon wrestled back and forth with God, seeking more and more confirmation that he was the one to do this great work of leading the resistance against the Midianites. At some point in it all, the Angel of the LORD spoke to Gideon and told him, **go in this might of yours, and you shall save Israel from the hand of the Midianites.**

Given the circumstances, it was strange thing to say: **Go in this might of yours**. Though it didn't look like it to many, Gideon was already mighty in many ways.

Gideon had the **might** of the *humble*. When the LORD came to Gideon, he was threshing wheat on the winepress floor. This was both difficult and humiliating. Wheat was threshed in open spaces, typically on a hill-top so the breeze could blow away the chaff. Wheat was not normally threshed in a sunken place like a winepress. In this humble place, Gideon was mighty.

Gideon had the **might** of the *caring* because he cared about the low place of Israel. When the LORD came to Gideon, he wanted to know why Israel was in a low place. Gideon cared about the low place of Israel and was interested in doing something about it. In this caring place, Gideon was mighty.

Gideon had the **might** of the *spiritually hungry* because he wanted to see God to great works again. Gideon asked the LORD, "We heard of these great things in the past, but we want to see God's greatness among us now." This hunger for more of what God could do was a trigger for future action. In this hungry place, Gideon was mighty.

Gideon had the **might** of the *teachable* because he listened to what the LORD said. After this conversation, Gideon set about doing the will of God. This showed he really was teachable. In this teachable place, Gideon was mighty.

More than anything, Gideon had the **might** of the *weak*, and God's strength is perfected in weakness (2 Corinthians 12:9). He knew he was weak, and this made him wise enough to trust the strength of God. In this weak place, Gideon was mighty.

Looking at it with the eye of man, Gideon was weak, and God's message was sarcastic. But looking at it through God's wisdom, we see that Gideon really could go forth in might – because it was the might of the weak relying on the strength of God.

Today, go forth in **this might of yours** – just make certain that it is really the strength of your mighty God.

April 25

The Model Prayer

In this manner, therefore, pray: Our Father in heaven, hallowed be Your name. Your kingdom come. Your will be done on earth as it is in heaven. Give us this day our daily bread. And forgive us our debts, as we forgive our debtors. And do not lead us into temptation, but deliver us from the evil one. For Yours is the kingdom and the power and the glory forever. Amen. (Matthew 6:9-13)

Jesus taught His followers how to give, pray, and fast in the right way. In this section dealing with prayer, Jesus began by correcting false ideas and practices about prayer. Now in this part, Jesus gave them a model prayer: **In this manner, therefore pray**.

The model prayer begins with the right way to address God: **Our Father in heaven**. The right kind of prayer comes to God as a **Father in heaven**. It rightly recognizes Whom we pray to, beginning with a special title that demonstrates a privileged relationship. It was unusual for many Jews to call God "Father" because it was considered too intimate. One commentator even says that there is no evidence of anyone before Jesus using this term to address God. When it came to prayer, Jesus was a true revolutionary.

So happily, we can call Him **Father**. It is true that God is the mighty Sovereign of the universe, who created, governs, and will judge all things – but He is also to us a Father.

Yet we remember what kind of Father He is. He is our Father, but He is our **Father in heaven**. When we say **in heaven**, we remember God's holiness and glory. He is our Father, but our Father in heaven.

We also notice that this is a prayer focused on community; Jesus said, **Our Father** and not "My Father." There is no reference to "I" or "me" or "my" in this prayer. The individual comes into the Father's presence, but then they pray as one member of a great family.

After the opening address, the model prayer continued: **Hallowed be Your name. Your kingdom come. Your will be done on earth as it is in heaven**. The right kind of prayer has a passion for God's glory and plan. His name, kingdom and will all have the top priority.

By instinct, each of us wants to guard their own name and reputation. But we must resist the tendency to protect and promote ourselves first and instead we must put first God's name, kingdom, and will.

Jesus wanted us to pray with the desire that God's will would be done **on earth as it is in heaven**. In heaven, there is no disobedience and no obstacle to God's will; on earth there is disobedience and are apparent obstacles to His will. The citizens of Jesus' kingdom want to see His will done as freely on earth as it is in heaven.

Today, let your prayer be, "Change me, Lord, wherever I don't understand or accept Your will."

April 26

Able to Save

Therefore He is also able to save to the uttermost those who come to God through Him, since He ever lives to make intercession for them. (Hebrews 7:25)

One day our daughter came home from school asking what a "witch's stand" was. We wondered what she was learning at school, and a little investigation revealed that she wasn't too sure about the U.S. Pledge of Allegiance and she thought it said: "and to the Republic, for witch's stands." Perhaps a similar thing has happened to you – you thought the words of a song went one way and were embarrassed to find out later that you sang the wrong thing all along.

Hebrews 7:25, is a perfect example. Most people think this verse says, "God is able to save us from the uttermost extent of sin." This isn't what Hebrews 7:25 is about. It really says that Jesus is able to complete your salvation – He can **save to the uttermost**. A famous evangelist, Billy Sunday, was a gutter drunk, and he used to quote this verse, "God can save from the guttermost." It is true that we can't out-sin God's ability to forgive or restore. The greatness of our sin is always less than the greatness of God's grace. You are never past God's forgiveness.

Hebrews 7:25 is not about what Jesus saves us *from*, it is about where He saves us *to*. Jesus **is able to save to the uttermost those who come to God through Him**. This is what is required of us – to keep coming to God through Jesus. Abiding in Jesus is the essential foundation of the Christian life. This is what the enemy of our souls wants us *not* to do – keep coming to God through Jesus. The devil may say, "Come to God – but not through Jesus." The devil may say, "Come to church – but don't come to God through Jesus." The devil may get you so busy or discouraged that you don't come to God through Jesus. So, combat the devil and build your life on that one foundation: keep coming to God through Jesus.

Remember that Hebrews 7:25 says that we have an intercessor in heaven. Do you remember that Jesus is praying for you in heaven? Jesus is not interceding for you because He is the "good cop" and the Father is the "bad cop." Jesus is not praying, "Please Father, forgive them one more time!" That forgiveness and payment for sin were forever purchased at the cross. Jesus is praying that we would be strengthened to know Him, love Him, and trust Him. Come to God through Jesus and receive that strength. He will see you through to the end.

This letter to the Hebrews was written to Christians who felt like giving up on the Christian life, and this is one of many passages that encourages them to hang in there because Jesus will not give up on them.

Jesus can save us from anything, but there is something special about knowing that He can **save us to the uttermost**.

April 27

How to Be Perfect

Therefore you shall be perfect, just as your Father in heaven is perfect. (Matthew 5:48)

In the Sermon on the Mount, Jesus challenged all His listeners to understand the Law of Moses properly. He dealt with our tendency to redefine the law in a way that makes it easier for us to keep.

At the end, Jesus said: **Therefore you shall be perfect**.

- He would never hate, slander, or speak evil of others.
- He would never lust in his heart or mind, and not covet anything.
- He would never make a false oath and always be completely truthful.
- He would let God defend his personal rights, and not take that on himself.
- He would always love his neighbors and even his enemies.

Jesus said that the person who did all this would be **perfect, just as your Father in heaven is perfect**. He would truly have righteousness greater than the scribes and the Pharisees (Matthew 5:20), exactly what we must have to enter God's Kingdom.

We can't deny it: there is only one Man who has lived like this, and it was Jesus Christ Himself. What about the rest of us? Are we left out of the kingdom of God?

Jesus was not trying to show what God requires of the Christian in his daily life. It was to say, "If you want to be righteous by the law, you must keep the whole law, internal and external – that is, you must be perfect."

Jesus demonstrated that we need a righteousness that is apart from the law. As the apostle Paul would later put it in Romans 3:21-22: *But now the righteousness of God apart from the law is revealed, being witnessed by the Law and the Prophets, even the righteousness of God, through faith in Jesus Christ, to all and on all who believe.*

This helps us to see what our current relation to the law is, as truly interpreted. We are exposed as guilty sinners who can never make ourselves righteous by doing good works Instead, we need to look to Jesus, Who was the only One to ever keep the law in perfection. As we put our trust in Him, His keeping of the law is credited to us.

By understanding the interpretation and the demands of the law, we should remember another aspect of Jesus' teaching on the law: in focusing on the command to love God and our neighbor, we will rightly understand the demands and details of the law (Matthew 22:37-40). This doesn't make the law easier to perfectly perform, but it does make it easier to understand.

We honor the law as the expression of God's beautiful standard for mankind – and then we look to Jesus, our perfect keeper of the law.

Only through Jesus can we keep the law, both as it is credited to us by faith and as He lives in and through us.

April 28

Like a Horse in Open Country

I will mention the lovingkindnesses of the Lord and the praises of the Lord, according to all that the Lord has bestowed on us, and the great goodness toward the house of Israel, which He has bestowed on them according to His mercies, according to the multitude of His lovingkindnesses.... As a beast goes down into the valley, and the Spirit of the Lord causes him to rest, so You lead Your people, to make Yourself a glorious name. (Isaiah 63:7, 14)

The last chapters of Isaiah are filled with hope. It isn't "don't worry, be happy" kind of hope; it isn't "things will somehow get better" kind of hope. Instead, it is hope that recognizes that a deep crisis will come; yet God will show Himself greater than the crisis.

The Kingdom of Judah was to be attacked, defeated, and conquered by the mighty Babylonian Empire. After that calamity would come deportation out of the beloved Promised Land and forced exile throughout the Babylonian Empire.

Isaiah prophetically placed a prayer in the mouth of a future Babylonian exile from Judah: **I will mention the lovingkindnesses of the Lord... according to all that the Lord has bestowed on us**. Despite the agony expressed later in the prayer, he first would **mention the lovingkindnesses of the Lord**. This is a glorious example of how, even in the lowest place, we can praise the Lord and remember His goodness. We see all his reasons to give thanks to God: *great goodness...mercies... He became their Savior... His love... His pity... He bore them and carried them.*

Isaiah 63:7 says He did it **according to the multitude of His lovingkindnesses**. This word is translated from the ancient Hebrew *hesed*. It is a steadfast love that is not merely felt but is also faithful, especially to the covenant it has made.

This future exile thought of all the ways God had shown His goodness to His people, despite the present low condition. He thought of God's past faithfulness to His people, especially saving them from Egypt in the exodus, through the wilderness, into the Promised Land. There was trust that God would also deliver His people from Babylon.

With this image of a **horse** and the **wilderness**, Isaiah spoke of the ease of progress that Israel made during the Exodus, and how God would bless Israel again in their regathering and restoration. The result will be that **the Spirit of the Lord causes him to rest**.

Do you feel stuck? The people of God were stuck in Babylon because they deserved it, and perhaps you "deserve" to be stuck as well. Nevertheless, even as God promised the Babylonian exiles that He would restore their progress, God may make this promise to you.

Today, pray for God to remove all hindrances and to restore your progress and your growth. The same God loves you with His steadfast, covenant love.

April 29

Having Nothing, Having Everything

Blessed are the poor in spirit, for theirs is the kingdom of heaven. (Matthew 5:3)

It isn't hard to convince people that it is better to be rich than it is to be poor. Not many people would choose poverty over riches – if they had the choice. Yet here Jesus tells us something remarkable: that there is a special blessing for those who are poor – that is, **poor in spirit**.

To be **poor in spirit** is somewhat like being poor when it comes to money. The poor in spirit recognize that they have no spiritual "assets." They know they are spiritually bankrupt. We might say that the ancient Greek had a word for the "working poor" and a word for the "truly poor." Jesus here used the word for the truly poor. It indicates someone who must beg for whatever they have or get. So the one who is **poor in spirit** recognizes that their spiritual value and strength must come to them from the outside; they don't have it in themselves on the inside.

To be **poor in spirit** is not to confess that we are by nature insignificant, or personally without value, for that would be untrue. Instead, it is a confession that we are in need. We don't have it in ourselves. Today, many people think that the key to spirituality is found deep inside oneself. They go on an inner search to dig down into the inner parts of their being because they think (or hope) that the answers are there. The one who is **poor in spirit** has given up on that. They know that if there is no money in the bank account, you can look at your bank statement all you want – you won't find anything. Something outside must come to be the needed resource.

We can also say that true poverty of spirit cannot be made up by trying to hate yourself; the Holy Spirit and our response to His working in our hearts bring it about. It is the work of God in us, and we respond to that work of God.

This beatitude is first. If you don't sense your own need and poverty, you will never hunger and thirst after righteousness, and if you have too high a view of yourself you will find it difficult to be merciful to others.

Poverty of spirit is an absolute prerequisite for receiving the **kingdom of heaven**. If we hold on to the dream of confidence in our own spiritual resources, we will never receive from God what we must have to be saved.

The **poor in spirit** are lifted from their low place and set in God's royal kingdom. It is indeed a happy poverty because it is a poverty rewarded richly.

God promises great things to those who stop looking for them within themselves and start looking to God instead. Look to Him for your needs today!

April 30

Wondrous Things

**Open my eyes, that I may see
Wondrous things from Your law.** (Psalm 119:18)

This simple line from the great Psalm 119 is a prayer for insight so that God's Word can be better understood. The psalmist prayed, **open my eyes, that I may see** because he recognized that he could not see what he could and should from God's Word without God bringing him light.

The idea is that our eyes (spiritually and even mentally speaking) are covered with a kind of curtain or veil that must be opened before we can see. Human effort and analysis of the Bible may be of little or no help unless that covering is removed.

This reminds us that it isn't the Bible that needs changing, as if it is obscure; we are the ones who are veiled and can't understand the Word of God apart from the work of the Hoy Spirit. Paul's eyes were unveiled when he was converted (Acts 9:18); it was as if scales had dropped from his eyes.

The psalmist didn't need a more understandable Bible or new revelation; he needed to see the revelation that was already given. He didn't need new eyes; he needed to see with the eyes he already had.

With those open eyes, he could see **wondrous things from Your law**. There are **wondrous things** in Scripture, but they can only be seen when God opens the eyes. This means that prayer is an important (and often neglected) part of Bible study.

It also means that not everyone sees the wondrous things in God's Word, but when one does see them, they should regard it as evidence of God's blessing and favor.

God has given man a sense of wonder, and certain things excite it. The new and unexpected can cause wonder; the beautiful and great can cause wonder, and the mysterious and unknown can cause wonder. We can say that God has provided for this sense of wonder by giving us His Word. The Holy Spirit can make us alive to the Bible and repeatedly see things that are new and unexpected; things that are great and beautiful, things that are mysterious and unknown. It is a shame that many Christians look for their sense of wonder to be satisfied without looking to the Word of God.

Think of all there is in the Bible that you don't see. Think of all the wonder, all the treasure there, but you don't see it. You can see such things, though you won't see everything, and sometimes you will think you see things that are not there. Yet those who see more than you are not necessarily smarter or better; their eyes are just more open.

Yet when God answers this prayer and gives us open eyes, it is our duty and privilege to study the Bible carefully and energetically. The gift of open eyes doesn't make study unnecessary; it makes it effective.

Pray this prayer with faith; then find some wondrous things.

May 1

Faith That Won't Quit

Then those who went before warned him that he should be quiet; but he cried out all the more, "Son of David, have mercy on me!" (Luke 18:39)

Jesus was on His way to Jerusalem, coming south from the region of Galilee. He knew that on this visit to Jerusalem He would be crucified, and His face was set in hard determination to love His people to the end.

With the weight of a coming betrayal, arrest, beating, and crucifixion on your mind, it would be easy to become annoyed at a pest, such as a blind man shouting at you. You could hardly blame the blind man; he sensed a highly charged excitement filling the air and asked a bystander what was happening. "Jesus of Nazareth is here," was the answer.

That's all the blind man needed, and he yelled out **Son of David, have mercy on me!** There wasn't an immediate answer, so he yelled it again. The people around him were annoyed – perhaps their ears hurt from the blind man's loud, desperate cry. "Be quiet!" they told him, but he wouldn't stop. Repeatedly he said, **Son of David, have mercy on me!** Luke even tells us that they **warned him** to stop. Maybe someone even threatened him with a punch in the mouth if he did not stop his shouting. But Luke notes, **he cried out all the more, "Son of David, have mercy on me!"**

What he shouted is important because it shows that the blind man knew who Jesus was. **Son of David** was a well-known Messianic title. The blind man said, "Jesus, You are the Messiah and I know You can help me."

What he shouted is important because it shows the blind man knew what he needed: mercy. He didn't come thinking that God owed him something; what he really wanted from Jesus was mercy.

Jesus came over to the blind man – probably smiling at the desperate man who wouldn't stop shouting and quiet down. Then, once He was close, Jesus asked him, "What do you want Me to do for you?" It was a strange question because the blind man's need seemed obvious. But Jesus wanted to hear it directly from the man's lips, and the blind man said, "Lord, that I may receive my sight." The blind man submitted himself to Jesus, calling Him "Lord."

Finally, Jesus healed him. He said to the blind man, "Receive your sight; your faith has made you well." How did the faith of the blind man save him?

- Because it was faith that wanted Jesus.
- Because it was faith that knew who Jesus was.
- Because it was faith that knew what he deserved from Jesus.
- Because it was faith that could tell Jesus what he wanted.
- Because it was by faith that he could call Jesus Lord.

Taken together, that is saving faith! The next time someone tells you to quiet down about Jesus, instead **cry out all the more**!

May 2
I Touched Him

When she heard about Jesus, she came behind Him in the crowd and touched His garment. For she said, "If only I may touch His clothes, I shall be made well." (Mark 5:27-28)

The law said that a woman in her condition made people and things unclean simply by a touch. They could only be made clean again through a special purification ceremony. Since the woman's condition never got better, she never became clean herself.

When this woman reached out to touch Jesus she would make this prophet, this miracle-worker – the Messiah Himself – unclean. But she touched Him with more than her hand; she touched Him with her faith. She knew that if she could only **touch His clothes** then she would **be made well**.

Was this woman correct in thinking she could be healed by touching the border of Jesus' garment? We have no scriptural evidence that Jesus healed this way before. Even though her faith had elements of error and superstition, she believed in the healing power of Jesus, and the border of His garment served as a point of contact for that faith. Her faith was in Jesus, and the object of faith is much more important than the quality of faith.

But Mark makes it clear. When she touched Jesus, then **immediately the fountain of her blood was dried up**. According to the thinking of the day, when this unclean woman touched Jesus, it would make Him unclean. But because of His nature and the power of God, when she touched His garment Jesus wasn't made unclean, the woman was made whole. When we come to Jesus with our sin and lay it on Him it doesn't make Him a sinner, but it makes us clean.

When the woman was healed, Jesus felt it. He asked who touched Him, and the disciples were amazed that Jesus could ask this question considering the crowds pressing in on Him. But the disciples didn't understand the difference between casual contact with Jesus and reaching out to touch Him in faith.

We can imagine someone who because of the press of the crowd bumped up against Jesus. When the woman's miracle was revealed, they might say, "I bumped into Jesus, I touched Him – yet I was not healed." But there is a big difference between bumping into Jesus and reaching out to touch Him in faith. You can come to church week after week and "bump into" Jesus. That isn't the same as reaching out to touch Him in faith.

Charles Spurgeon wrote, "It is not every contact with Christ that saves men; it is the arousing of yourself to come near to him, the determinate, the personal, resolute, believing touch of Jesus Christ which saves."

Jesus can tell the difference between the jostling of a crowd, and the heartfelt touch of a needy soul. You may "bump into" Jesus all the time.

Today, reach out to Jesus in real faith – beyond just "casual" contact.

May 3

Instead of Jesus

Little children, it is the last hour; and as you have heard that the Antichrist is coming, even now many antichrists have come, by which we know that it is the last hour. (1 John 2:18)

Most people in our modern culture don't know much about the Bible, but almost everyone has heard of the "Antichrist." We've seen the movies and have been told that the Bible predicts the rise of this frightening person.

This interest in the Antichrist is nothing new. Almost two thousand years ago, the apostle John wrote about him and expected the Christians of his day would understand him. John lived in the constant expectancy of Jesus' return, regarding his time as **the last hour** – an expectancy that we should also have, knowing that the Lord's return can come at any time. In this context, John warned: **the Antichrist is coming**.

What does the name "Antichrist" mean? In the ancient Greek language of the New Testament, the prefix "anti" can mean "the opposite of" or "instead of." The Antichrist is the "opposite Jesus"; he is the "instead of" Jesus.

Most people have focused on the idea of the "opposite Jesus." This has made them think the Antichrist will appear as a supremely evil person. It follows that in this thinking, that just as much as Jesus went around doing good, the Antichrist will do evil. As much as Jesus' character and personality were beautiful and attractive, the Antichrist's character and nature will be ugly and repulsive. As much as Jesus spoke only truth, the Antichrist will speak only lies. But the Antichrist will be more an "instead of" Jesus. He will look wonderful, be charming, and successful. He will be the ultimate winner and appear as an angel of light.

Some have wondered if this Antichrist will be an individual or a political system. This is a small distinction because the Bible tells us there will be both a person and a political system running the world before Jesus' return. There will be an individual and a state, and the two will be carefully identified.

John speaks of **the Antichrist** and **many antichrists**. There is a "spirit" of antichrist. This spirit of antichrist will one day find its ultimate fulfillment in the Antichrist, who will lead humanity in an end-times rebellion against God. Though the world still waits to see the Antichrist's eventual revealing, there are little previews of this man and his mission to come. These are the antichrists with a little "a."

What might be an "instead of" Jesus in your life? What might there be that you love or serve more than Him? Do not only look at the bad things. Something that looks good and attractive can take the place of Jesus in our lives and become an antichrist to us – something "instead of" Jesus. Many who would never dream of following the Antichrist in the last days are serving some antichrist today.

Is Jesus first in your life today?

May 4
A Tongue on Fire

Even so the tongue is a little member and boasts great things. See how great a forest a little fire kindles! And the tongue is a fire, a world of iniquity. The tongue is so set among our members that it defiles the whole body, and sets on fire the course of nature; and it is set on fire by hell. (James 3:5-6)

When James used the idea of a tongue starting a fire, he didn't mean it in a good way. He thought of a destructive, devastating fire – and thought of how the spoken word has often been used to destroy and devastate. The fire of the tongue has been used to burn many. Children are told, "sticks and stones may break my bones, but words can never hurt me." But that child's rhyme isn't true. The bitter pain of a word spoken against us can hurt for a lifetime, long after a broken bone has healed.

What we say to each other can last a long time, for good or for evil. The casual sarcastic or critical remark can inflict a lasting injury on another person. The well-timed encouragement or compliment can inspire someone for the rest of their life.

Proverbs speaks of the person who doesn't consider the destructive power of his words. *Like a madman who throws firebrands, arrows, and death, is the man who deceives his neighbor, and says, "I was only joking!"* (Proverbs 26:18-19)

James is not telling us never to speak or to take a vow of silence. In many ways, that would be easier than exercising self-control over the tongue. The bridle, the rudder, and the fire can all do tremendous good when appropriately controlled.

James rightly says, **the tongue is a fire, a world of iniquity**. There are not many sins that do not involve talking in some way. This gives us more reason to seek wisdom when it comes to what we say. One great source of wisdom in the Bible is the Book of Proverbs, and it has much to tell us about the spoken word. We could say that James echoes the testimony of Proverbs regarding the tongue:

- *In the multitude of words sin is not lacking, but he who restrains his lips is wise. The tongue of the righteous is choice silver; the heart of the wicked is worth little. The lips of the righteous feed many, but fools die for lack of wisdom.* (Proverbs 10:19-21)

- *Anxiety in the heart of man causes depression, but a good word makes it glad.* (Proverbs 12:25)

- *Pleasant words are like a honeycomb, sweetness to the soul and health to the bones.* (Proverbs 16:24)

- *Death and life are in the power of the tongue, and those who love it will eat its fruit.* (Proverbs 18:21)

God has put a lot of power into the spoken word – even the power of death and life.

Are you using that power for good, or using it to tear down?

May 5

Pride and Grace

But He gives more grace. Therefore He says: "God resists the proud, but gives grace to the humble." (James 4:6)

In the beginning of this verse, we see the idea, **He gives more grace**. That is a remarkable statement, but James does not end there. He continued: **God resists the proud**. With this, James reminds us that this grace only comes **to the humble**. Grace and pride are eternal enemies. Pride demands that God must bless me considering what I deserve, whether real or imagined. But grace will not deal with me based on anything in me – good or bad – but only based on who God is.

James used a powerful word in the phrase, **resists the proud**. God said the proud man fights against Him. Why is God so opposed to pride, and so honored by humility in man? In his book *Mere Christianity*, C.S. Lewis explains:

> According to Christian teachers, the essential vice, the utmost evil, is pride. Unchastity, anger, greed, drunkenness, and all that are mere fleabites in comparison: it was through pride that the devil became the devil. Pride leads to every other vice: it is the complete anti-God state of mind.

The strategy of Satan is to turn us into proud religious people. He works to build the heart that says, *God, I thank you that I am not like other men*, rather than having the attitude of the tax collector: *God, be merciful to me a sinner!* (Luke 18:9-14) The devil prizes a proud saint more than a flock of obvious sinners. When Satan looks at the believer who walks in pride, he can say, "Now there is a man like me! He is aware of spiritual things, yet he is utterly infected with the cancer of pride!"

One problem with pride is that it can be so subtle. We can be proud people yet have a spiritual image. How can we do a "pride check" in our lives? Here are some good questions to ask yourself.

- How much do I treasure the compliments of others?
- How devastated am I by the criticism of others?
- How often are my feelings hurt?
- How often do I wonder about my appearance?
- How often do I wonder what others are thinking of me?
- Am I usually miserable?
- Do I often feel neglected by others?
- Do I expect more from others than I do from myself?
- Am I generally disappointed in others?

If you want God to deal with pride in your life, do not expect it to be easy. Pride is like a weed with deep, strong roots, and it is hard to pull out. And when we think we pull it out, there is always a little bit left that will spring up later.

Don't wait – walk in humility before God today and receive His grace.

May 6
Always Praying, Never Losing Heart

Then He spoke a parable to them, that men always ought to pray and not lose heart. (Luke 18:1)

In Luke 18 Jesus told a story of a widow who came to an unjust judge, seeking justice in a legal dispute. The judge, though he did not regard God or man, eventually gave the widow justice because of her persistent requests. Jesus ended the parable with this application: *shall God not avenge His own elect who cry out day and night to Him, though He bears long with them?*

It's easy to lose heart in prayer because it is hard work. In Colossians 4:12, Paul praised Epaphras because he was *always laboring fervently…in prayers*. Paul knew that prayer required fervent labor. It is easy to lose heart in prayer because the devil hates prayer. If prayer were powerless, it would be easier to pray! It is easy to lose heart in prayer because we are not always convinced of the reality of its power; prayer too often becomes a last resort instead of a first resource. Despite all that, we **always ought to pray**.

In the parable, the only reason the judge gave the woman what she wanted was that she wouldn't stop bugging him. In wording of the ancient Greek, he complained that the woman was "beating" him or "stunning" him with her persistence. So eventually he answered her request. This parable has a unique approach. Obviously, God is not the unjust judge; but if the unjust judge will answer the persistent request, how much more will a righteous God? Charles Spurgeon said, "Too many prayers are like boy's runaway knocks, given, and then the giver is away before the door can be opened."

The woman had to overcome the judge's reluctance to help. We often *feel* that we must also overcome God's reluctance by our persistence. But this misses the point of the parable entirely. Jesus did not say, **that men always ought to pray and not lose heart** because God is reluctant, but because He isn't. Delays in answered prayer are not needed to change God, but to change us. Persistence in prayer brings a transforming element into our lives, building into us the character of God Himself.

Some promises of God take a long time to fulfill. Will we persevere in trusting God? George Mueller was a remarkable man of faith who ran orphanages in England. In a sermon he preached when he was 75 years old, he said that 30,000 times in his fifty-four years as a Christian he had received an answer to prayer on the same day that he prayed it. But not all his prayers were answered so quickly.

Mueller told of one prayer that had been brought to God about 20,000 times over eleven and a half years, and he was still trusting God for the answer: "I hope in God, I pray on, and look for the answer. Therefore, beloved brethren and sisters, go on waiting on God, go on praying." That's God's word to you today: go on praying!

May 7

Dealing Well According to His Word

You have dealt well with Your servant, O Lord, according to Your word. Teach me good judgment and knowledge, for I believe Your commandments. (Psalm 119:65-66)

This is such a wonderful thing to say, to know, and to believe: **You have dealt well with Your servant, O Lord, according to Your word**. These words have a note of deep gratitude. The psalmist found himself thankful for God's fair dealing toward him, and that it had come according to **Your word**.

We do not think about it enough, but it is wonderfully true that each believer can say to God, **You have dealt well with Your servant, O Lord**. Think of the many ways God has **dealt well** with us. He loves us, He chose us, He called us, and He drew us to Himself. He rescued us, He declared us righteous, He forgave us, He put His Spirit with us, and He adopted us into His family. He makes us kings and priests and co-workers with Him, and He rewards all our work for Him.

All these remarkable blessings came to the psalmist **according to Your word**. This implies that he not only knew the promises of God and appealed to them in prayer (as in Psalm 119:49); he also received the promises by faith and experienced them in his life.

We remember what Mary said to the angel Gabriel – who had just made the glorious promise that she would bear the Messiah. Mary said, *Behold the maidservant of the Lord! Let it be to me according to your word.* (Luke 1:38)

This should be the life experience of every child of God. They should know that God has dealt well with them, and they should know that it has been according to His Word.

In Psalm 119:65-66, the thinking moves from gratitude for the past and progresses to a prayer for the present, asking for **good judgment** and **knowledge**. This is the prayer of wisdom from a blessed life. Having received this well dealing from God, the psalmist understood the need to live in good judgment and knowledge. The blessing of God's dealing well with him was given for wise and obedient living for God's glory.

We too easily forget our great need to learn good judgment and knowledge, and we are far too ready to trust our own heart and conscience instead. But like every other aspect of our being, our conscience has been injured by the fall and does not always get it right. This is why we need to have our judgment and knowledge constantly informed by the Word of God.

The reason behind this is stated at the end of verse 66: **for I believe Your commandments**. The psalmist wanted God to teach him because he believed the commands and words of God.

That is a powerful thought: if we believe His Word, we want Him to teach us to live according to good judgment and knowledge. Today, let God teach you.

May 8

The Perfect Work of Patience

My brethren, count it all joy when you fall into various trials, knowing that the testing of your faith produces patience. But let patience have its perfect work, that you may be perfect and complete, lacking nothing. (James 1:2-4)

James wanted Christians – those who were his **brethren** – to **count it all joy when you fall into various trials**. James regarded trials as inevitable. He said, **when** not "if" you fall into various trials. These trials or times of adversity are a reason for joy, not a reason for a sense of defeat. We can **count it all joy** amid trials because those trials, the **testing of your faith**, can actually produce patience in us.

We take comfort in knowing that trials and adversity can have a good purpose. They are not meaningless or purposeless. Instead, **knowing that the testing of your faith produces patience**. Notice that faith is tested through trials, not produced by trials. If trials do not produce faith, what does? Romans 10:17 tells us: *So then faith comes by hearing, and hearing by the word of God.* Faith is built in us as we hear, understand, and trust in God's Word.

However, it is true that trials will reveal what our faith is in, and how much faith we have. God already knows what our faith is in and how much faith we have, but often we don't know those things. The **testing of your faith** doesn't teach God, it teaches us and those around us.

We notice that it is **faith** that is tested, showing us that faith is essential and precious – because only precious things are tested so thoroughly.

Trials do not produce faith, but when trials are received with faith, they produce **patience**. Patience is not automatically produced in times of trial. If difficulties are accepted with an attitude of unbelief and grumbling, trials can produce bitterness and discouragement. This is why James exhorted us to **count it all joy**. Counting it all joy is faith's response to a time of trial. James didn't tell us to enjoy our trials, or to say that we had to *feel* it all joy – instead, we decide to **count it all joy**.

James spoke wisdom to believers: **let patience have its perfect work, that you may be perfect and complete, lacking nothing**. The work of patient endurance comes slowly and must be allowed to have full bloom. Patient endurance is a mark of the person who is **perfect and complete, lacking nothing**. We are often in such a hurry that we never **let patience have its perfect work**.

Patience translates the ancient Greek word *hupomone*. This word does not describe a passive waiting, but an active endurance. It isn't so much the kind that helps you sit quietly in the doctor's waiting room, as it is the kind that helps you finish a marathon.

Make that your prayer today: "Lord, slow me down so that patience can have its perfect work in me."

May 9

Like a River, Like a Stream, Like a Mother

For thus says the Lord: "Behold, I will extend peace to her like a river, and the glory of the Gentiles like a flowing stream. Then you shall feed; on her sides shall you be carried, and be dandled on her knees. As one whom his mother comforts, so I will comfort you; and you shall be comforted in Jerusalem." When you see this, your heart shall rejoice, and your bones shall flourish like grass; the hand of the Lord shall be known to His servants, and His indignation to His enemies. (Isaiah 66:12-14)

Inspired by the Holy Spirit, Isaiah spoke wonderful words of comfort. When the Messiah returns in glory and triumph, the **peace** of Jerusalem will be like a gentle, powerful **river** that is never disturbed. If you have seen the flow of a mighty river, you understand the image. There is a calm, a glory, and strength in the flow of a big river that just says "peace." This is the peace God gives to those who turn to Him.

The promise doesn't end with Jerusalem. There is a sense in which God's plan of redemption began with the Jewish people, with the Father of Jews, Abraham. God established His covenant with Abraham, Isaac, and Jacob, and then with Jacob's twelve sons and their descendants. It was never God's intention to restrict that plan of redemption to the Jewish people. Rather through them, God would reach the whole world – the **Gentiles**. The Lord promised this in the very first words He spoke to Abraham (Genesis 12:1-3).

This was important for the Jewish people to remember, and sometimes they seemed to forget. Those who call themselves Christians today must remember the same principle; God blesses them and works in them so that He can bless others and work in them. We shouldn't think of ourselves as *containers* of God's blessing; instead, we should think of ourselves as *channels* of His blessing, with it passing through us and on to others.

Through Isaiah, God spoke with supreme tenderness to His faithful servants: **I will comfort you**. No one can comfort like a loving **mother**, and God will bring that kind of comfort to His people.

When the Messiah returns in glory and triumph, for some it will be a great blessing – and for others, it will be only judgment. Those who put their trust in Him; who have received His peace; those who receive His care and His comfort – these will receive the goodness of His hand: the **hand of the Lord shall be known to His servants**.

Yet for those who push God away and reject the message of hope and grace delivered through Isaiah, the sad news is that **indignation** from God awaits them. They have made themselves **enemies** of God and will be treated as such.

God gives you the choice – choose wisely. Today, receive the peace and comfort that comes from making the right choice.

May 10

The Need to Forgive

For if you forgive men their trespasses, your heavenly Father will also forgive you. But if you do not forgive men their trespasses, neither will your Father forgive your trespasses. (Matthew 6:14-15)

In His great Sermon on the Mount, Jesus gave us a model prayer – often called "The Lord's Prayer," but perhaps more accurately called "the Disciples' Prayer." In that prayer, Jesus gave a memorable line: *And forgive us our debts, as we forgive our debtors.* (Matthew 6:12)

With that line, Jesus linked together the way His disciples forgive and the way they are forgiven. Those who ask God for forgiveness must also be forgiving to those who have wronged them.

Now Jesus built on this idea in the verses immediately following the model prayer. First Jesus put it in the positive: **If you forgive men their trespasses, your heavenly Father will also forgive you**. Then Jesus put it in the negative: **But if you do not forgive men their trespasses, neither will your Father forgive your trespasses**.

If this was the only thing Jesus and the New Testament said about forgiveness, we might think that we have earned forgiveness from God because we forgive others. In many other passages (such as Matthew 9:2-6, 18:21-35, and Luke 17:3-4) Jesus tells us more about forgiveness. And the apostle Paul made it clear that the basis of forgiveness is what Jesus did for us on the cross, not anything we do (see Ephesians 1:7, Colossians 1:14).

Taking such passages into account, we see Jesus' point in this context: Forgiveness is required for those who have been forgiven. We are not given the luxury of holding on to our bitterness towards other people.

When we begin to see how greatly we have sinned against God and how great His forgiveness is towards us, then we properly see that what others have done against us is small by comparison. It is all a matter of perspective. The earth is big but compared to the sun it is small (the sun is 33,200 times bigger than the earth). So, the wrongs done against us may be big in our life, but compared to the wrongs we have done to God they are small. If we have an exaggerated view of the wrongs done against us, it proves we have too small a view of our own wrongs against God.

Forgiving others is often challenging – among the most difficult things we do. We can only do it if we really appreciate how greatly God has forgiven us. Yet we must do it, and in this passage, Jesus emphasizes the urgency of forgiveness; on the fact that it is not an option. Forgiveness is the right thing to do, being the only proper response of someone who is forgiven and wants to receive more forgiveness from God.

We also must forgive because forgiving others sets us free. You can live in the freedom of forgiveness today.

First, receive God's forgiveness, and then give it to others.

May 11
Showers of Blessing

Yet hear now, O Jacob My servant, and Israel whom I have chosen. Thus says the Lord who made you and formed you from the womb, who will help you: "Fear not, O Jacob My servant; and you, Jeshurun, whom I have chosen. For I will pour water on him who is thirsty, and floods on the dry ground; I will pour My Spirit on your descendants, and My blessing on your offspring; they will spring up among the grass like willows by the watercourses." (Isaiah 44:1-4)

Isaiah 43 ended with a severe warning of judgment, yet that did not mean that God took back His promise of hope and restoration. The people of God could still know the goodness of God if they would only turn back to Him.

When God told His people He was the one who **made** them, it reminds us that God is still active in creation. He didn't just create Adam and Eve and then stop. God has made each of us, so we have a personal obligation to Him as our Creator.

The words **fear not** were not only given to Jacob, but God also spoke to **Jeshurun**. The name Jeshurun means "the upright one." It is used here as a contrast to the name Jacob, even as the name Israel is sometimes used as a contrast to Jacob. It was a more gracious, merciful way for God to speak to His people (Deuteronomy 32:15, 33:5, 33:26).

God gave them reasons not to be afraid: **For I will pour water on him...I will pour My Spirit on your descendants**. This is a glorious promise to a humble, returning Israel. God will not simply give them His Spirit; He will **pour** out His Spirit on them as if water was poured over them.

Who receives this? God promised to **pour water on him who is thirsty**. When we are thirsty for the outpouring of the Spirit, ask for it and receive it in faith. God is looking for dry ground to pour out floods on!

This pouring out of God's Spirit is so great that it goes beyond the present generation. He says, **and My blessing on your offspring**. God doesn't only want to pour His Spirit; He also wants to pour His blessing, on our offspring and us. All we need to do is bring our dry ground to Him in faith and expect His poured-out Spirit, His shower of blessing.

God describes the effect of this poured out blessing: **They will spring up among the grass like willows**. The effect of the poured-out Spirit is life. Life springs up and grows where the Spirit of God is poured out. We need this shower of blessing to both start life and sustain it. Believe God for an outpouring of His Spirit – for true showers of blessing.

An old hymn cried out for "showers of blessings." You can cry out to God who wants to pour out His Spirit.

May 12

Not Ashamed at His Coming

And now, little children, abide in Him, that when He appears, we may have confidence and not be ashamed before Him at His coming. (1 John 2:28)

Have you ever arrived at a destination and been disappointed with the result? A police officer in Connecticut noticed a speeding car that matched the description of a robbery getaway car. He started a pursuit, and during the chase, the suspect made a wrong turn – into the MacDougall Correctional Institution, a high-security prison. He then jumped from his car and ran into the lobby. "I believe he thought it was a shopping mall," said the police officer. "But I've never seen too many malls with a razor wire across the top."

In 1 John 2:28, John presented a challenging idea. When we arrive at our eternal destination, some may be disappointed in the result. When Jesus returns, some people will be afraid because they never knew Jesus at all. But among those who do know Him, some will also be afraid; they will be **ashamed before Him at His coming**. They will realize that they have lived worldly, unfruitful lives. In one moment, the understanding will overwhelm them that whatever else they accomplished in life, they did not **abide in Him** as they could have.

Paul the apostle spoke of those who are barely saved: *He will suffer loss; but he himself will be saved, yet so as through fire* (1 Corinthians 3:15). There are those who, for at least a moment, the coming of Jesus will be a moment of disappointment rather than glory. It might only be a moment, but "suffering loss" or **be ashamed** are not ideas we want to connect to our meeting with Jesus.

Some might say, "What difference does it make? If we make it to heaven, we're good." Not really. How narrow is the distance between "barely saved" and "not quite saved"? When one asks, "How little can I do and still make it to heaven?" or "How far can I stray from the Shepherd and still be a part of the flock?" they are asking dangerous questions.

We wait for the return of Jesus and want to be ready for Him. But we also remember the best way to be prepared for His return. The best way to be ready is not to be a master of every prophecy in the Bible. The best way to be ready is not to retire to a monastery, away from the wicked world.

John 2:28 says it: If you want to be ready for the return of Jesus and know that you will not be ashamed before Him at His coming, then **abide in Him**. Live in Jesus. Make Him, and not yourself, the focus of your life. Then, no matter what hour Jesus comes for you – you will be ready and unashamed to stand before Him.

Do you want to be ready for the return of Jesus?

Then simply, faithfully, daily, live in Him.

Prayer, Earnest and Awake

Continue earnestly in prayer, being vigilant in it with thanksgiving; meanwhile praying also for us, that God would open to us a door for the word, to speak the mystery of Christ, for which I am also in chains, that I may make it manifest, as I ought to speak. (Colossians 4:2-4)

We know that the apostle Paul prayed for the Colossian Christians. An example of his prayer for them is found in Colossians 1:3-8. Paul prayed for them; now toward the end of his letter, he told them to keep on praying themselves.

Paul told them (and all Christians) to **continue earnestly in prayer**. This sort of earnest prayer is important but does not come easy. **Earnestly in prayer** speaks of great effort that is steadily applied. Much of our prayer is powerless because it lacks earnestness. Too often, we pray almost with the attitude of wanting God to care about things we don't.

Earnest prayer has power not because it persuades a reluctant God. Instead, it demonstrates that our heart cares passionately about the same things as God. This fulfills what Jesus promised in John 15:7: *If you abide in Me and My words abide in you, you will ask what you desire, and it shall be done for you.*

Our prayers are not only to be earnest but also **vigilant**. According to William Barclay, the idea behind the word translated **vigilant** is *awake*. In a sense, Paul told us not to fall asleep in prayer. Sometimes, because of the tiredness of our body or mind, we struggle against sleep when we pray. Other times we pray as if we were asleep, and our prayers sound and feel tired, sleepy.

Our earnestness and vigilance should also have **thanksgiving**. God gives us so much and blesses us with so much that we should always thank Him as we ask Him.

Paul went on to give them something specific to pray for – himself! He wrote, **meanwhile praying also for us**. Paul seemed to say, "As long as we are on the subject of prayer, please pray for us." But Paul didn't ask for prayer for his personal needs (which were many), but that God would open to us a door for the gospel. Paul knew that when God's Word was active and free to work, great things happened for God.

Finally, notice that Paul asked the Colossians to pray for his preaching so that he could **speak the mystery of Christ**, and do it as he ought to speak. When Paul wrote this, he was in chains for proclaiming the Word of God. He wanted Christians to pray that he would keep doing proclaiming God's Word and do it better all the time.

Today, pray that the Lord continues to give us open doors to spread God's Word and that we may proclaim His Word as we ought to speak. Pray earnestly; pray vigilantly.

If Paul needed that prayer, we need it much more.

May 14

For Me or For You?

Say to all the people of the land, and to the priests: "When you fasted and mourned in the fifth and seventh months during those seventy years, did you really fast for Me; for Me?" (Zechariah 7:5)

God knows who we are. Psalm 103:13-14 says: *As a father pities his children, so the LORD pities those who fear Him. For He knows our frame; He remembers that we are dust.* He knows that we need material, tangible things to help convince us of the reality of the spiritual. God cares about how we regard the material world; He wants us to use it for His glory instead of being a slave to material things.

One of the ways God helps us put the material world into perspective is by fasting. A time of fasting shows that we put our spiritual needs and concerns above our material needs and concerns. Yet we can twist a good gift like fasting and use it as an occasion for spiritual pride.

That was exactly the problem in Zechariah's day. The priests fasted, but they didn't fast for the right reasons. God asked them: **Did you really fast for Me; for Me?** God's Word through Zechariah rebuked the people of God for what their fasting had become – indulgent pity-parties instead of a time to genuinely seek God. As the prophet explained, their lives were not right when they did eat and drink – that they did it for themselves, not for the LORD. A few days of fasting every year could not make up for the rest of the year lived for self.

Isn't it challenging to think about how much we do for ourselves and not for the LORD? What might the LORD come to us about and say, **Did you really do this for Me, for Me?** We can pray in such a manner so that people will admire our prayer. We can sing songs of worship hoping people will hear our great voice – or worry about them hearing our poor voice. Either way, it's all about self, not God.

The great mistake they made in Zechariah's time was thinking that a day of ritualistic fasting could make up for an everyday life that ignored God. Later, the prophet asked, "Should you not have obeyed the words which the LORD proclaimed?" Because their hearts were not right with God, their rituals were not right before God. Everyday obedience would make their times of fasting meaningful, but their neglect of everyday obedience made their fasting hypocritical.

The point is that both the LORD God and His prophet Zechariah were not against fasting, they were against the wrong kind of fasting – fasting that was only a ritual, fasting that thought it could make up for a life that ignored God.

Used the right way, fasting is a wonderful part of our walk with God – just make sure you do it for the LORD, and not for self.

May 15

Excuses

Now it happened, as soon as he had finished presenting the burnt offering, that Samuel came; and Saul went out to meet him, that he might greet him. And Samuel said, "What have you done?" And Saul said, "When I saw that the people were scattered from me, and that you did not come within the days appointed, and that the Philistines gathered together at Michmash, then I said, 'The Philistines will now come down on me at Gilgal, and I have not made supplication to the LORD.' Therefore I felt compelled, and offered a burnt offering." (1 Samuel 13:10-12)

King Saul had a crisis and needed God's help. The Philistines invaded Israel with a massive army and were ready to destroy the army of Israel. King Saul and the prophet Samuel knew that spiritual preparation before the battle was essential, so Samuel told Saul to wait until the prophet came to the army camp and led Israel in sacrifice.

King Saul didn't wait. Afraid Samuel took too long, he offered the sacrifice himself. Yet, **as soon as he finished offering the burnt offering**, Samuel arrived. If he trusted God and waited an hour, how different things could have been! The last moments of waiting are usually the most difficult, and they tempt us to take matters into our own hands.

Guilty of impatience, presumption, and taking the priestly office to himself, King Saul should have repented before Samuel. He didn't. Therefore, Samuel asked, **"What have you done?"** All Samuel wanted to hear was confession and repentance. But Saul's response was a classic example of excuse-making and failure to trust God.

First excuse: **I saw that the people were scattered from me.** "I had to do something to impress the people and gain back their support." But if Saul had obeyed and trusted God, He would have brought victory over the Philistines with or without the people. He should have been more concerned with pleasing God.

Second excuse: **You did not come within the days appointed.** If Saul obeyed and trusted God, God would take care of Samuel and the timing. Even if Samuel was in the wrong, it didn't justify Saul's sin. We often blame our sins on others.

Third excuse: **The Philistines will now come down on me at Gilgal, and I have not made supplication to the LORD.** But if Saul would have obeyed and trusted God, the LORD would take care of the Philistines.

Fourth excuse: **Therefore I felt compelled.** Even though Saul felt compelled, he wasn't supposed to be ruled by his feelings. He didn't have to sin.

Often, it isn't our sin that sinks us – it's all the excuses we make afterward.

Today, leave all the excuses behind, and humbly confess and repent. Saul didn't, and it would be his ruin.

May 16

Right in All Things

Therefore I love Your commandments more than gold, yes, than fine gold! Therefore all Your precepts concerning all things I consider to be right; I hate every false way. (Psalm 119:127-128)

In the previous verses, the psalmist was disappointed over those who thought the Word of God was worthless and empty. He had a very different opinion; the great writer of Psalm 119 answered this low view of Scripture by saying, **Therefore I love Your commandments more than gold**. Though others regarded the Word of God as empty, the psalmist decided to love His commandments even more in response. He valued them **more than gold** – even more than much fine gold.

When the psalmist remembered what kind of men considered the Word of God as empty, it made him love the Word of God more. When we consider the monstrous men who have been enemies of God's Word – murdering tyrants such as Stalin and Mao – we knew that the Word of God is lovely. When wicked men hate the Word of God, it says something good in favor of the Scriptures.

Their rejection of the Bible makes me prize it even more. Yet, above even **fine gold**, God's Word has inherent value. There are blessings and goodness in God's Word to us that surpasses gold. Gold can't heal the broken heart; it can't truly relieve a wounded spirit. Gold can't give comfort on my deathbed, but God's Word can.

Considering this, the psalmist could say, **therefore all Your precepts concerning all things I consider to be right**. With great confidence, the psalmist proclaimed the inerrancy of God's Word. It was **right**, not wrong, and it was right **concerning all things**.

- When the Bible gives us history, it is right and true; the events actually happened as described.
- When the Bible gives us poetry, it is right and true; the feelings and experiences were real for the writer and ring true to our human experience.
- When the Bible gives us prophecy, it is right and true; the events described will come to pass, just as it is written.
- When the Bible gives us instruction, it is right and true; it truly does tell us the will of God and the best way of life.
- When the Bible tells us of God, it is right and true; it reveals to us what the nature and heart and mind of God are, or as much as we can comprehend.

With great affection for the right and true of God's Word, he could also say, **I hate every false way**. Because the psalmist loved and trusted the Word of God so much, he naturally hated **every false way**. He could not love the truth without also hating lies, and knowing the right and true Word of God, he could recognize the false way when he saw it.

No wonder it is worth more than gold, even fine gold.

May 17

Blessed Trouble

Blessed are those who are persecuted for righteousness' sake, for theirs is the kingdom of heaven. Blessed are you when they revile and persecute you, and say all kinds of evil against you falsely for My sake. Rejoice and be exceedingly glad, for great is your reward in heaven, for so they persecuted the prophets who were before you. (Matthew 5:10-12)

The Beatitudes that begin the Sermon on the Mount describe what a citizen of Jesus' kingdom looks like. The character traits described in the Beatitudes are not valued by our modern culture but describe the citizens of God's kingdom.

They will be poor in spirit, recognizing their need for God. They will mourn over their sinful condition and that of this lost world. They will have a meek, gentle attitude that trusts God more than self. They hunger and thirst after righteousness and show mercy to others, remembering mercy received. They have purity of heart, leading to a greater relationship with God and they will make peace with those who wrong them and those who wrong one another. When you think about this character profile, it describes a pretty wonderful person. What should these people expect out in this world?

Jesus told us: they should expect to be **persecuted** – and then **blessed**.

Jesus spoke of those **persecuted for righteousness' sake** and for Jesus' sake (**for My sake**), not for their own stupidity or fanaticism. Peter recognized that suffering might come to some Christians for reasons other than their faithfulness to Jesus (1 Peter 4:15-16), and this is not what Jesus addressed here. In Matthew 5:10 they are **persecuted for righteousness' sake**; in Matthew 5:11 they are persecuted for the sake of Jesus. This shows that Jesus expected that their righteous lives would be lived after His example, and in honor to Him.

We also notice how Jesus described persecution, and that it includes with being reviled, and having **evil** spoken against one **falsely**. Jesus brought insults and spoken malice into the sphere of persecution. We cannot limit our idea of persecution to only physical opposition or torture.

It did not take long for these words of Jesus to be fulfilled. Early Christians heard many enemies say all kinds of evil against them falsely for Jesus' sake.

Jesus told these persecuted how to react when mistreated: **Rejoice and be exceedingly glad**. Literally, we could translate this phrase to say that the persecuted should "leap for joy." Why? Because the persecuted will have great **reward in heaven**, and because the persecuted are in good company: the prophets before them were also persecuted.

The world persecutes good people because the values and character expressed in these Beatitudes are so opposite to the world's manner of thinking.

Our persecution may not be much compared to others, but if no one despises your Christianity or speaks evil of you, are these Beatitudes traits of your life?

May 18
Seeing God's Good When It Looks Bad

But I want you to know, brethren, that the things which happened to me have actually turned out for the furtherance of the gospel, so that it has become evident to the whole palace guard, and to all the rest, that my chains are in Christ; and most of the brethren in the Lord, having become confident by my chains, are much more bold to speak the word without fear. (Philippians 1:12-14)

Paul had a special relationship with the Christians in Philippi; they were not only part of a church he founded, but they were also his friends. Sometimes our friends are confused at what God is doing in our life – and sometimes we are even more confused! In Philippians 1:12-14, Paul wanted to reassure the Philippians that God was doing good even when it looked bad.

When Paul was in Philippi, he was arrested and imprisoned. But God miraculously freed him, and he continued preaching the gospel (Acts 16:25-34). When Paul wrote his letter to the Philippians, he was in a jail in Rome. Paul's Philippian friends were probably thinking, "God used a miracle to set Paul free before. Why doesn't God do it now? Is He letting Paul down, or is Paul in sin?" In Philippians 1:12-14, Paul assured them that God's blessing and power were still with him, even in prison – he was not out of God's will.

Considering how God set Paul free in Philippi, we shouldn't be surprised they wondered where the power of God was in Paul's present imprisonment. If Paul wasn't being advanced, that was all right – because his passion was to see the gospel advanced. Even though Paul was in prison, the circumstances around his imprisonment, and his manner during it, made it clear to everyone he was not just another prisoner, but he was an emissary of Jesus; this witness led to the conversion of many including his guards.

In fact, Paul's imprisonment gave the Christians around him, who were not imprisoned, greater confidence and boldness, because they saw that Paul could have joy amid adversity. They saw that God would take care of Paul and still use him even in prison. We also know this turned out for the **furtherance of the gospel** because during this time he wrote Ephesians, Philippians, and Colossians. When Paul was in bad circumstances, God was using him.

God didn't waste Paul's time in Rome. God never wastes our time, though we may waste it by not sensing God's purpose for our lives in our present situation. Are you in a bad place – even a "prison" of some sort? God can use you right where you are, and He wants to. Stop thinking your situation must change before God's power can be evident in your life. It can be evident right now.

God gave Paul the ability to see His good even in a Roman prison – this same God is with us today!

May 19

The Answer of Faith to the Advice of Fear

In the LORD **I put my trust; how can you say to my soul, "Flee as a bird to your mountain"? If the foundations are destroyed, what can the righteous do? The L**ORD **is in His holy temple, the L**ORD**'s throne is in heaven; His eyes behold, His eyelids test the sons of men.** (Psalm 11:1, 3-4)

In the years before he took the throne of Israel, David lived the life of a fugitive. King Saul hunted him, and he lived in constant danger. In such a time, his friends advised him, **Flee as a bird to your mountain.** They meant well, but David knew it was the wrong thing to do. So, David reacted with near outrage: **In the L**ORD **I put my trust; how can you say to my soul, "Flee as a bird to your mountain?"**

No matter how well-intentioned they were, David's friends gave him the advice of fear. This couldn't stand with the position of trust David had in God. David would rather face the danger of death than to show distrust in the LORD his God.

They asked him, **if the foundations are destroyed, what can the righteous do?**

David then gave the answer of faith to the advice of fear. First, David answered by remembering where God is: **The L**ORD **is in His holy temple.** David reminded himself, "God hasn't gone anywhere. I can go to His temple and meet with Him."

When the advice of fear comes on us, we can only arrive at the answer of faith by spending time with the LORD. When we think about our problems, the advice of fear often overwhelms us. When we pray about our problems, the answer of faith assures our hearts.

David had confidence in a holy, all-powerful, all-knowing God. David was asked, **what can the righteous do?** David answered with another question: What *can't* the righteous do when the LORD God is still on His throne?

David also remembered what God sees: **His eyes behold.** David didn't need to take the advice of fear because God saw his situation. David could have a greater cause than self-preservation because he knew that God was looking at him and taking care of him.

Finally, David remembered that even in this trial, God had a loving purpose. The **L**ORD **tests the righteous.** Again, David answered the question, **If the foundations are destroyed, what can the righteous do?** David answered, "The righteous can know that the LORD is testing them, and because a loving God is testing them, they can know they will not be pushed too far or forsaken. The righteous can know the LORD is in control."

The next time you are given the advice of fear, follow the same steps. First, remember where God is. Second, remember that God sees you. Then remember God's loving purpose.

Remembering those three things will help you give the answer of faith to the advice of fear.

May 20

From Defeat to Victory

When Your people Israel are defeated before an enemy because they have sinned against You, and when they turn back to You and confess Your name, and pray and make supplication to You in this temple, then hear in heaven, and forgive the sin of Your people Israel, and bring them back to the land which You gave to their fathers. (1 Kings 8:33-34)

At the grand opening of the temple, Solomon did everything possible to tell God, Israel, and the world that this was a special house for the Great God. 2 Chronicles 5:6 says they sacrificed so many sheep and oxen that they lost count. It also describes the spectacular music and heartfelt worship offered to God. God's glory filled the temple so completely that the priests couldn't minister.

Solomon was wise enough to know that as great as the dedication day was, it wouldn't be like that forever. Hearts on fire would grow cold and Israel would turn its heart away from God. In his great prayer, Solomon thought ahead to the future when the temple might not be a place of celebration, but of repentant confession and returning to God. Solomon asked God to listen to the prayers of His defeated people when they came to the temple to pray.

Solomon *expected* defeat would someday come (**When Your people Israel are defeated**). We are vulnerable to defeat until these bodies are resurrected and our salvation is complete. When we find ourselves in that place we should not be surprised. Some defeat is common to most Christian lives. The question is, "what are you going to do about it?" Don't feel condemned about being a defeated Christian. Convicted, yes – condemned, no.

Solomon knew where defeat came from (**because they have sinned against You**). Nothing can change in our Christian life until we realize defeat comes from us. Your trials or circumstances did not cause your defeat. Other Christians have gone through far worse and have emerged victorious. The problem is you. God may allow defeat as a gift to wake us up.

Solomon knew how to turn defeat into victory – you must turn back to God (**turn back to You**). Realize that in some way, you have turned away from Him and there is nothing more important than turning back to Him.

Then you must agree with God about who He is and what He thinks about your life (**confess Your name**). Change your thinking about whatever led you into defeat. Whether it was neglect of prayer, self-confidence, or not taking sin seriously – get God's mind on those things and confess the great name of God and He is right in all He does and thinks.

Finally, you must seek God passionately (**pray and make supplication to You**). He will reward the seeking heart; spend some extra – perhaps extraordinary – time in prayer and seeking God.

You held the cause of your defeat, but He holds the key to your victory. Seek God today!

May 21

The Gates of Hell

And I also say to you that you are Peter, and on this rock I will build My church, and the gates of Hades shall not prevail against it. (Matthew 16:18)

The dramatic statement of Jesus quoted above was made at Caesarea Philippi. It's important to understand that this was about 25 miles (46 km) north of the Galilee region, where Jesus lived and did most His preaching. Caesarea Philippi was not a Jewish-populated area; it was a center of pagan temples and worship.

Why did Jesus decide to go such a far distance and to such a pagan place to have an essential conversation with His disciples? This came during a season when crowds pressed in on Jesus more and more. He and the disciples were probably happy to get away to a place where Jesus wasn't known as much, and they could rest a bit.

Here Jesus promised Peter and the disciples that **the gates of Hades** would not prevail against His church. In the ancient world, the elders, judges, and rulers of the city often gathered at the city's gates. There they planned, decided, and made strategy. It is true that the plans and strategies of Hades (in this context, hell) would not and cannot prevail against Jesus' church.

Where Jesus chose to make this declaration is important – a large temple to the Roman god Pan who dominated Caesarea Philippi. The rear of the temple extended into a cave with a large crack or crevice in the floor of the cave. The pagan worshippers considered this large crack a portal to the underworld or a gate of Hades. Sacrifices were dropped down the crevice, and they waited for signs that the gods beneath received their sacrifice.

When Jesus said that the gates of Hades would not prevail against His church, one sense of it was to challenge the paganism of the Roman and Gentile world. Given the words and setting, it was as if Jesus said, "Just over there is the place where the pagans sacrifice to their idols, the place they consider the gates of Hades. None of that will prevail against My church, the community of My followers."

Up to then, the disciples mostly saw Jesus and His work as something among the Jewish people – and they thought of it that way for good reason. Jesus must have surprised them by challenging the old wineskin of the Judaism of His day and even the vast pagan world.

What began in an obscure corner of the Roman Empire came to spread over not only the Roman world but eventually all over the earth. Jesus wasn't content to merely reform the Jewish world of His day, but He would establish an unstoppable church (a community of His followers). Nothing could prevail against that community because it was His church that He built. Nothing can prevail against that community because it is His church that He builds.

Take joy in that today.

May 22

Fainting, Hoping

**My soul faints for Your salvation,
But I hope in Your word.
My eyes fail from searching Your word,
Saying, "When will You comfort me?"** (Psalm 119:81-82)

The psalmist spoke of the depth and desperation of seeking God. He said, **my soul faints for Your salvation**. His soul ached for God so much that it fainted in waiting for the salvation he needed – God's salvation, and nothing less.

The word **faints** has the idea of "coming to the end." It is the same verb in a slightly different form in Psalm 119:87: *They almost made an end of me*. Fainting is a loss of strength, a collapse. Here the psalmist felt his soul was so weak that it could not stand. He was not in despair because he told God that he had **hope in Your word**.

Being desperate yet not despairing is something known to the followers of God. The apostle Paul related this in 2 Corinthians 4:8-9: *We are hard pressed on every side, yet not crushed; we are perplexed, but not in despair; persecuted, but not forsaken; struck down, but not destroyed*. In it all, Paul could say, *we have the same spirit of faith* (2 Corinthians 4:13).

In contrast to the sense of weakness and failing, the psalmist found **hope** and strength in God's Word. This is the endurance of hope (1 Thessalonians 1:3), and the hope of salvation as a protective helmet (1 Thessalonians 5:8).

The singer of this psalm refused to give in to despair. There is nothing humble about despair; it is a twisted form of pride. When anyone doubts God's power to deliver them or gives self over to sin because they doubt God's power to work in their life, it is a strong example of setting self against God. Who are we to say that there is no hope for us when God promises there is?

The psalmist so diligently read and considered God's Word that he could say, **my eyes fail from searching Your word**. He studied so hard that his eyes hurt. One reason he loved God's Word so much was because he studied it so intently. God's Word yields its treasures to us in proportion to our seeking.

This was why the psalmist searched so diligently because he hoped to find **comfort** in his present distress. This sense of personal need is a greater motivation for diligent study than theological curiosity.

The psalmist knew there was **comfort** in God's Word and the promises found within. Yet sometimes the Word of God will lead us to rather practical answers to the question, **when will You comfort me?** In a sermon titled "God's Time for Comforting," Charles Spurgeon gave practical answers. Comfort will come when we do four things: Put away unbelief, finish our complaining, put away the sin that we tolerate, and fulfill the duties we have neglected.

Today, let God's Word lead you to His comfort.

May 23

Hands Stretched Out

And so it was, when Moses held up his hand, that Israel prevailed; and when he let down his hand, Amalek prevailed. But Moses' hands became heavy; so they took a stone and put it under him, and he sat on it. And Aaron and Hur supported his hands, one on one side, and the other on the other side; and his hands were steady until the going down of the sun. So Joshua defeated Amalek and his people with the edge of the sword. (Exodus 17:11-13)

The nomads of Amalek attacked Israel as they went through the wilderness, targeting their weak and helpless at the back of the huge procession. God ordered Israel to go to war against the Amalekites, and while Joshua led the battle, Moses supported the work in prayer. The fate of Israel in battle depended on Moses' intercession. In his early years, Moses thought the only way to win a battle was to fight. Now he would let Joshua fight, while Moses did more important work: pray for victory.

When Moses **held up his hand** it meant that he was in the Israelite posture of prayer, even as we might bow our heads and fold our hands. When Moses prayed, Israel won; when he stopped praying, Amalek prevailed. How could this be? How could life or death for Israel depend on the prayers of one man? God wants us to pray with that kind of passion, believing that life and death – perhaps eternally – may depend on our prayer.

It can be difficult to reconcile this with knowing God has a pre-ordained plan, but God didn't want Moses to concern himself with that – he was to pray because it really mattered. Just because we can't figure out how our prayers mesh with God's pre-ordained plan never means we should stop believing prayer matters.

Prayer is sometimes sweet and easy; other times it is hard work. This is why Paul describes the ministry of Epaphras as *always laboring fervently for you in prayers* (Colossians 4:12), and why Paul says we must *continue earnestly in prayer, being vigilant in it with thanksgiving* (Colossians 4:2).

The work of prayer was so important; the task was too big for just Moses. Aaron and Hur came alongside Moses and literally held his hands up in prayer; they helped him by partnering with him in intercession. He could not win the battle of prayer alone.

Because of this work of prayer, Israel was victorious over Amalek. If Moses, Aaron, and Hur had not done the work of prayer, the battle would not have been won and history would have been changed. Prayer matters. How much victory never happens because God's people will not pray?

Moses did pray, with his hands stretched out to God, and the battle was won. When Jesus accomplished His greatest victory over Satan, His hands were also stretched out on the cross.

Today, what battle is waiting to be won by your prayers?

May 24

Draw Near to God

Draw near to God and He will draw near to you. Cleanse your hands, you sinners; and purify your hearts, you double-minded. Lament and mourn and weep! Let your laughter be turned to mourning and your joy to gloom. Humble yourselves in the sight of the Lord, and He will lift you up. (James 4:8-10)

James, writing at the Holy Spirit's inspiration, gave us a remarkable promise: **Draw near to God and He will draw near to you.** The call to **draw near to God** is both an invitation and a promise. It is no good to submit to God's authority and to resist the devil's attack, and then fail to draw near to God. We have it as a promise: God will draw near to us as we draw near to Him.

Adam Clarke said it well: "When a soul sets out to seek God, God sets out to meet that soul; so that while we are drawing near to him, he is drawing near to us."

What does it mean to draw near to God? Charles Spurgeon considered a few ways:

- We draw near to God in worship, praise, and in prayer.
- We draw near to God when we ask counsel of Him.
- We draw near to God as we enjoy communion with Him.
- We draw near to God in the general course and experiences of life.

In one way, this text illustrates the difference between the old covenant and the new covenant. In the old covenant, God told Moses not to come closer to the burning bush and take off his shoes. Under the new covenant, God says to the sinner: "Draw near to Me and I will draw near to you." The ground between God and the sinner has been sprinkled with the blood of Jesus, and we can come close through that blood.

This shows what God wants to do for the sinner. It does not say, "Draw near to God and He will save you" or "Draw near to God and He will forgive you," though both are true. God wants to be near man, to have a close relationship and fellowship with the individual.

As James continued, he reminded us of an essential aspect of drawing near to God: **Cleanse your hands, you sinners; and purify your hearts, you double-minded. Lament and mourn and weep!** As we draw near to God, we will be convicted of our sin. So, we **lament and mourn and weep** as appropriate under the conviction of sin, and we are compelled to find cleansing at the cross.

James concludes the thought: **Humble yourselves in the sight of the Lord, and He will lift you up.** As we come as sinners before holy God (not as self-righteous religious people, as Jesus explained in Luke 18:10-14), we properly humble ourselves before God. Then He will lift us up, because God resists the proud, but gives grace to the humble, and grace – the undeserved favor of God – will always lift us up.

Today, get lifted up – by humbling yourself in the sight of God.

A Real Relationship

Truly our fellowship is with the Father and with His Son Jesus Christ. (1 John 1:3)

The idea of **fellowship** is an important concept in the Bible. In the New Testament, it translates the ancient Greek word *koinonia*, which speaks of sharing, communion, a common bond, and life. It has in mind a living, breathing, sharing, and loving relationship with another person.

In 1 John 1:3, John clearly and boldly said we can have **fellowship...with the Father and with His Son Jesus Christ**. To say one may have this kind of relationship with God was probably shocking to many of John's first readers, and it should also amaze us. The Greek mindset valued the idea of fellowship but restricted it to the human level – the concept of such a close relationship with God was revolutionary. In John's day, many people didn't know fellowship with God was either possible or desirable.

Jesus started the same kind of revolution among the Jews when He invited men to address God as *Father* (Matthew 6:9). We really can have a living, breathing connection with God **the Father**, and with **Jesus Christ**. He can be more than our Savior; He can also be our friend and our closest relationship.

For many people, this is unappealing. Sometimes it is because they don't know who God is. An invitation to a "personal relationship with God" is about as attractive to them as telling an eighth grader they can have a "personal relationship with the school principal." But when we know the greatness, the goodness, and the glory of God, we will want to have a relationship with Him.

Others may turn away from this relationship with God because they feel so distant from Him. They want a relationship with God, but they feel disqualified. Yet because of what Jesus did on the cross, God made it possible for us to draw near to Him. This is only possible because Jesus is who John says He is in 1 John 1:1-2: the eternal God. No one can have a genuine "spiritual" relationship with a dead person. But we can have a real relationship with the eternal God who became man.

In a sense, this relationship with God inspires His great plan for the ages. God's purpose in creating the world, with creating humans made in His image, allowing the fall of man, and bringing forth redemption, was all to have a real relationship with us. I wonder if God doesn't get frustrated sometimes, because sometimes we – like spoiled children – receive His gifts without wanting to spend time with Him and deepening our connection with Him.

But why would God want to have a relationship with me? Because He loves me. Why does He love me? Because He does. All the reasons are in Him, not in us.

Take some time today to quietly be in God's presence and ask Him to deepen your relationship with Him. It will fulfill the reason He created you.

May 26

A Different Kind of Righteousness

Whoever therefore breaks one of the least of these commandments, and teaches men so, shall be called least in the kingdom of heaven; but whoever does and teaches them, he shall be called great in the kingdom of heaven. For I say to you, that unless your righteousness exceeds the righteousness of the scribes and Pharisees, you will by no means enter the kingdom of heaven. (Matthew 5:19-20)

Jesus emphasized a correct understanding of God's law because it is essential for everyone to understand what God requires and what that understanding should guide us to do.

Jesus explained that anyone who **breaks** even **one of the least of these commandments** would **be called least in the kingdom of heaven**. We understand that we are to obey these commandments as explained and fulfilled by life and teaching of Jesus, not as in the legalistic thinking of the religious leaders Jesus spoke to. The law commanded sacrifice, but Jesus fulfilled this, so we don't run the danger of being called least in heaven's kingdom by not observing animal sacrifice.

Jesus wanted the citizens of His kingdom to know that the law remains essential. He reminded us that if anyone **does and teaches** God's commandments, **he shall be called great in the kingdom of heaven**. As a path for gaining a righteous standing before God, the Christian is done with the law. One passage that explains this is Galatians 2:21: *For if righteousness comes through the law, then Christ died in vain*. However, the law still stands as the perfect expression of God's ethical principles and the pattern of what He requires of man.

When we consider how carefully the scribes and Pharisees worked to keep the law as perfectly as they could, it might seem that we could never do what Jesus said we must. Jesus said that our **righteousness** must be *greater* than the **righteousness of the scribes and Pharisees**. We must do more than match their righteousness; we must exceed their righteousness or never enter the kingdom of heaven.

We can exceed their righteousness because our righteousness goes beyond that of the scribes and Pharisees in *kind*, not in *degree*. Paul describes the two kinds of righteousness in Philippians 3:6-9: *Concerning the righteousness which is in the law, [I was] blameless. But what things were gain to me, I have counted loss for Christ. But indeed, I count all things loss...that I may gain Christ, and be found in Him, not having my own righteousness, which is from the law, but that which is through faith in Christ, the righteousness which is from God by faith*.

The righteousness of the scribes and Pharisees was impressive to everyone who saw them – everyone except God. God could see the hypocrisy, pride, and self-focus that corrupted many of the good things they did. We aren't made righteous by keeping the law, but by the gift of Jesus' righteousness given to us and received by faith.

Be thankful that Jesus offers us a different kind of righteousness.

May 27

Almost an End

They almost made an end of me on earth, but I did not forsake Your precepts. Revive me according to Your lovingkindness, so that I may keep the testimony of Your mouth. (Psalm 119:87-88)

From time to time, we hear of people who have near-death experiences. We might say that the psalmist had his own near-death experience because he wrote **they almost made an end of me on earth**. In this section of Psalm 119, he cried out to God about his enemies, those who wished the worst for him.

Yet, notice his determination: **They almost made an end of me on earth, but I did not forsake Your precepts**. The point is emphasized by repetition. Nothing would make the psalmist forsake God's Word. He would cling to it in good times and in bad times.

There are many things that may cause a person to forsake the word of God in some way. It could be because of sinful compromise, or intellectual arrogance. It could come from mocking and persecution or a coldness of heart. Worldly distractions, love of material things, and chosen or allowed busyness can do this.

Many of us know the reality of most or all these things. Yet here, the psalmist was almost dead (**they almost made an end of me on earth**), yet he would not forsake the Word of God.

There is gold in that word **almost**. It reminds us that though our foes (especially our spiritual adversaries) may press for our destruction, God will preserve us. The Lord allows us to be attacked, yet at the same time, He sets a limit to the success of the attackers. **Almost** is a word of God's gracious protection.

The psalmist asked God to **revive** him **according to** God's own **lovingkindness**. He looked to God for a new life, for true revival. At the same time, the singer of this psalm knew that this was not deserved, even by someone as in love with God's Word as he was. Instead, he prayed **revive me according to Your lovingkindness**, and not according to what he deserved or what he had earned.

The psalmist spoke freely about his great love for God and His Word. Yet his trust was in the goodness and grace and lovingkindness of God, not in his love for God and His Word.

He then stated why he wanted this revived life: **So that I may keep the testimony of Your mouth**. Here the psalmist understood the purpose of a revived spirit within him. It wasn't merely to enjoy a season of spiritual excitement; it was for a more faithful, obedient walk with God. Many people look to revival as only a time of heightened spiritual excitement, which has little purpose other than to give people a sense of blessing and thrills. This mistaken idea of revival hinders the work of true revival.

Ask God for revival today – but do not ask because you deserve it, because you do not. Ask Him for revival so that you can better keep His Word.

May 28

Which Side Are You On?

You were perfect in your ways from the day you were created, till iniquity was found in you. By the abundance of your trading you became filled with violence within, and you sinned (Ezekiel 28:15-16a)

The Bible suggests that the beginning of evil was the rebellion of Satan. What was Satan's motive for rebellion? What triggered his proud rejection of God's authority? What was it specifically in the plan of God that Satan rebelled against?

Perhaps the occasion of Satan's rebellion came when he learned God's plan to create a completely different creature: Man. Satan would discover that humanity had a particular role in God's plan and a particular destiny.

- Man would be made lower than angels. (Psalm 8:5, Hebrews 2:7)
- Yet, angels would serve man. (Hebrews 1:14)
- Man would be made in the image and likeness of God (Genesis 1:26), something that is never said regarding angels.
- Redeemed men would be adopted in God's family and be made heirs with Him. (Romans 8:15-16; Galatians 4:4-7)
- One day, the redeemed will be glorified to a position above the angels, even being called kings and priests to God. (Revelation 1:6; 1 Corinthians 6:3)

It is not surprising that the most glorious being God created – Lucifer, the Day Star – would be offended by this. God first created glorious angelic beings, including Lucifer. Then, God's plan was to make strange "hybrid" beings – human beings. These beings would have spirits like angels, but bodies like animals. They would be lower than the angels, yet angels would have to serve them now, and one day they would be glorified above the angels. It makes some sense this plan would be an insult to Lucifer, and why he could find one-third of his fellow angelic beings to reject that plan.

Perhaps this is the reason why Satan rebelled against God. In the present day, we can't know for certain, because the Bible does not specifically tell us. But we do know Satan is permanently set against the purpose and plan of God, and we know Satan wants the opposite of God's planned relationship between men and angels.

Instead of angels serving man, Satan wants humanity to serve him. Through promoting sin and rebellion among men, Satan desires to obscure and deface the image of God in man. Satan seeks to keep as many as possible from being redeemed in Jesus so that they will not rule over him. Instead, they will be punished with him in Hell for eternity.

The question is simple – which side are you on? That isn't only an intellectual question; this question asks how you actually live. We can only be everything God wants us to be in Jesus, for He is the One who has ruined Satan, his power, and his schemes forever on our behalf. And we get to share in the victory!

Walk in it today – and look for ways to frustrate the devil's plans.

May 29
Imprisoned Angels

And the angels who did not keep their proper domain, but left their own abode, He has reserved in everlasting chains under darkness for the judgment of the great day. (Jude v. 6)

In warning Christians about dangerous people in their midst, Jude brought three examples before his readers. The examples were meant to show the certainty of judgment against these dangerous people, encouraging Christians to know that God and His cause would always win out in the end. In Jude v. 5 we read the first bad example: the rebellious children of Israel in the wilderness.

Jude v. 6 tells us of the second example of certain judgment: **the angels who did not keep their proper domain**. Jude's letter is famous for bringing up obscure or controversial points, and this is one of them. Jude wrote of angels who sinned, and who are now imprisoned and waiting a future day of judgment.

Who were these **angels who did not keep their proper domain** and therefore sinned? We only have two places in the Bible where it speaks of angels sinning. First, there is the original rebellion of some angels against God (Isaiah 14:12-14, Revelation 12:4). Second, there is the sin of the "sons of God" described in Genesis 6:1-2 – a controversial passage but consider an aspect of Jude v. 6 that is easy to agree on. These angels prompted God to uniquely imprison them. They are **reserved in everlasting chains under darkness for the judgment of the great day**. God judged these wicked angels, setting them in **everlasting chains**. Apparently, some fallen angels are in bondage while others are unbound and active among mankind as demons.

By not keeping their proper place, they are now kept in chains. Their sinful pursuit of freedom put them in bondage. In the same way, those who insist on freedom to do whatever they want are like these angels – so free that they are bound with everlasting chains! True freedom comes from obedience.

Consider this: If angels cannot break the chains sin brings on them, what make anyone think they can? Only Jesus can set captive humanity free.

This example teaches us two lessons. It assures us that those who cause trouble to the church will be judged, no matter what their spiritual status had been. These angels at one time stood in the immediate, glorious presence of God – and now they are in **everlasting chains**. If God judged the angels who sinned, He will surely judge those who deceive God's people. It also warns us that we also must continue walking with Jesus. If the past spiritual experience of these angels didn't guarantee their future spiritual state, then neither does ours. We must keep persevering and be on guard.

Don't get caught trusting in how things used to be with you and God. The imprisoned angels stand as examples of those who once enjoyed great privilege, but now are bound by their sin.

Today, how are things in your relationship with God?

May 30
Protection from the Proud

I have done justice and righteousness; do not leave me to my oppressors. Be surety for Your servant for good; do not let the proud oppress me. (Psalm 119:121-122)

It's easy to see pride – in other people. It isn't so easy to see it in us. When we see pride in others, it is often because they trouble us somehow. This was the problem of the psalmist.

He began by noting his own life: **I have done justice and righteousness**. This was not a claim to sinless perfection. It was confidence in the general righteousness of life. The psalmist knew he was dedicated to God, and his oppressors were not. The difference was in more than theology; it was in life. This confidence in one's spiritual condition and separation from those who didn't obey God is notable.

The psalmist asked God to defend and stand up for him, to **be surety** for him, a guarantee for his **good**. It was only through God defending him that he could avoid the oppression of the proud.

Those beautiful words, **be surety for Your servant** mean that he asked God to take up his interests and problems, and asked God to treat them as His problems. He wanted the proud people who troubled him to see that God was on his side.

This is evidence that his previous claim to justice and righteousness was not in an absolute sense. If he felt that he was completely just and righteous before God, he would not plead for God to stand as a surety for him – but he did. Even though he was upright, he still knew that he was a sinner before God and such a sinner that God must be his **surety**, his guarantee. He could not stand for himself; he needed God to stand for him.

The psalmist cried out to God as Job did: *Now put down a pledge for me with Yourself* (Job 17:3). The psalmist prayed that God would be to him what Jesus is to His people – a surety of the covenant, a guarantee of God's promise (Hebrews 7:22).

This was true for the psalmist in his present struggle, but it is also true in an even greater spiritual sense. The proudest creature ever to live is the devil himself, the father of all pride. Our proud accuser would crush us if the Lord Jesus had not stood between our spiritual enemy and us and become our promise of a better covenant.

He concludes by asking, **do not let the proud oppress me**. This verse (Psalm 119:122) is another rare example of a verse in Psalm 119 that does not mention God's Word in some way. It may be evidence of the tremendous mental and emotional anguish caused by the proud enemies of the psalmist. His eyes seem to be off the Bible and on his oppressors, but just for a moment.

Today, no matter how strong your adversaries, don't let them take your eyes off God and His Word!

May 31

Afraid and More Afraid

Therefore they cried out to the Lord and said, "We pray, O Lord, please do not let us perish for this man's life, and do not charge us with innocent blood; for You, O Lord, have done as it pleased You." So they picked up Jonah and threw him into the sea, and the sea ceased from its raging. Then the men feared the Lord exceedingly, and offered a sacrifice to the Lord and took vows. (Jonah 1:14-16)

It was a dreadful storm for the sailors on the ship headed to Tarshish. This storm was so fierce, so dark, and so evil that they knew it was more than a storm. It was the judgment of God on them all, or at least on *one* on board. Every man cried out to his god with all they had, knowing that only a miracle from the heavens could save them – or at least almost every man did. They found one sleepy stowaway, dragged him to the deck, and commanded him to pray to his God. Then someone thought, perhaps the wrath of God is on only one of us, and that one must pay for their sin so that the whole ship can be saved. Drawing straws, the short straw ended up in the hand of the sleepy stowaway. They found out he was a prophet on the run from the living God.

At that point, Jonah did a very brave thing. He offered to sacrifice himself for the sake of the perishing men on board the ship. He said, "Throw me in – let me bear the wrath of God and the sea, and you will be spared."

The sailors didn't want to throw Jonah into the sea because they believed his God was real and they feared throwing a prophet overboard. When all hope seemed lost, they took precautions (praying, **O Lord, please do not let us perish for this man's life, and do not charge us with innocent blood**) and threw Jonah into the sea.

Instantly, the sea ceased from raging. The sailors feared the Lord exceedingly, sacrificed to God, and made promises to serve Him. This pattern illustrates the salvation of every needy sinner when we examine the actions of the crew on this ship.

Why did Jonah ask to be thrown into the sea?

- Sinners, when they are tossed on the sea of conviction, make desperate efforts to save themselves.
- The fleshly efforts of awakened sinners must inevitably fail.
- The soul's sorrow will continue to increase if it relies on its own efforts.
- The way of safety for sinners is to be found in the sacrifice of another on their behalf.

You should know that the sacrifice of another on your behalf has turned away the wrath of God. If you have it received it, then by all means enjoy it as God's most precious gift to you and enduring proof of His great love.

June 1

What to Put On

Stand therefore, having girded your waist with truth, having put on the breastplate of righteousness, and having shod your feet with the preparation of the gospel of peace. (Ephesians 6:14-15)

The legions of ancient Rome were a powerful force, and they built a mighty empire around the Mediterranean Sea that extended to northern Europe. One reason the armies of Rome were so victorious was that they were well equipped. Like a modern soldier, the soldiers of ancient Rome wore armor that made them effective fighters.

In Ephesians 6, the apostle Paul described the spiritual armor that prepares the Christian to succeed in living the Christian life. Paul made analogies from the material world to the spiritual world, using the example of the armor worn by a Roman soldier. At the time Paul wrote this letter to the Ephesians, he saw a lot of Roman soldiers. He wrote this from his Roman imprisonment, as Roman soldiers guarded him. The connection between the Roman armor and the spiritual armor was a natural comparison for Paul to make.

Paul divided his description of this spiritual armor into two sections. First, he wrote about the armor to have, and then about the armor to take. The **breastplate of righteousness** is the second item listed, and it is one of the parts of the armor to have – that is, we keep it on, we have it always, as something constant in our life and experience. Using the connection Paul made, this means that we are to keep God's righteousness on us just as a Roman soldier kept his breastplate on him.

Note it well: righteousness is represented as a breastplate that provides essential protection for the most vital organs. We need God's righteousness to live as Christians. We can no sooner battle against spiritual enemies in our righteousness than a soldier can effectively fight without his breastplate.

This is not our own earned righteousness, not a feeling of righteousness, but righteousness received by faith in Jesus. It supplies a general sense of confidence and awareness of our standing and position. We know that our standing with God is based on who Jesus is and what He did, instead of who we are and what we have done. We put on the breastplate of righteousness by choosing to trust in Jesus but putting our faith in Him. Then – and only then – does this breastplate protect us.

As Martyn Lloyd-Jones wrote, "Thank God for experiences, but do not rely on them. You do not put on the 'breastplate of experiences,' you put on the breastplate of 'righteousness.'"

We are sometimes tempted to say to the devil, "Look at all I have done for the Lord." Sometimes it makes us feel good to say it, but that is shaky ground because feelings and experiences are always changing. God's righteousness does not change.

The breastplate of righteousness received from God is your essential protection.

Today, trust in the righteousness of God, not your own.

June 2

A Spiritual Sword

Above all, taking the shield of faith with which you will be able to quench all the fiery darts of the wicked one. And take the helmet of salvation, and the sword of the Spirit, which is the word of God. (Ephesians 6:16-18)

One by one, the apostle Paul used the pieces of a Roman soldier's fighting armor to illustrate important spiritual truths and principles.

- Truth is like the thick leather belt.
- Righteousness is like the metal breastplate.
- The gospel is like the sturdy sandals or shoes.
- Faith is like the large shield.
- Salvation is like the essential helmet.

Then, as the last spiritual analogy, Paul likened the Roman soldier's sword to be like the Word of God. He even calls God's Word **the sword of the Spirit**.

The idea is both simple and powerful: that the Holy Spirit provides a sword for you, and that sword is the **word of God**. To effectively use **the sword of the Spirit**, we can't regard the Bible as a book of magic charms or tie a Bible around our neck the way make-believe legends say garlic will drive away vampires.

To effectively use the sword, we must regard it as the **word of God**, as Paul wrote: **which is the word of God**. If we are not confident in the divine inspiration of Scripture and that the sword came from the Holy Spirit, then we will not use it effectively.

But we must also take **the sword of the Spirit** in the sense of depending on His help to use it. Not only did the Spirit give us the Scriptures but also, He makes them alive to us and equips us with the right thrust of the sword at the right time.

Think of a soldier or a gladiator in training, practicing sword thrusts, moves, and techniques. He must practice them ahead of time, and if he is a superior fighter with great fighting instincts, at the time of battle, he will instantly recall which move suits the precise moment. He will never be able to use the move in the fight if he has not first practiced it, yet he still needs to make a move at the moment.

Effectively using the sword takes practice. The great example of this was Jesus combating the temptation of Satan in the wilderness. Jesus could use **the sword of the Spirit** at the decisive moment because he had worked with it beforehand. In the same way, our study and interest in God's Word prepare us to use its truth and principles at the crucial moment. At the point of need, we can answer every lie that comes from the world, the flesh, and the devil with God's truth from heaven.

In those times, **the sword of the Spirit** – the **word of God** – is our offensive, attacking weapon, the only one given among the believer's complete spiritual armor.

June 3
Boldness in the Day of Judgment

Love has been perfected among us in this: that we may have boldness in the day of judgment; because as He is, so are we in this world. (1 John 4:17)

Have you ever stood before a judge? It is an intimidating experience. Just standing before a traffic court judge, or a small-claims court judge, has been enough to make my heart beat faster and my voice tremble.

But there is coming a day when everyone will have to stand before a far more important judge. If it is hard to have boldness before a human judge in an earthly court, how could anyone hope to be bold before God on the day of judgment? As amazing as it sounds, John tells us how we can have **boldness in the day of judgment**.

God's love works in us, and that work will be proven in the day of judgment. As much as we can know the completeness of God's love now, we will know it then even more. You may know you are a sinner now; you will know it more on the day of judgment. You may know now you are not better in yourself than those going to hell; you will know it more on the day of judgment. You may know the greatness of Jesus' salvation now; you will really know it on the day of judgment.

The work of God's love is so great that **we may have boldness in the day of judgment**. We might be satisfied to merely survive on the day of judgment, but God wants so to fill our lives with His love and His truth that we may have **boldness** on that day.

The Bible says one day, all humanity will gather before God's Great White Throne and face judgment. This day is coming; it is just as fixed in God's eternal calendar as any other day in world history. On that day, how could anyone have boldness? We can imagine Jesus being bold before the throne of God, but not us. Yet, if "we abide in Him, and He in us" (1 John 4:13), then our identity is bound up in Jesus: **as He is, so are we in the world**.

Think about it. How is Jesus now? He is glorified, justified, forever righteous and bold, sitting at the right hand of God the Father. Spiritually, we can have that same standing now, while we are in the world, because **as He is, so are we in the world**.

Indeed, this glory is in us now just in seed form; it has not yet fully developed into what it will be. But it is there, and its presence is demonstrated by our love for one another and our agreement with God's truth – and that all serves to give us boldness!

Does this boldness on the day of judgment seem impossible? God's love in your life can assure you of it right now.

Receiving Wisdom from God

If any of you lacks wisdom, let him ask of God, who gives to all liberally and without reproach, and it will be given to him. But let him ask in faith, with no doubting, for he who doubts is like a wave of the sea driven and tossed by the wind. For let not that man suppose that he will receive anything from the Lord; he is a double-minded man, unstable in all his ways. (James 1:5-8)

In every trial and difficulty of life, we need wisdom from God. We need to know if it is God's will for us to *escape* the difficulty, or if God wants us to *endure* the difficulty. That knowledge doesn't come easily, so we need wisdom from God.

Here James says that to receive wisdom, we simply **ask of God** – the one who gives wisdom to us generously, without despising us for asking. We also remember that God has given us the foundation for all wisdom in His Word. Our seeking after God's wisdom must always begin and end in the Bible; if we think God is guiding us any other way it must always be consistent with what He has already told us in the Bible.

We have this promise from God in James 1. Yet sometimes we feel that we ask God for wisdom, but we don't receive it. Why does that happen?

Our asking for wisdom must be made like any other request – we must ask in faith, without doubting God's ability or desire to give us His wisdom. For example, when we seek wisdom in the Bible, we must believe that what we read is God's Word, and we must believe that it speaks to us today.

When we come to God in faith, He is always ready to receive us. Don't be afraid to come to Him too often; God always wants to add new blessings to what He has given us before. Do you serve the god of the clenched fist or the God of the open hand?

If we come to God without faith, we have no foundation before Him. So, we are unstable and shouldn't expect to receive from Him. Are your doubts and fears hindering you before God? Be like the man we read about in Mark 9:24 who came to Jesus and said, *Lord, I believe; help my unbelief.* That man was not double-minded; he desired to believe, and he asserted his belief. Yet at the same time, he felt the inadequacy of his faith, so he asked Jesus for help so that he could trust Jesus the way he wanted to.

God is always ready to help our faith. What we need to do is come to Him with what faith we have, and humbly ask Him to give us more.

Today, take comfort in knowing that you can come to the God of the open hand, and not to the god of the clenched fist.

June 5
As the Rain Comes Down

For as the rain comes down, and the snow from heaven, and do not return there, but water the earth, and make it bring forth and bud, that it may give seed to the sower and bread to the eater, so shall My word be that goes forth from My mouth; it shall not return to Me void, but it shall accomplish what I please, and it shall prosper in the thing for which I sent it. (Isaiah 55:10-11)

When you think about this passage from Isaiah 55, every drop of rain is a reminder of God's beautiful promise: **For as the rain comes down.**

Using the figure of the water cycle, the Lord illustrated the essential principle that His Word **shall not return to Me void, but it shall accomplish what I please.** Rain and snow come down from heaven and don't return before serving their purpose on earth (they **water the earth, and make it bring forth and bud**). The rain and snow eventually do return to heaven, but not before accomplishing their purpose on earth. Even so, when He sends it down from heaven, God's Word doesn't return to Him void. Instead, it always fulfills His purpose on earth.

God is not just "all talk." The word of the Lord has power, and it never fails to accomplish His intended purpose.

God uses the rain from the sky to make plants **bring forth and bud** and the result is that will **give seed to the sower and bread to the eater**. These pictures illustrate the operation of God's Word, showing that God's Word brings forth fruit. It also indicates that the fruit has many different applications. The same grain that gives seed to the sower also provides bread to the eater.

The result is that God proclaims that His Word will **accomplish** what pleases Him. God's Word has something to **accomplish**. God doesn't just speak to hear Himself talk. His Word is not empty, nor does it lack in power. This also means that God's Word has a purpose. He didn't speak in unfathomable mysteries to confuse us or leave things up to any possible interpretation. When God speaks, He speaks to accomplish a purpose.

So, God can confidently say, **it shall prosper in the thing for which I sent it**. God's Word doesn't just merely get the job done. It shall **prosper** in the purpose God has for it. It is rich and full of life. God's Word always succeeds and always fulfills God's purpose.

This doesn't mean that it doesn't matter how God's Word is presented. Sometimes a terrible sermon has been excused by saying, "God's Word doesn't return void." The principle is clear and true from Isaiah's passage, but it is possible that because of the preacher's poor preparation or preaching, there may be little of God's Word put forth. The preacher can ignore, dilute, or obscure God's Word.

When little goes forth, that little will succeed – but how much better if more of the whole counsel of God went forth to succeed!

Let God's powerful word bear fruit in your life today.

June 6
The Wrong Way to Pray

And when you pray, do not use vain repetitions as the heathen do. For they think that they will be heard for their many words. Therefore do not be like them. For your Father knows the things you have need of before you ask Him. (Matthew 6:7-8)

In this section of the Sermon on the Mount, Jesus continued to teach His disciples – and us – the right way to pray. First, Jesus rebuked those who prayed more to be seen of men than to be heard by God. Now, Jesus exposes the wrong type of prayer that some people use: thoughtless repetition.

Jesus said, **when you pray, do not use vain repetitions**. The right kind of prayer does not use **vain repetitions**, which is any prayer made up of many words and little meaning; it is prayer that is all on the lips and not from the mind or heart.

The religious customs in the days of Jesus promoted the idea of praying long prayers just for the sake of praying long prayers. With this kind of religious environment, it does not surprise us that Jesus warned against prayers that were long just to be long.

One can pray long – but to the wrong god. In 1 Kings 18:26, Baal's prophets cried out, *O Baal, answer us* for half the day. In Acts 19:34, a mob in Ephesus shouted, *Great is Artemis of the Ephesians* for two hours. The true God is not impressed by the length or eloquence of prayer, but by truth faith and trust in God as we pray.

When we try to impress God (or people) with our many words, we deny that God is a loving, yet holy Father. Instead, we should follow the counsel of Ecclesiastes 5:2: *God is in heaven, and you are on earth; therefore let your words be few.*

The New International Version translates the words **vain repetitions** as "keep on babbling." That may be an accurate sense of the ancient Greek word *battalogeo*, a word that sounds like "babbling" and has the sense of "blah-blah-blah." This is just how some Christians pray: with a lot of "blah-blah-blah" to God.

Jesus told us to remember: **Your Father knows the things you have need of before you ask Him**. We don't pray to tell God things that He didn't know before we told Him. We pray to remind ourselves of our great need, to prompt and express our faith, to raise our soul from earth to heaven, and to commune with and appeal to a loving God who wants us to bring every need and worry before His throne.

In the following verses, Jesus explained the right way to pray. Yet before we can embrace the good, we must put away the bad – and when it comes to prayer that includes prayer that believes it can impress God merely with its length, and with prayer that uses empty repetition.

Having put those aside, you are ready to learn the right way to pray.

June 7

The Unappreciated Virtue

Blessed are the meek, for they shall inherit the earth. (Matthew 5:5)

With this third beatitude, Jesus proclaimed the blessedness of meekness. The gospel writer recorded the ancient Greek word *praus*. According to many (including the great Greek scholar William Barclay), it is impossible to translate this ancient Greek word *praus* with just one English word. It has the ideas of the proper balance between anger and indifference; of a powerful personality properly controlled; and of humility.

In the vocabulary of the ancient Greek language, the **meek** person was not passive or easily pushed around. The main idea behind the word **meek** was strength under control, like a strong horse trained to do a job instead of running wild. But the idea of being trained to do a job and serving others doesn't appeal to everyone. In general, the ancient Greeks thought that meekness was a fault and not a virtue.

Jesus went against the thinking of the culture of His day and said, **blessed are the meek**. Jesus knew something that the culture of His day did not: that there is a difference between true meekness and slave-like bondage; true meekness means freedom – freedom from hatred and vengeance.

To be **meek** means to show a willingness to submit and work under proper authority. It also shows a willingness to disregard one's own "rights" and privileges. It is one thing for me to admit my own spiritual bankruptcy, but what if someone else does it for me? Do I react meekly?

This blessed one is meek. They are meek before God, in that they submit to His will and conform to His Word. They are meek before men, in that they are strong – yet also humble, gentle, patient, and longsuffering.

We can only be meek, willing to control our desire for our rights and privileges because we are confident God watches out for us, that He will protect our cause. The promise **they shall inherit the earth** proves that God will not allow His meek ones to end up on the short end of the deal.

We might think that the meek would be devoured and run out of the world, but **they shall inherit the earth**. The wolves eat the sheep, but there are still many more sheep in the world than wolves, and the sheep keep multiplying and feeding in green pastures. The meek man or woman looks at the earth and realizes that it all belongs to the God who is his or her Father; and if it all belongs to their Father, it also belongs to them because they are heirs of God and joint heirs with Jesus Christ (Romans 8:17).

In this sense, we can have it all – we can inherit the earth, but only as God works in us and we are poor in spirit, mourning under our spiritual poverty, and properly meek before God and man.

Thank God – as truly meek ones in Him, you can inherit the earth.

June 8
Knowing but Not Knowing

So David's anger was greatly aroused against the man, and he said to Nathan, "As the LORD lives, the man who has done this shall surely die! And he shall restore fourfold for the lamb, because he did this thing and because he had no pity." (2 Samuel 12:5-6)

The man after God's heart – King David – endured a year of his heart chilling towards God. The psalmist of Israel was silent, conscious of his sin but not truly convicted of it. God mercifully reached from heaven and prompted David's friend, the prophet Nathan, to come and tell him a story.

A rich man with many sheep stole the dear lamb of his poor neighbor simply because he couldn't say "no" to his greedy impulses. When he heard this, **David's anger was greatly aroused**. Nathan didn't ask David for a judicial decision, and David assumed the story was true. David immediately passed sentence on the thief. Though David was guilty of a far greater crime than lamb-stealing, he had no trouble passing a harsh sentence on someone guilty of a lesser crime. David did what most of us do at one time or another – we try to clear our guilty consciences by passing judgment on someone else.

David's sense of righteous indignation was so affected by his own guilt that he commanded a death sentence, even though stealing a lamb wasn't a death-sentence crime. David's use of the oath **as the LORD lives** shows he called God to witness the righteousness of his sentence on the rich man.

In condemning the man's sin, David condemned himself. When David later saw this, it was an important step in his restoration. David had to condemn his own sin before he could find forgiveness. We often try to find refuge in excusing, minimizing, or deflecting the blame of our sin and we do not condemn sin in ourselves.

David said, **he shall restore fourfold for the lamb**. This shows that David knew the truth about repentance. David knew that penalizing the rich man – even with death – wasn't enough. The guilty man also had to **restore** something to the man he stole from. True repentance means restitution.

David's sin and hardness of heart did not diminish his knowledge of the Bible and what it says about those who steal sheep: *If a man steals an ox or a sheep, and slaughters it or sells it, he shall restore five oxen for an ox and four sheep for a sheep* (Exodus 22:1). David knew the words of the Bible but was distant from the Author.

A person can be a Bible scholar yet still be out of fellowship with the Author of the Bible. Knowing the words of truth doesn't necessarily mean that you know the God of truth. David had to bring his relationship with God back into line with his knowledge of God.

Today, bring your relationship with God in greater alignment with the truth about God.

June 9

God of the Second Chance

Now the word of the L<small>ORD</small> came to Jonah the second time, saying, "Arise, go to Nineveh, that great city, and preach to it the message that I tell you." (Jonah 3:1-2)

It's hard to find a more wonderful line in the Bible than this: **Now the word of the L<small>ORD</small> came to Jonah the second time**. This shows the amazing love of God to His wayward people. Though Jonah did everything he could to resist the first call of God after Jonah repented God called him again – though God was under no obligation to do it. He did it out of mercy and grace.

This is especially remarkable when we remember how the Book of Jonah began: *Now the word of the L<small>ORD</small> came to Jonah the son of Amittai, saying, "Arise, go to Nineveh, that great city, and cry out against it; for their wickedness has come up before Me"* (Jonah 1:1-2). Do you see the similarity? First, *the word of the L<small>ORD</small> came to Jonah*. Then, **Now the word of the L<small>ORD</small> came to Jonah a second time**. Thank God for that second time!

Many of us who believe God has given us a word to bring to others are especially thankful for that **second time** – or the one-hundred-and-second time! This is pure grace from God. He has every right to exclude us and never use us again when we fail, but He is the God of the second chance and the one-hundred-and-second chance.

A city needed to be reached, so God raised up one man – and by amazing persistence and amazing grace He made that one man qualified to do the job. Notice what God told Jonah to do the second time: **Preach to it the message that I tell you**. In Jonah 1, God told the prophet to *cry out against Nineveh*, but this time God told Jonah to go there and wait for further instructions. God often works this way, and our stubborn nature finds it irritating. We want it all explained long before we take the first step, but God often doesn't deal with us that way.

In fact, the story of Jonah demonstrates why God so often leads us one step at a time without telling us more. When God told Jonah what he would say in Nineveh, Jonah rejected the call. God often only tells us what we can handle at the moment.

We commonly thank God for His Word and what He shows us. When was the last time you thanked Him for what He *didn't* tell you? Sometimes His greatest kindness is shown by what God doesn't say because He knows we aren't ready to receive it.

Today, spend some time thanking God for all the second chances He has given you. Then, spend some more time thanking Him for the things He has mercifully not revealed to you.

Trust this today: Your heavenly Father really does know best.

June 10
A Song of Salvation

Behold, God is my salvation, I will trust and not be afraid; "For Yah, the Lord, is my strength and song; He also has become my salvation." (Isaiah 12:2)

Isaiah chapter 11 spoke powerfully of the reign of the Messiah as king over all the earth. Now, in Isaiah 12, we have a chapter of praise coming from the heart of one that has surrendered to the Messiah as king, and who enjoys the benefits of His reign.

The song begins with **behold**. It is an invitation to see what the worshipper sees. Isaiah is excited about what God has done in his life and invites all to behold the work of the Lord.

Then he declares, **God is my salvation**. To say God is my salvation is also to say, "I am not my own salvation. My good works, my good intentions, my good thoughts do not save me. God is my salvation." Many don't ever feel the need for salvation. Instead, they think their lives are fine, and they come to God for a little help when they feel the need for it. But they never see themselves as drowning men in need of rescue or as hell-destined sinners in need of salvation.

The worshipper declares: **I will trust and not be afraid**. This is the peace and security that comes from knowing that **God is my salvation**. When God is our salvation, we can **trust and not be afraid**. The apostle Paul repeated the same idea when he wrote in Romans 5:1: *Therefore, having been justified by faith, we have peace with God through our Lord Jesus Christ*. The place of peace and trust and "no fear" comes only from seeing our salvation in God, and not ourselves.

The worshipper emphasizes the idea, **I will trust and not be afraid**. This confidently reflects the choice of the worshipper. He is deciding to **trust and not be afraid**. There are feelings of trust, but those are different than the decision to trust. We can say to our will, **I will trust and not be afraid**. There is no place in the Bible where it says, "feel and believe"; instead, it simply tells us to put our faith in Jesus Christ. Don't wait for the feelings you think you should have with faith; instead proclaim **I will trust**.

The worshipper continued, **for Yah, the Lord, is my strength and my song**. The Lord is not only the worshipper's salvation; He is also his **strength** and **song**. Some consider the Lord their salvation in a distant "someday-I'll-make-it-to-heaven" way rather than taking Him as their **strength** and **song** now.

When the Lord is our **strength**, it means that He is our resource; He is our refuge. We look to Him for our needs and are never unsatisfied. When the Lord is our **song**, it means that He is our joy and our happiness. We find our purpose and life in Him, and He never disappoints.

You can make this your song too.

June 11
Learning from Others

"Hear and testify against the house of Jacob," says the Lord God, the God of hosts, "That in the day I punish Israel for their transgressions, I will also visit destruction on the altars of Bethel; and the horns of the altar shall be cut off and fall to the ground. I will destroy the winter house along with the summer house; the houses of ivory shall perish, and the great houses shall have an end," says the Lord. (Amos 3:13-15)

If ever there was a prophet with a social conscience, it was Amos. This sheepherder from ancient Israel looked at the greed and materialism that marked his age and spoke out boldly against the rich who oppressed the poor and promised that God would judge them for their greed.

It is easy to think that because we perform some religious ceremony that we will be spared judgment. Think of a greedy, selfish man who cheats and steals to gain and maintain his wealth. The greedy man tells himself that God gives him a free pass on such sins because he regularly attends church. "God is pleased by my religious observance," he thinks. But he is blind to the fact that a religious facade cannot cover over a corrupt life.

The greedy in ancient Israel found refuge in their religious observance, but God saw right through it. They would not find refuge in their idol worship. Instead, the altars of dedication to idols would be destroyed by God's judgment. When we build a place of idolatry, we invite God to destroy it. The horns of the altar at each corner and were thought to represent the "strength" of the altar, just as horns represent the "strength" of an animal.

It is easy to think that because we have wealth that we spared from God's judgment. The greedy man looks at his big house and his fancy car and believes that somehow these things protect him from the troubles others may endure. He tells himself that his material prosperity is God's mark of approval and that it is his security against a coming calamity.

To these greedy men who trusted in their wealth, God said through Amos: **The great houses shall have an end**. God's judgment would not stop at places of idol worship; it would also extend to places built and enjoyed through oppression and robbery.

We live in a greedy and materialistic age, but most of us think that we could never be judged for such things. It's a matter of the heart much more than a matter of the bank account. The important thing for us to do is to learn from the warnings that others received, instead of only learning from our own judgment.

We should learn from God's warning to the greedy and materialistic people in ancient Israel through the prophet Amos.

We should get right with God now because we can't find refuge in religious appearance or in our own material success.

June 12

The Doctor Is In

Those who are well have no need of a physician, but those who are sick. I did not come to call the righteous, but sinners, to repentance. (Mark 2:17)

Jesus was accused of associating with sinners, and worst of all – at least the worst to His critics – the sinners liked being with Jesus! The scene here in Mark 2 was a going-away party thrown by Matthew, who was a new disciple of Jesus who quit his job as a tax collector. Matthew – also known as Levi – invited all his friends to meet Jesus before he left home to follow the Master. In his circle of friends, Matthew had a lot of tax collectors and notorious sinners, but when these people met Jesus many of them also wanted to follow Him (Mark 2:15). This association with sinners outraged the religious leaders, and when they accused Jesus of being a sinner because of it all, the Son of God answered with cool, unanswerable logic: a doctor should be among the sick.

This gives us a lot to think about. Jesus, the great physician, is our doctor. Our disease is sin. As a doctor, Jesus receives new patients; so, why don't more people come to Him?

Some sick people don't know they are sick. You can feel fine, yet still be in critical condition because of the disease of sin. Jesus performs an MRI scan on us – a Moral Resonance Image – and finds that we don't measure to God's standard. We need the doctor, and the doctor is in.

Some sick people think they will get better on their own. They trust in the power of their bodies to heal themselves. Our bodies can do amazing things, but we can never heal ourselves of the sin disease. We need a doctor, and the doctor is in.

Some sick people don't know that a doctor can help them. Perhaps they have been to a few bad doctors and are discouraged with all doctors. But Jesus isn't just any doctor; He is the Great Physician. We need a doctor, and the doctor is in.

Some sick people don't go to the doctor because they can't pay the bill. Some doctors charge a lot of money. But Jesus is the greatest doctor because He is always available, He always makes a perfect diagnosis, He provides a complete cure, and He even pays the bill!

Some sick people don't go to the doctor because they know what the doctor will tell them to do, and they just don't want to do it. So, they put it off, and tell themselves they really will make an appointment someday, and get that sin thing looked at, and so forth. But at the end of it all, they never come to the great physician. You can say a lot about that, but you certainly cannot say that it is the doctor's fault. We need a doctor, and the doctor is in.

Jesus, the Great Physician, is ready to see you now!

June 13
Waiting for a Promise

And being assembled together with them, He commanded them not to depart from Jerusalem, but to wait for the Promise of the Father, "which," He said, "you have heard from Me; for John truly baptized with water, but you shall be baptized with the Holy Spirit not many days from now." (Acts 1:4-5)

Right before He ascended to heaven, Jesus commanded His disciples to stay in Jerusalem. Remaining there, they were to wait for the coming of the Holy Spirit (here called the **Promise of the Father**). Jesus knew that they really could do nothing effective for the kingdom of God until the Spirit came on them.

Jesus commanded them to wait, and there is much meaning in that command.

- To wait means the Father's promise of the Holy Spirit was worth waiting for.
- To wait means they must receive the Spirit; they couldn't create an experience themselves.
- To wait means they would be tested by waiting, at least a little.

It is significant that this coming, filling, and empowering of the Holy Spirit was called the **Promise of the Father**. Even though there is a sense in which this was now also the promise of the Son of God, there is meaning in the phrase, the **Promise of the Father**.

- It shows that we should wait for it with eager anticipation because a Promise of the Father who loves us so much can only be good.
- It shows that it is reliable and can be counted on; a loving and powerful Father would never Promise something that He could not fulfill.
- It shows that this Promise belongs to all His children since it comes from God as our Father.
- It shows that it must be received by faith, as is the pattern with the promises of God throughout the Bible.

Jesus explained more about this Promise when He added: **you shall be baptized with the Holy Spirit**. Being baptized is to be immersed in or covered over in something. Even as John baptized people in water, these disciples would be "immersed" in the Holy Spirit.

When would it happen? As Jesus said this right before He ascended to heaven, He added: **Not many days from now**. They knew that this Promise of the Father would come, but not immediately. It would be days away, but not many days.

Jesus had a purpose in not telling them exactly when it would come. One objective was so the disciples would learn to wait in expectant faith. Even so, we should resist "creating" a move of the Spirit. Instead, we trust the Promise of the Father and have expectant faith regarding the outpouring of the Holy Spirit in our life.

The real move of the Holy Spirit is worth it.

June 14

Like Dross

You reject all those who stray from Your statutes, for their deceit is falsehood. You put away all the wicked of the earth like dross; therefore I love Your testimonies. My flesh trembles for fear of You, and I am afraid of Your judgments. (Psalm 119:118-120)

The author of Psalm 119 loved the Word of God. He read the Scriptures, prayed them, thought deeply on them, and did his best to live and obey them. Yet his time with the Scriptures taught him a sometimes-uncomfortable truth: that God is a righteous judge, and it is part of His character to judge evil and evildoers, eventually.

That's why he wrote, **You reject all those who stray from Your statutes**. The psalmist here saw the righteous judgment of God. He understood that God uses His Word (**statutes**) as a measuring line for His judgment and will eventually reject all who depart from His Word and the principles it reveals.

Then, with his mind on God's judgments, he used a picture to communicate the idea: **You put away all the wicked of the earth like dross**. This shows us that the judgments of God have a purifying purpose and effect. He will cleanse the earth from the wicked, treating them **like dross** – as impurities that need to be removed.

Dross is the scum layer that floats to the top of melted precious metal when it is refined. The metalsmith heats the gold or silver into a liquid and keeps heating it. At just the right temperature, the dross comes to the surface and is carefully scraped away.

In many ways, sin is like dross. Dross takes away from the shine and glory of metal; it makes it dull. Dross is deceptive: it is not silver, but it seems like it; it is not gold, but it looks like it. Dross is not made better by the fire; the fire helps remove the dross, not improve it. Dross is worthless. It has no real value or purpose. Dross is damaging to metal because it brings an opportunity for rust. Metal with dross in it will be eaten away.

With the thought of the eventual judgment of the wicked, the psalmist responded: **Therefore I love Your testimonies**. When the author of Psalm 119 thought about these righteous judgments, it made him praise God even more. He gave glory to God and His Word (**Your testimonies**) as righteous measures of judgment.

It also made him think about his own life: My flesh trembles for fear of You, and I am afraid of Your judgments. As the psalmist considered God's righteous judgments, he looked to his own life and understood that it was not entirely righteous. Ideally, this sense of trembling fear made him run to God for His promise of an atoning, covering sacrifice.

The psalmist didn't celebrate the judgment of the wicked; it made him tremble in holy fear himself.

That's something wise for all of us.

June 15
Total Winners

For whatever is born of God overcomes the world. And this is the victory that has overcome the world; our faith. Who is he who overcomes the world, but he who believes that Jesus is the Son of God? (1 John 5:4-5)

We would think it strange if the child of wealthy parents was poor, or if the child of tiny parents grew to be very large. We expect children to follow, at least in some way, after their parents. It's the same way with those who are born of God. John wants us to see that if we are born of God, we will overcome the world. The idea that the world could defeat anything born of God seemed strange to John, and it should also seem strange to us.

How do we become overcomers? By faith. The one who **believes** in the true Jesus is the one who **overcomes the world**. The life of abiding faith and trust in Jesus Christ is the life that overcomes the pressures and temptations of the world. As we know who Jesus is – not just as a matter of facts or information, but also as food for life – He will fill our soul so powerfully that this world's temptations no longer have the same power over us. Those temptations are still there, but we are different people.

This means we overcome because of who we are in Jesus, not because of what we do. We overcome because we are **born of God**, and we are born of God because we believe **that Jesus is the Son of God**. We believe this in more than an intellectual sense, but we place our lives on the fact that Jesus is the Son of God.

To be one who overcomes the world is a big idea. In what ways are we world-overcomers in Jesus?

First, Jesus said, *In the world you will have tribulation; but be of good cheer, I have overcome the world* (John 16:33). Because Jesus has overcome the world, as we abide in Him, we are overcomers in Jesus.

Second, John said of those growing in their walk with Jesus: *You have overcome the wicked one* (1 John 2:13-14). As we walk with Jesus and grow in that walk, we will overcome our spiritual opposition – the devil, that wicked one, with all his agents.

Overcomers have a special place in the world to come. Jesus promised, *To him who overcomes I will grant to sit with Me on My throne, as I also overcame and sat down with My Father on His throne* (Revelation 3:21). This is a privileged reward.

Finally, overcomers overcome because the blood of Jesus overcomes Satan's accusations, the word of their testimony overcomes Satan's deceptions, and loving not their lives overcomes Satan's violence (as in Revelation 12:11).

Jesus is the complete winner, and the good news is He shares His victory with believers. As you live your lives in Him, you can't lose.

The Character of Heavenly Wisdom

But the wisdom that is from above is first pure, then peaceable, gentle, willing to yield, full of mercy and good fruits, without partiality and without hypocrisy. Now the fruit of righteousness is sown in peace by those who make peace. (James 3:17-18)

In pressing the need for all Christians to live with wisdom – but especially teachers and leaders among God's people – James exposed the bad results from earthly wisdom. Here he made the contrast of earthly wisdom with heavenly wisdom, **the wisdom that is from above**.

Earthly wisdom has its results, but God's wisdom also has fruit. James here defined what he meant by the meekness of wisdom back in James 3:13.

This wisdom is **first pure, then peaceable, gentle, willing to yield, full of mercy and good fruits, without partiality and without hypocrisy**. The character of this wisdom is wonderful. It is full of love and a giving heart, consistent with the holiness of God.

This wisdom is **first pure**. The idea here is not so much of sexual purity, but wisdom free from sinful attitudes or motives.

This wisdom is then **peaceable**. According to one commentator, this word has a royal association; the wisdom of a great king who has the right to make war but chooses peace and kindness.

This wisdom is **gentle**. William Barclay said this was the man who knew how to forgive when strict justice gave him the perfect right to condemn.

This wisdom is **willing to yield**. It is not stubborn; it knows when to bend and to respond to an appeal.

This wisdom is **full of mercy**. It does not judge others strictly based on the law but will extend a generous hand full of mercy. It knows the same measure of mercy we grant to others is the same measure God will use with us (Matthew 7:2).

This wisdom is **full of...good fruits**. This wisdom can be seen by the fruit it produces. It is not just the inner power to think and talk about things the right way; it is **full of...good fruits**.

This wisdom is **without partiality**, or "without judging." The idea is that it does not have a curious inquiry into the faults or failings of others.

This wisdom is **without hypocrisy**. It does not pretend to be something that it is not; it never works under a mask.

When people think of wisdom, they often think of the theoretical and speculative. They think of a detached philosopher putting forth fancy ideas. Yet heavenly wisdom – biblical wisdom – is completely practical. It translates into real life and makes for people (and leaders) who are full of love and goodness.

This heavenly wisdom is for you, today.

June 17

If Water is Wet and Rocks are Hard

Therefore if there is any consolation in Christ, if any comfort of love, if any fellowship of the Spirit, if any affection and mercy. (Philippians 2:1)

Philippians 2 begins with the nature and work of Jesus in a powerful and poetic way. But Paul's purpose was to help the Christians of that church to get along better. He challenged them by introducing the basis for unity, humility, and love among believers. If the Philippian Christians had received the things he mentioned in Philippians 2:1, then they have a responsibility to do what he is about to teach them.

If there is any consolation in Christ. Is there **any consolation in Christ**? Of course, there is! Every Christian should know what it is to have Jesus console their soul. Luke 2:25, says Jesus is *the Consolation of Israel.* And in 2 Corinthians 1:5, *For as the sufferings of Christ abound in us, so our consolation also abounds through Christ.* 2 Thessalonians 2:16, says that God *has loved us and given us everlasting consolation and good hope by grace.* Of course, there is consolation in Christ – but are you experiencing it?

If there is any... comfort of love. Is there any **comfort of love**? Of course there is! Every Christian should know what it is to have Jesus give them the comfort of love. 2 Corinthians 1:3, says God is the *God of all comfort.* There is no circumstance beyond His reach to comfort. The word **comfort** in this passage is the ancient Greek word *paraklesis*. The idea behind this word in the New Testament is more than sympathy. It has the idea of strengthening, helping, and making strong. The love of God in our life makes us strong and brave. Of course, there is **comfort of love** – but are you experiencing it?

If there is any... fellowship of the Spirit. Is there any **fellowship of the Spirit**? Of course there is! Every Christian should know what it is to have the fellowship of the Spirit. Fellowship is the ancient Greek word *koinonia*. It means the sharing of things in common. We share life with the Spirit of God that we never knew before. The Holy Spirit fills, guides, and moves in our lives in a powerful and precious way. Of course, there is **fellowship of the Spirit** – but are you experiencing it?

If there is any... affection and mercy. Is there any **affection and mercy**? Of course there is! Every Christian knows something of the affection of God, and the mercy of God – but are you experiencing them?

Paul suggests that they should all be obvious parts of the Christian's experience. These things should be just as real in our lives as the wetness of water, the hotness of fire, and the hardness of rocks.

Are they obvious parts of your life?

June 18

What We Are, What We Do

With it we bless our God and Father, and with it we curse men, who have been made in the similitude of God. Out of the same mouth proceed blessing and cursing. My brethren, these things ought not to be so. Does a spring send forth fresh water and bitter from the same opening? Can a fig tree, my brethren, bear olives, or a grapevine bear figs? Thus no spring yields both salt water and fresh. (James 3:9-12)

In his general letter to all Christians, the apostle James spent a lot of time writing about what we say, and he used the human tongue as a representation of the words we speak. In considering the tongue, James observed that with it we both **bless our God** and we also **curse men**. Our words can be used for the highest calling (to **bless our God**), and they can be used for the lowest evil (to **curse men**). In those who are born again, it shouldn't be said that **out of the same mouth proceed blessing and cursing**.

A good illustration of this comes from the life of one of the other apostles. As a disciple, Peter's tongue confessed Jesus as the Messiah, the Son of the living God, and the same tongue denied Jesus with curses.

What does James say about this? **These things ought not to be so**. Our speech should be consistently glorifying to God. We shouldn't use one vocabulary or one tone of speaking at church and a different one at home or on the job. Like a spring of water, our mouths shouldn't **send forth fresh...and bitter from the same opening**.

Some commentators wonder if James had suffered from the attack of bitter and hurtful words himself. The war of words in the community of faith can certainly make a man plead that we should all speak with more thought and more love.

Notice: **no spring yields both salt water and fresh**. James points to the ultimate impossibility of such a contradiction. If bad fruit and bitter water continue to come forth, it means that there is something is wrong at the source. The tree is bad, and the spring is bad. After all, Jesus taught in Matthew 12:34-37 that a man's words are a true revelation of his inner character. What we say can indicate what we are.

As James observed, a freshwater spring doesn't bring forth saltwater. A fig tree doesn't bear olives. The reality of our spiritual claims can be tested by what comes forth from our life.

Unless God changes who we are on the inside, we will never be different on the outside. He makes us new people in Jesus Christ; then, we are told to go and live that new life. Our part is to receive that newness of life by faith, and then in the same faith to live it.

If you do, one place it will show is in the words you say.

June 19

In But Not Of

Depart from me, you evildoers,
For I will keep the commandments of my God! (Psalm 119:115)

There is a constant challenge in the Christian life: to be in the world, but not of the world. To be "in the world" (as in Philippians 2:15) means that we have a presence in culture and society, and we shine as lights for God's love and truth. To be "of the world" (as in John 15:19) means that we let the culture surrounding us tell us what our values and principles are. God wants us to keep both our values and our influence.

In Psalm 119, the psalmist made a rare departure in his ongoing conversation with God about His Word. He addressed the **evildoers** that brought him such trouble. He knew that the best remedy was to put space between him and these evildoers, so he boldly told them, **depart from me**.

The psalmist was careful in choosing his friends. It's been said, "Show me your friends, and I will show you your future." Whether we feel it or not, we take on some of our friends' qualities, good and bad.

We don't feel that the psalmist never encountered those who didn't know or dishonored God; it just that he knew there were limits to the influence he allowed in his life. Instead, the psalmist was committed to obedience in keeping the **commandments** of God.

This second line of the verse connects with the first line. The psalmist found it more challenging to keep God's commandments in the close company of evildoers, so he sent them away. He felt that he had to keep the commandments of God, but he didn't have to keep close company with anyone or everyone.

This was very much the spirit of Jesus when He steadfastly resisted the devil when tempted in the wilderness (Matthew 4). He told the devil to go away (Matthew 4:10) and repeatedly relied on the Word of God (Matthew 4:4, 7, 10).

It's possible that for some reading this, what the psalmist described isn't relevant. Some followers of Jesus are too isolated from those to whom they could be a light. For many, this is precisely what they need to do. They think, "Jesus was around sinners all the time, and so can I be." There's a significant difference: Jesus was around sinners, but as a physician, to love them and heal sinful hearts (Luke 5:29-32). If we make company with those who don't know God, it should be as physicians (or physicians assistants), and not as evildoers ourselves.

This can only be done as we stay close to God. In this massive Psalm, the word "God" only appears once in this verse. When "God" is mentioned, it is in the personal sense – **my God**.

Today, your close, intimate connection with God, can give you the wisdom to be in the world, but never of it.

June 20

The Decision Between Two Builders, Two Destinies

Therefore whoever hears these sayings of Mine, and does them, I will liken him to a wise man who built his house on the rock: and the rain descended, the floods came, and the winds blew and beat on that house; and it did not fall, for it was founded on the rock. But everyone who hears these sayings of Mine, and does not do them, will be like a foolish man who built his house on the sand: and the rain descended, the floods came, and the winds blew and beat on that house; and it fell. And great was its fall. (Matthew 7:24-27)

Jesus used the close of His Sermon on the Mount to call His listeners to an important decision between two destinies. Jesus described the person who hears and does what He says. That one was **wise man**, who built his house on a reliable foundation – a **rock**. Another man built on an untrustworthy foundation, one of **sand**. That illustrates the man who hears what Jesus said but did not do it.

Each house looked the same outwardly. Both the wise man and the foolish man built houses, likely of similar design. The difference was not in the workmanship or the materials but in the foundation. Our life's foundation is typically hidden and is only proven in the storm, and those storms come from both heaven (**rain**) and earth (**floods**).

In good weather, there seemed to be no difference between the two foundations. But there came a time when the weather changed for the worse with **rain, floods**, and **winds**. Jesus warned that the foundations of our life would be shaken at some time or another, both now (in our troubles), but also in the ultimate judgment before God.

Time and the storms of life will prove the strength of one's foundation, even when it is hidden. We may be surprised when we see who has truly built on the firm foundation. It's better to test our life's foundation now rather than later, at our judgment before God, when it's too late to change our destiny.

The people who built on a weak foundation were **everyone who hears these sayings of Mine, and does not do them**. Merely hearing God's Word isn't enough to provide a secure foundation. We must also be doers of His Word. If we are not, we commit the sin that will surely find us out, the sin of doing nothing (Numbers 32:23) – and great will be our fall.

The second builder's problem was not that he deliberately wanted to build on a bad foundation. Instead, he didn't think it was so important. The choice isn't between choosing a good foundation or a bad one but paying close attention to our foundation or paying no attention.

We need to hear His words and do what He says – focused on trusting Him in both Who He is and what He has done for us.

That is your secure foundation.

June 21

A Better Measure Than Success

And Moses and Aaron gathered the assembly together before the rock; and he said to them, "Hear now, you rebels! Must we bring water for you out of this rock?" Then Moses lifted his hand and struck the rock twice with his rod; and water came out abundantly, and the congregation and their animals drank. (Numbers 20:10-11)

You can't live very long without water. God knew it, Moses knew it, and the thirsty nation of Israel knew it. So, when the people complained again to Moses about their lack of water, it addressed a real problem. Moses must have felt the pressure of always being the "lightning rod" for the problems of Israel. The way the people presented the problem didn't help – steeped in unbelief, looking to Moses instead of looking to the Lord, and longing for Egypt all over again.

Moses sought the Lord, falling on his face before God at the house of the Lord, experiencing a fresh encounter with the glory of the Lord. God told him what to do, and Moses began by doing exactly what the Lord had told him to do. He took the rod and gathered the people of Israel.

But God never commanded Moses to speak to the nation, and he did: **Hear now, you rebels! Must we bring water for you out of this rock?** Moses felt it was time for a lecture, and he spoke harshly to the people of God. The lecture itself was bad enough; the attitude of heart it showed was even worse – one of anger and contempt for the people of God, a bitter heart.

Previously, Moses fell on his face before God when the people rebelled (Numbers 16:4). At Meribah, when the people contended with Moses because there was no water Moses cried out to the Lord, not against the people (Exodus 15:22-25).

But here, Moses disobeyed God directly by striking the rock instead of speaking to it (Numbers 20:8). When he struck the rock at the beginning of the Exodus journey, he only had to strike it once. Now out of anger and frustration, he did it twice.

Despite the lapse of Moses into sinful attitude and action, God still provided abundantly for the people. This teaches us that God's love for His people is so great that He will use truly imperfect instruments. The fact God uses someone is no evidence that they themselves are right with God or ministering according to God's heart. Sometimes God works despite His servants, not because of them.

But what works is not the best measure of what is right before God. In our moment of success, we may not be clear-headed enough to discern if we did it according to God's heart. Moses provided water and it came miraculously – yet God knew Moses didn't act according to His heart. Moses learned there was a better measure than simple success.

Are you learning that heaven's applause is more important than success in this world?

June 22

Choosing the Poor of This World

Listen, my beloved brethren: Has God not chosen the poor of this world to be rich in faith and heirs of the kingdom which He promised to those who love Him? But you have dishonored the poor man. Do not the rich oppress you and drag you into the courts? Do they not blaspheme that noble name by which you are called? (James 2:5-7)

People find it easy to favor the rich – it comes naturally. But that isn't how God works. Instead, there is a real sense in which God has **chosen the poor of this world**. How are the poor chosen by God?

They are chosen **to be rich in faith** because the poor have more opportunities to trust God. They may be richer in faith than the rich man. There is a sense in which the rich person *might* trust God, but the poor man *must* trust God.

They are chosen to be **heirs of the kingdom** because Jesus said that being rich made it harder to enter the kingdom of heaven (Matthew 19:24). The poor more readily respond to God in faith, having fewer obstacles to the kingdom.

God chose the poor when He added humanity to His deity and came to earth (2 Corinthians 8:9). Many people dread poverty and will do anything to escape it. Yet the Son of God chose poverty. He chose to be born into a family and a life of humble resources.

James taught us why Christians should not be biased against the poor, because it is more likely that the rich **oppress you and drag you into the courts**. James reminded his readers that the rich often sin against others because the love of money is the root of all kinds of evil (1 Timothy 6:10). For this reason alone, the rich are not worthy of the favoritism often shown to them.

Of course, God has not *only* chosen the poor. We may say that He has chosen the poor first in the sense Paul spoke of in 1 Corinthians 1:26: *For you see your calling, brethren, that not many wise according to the flesh, not many mighty, not many noble, are called.*

We should also remember that God also never calls for partiality against the rich. If one must judge in a dispute between a rich man and a poor man, they should let the law and the facts of the case decide the judgment, instead of the economic class of those in the dispute.

When we choose people by what we see on the surface – rich or poor – then we miss the mind of God. Judas appeared to be much better leadership material than Peter was. If one is poor in this world, let them regard it as an opportunity to be rich in heaven (and improve their lot on earth).

If one is rich in this world, let them remember that this is no promise of riches in eternity, and they must handle what God gives them rightly.

June 23
Why to Not Worry

Look at the birds of the air, for they neither sow nor reap nor gather into barns; yet your heavenly Father feeds them. Are you not of more value than they? Which of you by worrying can add one cubit to his stature? So why do you worry about clothing? Consider the lilies of the field, how they grow: they neither toil nor spin; and yet I say to you that even Solomon in all his glory was not arrayed like one of these. Now if God so clothes the grass of the field, which today is, and tomorrow is thrown into the oven, will He not much more clothe you, O you of little faith? (Matthew 6:26-30)

Most people know that it is bad to worry, and there is a lot of advice given to remind us that we shouldn't worry. When someone says, "Just think positive" or "Think happy thoughts" or "Don't worry, be happy," there often isn't much substance to their advice.

When Jesus, in the Sermon on the Mount, told us not to worry, He did more than give empty advice. He gave us good, solid reasons why we shouldn't worry. **Look at the birds of the air...your heavenly Father feeds them**. Jesus reminded us that God provides for the birds, and He takes good care of them. Therefore, we should expect that God would also take care of us.

We should take note: The birds don't worry, but they do work. Birds don't just sit with open mouths, expecting God to fill them. They go out and work for the food that God has provided for them.

Jesus reminded us that we are of **more value** than the birds. The worry many people have over material things is rooted in a poor understanding of their value before God. They don't understand how much He loves and cares for them.

Jesus also reminded us that worry accomplishes nothing; we can **add** nothing to our lives by **worrying**. There might be bigger sins than worry, but there are none more self-defeating and useless. If God takes care even of the **grass of the field**, He will certainly take care of those who trust Him.

The ancient Greek words translated **can add** may mean, "adding to life" instead of "adding to height," but the thought is the same. Instead of adding to our life, we can harm ourselves through worry. Stress is one of the great contributors to disease and poor health.

Jesus made a case for trusting God, and for refusing to worry. He closed this brief rebuke of worry with some sobering words when He said, **you of little faith**. It is fair to say that **little faith** is not a little problem.

Today, treat God as if He can really be trusted. He is trustworthy – and He can take care of you.

June 24

God's Righteousness, Our Friend

For in it the righteousness of God is revealed from faith to faith; as it is written, "The just shall live by faith." (Romans 1:17)

In August of 1513, a German monk teaching at a seminary was lecturing on the book of Psalms, but his inner life was in great turmoil. In his studies, the monk came across Psalm 31:1: *Deliver me in Your righteousness*. The passage confused him; how could God's righteousness do anything but condemn humanity to Hell as a deserved punishment for sin? The monk had legal training before going into the monastery, so he knew what it meant that God is a righteous judge – a judge who would surely condemn the guilty.

As he thought on this, the monk's mind was repeatedly drawn to Romans 1:17, which says that in the gospel, **the righteousness of God is revealed from faith to faith; as it is written, "The just shall live by faith"** (the last portion is a quote from Habakkuk 2:4). The monk described his thoughts: "Night and day I pondered until…I grasped the truth that the righteousness of God is that righteousness whereby, through grace and sheer mercy, he justifies us by faith. Therefore I felt myself to be reborn and to have gone through open doors into paradise…. This passage of Paul became to me a gateway into heaven." The German monk's name was Martin Luther and through understanding the good news of righteousness by faith he was born again. You could say that this was when the Reformation began in Martin Luther's heart.

Many people don't think that God is truly righteous. They suppose that God will just excuse all sin because He is supposed to forgive people. Perhaps God is mad at a few things, but not anything they would do.

It is true that God is love; but He is also a completely righteous judge. The means God is just and fair, and it isn't fair to let the guilty go. If someone is guilty, the righteousness of God seems only to condemn them. Therefore, if God is completely fair, it doesn't seem like this fairness is our friend.

But here is the good news of the gospel: God has righteously dealt with the sin of His people by putting on Jesus the punishment they deserve. Their sin is righteously and fairly punished – but it is judged in Jesus, not in the believer.

Because of this, God's fairness now is the believer's friend instead of their enemy. Because their sin is already settled in Jesus, it wouldn't be fair for God to hold those sins against His people.

Because God is righteous, the one who puts their trust in Jesus Christ and His work on our behalf can be confident He will never leave us or forsake us, and He will always be for us. Why not receive – and thank God for – all Jesus did for us to make God's fairness, His righteousness, our friend instead of our enemy.

This is the good news – God's righteousness delivers those who put their trust in Him, and not in themselves. Live by this faith and this righteousness today.

June 25
Asking, Seeking, Knocking

Ask, and it will be given to you; seek, and you will find; knock, and it will be opened to you. For everyone who asks receives, and he who seeks finds, and to him who knocks it will be opened. (Matthew 7:7-8)

Earlier in the Sermon on the Mount, Jesus dealt with the subject of prayer (Matthew 6:5-15). Here Jesus came back to the idea of prayer because it is such a vital part of life in His Kingdom.

Jesus described prayer in three pictures: **Ask, seek,** and **knock**. In these, we see a progressive energy, going from **ask** to **seek** to **knock**. With this, Jesus told us to have intensity, passion, and persistence in prayer. In this three-fold description of prayer as asking, seeking, and knocking, we see different aspects of prayer and different aspects of its reward.

- Prayer is like asking in that we make our requests known to God and everyone who asks receives. Receiving is the reward of asking.
- Prayer is like seeking in that we search after God, His Word, and His will, and he who seeks finds. Finding is the reward of seeking.
- Prayer is like knocking until the door opens, and we seek entrance into the magnificent heavenly palace of our Great King. Entering through the opened door into His palace is the reward of knocking, and the best reward of all.

The idea of knocking also implies that we may sense resistance as we pray. After all, if the door were already open, there would be no need to knock. Yet Jesus encouraged us, "Even when you sense that the door is closed and you must knock, then do so and continue to do so, and you will be answered."

The image of knocking also implies that there is a door that can be opened. The door to God and the prayers He answers are meant to be open; they are intended to be an entrance. It is of no use to knock at a wall, but Jesus told us to "knock" in prayer as if we were at a door with hinges and hardware ready to be opened.

We come to God's door, and all we must do is knock. If it were locked, we would need a burglar's tools to break in, but that isn't necessary; all we must do is knock, and even if I don't have a burglar's skills, I can still knock.

Jesus said, **ask and it will be given to you**. Here God promised an answer to the one who diligently seeks Him. Many of our passionless prayers are not answered for a good reason; because it is almost as if we ask God to care about something for which we care little or nothing.

So do it – and keep doing it. **Ask**, **seek**, and **knock**. God will meet you in your need and answer according to His love, power, and wisdom.

He promised to do so.

June 26

I Confess

So David said to Nathan, "I have sinned against the LORD." (2 Samuel 12:13)

David's confession of sin is an example for all of us: **I have sinned against the LORD.** He placed the blame squarely on himself. He did not make less of his offense. David realized that he especially sinned against God.

In the Hebrew, David's words, **I have sinned against the LORD** are two words: *hata al-Yahweh*. These two words, and the heart they reflect, show the basic difference between David and Saul. If you compare David's confession to King Saul's confession in 1 Samuel 24:16-21, you see Saul was eloquent with words but not sincere in his heart. Confession does not need to be long to be genuine.

This was an excellent response from a man of David's standing. When confronted with sin, kings often say, "Off with their head." David proved that God was working on his heart all along, and Nathan's confrontation was simply the last piece of that work. Other kings would have killed Nathan and gone their way, but not the man after God's heart. Look at the confession:

- **I**: David spoke of himself. It isn't "we," though it was true that he was not the only sinner. David knew that he had to deal with his sin. David shows personal responsibility.
- **Have sinned**: David didn't use elaborate vocabulary. He **sinned**. It wasn't a mistake, an error, a mess-up, an indiscretion, or a problem.
- **Against the LORD**: This expressed the enormity of David's sin. His sins against Bathsheba, Uriah, Ahithophel, his wives, his children, and the nation were great. But his sin against the LORD was greatest of all. There are no small sins against a great God, and great sins are even greater.

David eloquently expressed his repentance in Psalm 51:

Have mercy upon me, O God, according to Your lovingkindness; according to the multitude of Your tender mercies, blot out my transgressions. Wash me thoroughly from my iniquity, and cleanse me from my sin. For I acknowledge my transgressions, and my sin is ever before me. Against You, You only have I sinned, and done this evil in Your sight — that You may be found just when You speak, and blameless when You judge.... For You do not desire sacrifice, or else I would give it; You do not delight in burnt offering. The sacrifices of God are a broken spirit, and broken and contrite heart — these, O God, You will not despise. (Psalm 51:1-4; 16-17)

David's awareness of sin, desire for cleansing, recognition of God's righteous judgment, and understanding of what God wants are clear in Psalm 51. David found wonderful restoration. He admitted he was lost and knew he was a sinner.

God came to save sinners, not the righteous. David found great peace and resolution in being completely honest with God.

Today, a loving God offers you an excellent opportunity to be honest with Him.

June 27

What to Live By

Behold the proud, his soul is not upright in him; but the just shall live by his faith. (Habakkuk 2:4)

Habakkuk knew that judgment was coming on Judah, and that God would use the Empire of Babylon to bring the judgment. Knowing this, Habakkuk wondered why God would use Babylon – a nation even more sinful than Judah – to bring judgment against Judah. He saw Babylon as the proud nation – proud, yet still used by God to bring judgment to Judah. In answering the prophet, God first assured him that He sees the proud, and knows that **his soul is not upright in him**.

Pride is everywhere and takes all manner of shapes. Here is the rich man, proud of what he has, and there is the poor man, proud of his honor in having less. Here is the talented man, proud of what he can do, and there is the man of few talents, proud of his hard work. Here is the religious man, proud of his religion, and there is the unbeliever, proud of his unbelief. Here is the establishment man, proud of his place in society, and there is the counter-cultural man, proud of his outcast status. Here is the learned man, proud of his intelligence and learning, and there is the simple man, proud of his simplicity.

A brother can be proud of his ability to pray, his growth, or his humility.

Thankfully, not everyone is among the proud: **but the just shall live by his faith**. In wonderful contrast to the proud, there are **the just**. The principle of their life is faith, instead of pride that looks to self. True faith looks outside of self and looks to the LORD God.

This statement from the prophet Habakkuk is one of the most important, and most quoted Old Testament statements in the New Testament. Paul used it to show that the just live by faith, not by law. Being under the law isn't the way to be found just before God, it is only living by faith. If you are declared just – that is, approved – before God, it happens through a relationship of faith. If your life is all about living under the law, then God does not find you approved.

Martin Luther said: "Before those words broke upon my mind I hated God and was angry with him because, not content with frightening us sinners by the law and by the miseries of life, he still further increased our torture by the gospel. But when, by the Spirit of God, I understood those words – 'The just shall live by faith!' 'The just shall live by faith!' – then I felt born again like a new man; I entered through the open doors into the very Paradise of God."

Some Christians live by devotions, and some live by works. Some Christians live by feelings, and some live by circumstances. Each of these is meaningless and perhaps dangerous without faith.

God's just ones live by faith. What do you live by?

June 28

Strong in the Lord

Finally, my brethren, be strong in the Lord and in the power of His might. (Ephesians 6:10)

It is a wonderful phrase: **be strong in the Lord and in the power of His might**. Literally, Paul wrote, "strengthen yourselves in the Lord." He probably took the idea from 1 Samuel 30:6, where it is said that David *strengthened himself in the* L%%ORD%% *his God.*

The detailed teaching of spiritual battle in this passage presents two essential components. First, the believer must **be strong in the Lord and in the power of His might**. Then, they must "put on the whole armor of God" (as it will say in the next verse). The two are essential, and much teaching on spiritual battle neglects the first. If you take a weak man who can barely stand and put the best armor on him, he will still be an ineffective soldier. He will be easily beaten. Equipping for Christian combat must begin with **be strong in the Lord and in the power of His might**.

Before a soldier is given a gun or shown how to fire a missile, he or she goes through basic training. One great purpose for basic training is to build up the recruit's physical strength.

This strength is found **in the power of His might**. This does not happen just by saying the words. It is not magic or a spell. You can't just walk around saying, **be strong in the Lord and in the power of His might** repeatedly and see it happen. Christianity is not one of those self-help formulas where you go around saying positive things to ourselves. Those kinds of mental games can accomplish something, but it certainly was not what Paul meant here.

Might is inherent power or force. A muscular man's big muscles display his might, even if he does not use them. It is the reserve of strength. **Power** is the exercise of might. When the muscular man uses his might to bend an iron bar, he uses his power. It means that the reserve of strength is in operation.

God has vast reservoirs of **might** that can be realized as the **power** in our Christian life. But His strength does not work in me as I sit passively. His **might** works in me as I rely on it and step out to do the work. I can depend on it and do no work. I can do work without relying on it. But both of these fall short. I must rely on His **might** and then do the work. It is not:

- I do everything, and God does nothing.
- I do nothing, and God does everything.
- I do all I can, and God helps with what I can't do.

Each of those approaches falls short.

The key is for you to rely on His might by faith and depend on it more and more – and then do the work.

June 29
The Successful Failure

In the eighteenth year of King Jeroboam the son of Nebat, Abijam became king over Judah. He reigned three years in Jerusalem. His mother's name was Maachah the granddaughter of Abishalom. And he walked in all the sins of his father, which he had done before him; his heart was not loyal to the Lord his God, as was the heart of his father David. (1 Kings 15:1-3)

The line of kings over Israel began with Saul, but he disqualified himself, so the dynasty of Saul ended with Saul. Then came David, who was perhaps Israel's greatest ancient king; followed by Solomon, the son of David who built the glorious temple.

After Solomon, came a disaster in the name of Rehoboam. He sunk the kingdom into carnality and civil war, and because of the division there soon were two kingdoms made up of the twelve tribes of Israel. The king described in 1 Kings 15:1-3 was the son of Rehoboam and he sat on the throne of the southern kingdom, called Judah. This son of Rehoboam only reigned three years, showing that God did not bless his reign.

Comparing this account with 2 Chronicles 13 we learn that Abijam knew somewhat of the Lord, and how to preach – but he did not uproot the idolatry and sexual immorality that was introduced by Rehoboam. The successor of Abijam (Asa) removed the centers of the sexually charged idolatry that were so common in the land (1 Kings 15:12-13).

The real problem with Abijam's reign was his lack of a relationship with God. King David sinned during his reign, but his heart stayed **loyal to the Lord his God**. The same could not be said of Abijam.

2 Chronicles 13 explains there was war between Jeroboam of Israel and Abijam of Judah, and how Abijam challenged Jeroboam on the basis of righteousness and faithfulness to God. Jeroboam responded with a surprise attack, and victory seemed certain for Israel over Judah. But Abijam cried out to the Lord, and God won a victory for Judah that day. 2 Chronicles 13:18 says, *Thus the children of Israel were subdued at that time; and the children of Judah prevailed, because they relied on the Lord God of their fathers*. God blessed Abijam's reign even when it seemed that he didn't deserve it.

Chronicles also explains his standing at the end of his brief reign: *Abijah grew mighty, married fourteen wives, and begot twenty-two sons and sixteen daughters* (2 Chronicles 13:21). Amid his victory and good leadership for Judah, he never had the right relationship with the Lord.

We could say that Abijam is a classic example of an increasing phenomenon: the successful failure. He both succeeded and failed at the same time. Abijam thought that the most important thing in life was being a good king; he missed what really mattered most: his personal life with God.

Don't make the same mistake in your own life.

June 30

What Comes from God

Every good gift and every perfect gift is from above, and comes down from the Father of lights, with whom there is no variation or shadow of turning. Of His own will He brought us forth by the word of truth, that we might be a kind of firstfruits of His creatures. (James 1:17-18)

In writing about temptation, James wanted us to know that temptation to evil never comes from God. To emphasize that, He used a point of contrast to tell us what comes from God: **every good gift and every perfect gift**. We expect no pure goodness from our own fallen natures and from those who would entice us. But **every good and every perfect gift** comes from God the Father in heaven.

Of course, we must measure the ultimate goodness of any gift on an eternal scale. Something that may seem to be only good (such as winning a lottery) may cause our destruction.

James wrote, **with whom there is no variation or shadow of turning**. God's goodness never changes. There is no variation with Him. Instead of shadows, God is the **Father of lights**.

The sun and stars never stop giving light, even when we can't see them. Even so, there is never a shadow with God. When night comes, the darkness is not the fault of the sun; it shines as brightly as it ever does. Instead, part of the earth turns from the sun, and darkness comes.

Simply said, this means that God never changes.

James understood that the gift of salvation was given by God and not earned by the work or obedience of man. It is of **His own will** that He **brought** forth His people for salvation. We can see God's goodness in our salvation, as He initiated our salvation of His own will and brought us forth to spiritual life by His Word of truth, that we might be to His glory as firstfruits of His harvest. In the previous verses, James told us what the lust of man brings forth: sin and death. Here he tells us what the will of the good God brings: salvation to us, as **a kind of firstfruits of His creatures**.

With the term **firstfruits**, James may refer to his generation of believers, who were primarily Christians from a Jewish background. The fact that these Christians from Jewish backgrounds were **firstfruits** (Deuteronomy 26:1-4) shows that James expected a later and greater harvest of Christians from a Gentile background.

Think about it: God will often do a work, and He means it to be a small sign and evidence of a greater work to come.

What God wants to do in your life today is an indication of a much greater work He wants to do in and through you.

July 1
Gold for the Golden Rule

Therefore, whatever you want men to do to you, do also to them, for this is the Law and the Prophets. (Matthew 7:12)

As He began the conclusion to his Sermon on the Mount, Jesus said one of the most memorable lines in the entire Bible, often known as "The Golden Rule."

He said, **whatever you want men to do to you, do also to them**. The negative way of stating this command was known long before the time of Jesus. It had long been said, "You should not do to your neighbor what you would not want him to do to you." But it was an important advance for Jesus to put it in the positive, to say that we should do to others what we want them to do to us, making the command much broader.

Jesus described the judgment of the sheep and the goats at the end of the age (Matthew 25:31-46). The guilt of the unfortunate "goats" was that they did not do what they should have done. Under the negative form of the Golden Rule, the goats spoken of would be found "not guilty." Under Jesus' positive form, they would indeed be found guilty.

No wonder this rule is called "golden." How the world would be different if people followed it! No one would steal, cheat, or lie. No murderer wants to be killed. Even the worst thief does not want to be robbed. There would be much more kindness and companionship in a world ruled by the Golden Rule. The person who wants a friend would reach out in friendship to another; the person who needs comfort would seek someone out who needs it. Multiply this principle person by person through a community, through a nation, through the world – and it would be almost heaven on earth.

Jesus showed that this simple principle summarized all that the **Law and the Prophets** say about how we should treat others. If we would treat others the way we would want to be treated, we would naturally obey all the law says about our relationships with others.

Simple? Of course, it's simple to grasp. This explanation of Jesus makes the law much easier to understand, but it doesn't make it easier for us to obey. No one has ever consistently done to others as they would like others to do to themselves. Where do we begin with the Golden Rule? We should start by asking God to forgive us for not keeping it, and we should realize that this failure to keep something so simple and easy to understand means we need a Savior – Jesus Himself.

This brief, authoritative word from Jesus points us in the right direction, but it also exposes our need for Him as savior and strength. It's a Golden Rule, but I'm bankrupt.

Today, let Him be your gold (Revelation 3:18), and He will help you live His Golden Rule.

All the Armor

Put on the whole armor of God, that you may be able to stand against the wiles of the devil. (Ephesians 6:11)

The apostle Paul, inspired by God, began this section about spiritual struggle by telling us to be *strong in the Lord and in the power of His might* (Ephesians 6:10). After that, Paul explained the goal of our battle – **that you may be able to stand against the wiles of the devil.** We express the strength we have in God by standing **against the wiles of the devil**. The schemes of our spiritual adversaries come to nothing when we stand against them in the power of God.

So, **put on** all of God's **armor**. Paul wrote using a metaphor, a word-picture. Just as a Roman soldier had armor that made him ready to fight, the follower of Jesus has spiritual resources and equipment that prepare him to survive and win spiritual conflicts.

This armor of God will be explained fully in the next verses, but the emphasis here is on **the whole armor of God**. God gives the believer a full set of spiritual equipment, and He sends us out into battle with everything we need at our disposal.

This ancient Greek word for armor is used in only one other place in the New Testament. In Luke 11:21-22, Jesus spoke of the *strong man who is fully armed*, but is stripped of *all his armor* when a stronger one comes and defeats him. We know that at the cross, Jesus disarmed all spiritual authorities and powers that oppose us (Colossians 2:15).

So, we are to **put on the whole armor of God**. This armor is **of God** both in the sense that it is from Him, and in the sense that it is His actual armor. In the Old Testament, it is the LORD who wears the armor (Isaiah 59:17). He now shares that armor with us – no wonder Romans 8:37 says we are more than conquerors!

In the book of 1 Samuel, there is a story of a king who gave a boy his armor before a battle. The armor must have been good because it belonged to a king. Yet the boy didn't want to fight in the king's armor, no matter how good it was. The boy – who would later become a king himself – explained that he didn't want to use the king's armor because he had not tested it (1 Samuel 17:29).

The boy, David, went on to fight against Goliath in armor that he had tested before. David had trusted God to protect him, give him courage, and to provide him with skill in battle before. That trust was part of a tested, proven armor for David, and he won the battle against Goliath.

The armor God gives you won't be effective until you use it; until you test it. The more you use it, the more effective it will be.

Just make sure you take **the whole armor of God**.

July 3
The Law That Brings Liberty

For whoever shall keep the whole law, and yet stumble in one point, he is guilty of all. For He who said, "Do not commit adultery," also said, "Do not murder." Now if you do not commit adultery, but you do murder, you have become a transgressor of the law. So speak and so do as those who will be judged by the law of liberty. For judgment is without mercy to the one who has shown no mercy. Mercy triumphs over judgment. (James 2:10-13)

We usually don't think that law and liberty go together. This modern kind of thinking is wrong and harmful. We too often believe that the key to real liberty is ignoring or breaking God's law and then doing whatever comes in our mind to do. Yet James reminds us that this isn't correct at all.

James guards us against selective obedience. The **whole law** is of concern to the believer. We can't pick and choose which commands of God should be obeyed and which can be safely ignored. We can't say, "I like God's command against murder, so I'll keep that one. But I don't like His command against adultery, so I will ignore it." God cares about the whole law.

In addition, believers are under the **law of liberty** and will be **judged** by that law. It has liberty, yet it's still a law that must be obeyed and that we will be judged by at the judgment seat of Christ (2 Corinthians 5:10). One might call it the **law of liberty** because it comes freely from the life of those God has redeemed.

As those who will be judged by the law of liberty, we should always show **mercy** to others by refraining from partiality. The mercy we show will be extended to us on the day of judgment, and that **mercy triumphs over judgment**. In this, James related another principle of Jesus from the Sermon on the Mount: *For with what judgment you judge, you will be judged; and with the measure you use, it will be measured back to you.* (Matthew 7:2)

Yet, God empowering us, if we walk in this Christ-life, when we are judged, we will find mercy. We will see that **mercy triumphs over judgment**. The life that has shown mercy will triumph in the face of judgment, even as Jesus said in the Sermon on the Mount.

Do you want to see God's mercy win in your life? Then depend on God, look to Him, and set yourself to live out the kind of love suggested by the perfect law of liberty. This loving law keeps us in freedom, unbound by the chains of sin, prejudice, and bitterness.

Today, you can know the liberty of obedience; you can understand it well enough to avoid the bondage of disobedience.

July 4

Set Free for a Purpose

But at night an angel of the Lord opened the prison doors and brought them out, and said, "Go, stand in the temple and speak to the people all the words of this life." (Acts 5:19-20)

God was working in a powerful way through the apostles, and the religious leaders in Jerusalem didn't like it. Acts 5:17-18 says the high priest arrested the apostles and put them all in prison.

They didn't stay in prison long. An **angel of the Lord** set them free. This was easy for God to arrange. Angels are all ministering spirits sent forth to minister for those who will inherit salvation (Hebrews 1:14). God sent forth this angel to minister for the apostles. Locked doors are nothing for God or for those who He uses.

To do the work, God sent an **angel**. Possibly, they only understood this was an angel as they looked back. Angels often come in human appearance, and it may not always be easy to recognize an angel (as in Luke 24:3-7 and Hebrews 13:2).

The angel didn't only open doors, he also had a message: **Go, stand in the temple and speak to the people all the words of this life**. The angel freed them from prison, but he wasn't going to do the work of preaching. That was up to the apostles, and it is also up to us.

Their rescue from prison was wonderful, but for a purpose – so they could continue their work. God didn't set them free primarily for their safety or comfort. They were set free for a reason. In the future, they were not always delivered.

The later history of these apostles – and others associated with them in the early church – shows that sometimes God delivers by a miracle, sometimes He does not. According to church history and tradition, miraculous angels did not always deliver them.

Matthew was beheaded with a sword. Mark died in Alexandria after being dragged through the streets of the city. Luke was hanged on an olive tree in Greece. John died a natural death, but they unsuccessfully tried to boil him in oil. Peter was crucified upside-down in Rome. James was beheaded in Jerusalem. James the Less was thrown from a height then beaten with clubs. Philip was hanged. Bartholomew was whipped and beaten until death. Andrew was crucified and preached at the top of his voice to his persecutors until he died. Thomas was run through with a spear. Jude was killed with the arrows of an executioner. Matthias was stoned and then beheaded – as was Barnabas. Paul was beheaded in Rome.

This reminds us that we should trust God for miraculous things and wish to see them more and more; but we do this knowing that God also has a purpose when He does not deliver with a miraculous hand.

We also see that we, like the apostles, are given freedom for a purpose – not merely to live for ourselves. Celebrate the freedom God gives – then use it to further the work of His kingdom.

July 5

Life With and Without Meaning

In the beginning, God created the heavens and the earth. (Genesis 1:1)

When we realize who God is and who we are, it sets a foundation for a life full of meaning. Why is there a universe at all? Why is there something, instead of nothing? The answer to those questions can lead one either to a life full of meaning, or a life without meaning. If everything around us, including ourselves, is the result of random, meaningless occurrences, apart from the work of a creating God, then it says something about who I am – and where I, and the whole universe is going. Then the only dignity or honor we bestow on men is only sentimental because I don't have any more significance than a worm. Then, there is no greater law in the universe than survival of the fittest.

Genesis 1:1 simply and straightforwardly declares that the world did not create itself or come about by chance; it was created by God – who, by definition, is eternal and has always been. If God created this world, and He has a plan for both the world and for us as individuals. We can find meaning in our lives by fulfilling the purpose our Creator made for us. If I take a screwdriver and try to use it as a hammer, it won't work very well and may break the screwdriver. The screwdriver is not fulfilling its created purpose, and all we have is frustration. When we look to our Creator and His Word, we discover His purpose for us.

Many people think Genesis 1:1 doesn't have anything to do with scientific facts. They look to other things for meaning in life. One day, students in the class of a great scientist spoke among themselves and decided that there was no God. The scientist asked them how much of all the knowledge in the world they had among themselves collectively, as a class. The students discussed it for a while and decided they had 5% of all human knowledge among themselves. The scientist thought that their estimate was a little generous, but he replied: "Is it possible that God exists in the 95% that you don't know?"

Some 100 years ago, there was a great German philosopher named Arthur Schopenhauer. He was sitting on a park bench in Berlin, deep in thought. A policeman asked the philosopher "Who are you?" Schopenhauer answered, "I wish to God I knew." The only way we can ever really find out who we are is to learn it from God – and the place to begin is Genesis 1:1.

Today, spend some special time considering what it means that God is your Creator, and you are His creature. Then look to His Word to learn more about His purpose for you. God did not make a mistake or roll the dice when He made you.

You have an important place in His plan, and Jesus' death for you on the cross shows how important you are to God.

How to Ask God for Help

But now, O LORD, You are our Father; we are the clay, and You our potter; and all we are the work of Your hand. Do not be furious, O LORD, nor remember iniquity forever; indeed, please look; we all are Your people! (Isaiah 64:8-9)

This verse begins with a passionate prayer for mercy, and then an honest recognition of why the people of God were in such a low place – because of their own sin and rejection of God. They felt that God was hiding His face from them, but they had turned away from Him first – and the people of God came to understand that this was true. They were the problem, not God.

Then, Isaiah shows how to pray, even when you know you don't deserve God's help. Consider it phrase by phrase:

But now, O LORD, You are our Father. This praying one was in a desperate place; knowing they need the mercy of God because the justice of God condemned him. Therefore, in the appeal for mercy, he first reminded God, "You are our Father. Please, LORD, have mercy on us as a loving Father." When we cannot appeal to our goodness, when we cannot appeal to our obedience, when we cannot appeal to anything in us, we can appeal to something in God, and come to Him as our Father.

We are the clay, and You our potter. Next, the praying one appealed to God's mercy because of God's sovereign power over each life. It is like saying, "LORD, deal gently with us, and mold us according to Your mercy." It is somewhat like the appeal to God as our Father, but with more of an emphasis on the power and majesty of God as the creator and shaper of all.

A father can never truly disown his children. A potter cannot disown the clay pot that he made; it is only there because he made it. This was Isaiah's way of saying, "You're stuck with us, LORD! You are our Father; You are our Potter – so do something with us."

Do not be furious, O LORD, nor remember iniquity forever. Here the praying one asked for mercy on account of "time already served." The "time already served" in jail may count as part of a penalty, even though it was already past. It was as if he prayed, "LORD, You had a right to be furious with us for a time but it has been long enough already."

Indeed, please look – we all are Your people! The praying one made his final appeal for mercy on these simple grounds: "LORD, we all are Your people. We are sinners and deserve Your judgment, but we are still Your people. We belong to You."

It's no use coming to God as if we deserve His blessings and help. Instead, come just as you are – with you sins, faults, weaknesses, everything.

Today, pray with the same heart as Isaiah's praying one, and see God answer.

July 7
This Same Jesus

Now when He had spoken these things, while they watched, He was taken up, and a cloud received Him out of their sight. And while they looked steadfastly toward heaven as He went up, behold, two men stood by them in white apparel, who also said, "Men of Galilee, why do you stand gazing up into heaven? This same Jesus, who was taken up from you into heaven, will so come in like manner as you saw Him go into heaven." (Acts 1:9-11)

About 40 days after His resurrection, Jesus gathered His disciples on the Mount of Olives and spoke with them about their duty to be witnesses to Him in all the earth. After finishing that important final command, Jesus did something remarkable. His physical body was lifted into heaven, even as His disciples watched. He went up, up, and up further until He faded into the clouds and could be seen no more.

In the Gospel of Luke, another point is added: that Jesus lifted His hands to bestow a blessing on His disciples, and that while He was blessing them, He was carried up into heaven (Luke 24:50-51).

Acts 1:9 says that Jesus was **taken up** while **they watched**. It was important for Jesus to leave His disciples this way. He could have simply vanished to heaven and the Father's presence in secret. By ascending in this manner, Jesus wanted His followers to know that He was gone for good, as opposed to how He had appeared and reappeared during the 40 days after His resurrection.

Remember Jesus' words to His disciples in John 16:7: *It is to your advantage that I go away; for if I do not go away, the Helper will not come to you; but if I depart, I will send Him to you.* Now the disciples could know that that promise would be fulfilled. The Holy Spirit was coming because Jesus promised to send the Spirit when He left, and the ascension was a way to demonstrate that Jesus was gone.

As the disciples stood staring up into the sky, two men – who were angels – asked them, **why do you stand gazing up into heaven?** They told the disciples to put their attention in the right place (obedience to Jesus' command to return to Jerusalem), not in wondering where and how Jesus went. Jesus told them to go to the ends of the earth, and they stood **gazing up into heaven**.

The two men called the One who had just ascended into heaven, **this same Jesus**. The same Jesus that ascended to heaven and was seated at the right hand of God, the Father, is the same Jesus of the Gospels. He is the same Jesus of love, grace, goodness, wisdom, and care. The Jesus in heaven is **this same Jesus**.

Then they stated that Jesus **will so come in like manner as you saw Him go into heaven**. This Jesus will return just as He left.

Be ready for His return – come quickly, Lord Jesus!

July 8

Never Ending Faithfulness

Forever, O Lord, Your word is settled in heaven. Your faithfulness endures to all generations; You established the earth, and it abides. They continue this day according to Your ordinances, for all are Your servants. (Psalm 119:89-91)

It's good for a man or a woman to have some things settled in their mind. Significant doubts are passed, and one is at peace with a matter that has been carefully weighed, and then a conclusion is finally reached.

For the author of Psalm 119 – inspired by the Holy Spirit of God – God's Word was settled, and it was **settled in heaven**. That settled state of heart and mind led to a logical conclusion. He said to the God of a settled word, **Your faithfulness endures to all generations**. The psalmist believed that God's settled word was a demonstration of His faithfulness, and that faithfulness extends across all generations.

We recognize this truth when we look at generations past, present, and future. We trace the line of God's incredible faithfulness to each generation, despite man's worst desires and works. We recognize the truth of this when we consider how God has preserved His Word through the generations. There have been seasons (and are still today) when merely possessing a Bible was a crime punishable by death.

Remember that for most of its existence, the Bible was the target of hatred and persecution. Kings, skeptics, and religious men of all sorts tried to destroy the Word of God. Sometimes they attacked it with force and fire, sometimes with arguments and mockery meant to discredit the Bible. Despite it all – the Bible not only survives; it thrives.

The psalmist continued: **You established the earth, and it abides. They continue this day according to Your ordinances**. This means that the Word of God (**Your ordinances**) is what established the earth and causes it to abide. The world and all of creation began with a word from God (Genesis 1); it is no surprise that they are also sustained and endure according to God's Word.

According to Isaiah 40:8 and Matthew 24:35, God's Word will stand even when heaven and earth will pass away. These passages put God's Word outside the created world and indicate that His Word is more permanent and enduring than creation. Since the created world came into being and is sustained by His Word, this makes perfect sense.

For all are Your servants means the psalmist looked at the created order and understood that all creation ultimately serves God and His purpose. The earth, which He established, and which abides, obeys His Word. There is a wonderful and inspiring link between the beauty, power, and order of creation and the beauty, power, and order of God's Word.

As one of His creatures, do something today: read, meditate on, and believe God's enduring word.

July 9

Like a Meteor on a Dark Night

And Elijah the Tishbite, of the inhabitants of Gilead, said to Ahab, "As the Lord God of Israel lives, before whom I stand, there shall not be dew nor rain these years, except at my word." (1 Kings 17:1)

The times were so chaotic that the Kingdom of Israel had seen four dynasties rise in rapid succession. It was a crucial time in Israel's history. It looked as if the worship of the true God might be virtually eliminated in the northern kingdom. It was a time when the whole nation seemed to be apostate. As it was later discovered, there were seven thousand who had remained faithful to God, but those were well hidden, and Elijah had every reason to feel alone.

At this crucial time in the history of Judah and Israel, the prophet Elijah suddenly appeared, shining like a meteor on a black night. He became the dominant spiritual force in Israel during the dark days of Ahab's apostasy. Even the name Elijah means "Yahweh is my God."

Elijah said, **there shall not be dew nor rain these years, except at my word.** This was a dramatic demonstration against the pagan god Baal, who was thought to be the god of the weather. Elijah showed that through his prayers to the God of Israel, Yahweh was mightier than Baal.

Elijah was not merely the prophet of this drought. In the sense of prayer, he was also the cause of the drought. James 5:17-18 makes this clear: *Elijah was a man with a nature like ours, and he prayed earnestly that it would not rain; and it did not rain on the land for three years and six months. And he prayed again, and the heaven gave rain, and the earth produced its fruit.*

Elijah revealed the source of his strength: **as the Lord God of Israel lives, before whom I stand**. It is specifically said, *Elijah was a man with a nature like ours* (James 5:17). Yet he showed a strength greater than most of us in our lives with God. We must pay attention to these two indications revealing the source of Elijah's strength.

First, he said, **As the Lord God of Israel lives**. Everyone else felt that the Lord was dead, but for Elijah, the Lord lived. He was the supreme reality of Elijah's life.

Second, he said, **before whom I stand**. Elijah stood in the presence of Ahab, but he was conscious of the presence of Someone greater than any earthly king. Gabriel himself could not choose a higher title (Luke 1:19).

It is easy to see that we also live in a dark day. Should we not expect God to raise up new Elijahs today – men and women of such moral and spiritual strength that they shine like a meteor on a dark night?

Today, remember that Elijah was a person just like you; if he had your weaknesses then you – with God's blessing – can have his strength.

The Light-Giving Word

The entrance of Your words gives light; it gives understanding to the simple. I opened my mouth and panted, for I longed for Your commandments. (Psalm 119:130-131)

It is a theme mentioned before in Psalm 119, but in these verses, the author of the great psalm repeated it: **the entrance of Your words gives light**. The idea is simple: God's Word brought light to him. The Word of God makes things clearer not cloudier. When the Bible came in, light and clarity also came.

The Hebrew word translated **entrance** here can have two meanings, depending on how it is pronounced. With one sound, the word means, "door," and with another pronunciation, it means "revelation." According to James Boice, the reason for this double meaning was that for centuries the Jewish people lived in tents, and when the door to the tent was opened, light came in, and the light revealed everything in the tent. Martin Luther translated this phrase as, "When Your word is revealed."

With the Word of God, the door must be opened – then the light can come. Sometimes the door to our understanding is blocked by pride, prejudice, or apathy. When the obstacles are removed, and we give proper attention to God and His Word, light enters.

That's why the psalmist could write, **it gives understanding to the simple**. The idea of **simple** does not mean someone who is stupid, but just an everyday person, and perhaps someone who doesn't have much life experience. The Word of God is so clear and light-giving that even simple people gain understanding from it. It does not take great intellect or mental powers to benefit from God's Word.

It's beautiful to see God's concern for the simple, and the Bible is for them.

- This is a *blessing* for the simple; God does not forget them. He has not made salvation or growth in godliness primarily a matter of the intellect.
- This is a *promise* for the simple; they can approach God's Word with confidence, expecting God to give them understanding.
- This is a *responsibility* for the simple; they cannot make excuses for their average (or less) intellect or mental powers. They are still responsible for seeking God in His Word.

This is why he wanted God's truth so much: **I opened my mouth and panted, for I longed for Your commandments**. Because the Word of God is light-giving and clear enough even for the simple, the psalmist wanted God's Word, in the same way a thirsty animal pants after water. He may have panted because of thirst, or he may have panted gasping for air, but either way, panting means desire.

The word **opened** has a particular idea, describing the eager thirst of an animal. Think of a dog or a horse after a run, and how they go straight for their drinking water. The psalmist was thirsty for God and His Word in the same way.

Do you get thirsty for God and His Word?

July 11
Looking Outward

And on some have compassion, making a distinction; but others save with fear, pulling them out of the fire, hating even the garment defiled by the flesh. (Jude v. 22-23)

Jude is one of the shortest books in the New Testament – but in this brief letter Jude spent most of his time explaining the character and the fate of certain dangerous men who threatened the early church and God's people.

Jude didn't recommend a search and destroy mission against these dangerous men. While he wanted Christians to guard against them, he never wanted the focus of God's people to be on possible deceivers.

Consider what Jude recommended considering the present danger. He told us that on some we should **have compassion**. With this, Jude told us what we should do with those who have been influenced by dangerous men and their ideas. We must do it wisely, making a distinction, based on their circumstances and spiritual condition.

This reminds us that using wisdom, we approach different people in different ways. By being sensitive to the Holy Spirit, we can know when we should comfort and when we should rebuke. Certainly, in many cases, the correct response is **on some have compassion**.

This means loving them. No matter how bad a person is or how misleading and terrible their doctrine might be, we still are not allowed to hate them – or to be unconcerned for their salvation and spiritual well-being. Christians should not abandon a friend flirting with false teaching. They should help them through the difficult season in love instead of treating them like a spiritual leper.

There are also those whom we must **save with fear**. This second group must be confronted more strongly – but in fear, not with a sanctimonious superiority. You may need to pull them out of the fire, but never do it in pride. Any correction must be done with a humble heart – one that cares about spiritual purity (**hating even the garment defiled by the flesh**) but will do it humbly before God (**with fear**).

The apostle Paul communicated much the same idea in Galatians 6:1: *Brethren, if a man is overtaken in any trespass, you who are spiritual restore such a one in a spirit of gentleness, considering yourself lest you also be tempted.* The overtaken ones need to be restored. They are not to be ignored. They are not to be excused. They are not to be destroyed. The goal is always restoration.

This outward look is important. Are you only concerned about your own spiritual welfare? Or do you care about other Christians who are edging towards significant error? Some only want to take the inward look Jude mentioned in Jude v. 20-21, yet we should never neglect the outward look he directs us to in Jude v. 22-23.

Today, the love and the nature of Jesus calls you to look outside yourself to care about others.

July 12

Asleep in the Storm

Then the mariners were afraid; and every man cried out to his god, and threw the cargo that was in the ship into the sea, to lighten the load. But Jonah had gone down into the lowest parts of the ship, had lain down, and was fast asleep. So the captain came to him, and said to him, "What do you mean, sleeper? Arise, call on your God; perhaps your God will consider us, so that we may not perish." (Jonah 1:5-6)

The thought of an exhausted Jesus sleeping in the boat on the stormy Sea of Galilee is touching. The thought of rebellious, disobedient Jonah asleep in the boat is not. What a curious and tragic scene! All the sailors were religious men, devout in prayer to their gods. Yet their gods were nothing and could do nothing. There was one man on board who had a relationship with the true God, who knew his Word, and who worshipped Him – yet he was asleep!

With the storms whipped up by the world, the flesh, and devil there is no proper place for a sleeping Christian. Yet some are like Jonah and have no problem sleeping while the storm rages around them and lives hang in the balance. The nature of Jonah's sleep can teach us because it is all too much like the sleep of the careless Christian:

- Jonah slept in a place where he hoped no one would see him or disturb him, and sleeping Christians like to "hide out" among the church.
- Jonah slept in a place where he couldn't t help with the work that needed to be done, and sleeping Christians stay away from the work of the Lord.
- Jonah slept while there was a prayer meeting up on deck. Sleeping Christians don't like prayer meetings.
- Jonah slept and was oblivious to the problems around him. Sleeping Christians have their eyes closed to what is really happening around them.
- Jonah slept when he was in great danger. Sleeping Christians are in danger, but don't know it.
- Jonah slept while the heathen needed him. Sleeping Christians snooze on while the world needs their message and testimony.

Some sleeping Christians protest that they are not asleep at all, but there is a way to test this. Perhaps the best way to know you are fully awake is to see if you live with a true, thorough consciousness of spiritual things. Are heaven and hell real to you, or are they just vague ideas? Is the soul of another person less real to you than their physical form? Truly awake Christians live with a full and proper awareness of the things that matter, the things of eternity. They think and act considering eternal matters, not in passing shadows and dreams.

Perhaps it is time for us to hear what the captain of the ship said to Jonah: **What do you mean, sleeper? Arise, call on your God.**

Today, **call on your God** and ask Him to make you fully awake.

July 13

Bitter Made Sweet

So Moses brought Israel from the Red Sea; then they went out into the Wilderness of Shur. And they went three days in the wilderness and found no water. Now when they came to Marah, they could not drink the waters of Marah, for they were bitter. Therefore the name of it was called Marah. And the people complained against Moses, saying, 'What shall we drink?' So he cried out to the Lord, and the Lord showed him a tree. When he cast it into the waters, the waters were made sweet. (Exodus 15:22-25)

The miracle of the Red Sea was spectacular, but three days is time enough to forget the victory. Wow Israel faced a long trip through a challenging, dry desert. After three parched, thirsty days, they finally came to water. But when they found the pool of water, it must have seemed like a cruel joke. To eventually come to water, and then to find that the water undrinkable! The water tasted sour, so they named the place **Marah**, – which means "bitter."

But God had a plan. He directed Moses to take **a tree** – or perhaps a portion of the tree – and cast it into the polluted pool. Somehow, the tree made the waters drinkable, and God supplied their need.

How did the tree work? In his book on the Exodus journey, author Jamie Buckingham believed that the chemicals in the sap of the broken limb drew the mineral content down to the bottom of the pool and left only good water on top. Based on the mineral composition of water pools in that part of the world, he thought that though the waters were now drinkable, they still had a significant magnesium and calcium content. These chemicals would purge their bodies from common Egyptian ailments such as dysentery and other weakening diseases. Also, the calcium and magnesium form the basis of a supplement called dolomite – used by some athletes to enhance their performance in hot weather conditions. If Buckingham is correct, then at Marah, God provided the precise medicine to clean out their systems and prepare them for the long, hot march to Sinai.

One way or another, the point is evident. God was not only interested in getting the children of Israel out of Egypt. He also wanted to get Egypt out of the children of Israel – both physically and spiritually. God planned the transformation a slave people into a Promised Land people. He used some tough times in the desert to accomplish that goal, but God always had that goal in sight. His goal was not to make them thirsty at Marah but to make them Promised Land people.

God's work is essentially the same in believers today. That means God must take us out of a sinful environment, and then He must take a sinful environment out of us.

What does God want to work out of you to make you more of a Promised Land kind of person?

The Way Moses Prayed

July 14

Now if You kill these people as one man, then the nations which have heard of Your fame will speak, saying, "Because the Lord was not able to bring this people to the land which He swore to give them, therefore He killed them in the wilderness." And now, I pray, let the power of my Lord be great, just as You have spoken, saying, "The Lord is longsuffering and abundant in mercy, forgiving iniquity and transgression... Pardon the iniquity of this people, I pray, according to the greatness of Your mercy, just as You have forgiven this people, from Egypt even until now." Then the Lord said: "I have pardoned, according to your word." (Numbers 14:15-20)

Israel had rejected God – again! Numbers 14 describes how they not only refused to believe what God had told them, but they also accused God of plotting the murder of Israel's children. Enough was enough, and God told Moses of His intention to wipe out the nation and start all over again – making Moses the father of a brand new, better nation. That's when Moses began to pray.

Moses prayed with a zeal for God's glory. He knew that if God wiped out the present nation and started again with Moses, it would be a "black mark" on His reputation before the nations – especially Egypt. Could then the nations claim that the Lord was not able to bring this people to the land? Is the sin and rebellion of man greater than the power and goodness of God?

Moses cared about God's glory and reputation and prayed with an understanding of God's power to wipe out Israel in an instant. He gloried in the power of God but asked that God would use His power by showing mercy and longsuffering to a rebellious Israel. Do we know God is powerful and ask Him to use it in the right ways?

Moses prayed with trust in God's Word. In his prayer, he quoted what God said about Himself in His dramatic encounter with Moses in Exodus 34:6-8: *God is longsuffering...abundant...forgiving iniquity and transgression...by no means clears the guilty...great in mercy*. Moses basically said: "Lord, You have revealed Yourself to me by Your word. Your word declares who You are. Now Lord, please act towards Israel according to who You have declared Yourself to be in Your word."

Moses knew God's glory and appealed to it; he knew God's power and appealed to it; Moses knew God's promise and appealed to it. What a great example of intercession! What made this intercession impressive was not primarily Moses' method but his heart. Moses was completely others-centered, not concerned for his own glory, but only for Israel.

This, of course, was God's intention all along: to develop and draw out of Moses just this kind of heart, transforming him into the image of His Son (Romans 8:29), far before the time of Jesus.

Make this your prayer today.

July 15

Real Reasons for Comfort

"**Comfort, yes, comfort My people!**" Says your God. "**Speak comfort to Jerusalem, and cry out to her, that her warfare is ended, that her iniquity is pardoned; for she has received from the Lord's hand double for all her sins.**" (Isaiah 40:1-2)

Isaiah spoke to hurting hearts when he cried out, **comfort, yes, comfort My people!** Isaiah knew what it was to warn and instruct God's people, but the Lord also wanted His people to receive His **comfort**. 2 Corinthians 1:3 speaks of our Lord as the God of all comfort; God wants His messengers to speak comfort to His people.

God told him to **Speak comfort to Jerusalem**. This means that Jerusalem needed a word of comfort. God always gives His people reasons for comfort.

The announcement, **her warfare is ended** may have been a prophetic word. Even though there was still an army against them, as far as God was concerned, her warfare was ended. God says we can be more than conquerors through Him who loved us (Romans 8:37). The battle still looms, but as far as it concerns the believer in Jesus Christ, her warfare is ended, because *You are of God, little children, and have overcome them, because He who is in you is greater than he who is in the world* (1 John 4:4). This is reason for comfort.

God also announced that Israel's **iniquity** was **pardoned**. When Isaiah spoke this, Jerusalem was aware of her sin – Isaiah had made that clear. Yet, the prophet spoke of a day when comfort could be offered because **her iniquity** was **pardoned**. This is real comfort – to be recognized as a sinner, one having iniquity – knowing just as certainly that our iniquity is pardoned. This was reason for comfort.

There was a basis for the pardon of iniquity – sin has been completely paid for. Israel had **received from the Lord's hand double for all her sins**. Isaiah, speaking in old covenant terminology, spoke of Jerusalem bearing the curse for disobedience described in passages like Leviticus 26 and Deuteronomy 28. But the same principle applies to the believer under the new covenant; our iniquity is pardoned because our sin has been paid for. This is reason for comfort.

Does it seem unfair that God would have a double payment for sin? One Old Testament scholar said that double here means, "to fold over, fold in half" (as in Exodus 26:9). When something is folded over, each half corresponds exactly with the other half. There is an exact correspondence between sin and payment.

Under the new covenant, it is not the believer who has **received from the Lord's hand double for all her sins**; it was their sin-bearing Savior Jesus Christ, who received the cup of wrath from the Lord's hand double for all their sins.

All this is much more than wishful thinking; God gives us real reasons for comfort.

Take those reasons to heart today.

July 16

Don't Conform, Transform

And do not be conformed to this world, but be transformed by the renewing of your mind, that you may prove what *is* that good and acceptable and perfect will of God. (Romans 12:2)

Romans 1 through 11 is heavy on right thinking, on good theology. Starting with chapter 12, the apostle Paul focused more on living out the truth already presented. Because of what God has done in the believer, they should **not be conformed to this world**. This warns us that the popular culture and thinking that is in rebellion against God will try to conform us to its ungodly pattern, and we must resist that process.

The opposite of being **conformed to this world** is to **be transformed by the renewing of your mind**. The battleground between conforming to the world and being transformed is in the **mind** of the believer. *Christians must think differently.* "I don't want to be conformed to this world. I want to be transformed. How do I do it?" **By the renewing of your mind**. The problem with many Christians is they live based on *feelings*, or they are only concerned about *doing*.

The life based on *feeling* says, "How do I feel today? How do I feel about my job? How do I feel about my marriage? How do I feel about worship? How do I feel about the preacher?" This life by feeling will never know the transforming power of God because it neglects the **renewing of the mind**.

The life based on *doing* says, "Don't give me your theology. Just tell me what to *do*. Give me the four points for this and the seven keys for that." This life of doing will never know the transforming power of God, because it neglects the **renewing of the mind**.

God is never against the principles of feeling and doing. He is a God of powerful and passionate feeling, and He commands us to be doers. Yet feelings and doing are completely insufficient *foundations* for the Christian life. The first questions cannot be "How do I feel?" or "What do I do?" Rather, they must be "What is true here? What does God's Word say?" This is how minds are renewed and lives are **transformed**.

As we are **transformed** on the inside, the *proof* is evident on the outside, as others can see what the **good and acceptable and perfect will of God** is through our life.

Here is how to live out the will of God:

- Keep in mind the rich mercy of God to you – past, present, and future.
- As an act of intelligent worship, decide to yield your entire self to Him.
- Resist conformity to the thoughts and actions of this world.
- As you focus on God's truth and follow Jesus, God will transform your life.
- Your life will **prove** the **good and acceptable and perfect will of God**.

Don't conform – transform by the power of God's Spirit and His truth.

July 17

Tired Eyes for a Good Reason

My eyes fail from seeking Your salvation and Your righteous word. Deal with Your servant according to Your mercy, and teach me Your statutes. I am Your servant; give me understanding, that I may know Your testimonies. (Psalm 119:123-125)

If you look at something for a long time, your eyes may begin to hurt. The poet-author of Psalm 119 loved and looked at God's Word so intently that he could say, **my eyes fail from seeking Your salvation and Your righteous word**. This was another indication of how committed the psalmist was to the Word of God, and how much he valued the salvation he found from it.

It was not just that he read God's Word; he also sought God's **salvation** found in it. The psalmist had many oppressors and enemies, and he sought help in and from God's Word. The good news is that even if our eyes fail, God will never fail, and God's eyes never fail to see us and look on us with sympathy and compassion.

This waiting expectation shows us that *faith* came before *experience*. The psalmist was willing to have faith until the experience came, and would wait for God's salvation, and wait for as long as it took.

As he sought God in His Word, the psalmist made a request: **Deal with Your servant according to Your mercy, and teach me Your statutes**. The singer understood that when God teaches His people, it is evidence of His great **mercy**. God has no necessary obligation to teach us anything. Yet out of the merciful compassion of His heart, He does so.

Then the psalmist cried out, **I am Your servant; give me understanding**. For the third time in five verses, the psalmist called himself a **servant** of God. He understood that this meant he had obligations to God, and that God – as his Master – had obligations to him. Therefore, he could ask for **understanding**. It is only right that a master would teach his servant the meaning of his orders, and God is the right Master to us.

All this made the psalmist continue his prayer by asking, **give me understanding, that I may know Your testimonies**. The psalmist wanted to understand, but not so much as to know the future or some hidden secrets of his soul or those of anyone else. He wanted this **understanding** so that he would understand the testimonies of God better.

He believed that with the help of God, the Word of God could be understood. He also believed that understanding God's Word was of great importance because it would lead him to wisdom and the knowledge of life.

The psalmist was right. God's Word can be understood, perhaps not in every detail, but it is evident in its grand themes and subjects. It's also true that understanding God's Word leads us to greater wisdom and understanding for all of life.

It is so valuable that it is worth getting tired eyes every so often.

July 18
No Prayer, Selfish Prayer, and Real Prayer

Where do wars and fights come from among you? Do they not come from your desires for pleasure that war in your members? You lust and do not have. You murder and covet and cannot obtain. You fight and war. Yet you do not have because you do not ask. You ask and do not receive, because you ask amiss, that you may spend it on your pleasures. (James 4:1-3)

James wrote about the destructive desires that make for conflict among people, including the people of God. He first reminded us of the fact of conflict. Then he exposed the reason for the conflict: the frustrated **desires for pleasure** that bring us into battle with one another.

James explained the reason for the frustrated, destructive desires among the followers of Jesus: **you do not have because you do not ask**. The reason these destructive desires exist among Christians is that they don't seek God for their needs (**you do not ask**). James reminds us of the great power of prayer and why one may live unnecessarily as a spiritual pauper simply because they do not pray or ask when they pray.

We might state almost as a virtual spiritual law: that God does not give unless we ask. If we possess little of God and His Kingdom, almost certainly, we have asked little. We expect little of God, ask for little from God, and we are answered according to our expectations and asking.

James addressed the problem of selfish prayer: **You ask amiss, that you may spend it on your pleasures**. When they did ask, they asked God with purely selfish motives.

It is seen even more clearly when we look at the word James used, translated here as **spend**. It is the same verb used to describe the wasteful spending of the Prodigal Son in Luke 15:14. Destructive desires persist even if we pray, because our prayers may be self-centered and self-indulgent.

We must remember that the purpose of prayer is not to persuade a reluctant God to do what we want. The purpose of prayer is to align our will with His, and in partnership with Him, to ask Him to accomplish His will on this earth (Matthew 6:10).

That great preacher of Victorian England, Charles Spurgeon, eloquently said: "If you may have everything by asking, and nothing without asking, I beg you to see how absolutely vital prayer is, and I beseech you to abound in it.... All heaven lies before the grasp of the asking man."

When we guard ourselves against the danger of no prayer and against the danger of selfish prayer, we are ready to pray and receive. As we pray and receive, the destructive presence of frustrated desire fades away, and we are in the right frame of mind and spirit to get along with others.

Today, remember the great power and privilege there is in prayer.

July 19

Take Him as He Was

They took Him along in the boat as He was. (Mark 4:36)

At this point in His ministry, Jesus was so popular that the crowds mercilessly pressed on Him. To teach more effectively, Jesus used a boat for His pulpit. The crowd gathered on the shore and Jesus sat in a boat and taught them, just a few yards offshore. After a long day of teaching, Jesus wanted to finish. Instead of returning to shore where the crowds gave Him no rest, Jesus said to the disciples, "Let's go to the other side of the Sea of Galilee." So, the rest of the disciples climbed into the boat, taking Jesus **along in the boat as He was.**

They did not stop for supplies or send a messenger ahead. They were tired and hungry – especially Jesus – but **they took Him along in the boat as He was**.

We must take Jesus **as He was**. Almost every world religion has something kind to say about Jesus. They want to take Him, but not **as He was**.

Some people take Jesus as they *wish* He was. They imagine Him as "Jesus the political reformer," and they create a Jesus of their imagination by what they leave out of His teaching. People do the same thing when they create "Jesus the moral reformer" or "Jesus who never offended anyone." But we can't do that; we must take Jesus **as He was**.

Some people take Jesus as others present Him. But even the best sermon about Jesus falls short of Jesus Himself. Teaching about Jesus is good if it helps us to take Him **as He was**, but no one's teaching – no matter how good – can do the whole job. This is why we must come to the Word of God and Jesus the Word, again and again, asking God to help us take Jesus **as He was**.

Some people take Jesus as they see Him in the lives of others. Every Christian has the responsibility to reflect Jesus in their life, but no one does it perfectly. If you look at a strong area of my life, you may see some of Jesus reflected there. But if you look for Jesus in a weak area of my life, you may not see Him as well. If we only take Jesus as He is reflected in the lives of others, we won't get a true representation of who He is. We must take Him **as He was**.

A.W. Tozer wrote, "What comes to our minds when we think of God is the most important thing about us." If we will be correct about what comes to our minds when we think of God, we must take Jesus **as He was**.

Not as we wish Jesus was.

Not as others may present Jesus.

Not as you might see Him in the lives of others.

What keeps you from taking Jesus as He was?

July 20

The Spirit and the Word

So Ezra the scribe stood on a platform of wood which they had made for the purpose; and beside him, [godly men].... And Ezra opened the book in the sight of all the people, for he was standing above all the people; and when he opened it, all the people stood up. And Ezra blessed the LORD**, the great God. Then all the people answered, "Amen, Amen!" while lifting up their hands. And they bowed their heads and worshipped the L**ORD** with their faces to the ground.** (Nehemiah 8:4-6)

The great scholar of religious awakening J. Edwin Orr defined revival as: "The Spirit of God working through the Word of God, in the lives of the people of God." Nehemiah 8 gives us a great example of this. The Spirit of God was working in the people of God, and at the center was the Word of God. Notice how the people received the Word of God.

First, they prepared to hear the Word of God. They built a **platform of wood** so the Word of God could be heard. They did practical things so God's Word would have the greatest effect. Consider some practical things you can do to receive the word more effectively.

Second, people supported the presentation of God's Word. On the right and left hand of Ezra stood men supporting him in his ministry of teaching God's Word. The ministry of God's Word has the greatest effect when people can see others supporting and obeying it.

Next, they had respect for God's Word. When Ezra opened the scroll, all the people stood up. They recognized it as the Word of God, not the word of man. In some old churches, when the preacher was ready to speak, a trusted deacon would walk from the back, up the center aisle to the pulpit, carrying a huge Bible. The congregation stood as the Bible came down the aisle and the deacon placed it on the podium, and then the preacher began to speak. This showed that the preacher's authority came to him from the Bible and the respect the people had for the Word of God. God wants us to honor it in the best way possible – by believing it and living it.

In Nehemiah 8, the Word of God had real results. The people thanked God (by saying **Amen** when Ezra blessed the LORD), they prayed (by **lifting up their hands**), and they worshipped (by bowing down before Him). Thanksgiving, prayer, and praise reveal how the Spirit of God and the Word of God are working in us.

Many of us really want to see revival, to see the Spirit of God working through the Word of God and touching the lives of the people of God. We should do what an old evangelist recommended: "go home, draw a circle around a chair, and sit in the chair. Then pray for revival and ask God to start right in that circle."

As you do that – do not forget your Bible!

July 21

Three Signs

Then it will be, if they do not believe you, nor heed the message of the first sign, that they may believe the message of the latter sign. And it shall be, if they do not believe even these two signs, or listen to your voice, that you shall take water from the river and pour it on the dry land. And the water which you take from the river will become blood on the dry land. (Exodus 4:8-9)

Moses was on a mission from God, but he had to persuade the rest of the people of Israel. Moses couldn't lead them out of Egypt unless they wanted to go. He had to prove himself, so God gave Moses three signs to provide the proof.

The first sign was for Moses to take his shepherd's staff, throw it on the ground, and God would miraculously change the staff into a real snake. Then Moses was to pick up the snake by the tail (a dangerous thing to do) and the snake would turn into a shepherd's staff again.

The second sign was for Moses to take his hand and put it inside his robe. When he pulled it out, it would be white with leprosy. When he put the leprous hand back in his robe and pulled it out again, it would be just as healthy as before.

Each of the first two signs had to do with *conversion*. In each, something good and useful (a rod or a hand) was converted to something evil (a serpent or a leprous hand). Then, miraculously, it was converted back into something good and useful again.

There was a real message in the first two signs. The first sign said, "Moses, if you obey Me, your enemies will be made powerless." The second sign said, "Moses, if you obey Me, your pollution can be made pure." God gave Moses these signs because he was worried in both areas. He thought, "I can't go back to Egypt, because I have enemies there" and, "I can't go back to Egypt, I have a criminal record there." Before these signs touched the heart of anyone else, they touched the heart of Moses. This is always the pattern with God's leaders. They can't touch the hearts of others until their hearts are touched.

The third sign was a sign of judgment. Pure waters were made foul and bloody by the work of God – and they did not become pure again. If the miracles of conversion did not turn the hearts of the people, then perhaps the sign of judgment would. But the sign of judgment was only given when unbelief persisted in the face of the miracles of conversion.

God has put miracles of conversion right in front of you. Perhaps He has even put a miracle of conversion in your mirror!

Today, learn from God's miracles of conversion, and trust Him. Then you won't need to learn through a sign of judgment.

Why We Love Jesus

We love Him because He first loved us. (1 John 4:19)

"I just love Jesus." I've heard it many times from many people. Often, they mean it like this: "I don't care much about church or the Bible or organized religion or theology. I simply love Jesus." But simply, truly loving Jesus is full of meaning. Why? Why does anyone truly love Jesus? John gives us the answer in eight easy words: **We love Him because He first loved us**.

First, there is a fact stated: **We love Him**. John begins by declaring the heart of every true follower of Jesus Christ. Simply and boldly put, **we love Him**. This is true of every genuine disciple of Jesus. It is something that every Christian should be unafraid to proclaim: "I love Him; I love Jesus." Can you say that? Are you embarrassed to say it? Can you say, "I love Jesus"?

This verse not only declares our love for Jesus, it tells us *when* He loved us: **He first loved us**. Some people imagine that Jesus loved us because He knew we would love Him and come to faith in Him. But He loved us long before that, and even before the worlds were created, when our only existence was in the mind and heart of God. Even then, Jesus loved us. He loved us when we were still sinners.

This verse tells us where our love for Jesus comes from. It comes from Him! **We love Him because He first loved us**. Our love for God is always in response to His love for us; He initiates, and we respond. We never have to draw God to us; instead, He draws us to Himself.

This verse tells us why we love Jesus and how we can love Him more: **We love Him because He first loved us**. The great preacher of Victorian England Charles Spurgeon said something very helpful here: "Yet we must not try to make ourselves love our Lord, but look to Christ's love first, for his love to us will beget in us love to him. I know that some of you are greatly distressed because you cannot love Christ as much as you would like to do, and you keep on fretting because it is so. Now, just forget your own love to him, and think of his great love to you; and then, immediately, your love will come to something more like that which you would desire it to be."

Did you get that? Instead of working hard to love Jesus more, meditate more on His great love for you. Based on this principle of 1 John 4:19, you can be assured that greater love for Him will begin to rise within you as you consider more fully how much He loves you.

Finally, if **He first loved us**, then it is true that He loves us now. Do you believe it?

Today, let it sink down deep into your heart: **we love Him because He first loved us**.

July 23

Angry – But Is It Right?

Then the Lord said, "Is it right for you to be angry?" (Jonah 4:4)

Jonah had results the most ambitious preacher would be proud of – after a short, harsh sermon constantly repeated, a city repented so radically that even their livestock got right with God. God's mercy held back the promised punishment because every warning of coming judgment is an implied invitation to repent.

Even with these impressive results, Jonah wasn't happy. He was more depressed and angrier than ever because God spared the Assyrians of Nineveh. The Assyrians were infamous for their cruel and brutal treatment of other nations, and God's people in Judah and Israel felt some of their terror. Jonah wanted the Ninevites buried under God's judgment, and it made him angry when they repented.

The prophet stewed in his anger for a while. He even complained that the burden of living with the spared city of Nineveh was more than he could bear, and he begged God to take his life (Jonah 4:3). Jonah then heard the word of the Lord again but this time it was for him, not for the people of Nineveh. It was a simple question: **Is it right for you to be angry?** As Jonah expressed his anger against God, it was good that he was honest about his feelings; nevertheless, we should never think that all our feelings towards God are justified.

God likes to ask questions because they reveal the heart of men and women:

- Where are you? Who told you that you were naked? What is this you have done? (Genesis 3)
- Where is your brother Abel? What have you done? (Genesis 4)
- Why did you despise the word of the Lord by doing what is evil in his eyes? (2 Samuel 12)
- Whom shall I send? Who will go for us? (Isaiah 6)
- Who do you say that I am? (Matthew 16)
- What do you want Me to do for you? (Matthew 20)
- Are you betraying the Son of Man with a kiss? (Luke 22)
- Why are you persecuting Me? (Acts 9)

Sometimes when others question us, we feel defensive and wonder just who they think they are to question us. When God asks the questions, we know He has every right to ask – and we know that every question He asks has a loving purpose behind it.

If we are angry against God, He will ask us the same question He asked Jonah: **Is it right for you to be angry?** And the answer must always be "No, Lord. All Your ways are right even if I don't understand them."

Remember that God has never sinned against us, and we can trust Him even when we don't understand what He is doing.

July 24

Doing Good for the Right Motives

Take heed that you do not do your charitable deeds before men, to be seen by them. Otherwise you have no reward from your Father in heaven. (Matthew 6:1)

As Jesus continued the Sermon on the Mount, He described the character and lifestyle of the "citizens" of His kingdom. It was as if Jesus said, "I come as a King, but not the kind of king you expected. Let Me tell you how My reign impacts the lives of those who follow Me; let Me describe the character of My kingdom."

In the previous section of this sermon, Jesus explained the true interpretation of the law of God. Many people in His day had the habit of re-explaining God's law in a way that made it easier to obey, but essentially stripped the law of its God-intended meaning. So, Jesus showed us the kind of understanding of the law that really honors God.

After showing God's righteous standard in its true understanding, perhaps Jesus anticipated the thoughts in the minds of the listeners: "Wouldn't everybody be impressed if I was like that?" So here Jesus addressed the danger of cultivating the mere image of righteousness. It is almost impossible to do spiritual things in front of others without thinking what their opinion is of us as we do those things, and how they are thinking better or worse of us as we do what we do.

Therefore, Jesus said, **take heed that you do not do your charitable deeds before men**. The word translated **charitable deeds** is actually the word "righteousness." Jesus told us to not do righteous things for the sake of display or image (**to be seen by them**).

It should be noted that this does not contradict His previous command to *let your light so shine before men* (Matthew 5:16). Although the followers of Jesus are to be seen doing good works, they must not do good works simply to be seen.

Jesus explained: **Otherwise you have no reward from your Father in heaven**. The idea is when we do righteous deeds for the attention and applause of men, their attention and applause is our reward. It is much better to receive a **reward from your Father in heaven**.

There are some people who say, "All that is important is the doing of the deed. How I do it is much less important than the doing of it." It is true that in some cases it would be better to do the right thing in the wrong way or out of the wrong motive than to do the wrong thing, but Jesus' point is clear: God cares about how we do our good works, and with what motive we do them.

Jesus thus begins to deal with three spiritual disciplines: giving, prayer, and fasting. As He does, we shouldn't forget this fundamental principle: God cares about how we do our good works, and with what motive we do them.

Today, ask God to work on your motives in doing what you do for Him.

July 25

Never Forgotten

Can a woman forget her nursing child, and not have compassion on the son of her womb? Surely they may forget, yet I will not forget you. See, I have inscribed you on the palms of My hands; your walls are continually before Me. Your sons shall make haste; your destroyers and those who laid you waste shall go away from you. Lift up your eyes, look around and see; all these gather together and come to you. "As I live," says the LORD, "You shall surely clothe yourselves with them all as an ornament, and bind them on you as a bride does." (Isaiah 49:15-18)

It is a strange and terrible thing for a mother to abandon her baby; therefore God, speaking through the prophet Isaiah, asked: **Can a woman forget her nursing child**? Though bizarre accounts of unspeakable cruelty surface from time to time, everyone knows that a woman will never forget her nursing child. Yet the LORD says, **surely they will forget, yet I will not forget you**. The LORD's affection for His people is greater than the devotion a woman has for her nursing child!

God told His people He had **inscribed** them **on the palms** of His **hands**. This has obvious and beautiful fulfillment in the nail-scarred hands of Jesus. As Jesus told Thomas in a post-resurrection appearance, *look at My hands* (John 20:27). When we see the nail-scarred hands of Jesus, we see how He has inscribed us on the palms of His hands. With such love, how could God ever forget His people?

Then God said: **Your walls are continually before Me**. The **walls** refer to the walls of the city of Jerusalem, which figuratively speak of the health, strength, prosperity, and security of God's people. God is always mindful of the condition of His people, despite the objections of a doubting Zion.

It is a deeply painful thing to feel alone and forgotten, and seasons of crisis make us feel this way even more. God wanted His people to know that He had not forgotten them, and He would never forget about them. This was especially relevant for the people Isaiah originally wrote to because they were headed for exile and captivity under the mighty Babylonian Empire. God knew that amid this crisis they would tend to feel forgotten, so He gave great assurance to His people.

The LORD would bring back the exiled and captive sons of Zion to the Promised Land, and this will be an **ornament** for God's people. They would come quickly, in **haste**. The LORD's love and faithfulness for Zion is also shown by His promise for their future. It isn't just demonstrated by the past and the present, but also by His future plans.

This was true of God's ancient people in the Kingdom of Judah; it is also true of His people today.

Today, remember this: past, present, or future – God has not forgotten you.

What You Say

These are grumblers, complainers, walking according to their own lusts; and they mouth great swelling words, flattering people to gain advantage. But you, beloved, remember the words which were spoken before by the apostles of our Lord Jesus Christ: how they told you that there would be mockers in the last time who would walk according to their own ungodly lusts. (Jude v. 16-18)

Jude warned the early church about dangerous people in their midst, and his warning echoes across the centuries to us today.

Jude described the actions of these dangerous men among the Christians. He said they were **grumblers, complainers** and that **they mouth great swelling words, flattering people**. It shows us how much trouble our words can cause for ourselves and for others. James warned us that our tongue can be like a match that can light a whole forest on fire. The match is a small thing, but it can bring massive destruction (James 3).

Jude says, **these are grumblers, complainers**. It has rightly been said, "Whenever a man gets out of touch with God, he is likely to begin complaining about something." Our grumbling and complaining is an insult to God. He gives us all things and has promised that nothing can separate us from His love. When we live with a sour, complaining attitude we may as well tell God that He doesn't care about us and that His promises are lies.

Their tongue-problem went further than just complaining. They also were guilty of **flattering people**. These certain men knew how to use smooth, flattering words to get an advantage over other people. They would say anything – good or bad – to get an advantage. This is a different misuse of the tongue, but an evil one just the same.

Jude believed that Christians should be different. We are to remember what Jesus and the apostles taught. The Word of God is always the answer to dangers in or out of the church. When your mouth is filled with God's Word it is much less likely to be filled with grumbling or empty flattery.

When we remember the words of the apostles, they warned us **there would be mockers in the last time**. Perhaps Jude had in mind those who mocked the idea of Jesus' return. These were **mockers...who would walk according to their own ungodly lusts**, who often love to mock those who want to please God. Jude wanted Christians to expect this kind of mocking, so they wouldn't be surprised by it.

How about your words? With what you say, are you building others up or are you tearing them down? Perhaps you think you are quite a prophet, and God has given you the ministry of criticizing and exposing wrongs. Think again about the New Testament description of prophetic ministry: he who prophesies speaks edification and exhortation and comfort to men (1 Corinthians 14:3).

Today, use your words to build up rather than to tear down.

July 27

Truth and Godliness, In One Accord

Paul, a bondservant of God and an apostle of Jesus Christ, according to the faith of God's elect and the acknowledgment of the truth which accords with godliness. (Titus 1:1)

The apostle Paul had many associates and co-workers. One of them was a younger man named Titus. They worked together spreading the good news of Jesus Christ and establishing churches among the believers on the island of Crete.

When Paul had to leave, and Titus was left behind to continue a challenging work, he wanted to instruct and encourage his young co-worker. Inspired by the Holy Spirit, this letter was helpful for Titus and God's people through all the ages.

Because this writing was inspired by the Holy Spirit and rightfully including among the writings of the New Testament, each word and phrase has depth and meaning. We can learn from both its broad themes and individual words and phrases. The first line of Titus 1:1 is an excellent example of how, under the Holy Spirit's inspiration, so much can go into a few words.

First, we see how Paul referred to himself: both a **bondservant of God** and an **apostle of Jesus Christ**. It is hard to think of a lower title than **bondservant**. The original word speaks not only of a lowly slave (one Greek scholar called it "the most abject, servile term in use among the Greeks for a slave"); it was also the word for a slave by choice. Paul took glory in such a humble title – he was a willing servant, a slave, of God. Yet he was also an **apostle**, a uniquely designated ambassador of God, one of those commissioned by God to lay that one-time foundation of the church (Ephesians 2:20).

Paul said that his calling as a bondservant and an apostle was **according to the faith of God's elect and the acknowledgment of the truth**. His calling was not *because* of the faith of God's elect, but in harmony with **the faith** (the belief, the truth) shared among God's elect. We can know who the elect are because they make this acknowledgment of the truth – they believe and confess the truth about Who Jesus is and what He came to do for us, especially His work on the cross.

Paul was careful to write that the truth acknowledged by God's elect **accords with godliness**. It is consistent with a godly, moral life. An ungodly life, marked by sin and moral compromise, does not acknowledge the truth of God. This truth brings us to one of the big themes of Paul's letter to Titus: the link between sound doctrine and godly living.

Truth and godliness should always be in one accord. Do I believe the truth, especially about Jesus and His work for me? Do I walk in godliness, consistent with the truth and nature of God?

Today, remember that both are important, and there is a real connection between right belief and right living.

July 28
Building a House

Now therefore, thus shall you say to My servant David, "Thus says the LORD of hosts: 'I took you from the sheepfold, from following the sheep, to be ruler over My people, over Israel.... Also the LORD tells you that He will make you a house.'" (2 Samuel 7:8, 11)

When David came to the throne of Israel, he soon had rest from all his enemies. It was one victory after another. When David conquered Jerusalem, he made it his capital and brought the Ark of the Covenant there. He built himself a fine palace made of the best wood. One day David looked out from his home and saw the tabernacle of God – a tent representing the house of God among the people of Israel. David was troubled that he lived in a nicer house than the Ark of the Covenant representing God's presence.

David told the prophet Nathan that he wanted to build a temple to replace the tabernacle. The tent of meeting – also known as the tabernacle – was perfectly suited for Israel in the wilderness, because they constantly moved. Now that Israel was securely in the land and the tabernacle was in Jerusalem, David thought it was more appropriate to build a temple to replace the tabernacle. Nathan told David to do it, but that night God told Nathan he spoke too quickly – that David was not to build this house for Him.

Instead, God promised David that he would build *him* a house in the sense of establishing a dynasty for the house of David. This was an enduring legacy for David long after his death. The temple would be destroyed, but the house of David would live on.

David was a man of war and God wanted a man of peace to build His temple. *But the word of the LORD came to me, saying, "You have shed much blood and have made great wars; you shall not build a house for My name, because you have shed much blood on the earth in My sight... a son shall be born to you, who shall be a man of rest... He shall build a house for My name."* (1 Chronicles 22:8-10)

David made his soul content saying "God has a reason He does not want me to build the temple. I cannot know it or understand it now, but I accept it as a wise and loving reason from God."

God honored what David gave him, even though David only gave it to God in his sincere intention. There are some things that we want to give God but are prevented from giving. In these cases, God receives the intention as the gift.

The important thing is to have the same kind of heart David had, the heart that will say: "God, You have given me so much. What can I do for You?"

God grants that kind of heart to the seeking soul – ask Him for such a heart today.

July 29
A Fool and His Money

Then Nabal answered David's servants, and said, "Who is David, and who is the son of Jesse? There are many servants nowadays who break away each one from his master. Shall I then take my bread and my water and my meat that I have killed for my shearers, and give it to men when I do not know where they are from?" So David's young men turned on their heels and went back; and they came and told him all these words. (1 Samuel 25:10-12)

In the years David lived as a fugitive on the run from Saul, he roamed around Israel, keeping a step ahead of the king who wanted to kill him. In 1 Samuel 25, David came to the area of Paran and Moan. There he met a man named Nabal.

Nabal was a wealthy man and had many servants watching over his livestock. David had many men following him. At first, David's men met with Nabal's servants. When the Philistines and many bandits troubled the land, David's men provided Nabal's servants and flocks valuable protection for many months.

When it was sheep-shearing time, David politely presented a bill for the services provided to Nabal. At that time, there was nothing unusual about what David did.

What was unusual was the way that Nabal responded. In an insulting way, he refused to pay David. He asked, **who is David, and who is the son of Jesse?** Nabal pretended that he didn't even know who David was – even though David was famous throughout Israel (1 Samuel 18:5-7). Nabal said this as a direct insult to David – knowing who he was but refusing to recognize him. Then Nabal said, **there are many servants nowadays who break away each one from his master.** This deepened that insult, saying that David was simply a runaway slave.

Finally, Nabal showed how greedy he was. In refusing to pay David what he rightfully owed to him, he said, **Shall I then take my bread...my water...my meat...my shearers, and give it?** He looked at everything as his, instead of the Lord's. Biblical generosity does not think, "This is mine and I will share it with you." It thinks, "All that I have belongs to the Lord so you can have some of it also."

1 Samuel 25:2 says that Nabal was *very rich*. There are four kinds of riches.

- Riches in what you own.
- Riches in what you do.
- Riches in what you know.
- Riches in what you are – riches of character.

Nabal was a rich man, but only rich in what he owned. He had the lowest kind of riches. The name "Nabal" means "Fool." Nabal was a man who lived down to his name. Do not be a Nabal. Make sure you pursue the greatest riches.

Today, understand that all you have belongs to God, and show it by your generosity.

July 30

When a Rite Is Wrong

Now when they saw some of His disciples eat bread with defiled, that is, with unwashed hands, they found fault. For the Pharisees and all the Jews do not eat unless they wash their hands in a special way, holding the tradition of the elders. (Mark 7:2-3)

"Cleanliness is next to godliness." John Wesley first recorded this saying in a sermon in 1778, but the idea is ancient, found in Babylonian and Hebrew religious writings. But it certainly isn't in the Bible.

In Jesus' day, He got into a conflict with the religious leaders over the issue of washing hands. It had nothing to do with cleanliness, but complicated ceremonial washings. The observant Jews of that day strictly observed a rigid, extensive ritual for washing before meals. The disciples didn't follow these ceremonies, and so the Pharisees criticized the Master of the disciples. Jesus rebuked the religious leaders for their hypocritical emphasis on outward rituals, while neglecting inward godliness.

For these ceremonial washings, special stone vessels of water were kept, because ordinary water might be unclean. To wash your hands, you started by taking enough of this water to fill one and one-half eggshells. Then, you poured the water over your hands, starting at the fingers and running down towards your wrist. Then you cleaned each palm by rubbing the fist of the other hand into it. Then you poured water over your hands again, this time from the wrist towards the fingers. These rules were thought to be so important they said bread eaten with unwashed hands was no better than excrement.

It's easy for us to think these religious leaders were strange for their emphasis on traditions like this. But we don't realize how subtly these things emerge, and how spiritual they seem to be, especially in their beginning. It all started with Exodus 30:19 and 40:12. Those passages speak of the need for the priests of Israel to wash their hands and their feet in the course of their priestly duties.

Didn't God command the priests to wash their hands before serving Him? Shouldn't every faithful follower of God have the same devotion as a priest? Isn't every meal sacred to God?

Doesn't God say, *Who may ascend into the hill of the LORD? Or who may stand in His holy place? He who has clean hands and a pure heart?* (Psalm 24:3-4)

When the questions are put this way, it's easy to say, "Yes, yes, yes," until you have agreed with the logic supporting the tradition. But if in the end you have a word of man, a tradition of man, a ritual of man, that is given the same weight as the Word of God, you're wrong. Your "spiritual logic" doesn't matter. You are wrong.

It's good to take a deep breath and say, "Lord, Your Word is high above everything else. It's above traditions, it is above rituals, it is above what I think are my personal revelations. Help me to hold to Your word far above anything else."

July 31

A Three-Way Work

Jude, a bondservant of Jesus Christ, and brother of James, to those who are called, sanctified by God the Father, and preserved in Jesus Christ. (Jude v. 1)

Jude saw deceptive and dangerous teaching creeping in among God's people. He could not stay silent; he had to warn his fellow Christians so they could prepare against the coming storm of false doctrine.

Jude preached against dangerous practices and doctrines that put the gospel of Jesus in peril. These were – and still are – serious issues. Jude looked at dangerous people and faced them head-on.

The name Jude is literally "Judas." But to avoid any connection with Judas Iscariot – the one who betrayed Jesus – many translations use the name **Jude**. Most people believe that this Jude is the one mentioned in Matthew 13:55 and Mark 6:3, the one who didn't believe in Jesus as Messiah until after His resurrection (John 7:5; Acts 1:14).

He introduced himself as **a bondservant of Jesus Christ**. This says something because Jude was a blood relative of Jesus, but he considered himself only His **bondservant**. Few things are more revealing than the titles by which a person wants to be known. Jude could have said, "here I am, the half-brother of Jesus, listen to me!" But he was fully content to be known simply as Jesus' **bondservant**. More valuable to him was his new relationship with Jesus. The blood of the cross that saved Jude was more important than the family blood in his veins.

Jude wrote to Christians, **those who are called**. A person is a Christian because God has called them. It starts with God's initiative, not man's. We don't look for God until He puts it in our hearts to search for Him. The important thing is to answer the call when it comes. Christians are those who have heard God calling and have responded.

Jude says God the Father has **sanctified** them. **Sanctified** is a very religious sounding word, but the meaning is simple. It means that Christians are set apart – set apart *from* the world and set apart *to* God. When Christians act as if they belong to the world and not God, then they are not living as if they are sanctified.

Finally, we see they are **preserved in Jesus**. Jesus Christ is their guardian and protector. As they stay faithful to God, Christians know this isn't because they are so great and so faithful. It is because Jesus Christ is faithful, and He preserves us.

Jude didn't mean to spell out a detailed doctrine of the Trinity as he opened his brief letter. Yet because the Trinity is true, it constantly finds itself woven into the fabric of the Bible. The Spirit calls, the Father sanctifies, and Jesus preserves. Our salvation is the work of the Triune God. This is what God works in His people; our job is to let it out in full display.

Can others see that you are called, sanctified, and preserved?

August 1

A Prepared Place

Behold, I send an Angel before you to keep you in the way and to bring you into the place which I have prepared. Beware of Him and obey His voice; do not provoke Him, for He will not pardon your transgressions; for My name is in Him. (Exodus 23:20-21)

Moses received the law from God and brought it down from Mount Sinai to the people of Israel. In Exodus 23, God looked ahead to their progress into the Promised Land. Israel had God's Law, but the law alone could never bring them into the rest and blessing the Promised Land was meant to be. They needed a *person* to bring them in, and that person was **an Angel before you to keep you in the way and to bring you into the place which I have prepared**.

This special Angel would keep Israel on the right path, lead them into the Promised Land, command their obedience, have the authority to forgive or retain sins, and had God's name in His own Person.

In Exodus 23:21, God identified this Angel saying, **My name is in Him**. We only know a few angels by name. Jude v. 9 mentions Michael, and Luke 1:19 mentions Gabriel. There is a sense in which each of these had the name of God "in" them. The generic Hebrew word for God is "El," and these two are named Micha-el and Gabri-el, each having God's name within their name.

But Michael nor Gabriel could not command obedience from Israel or presume to sit in judgment over them. The Angel mentioned in Exodus 23:20-21 was the specific Angel of the Lord, Jesus appearing in the Old Testament, before His incarnation in Bethlehem, who often speaks directly as the Lord. Yahweh's name is in Jesus; His name is Yah-shua – "The Lord is salvation."

Jesus is occasionally called an Angel because the word "angel" means "a messenger." Jesus is much more than that, but He is heaven's ultimate Messenger. When we say Jesus is an Angel, we do not mean that He is an angelic being, like other angels described in the Bible. We mean that He has a unique role as heaven's most special Messenger.

Since the Angel was Jesus, it means Jesus was with Israel in all their wilderness experience and brought them into the Promised Land, and He was the One to be obeyed. It means that Jesus had the power to forgive or retain sins. Jesus was each of these things for ancient Israel in the wilderness, and for us.

The Angel went before them **into the place which I have prepared**. Not only is it true that Jesus goes before us to prepare a place for us in heaven (John 14:2-3), but God prepared the place you walk in today, and He prepares where you will walk tomorrow.

Instead of worrying about today or tomorrow, look to Jesus, and He will make sure you are in a place prepared by Him.

August 2

We Packed and Went

And after those days we packed and went up to Jerusalem. (Acts 21:15)

Paul and his companions were on their way to Jerusalem. They had traveled a long way, mostly across the Mediterranean Sea. Now they were on the last part of their journey, going from Caesarea on the coast inland toward Jerusalem.

Luke traveled with Paul, indicated by the use of **we** in this sentence. In writing about this part of the trip, Luke said something small, yet in my mind, significant. He noted, **we packed**. This is noticeable because this was the end of a long journey, yet Luke never before stated that they packed. They sailed from Miletus to Cos, from Cos to Rhodes, from Rhodes to Patara, from Patara to Tyre, Tyre to Ptolemais, and then finally from Ptolemais to Caesarea. They packed and unpacked at each step along the way, but Luke never mentioned it. Only here he did, as they prepared to leave Caesarea and go to Jerusalem.

This makes me think that this was the first time Luke visited Jerusalem, and like any follower of Jesus, he was excited. He knew this was the famous City of David, the location of the great temple, and the place where Jesus taught, did miracles, died, rose again, and ascended to heaven. Luke thought that every detail of this last part of their long journey was exciting, and like an excited tourist, he even mentioned, **we packed**.

There are a few other things to consider about **we packed and went**.

It shows us that God loves order, and packing merely is ordering what we have in preparation for travel. God is a God of order and planning, and our desire to have things in order reflects His image in us. We should never make order and organization an idol, but it is essential to be mindful of them because God is full of order and organization.

It shows us that it is wise to prepare for where we are going. Paul, Luke, and the others traveling with them knew that packing would help them be ready for their travel to Jerusalem and their time there. Therefore, they took the foresight to get prepared by carefully packing. The same principle is true for us. We all have an appointment with the future. This is true for the near future, and it is wise for us to prepare for what lies ahead in this life.

It is even more valid for our eternal future. Each of us has an appointment with eternity, one that no one escapes. It would be best if you did your packing for that journey. Give your attention to eternal things right now. That means:

- Attention to God Word, which is eternal.
- Attention to people, who are eternal.
- Attention to giving, to send treasure ahead to heaven.

Before you go up to the New Jerusalem, make sure you have packed and prepared for the trip.

August 3

A True Miracle

Then Moses stretched out his hand over the sea; and the Lord caused the sea to go back by a strong east wind all that night, and made the sea into dry land, and the waters were divided. (Exodus 14:21)

This great event has been acted out in movies (*The Ten Commandments* or *The Prince of Egypt*) and has been displayed in paintings. Some wonder if Moses really did stretch out his hand over the sea and if it did really part in two, allowing Israel to pass through the Red Sea.

We do not know exactly where the place was, and what the exact geography was. This is especially true because an area like this will change every flood or drought season. We do know there was enough water there to trap the Israelites and enough to drown the Egyptians later. We can suppose that this was at least 10 feet (3 meters) of water. We can also suppose that the distance across was not so wide that it allowed the large group of Israelites to cross over in one night.

No matter where it happed, it is entirely reasonable to believe that it did happen. Many years ago in the *Los Angeles Times*, Thomas Maugh wrote an article titled, "Research Supports Bible's Account of Red Sea Parting":

> Sophisticated computer calculations indicate that the biblical parting of the Red Sea, said to have allowed Moses and the Israelites to escape from bondage in Egypt, could have occurred precisely as the Bible describes it. Because of the peculiar geography of the northern end of the Red Sea, researchers report Sunday in the Bulletin of the American Meteorological Society, a moderate wind blowing constantly for about 10 hours could have caused the sea to recede about a mile and the water level to drop 10 feet, leaving dry land in the area where many biblical scholars believe the crossing occurred.

That could be an adequate scientific description of how it might have happened. But I much prefer God's narrative, found in Psalm 77:16-20:

> *The waters saw You, O God; the waters saw You, they were afraid; the depths also trembled. The clouds poured out water; the skies sent out a sound; Your arrows also flashed about. The voice of Your thunder was in the whirlwind; the lightnings lit up the world; the earth trembled and shook. Your way was in the sea, Your path in the great waters, and Your footsteps were not known. You led Your people like a flock by the hand of Moses and Aaron.*

It usually is not wrong to analyze God's work, whether His work is in history or in day-to-day life. But it should never rob us of the wonder and glory we find in just praising God for His marvelous works, no matter how He chooses to do them.

The same miracle-working God, the one who led His people like a flock by the hands of Moses and Aaron, is also here to lead you today.

August 4

No Hammer Was Heard

And the temple, when it was being built, was built with stone finished at the quarry, so that no hammer or chisel or any iron tool was heard in the temple while it was being built. (1 Kings 6:7)

It was an amazing building project – the construction of one of the most beautiful buildings in the ancient world. Solomon's temple was built with almost unlimited resources and designed according to the general pattern of the tabernacle – the tent that for more than 500 years was the center of worship for the tribes of Israel.

God was not only interested in the result but also in the process of construction. This is an important principle in God's work. Sometimes God's servants get so caught up in the result that they think any method justifies a good result. This principle from the building of the temple is a good warning against the false idea that God is more interested in the product of our service than the process.

Therefore, we read that **no hammer or chisel or any iron tool was heard in the temple while it was being built**. This means that the stones used to build the temple were all cut and prepared at another place. At the actual building site of the temple, the stones were only assembled. They were fashioned in one place and arranged in another, at their final resting place.

This speaks to the way God wants His work to be done. The temple had to be built with human labor. God did not send a team of angels to build the temple. Solomon did not want the sound of man's work to dominate the site of the temple. He wanted to communicate, as much as possible, that the temple was of God and not of man. This means we should do what we can to point people to God and not directly to His servants. That is not easy to do in a culture dominated by superstars and the cult of celebrity.

Often the greatest work in the kingdom of God happens quietly. Yet the building site of the temple was only quiet because there was a lot of noise and diligent work at the quarry. When the spiritual environment seems quiet it is easy to think that God isn't doing much, but that may be a wrong conclusion. The work of God may be extremely active and effective, only in a hidden place. We should not be too quick to judge where God is working and isn't working.

God works among His people, cutting and shaping them here, preparing them for a place in heaven. Jesus said that He went to prepare a place for us, but it is also true that He prepares us for that place. This shaping work will be complete in heaven, and no hammer is heard there.

God knows what He is doing as He shapes your life into the likeness of Jesus Christ today.

August 5

A Warning to Bible Teachers

My brethren, let not many of you become teachers, knowing that we shall receive a stricter judgment. For we all stumble in many things. If anyone does not stumble in word, he is a perfect man, able also to bridle the whole body. (James 3:1-2)

James wrote about the proof of a living faith, real faith that saves for eternity and does some good in this life. Making our way into chapter 3, we see that James focused on one aspect of a living faith: it would affect how we talk.

He begins with, **let not many of you become teachers**. James had a sober warning for those who would become teachers in the church. They must take the responsibility seriously because their accountability is greater, and they shall receive a stricter judgment.

It is easy to take the teacher's position lightly in the church, without considering its cost in terms of accountability. Jesus warned, *to whom much is given, from him much will be required; and to whom much have been committed, of him they will ask the more.* (Luke 12:48)

The words of Jesus and James remind us that being among the teachers in God's church is more than a matter of having natural or even spiritual gifts; there is an additional dimension of appropriate character and right living. Therefore, teachers were both tested more and would be judged more strictly.

Then James explained another reason why it was so important for teachers to take this seriously. He reminds us, **for we all stumble in many things**. The greater accountability of teachers is especially sobering considering our common weaknesses. After all, **we all stumble in many things**. The ancient Greek word translated stumble doesn't imply a fatal fall, but something that trips us up and hinders our spiritual progress.

Notice that James wrote, **we** and not "they." **We all stumble** means that James included himself among those who could stumble. Yet he did not excuse his or our stumbling. We know that **we all stumble**, but we should all press on to a better walk with the Lord, marked by less stumbling.

Then James provided a way to measure spiritual maturity for teachers and all Christians: **If anyone does not stumble in word, he is a perfect man**. We stumble in word about ourselves with our boasting, exaggeration, and selective reporting. We **stumble in word** about others with our criticism, gossip, slander, or flattery.

To **not stumble in word** shows real spiritual maturity. This is especially relevant to teachers, who have so much more opportunity to sin with their tongue. We could say it firmly to any teacher: *Watch what you say. Your words are important.* That is something we all need to hear, as James explains in the verses that follow.

Yet teachers need to listen to this; they can help or hurt others for now and eternity by their words.

August 6

The Very Pure Word

My zeal has consumed me,
Because my enemies have forgotten Your words.
Your word is very pure;
Therefore Your servant loves it. (Psalm 119:139-140)

Psalm 119 is the great psalm that tells of the glory and goodness of God's Word, and it understands God's Word in the real world. The author of Psalm 119 had enemies, problems, and challenges like the rest of us, but he understood how God's excellent word speaks to every challenge of life.

Notice this phrase from Psalm 119: **My zeal has consumed me because my enemies have forgotten Your words**. The more the psalmist's enemies rejected the Word of God, the more he was determined to be zealous for those words. The psalmist had decided to make sure that he honored God's Word even if others did not.

The word **zeal** implies energy and action. The appreciation of the psalmist for the Word of God was not passive. The living and active Word of God made for a living and active response from the psalmist. People are zealous for any number of things, but the man of God and the woman of God will have a zeal for God's Word.

The psalmist also understood and appreciated the purity of God's Word. He wrote, **Your word is very pure; therefore Your servant loves it**. As the biblical authors wrote by the inspiration of the Holy Spirit (2 Timothy 3:16), what they originally wrote was perfectly pure, being inspired by God. What we have today of those original writings is also pure because we have incredibly reliable copies of those original writings.

For the Hebrew Scriptures, the quality of the text was preserved by the diligent practices of the professional scribes. Regarding the Greek Scriptures, there is also a similar astonishing degree of accuracy. In part, this is because of the vast number and quality of the ancient Greek manuscripts, and the existence of relatively early copies. Indeed: **Your word is very pure, therefore Your servant loves it**.

All in all, we see that the Bible gives us almost unending reasons to love the word God and the God who gave His Word – to us.

It is the word of the Lord (Genesis 15:1) and the Word of God (Luke 8:11). It is the word of the kingdom (Matthew 13:19) and the word of salvation (Acts 13:26). It is the word of grace (Acts 14:3) and the word of the gospel (Acts 15:7). It is the word of faith (Romans 10:8) and the word of the cross (1 Corinthians 1:18).

It is the word of reconciliation (2 Corinthians 5:19) and the word of truth (2 Corinthians 6:7). It is the word of life (Philippians 2:16), the word of Christ (Colossians 3:16), and the word of His power (Hebrews 1:3).

Understanding all these remarkable qualities of the Bible, we agree with what the psalmist wrote: **Your word is very pure; therefore Your servant loves it**.

August 7

Pray in This Manner

In this manner, therefore, pray: Our Father in heaven, hallowed be Your name. Your kingdom come. Your will be done on earth as it is in heaven. Give us this day our daily bread. And forgive us our debts, as we forgive our debtors. And do not lead us into temptation, but deliver us from the evil one. For Yours is the kingdom and the power and the glory forever. Amen. (Matthew 6:9-13)

In this part of the Sermon on the Mount, Jesus described a model for prayer. He said that we should pray like this: **Give us this day our daily bread. And forgive us our debts, as we forgive our debtors. And do not lead us into temptation, but deliver us from the evil one**. This means that the right kind of prayer will freely bring its own needs to God. This will include what we need to get by every day, forgiveness, and strength in the face of temptation.

When Jesus spoke of **daily bread**, He meant real bread that we need for food daily. Some early theologians thought **bread** here referred to communion, the Lord's Supper. Or some thought it referred to Jesus Himself as the Bread of life. Others thought it spoke of the Word of God as our daily bread. We need all those, but there is no reason to believe Jesus didn't mean normal bread. God cares about everyday things, and we should pray about them.

Jesus then addressed forgiveness, instructing the disciple to ask God to **forgive us** and to help us **forgive** others. The one genuinely forgiven will show forgiveness to others. Jesus used the idea of a debt to describe our sin. Unforgiven sin means that someone owes something to God. Those freely forgiven should freely forgive.

The disciple of Jesus should pray for help in **temptation**. The word **temptation** means a test, not always an invitation to do evil. God has promised to keep us from any testing that is greater than what we can handle (1 Corinthians 10:13). In prayer, we should always remember our own weakness and pray for constant protection amid every testing.

If we rightly pray **lead us not into temptation**, it will be lived out in several ways:

- We will not boast in our own strength.
- We will not seek out temptation.
- We will not lead others into temptation.

The right kind of prayer will also praise God, properly giving Him credit for the **kingdom and the power and the glory**. This kind of statement of praise to God is often called a *doxology*. There is some dispute about whether this doxology is in the original manuscript Matthew wrote or was added later by a scribe. Even if this is so, the thought is still beautiful. Sincere prayer recognizes that it all belongs to God – the **kingdom**, the **power**, and the **glory** are all His.

This model prayer invites us to do something: to pray. Knowing all about prayer matters little if we don't pray. So do it – and do it remembering the model Jesus provided for us.

August 8

Understanding the Creator

Your hands have made me and fashioned me; give me understanding, that I may learn Your commandments. (Psalm 119:73)

It is hard to say if we could rightly call the author of Psalm 119 a scientist. Indeed, he was a man of research and careful thought, and he thought deeply about his Creator. The psalmist knew that whatever was the precise mechanism behind his being, he could confidently say: **Your hands have made me**.

When he wrote **Your hands have made me and fashioned me**, the psalmist intended to make us think of Genesis 2:7, where it says that God fashioned the first man: *and the* LORD *God formed man of the dust of the ground*.

The psalmist clearly understood that God was his Creator, and he did not come to exist by chance or accident. The author of Psalm 119 also seemed to understand that he had certain obligations because the hands of God had fashioned him.

With its widespread denial of a Creator God, the modern age has almost no sense of obligation to God as Creator. Despite the deeply seated rejection of God as Creator, the accountability we have to our Maker remains. The psalmist understood what many today forget or choose to deny.

To say that God is our Creator is to recognize:

- We are obligated to Him as the One who gives us life.
- We respect Him as One who is more significant and smarter than we are.
- God, as our designer, knows what is best for us.
- Since our beginning is connected to the world beyond our sight, so our end will also be.

When we remember the work of God's hands in our creation, we also remember the work of the hands of our Savior in our redemption. Those hands were nailed to a cruel cross, as Jesus willingly made Himself the target of the judgment we deserve. We ask God to look on us as the work of His own hands, and on the wounds in His own hands as the satisfaction of justice against us.

He continued his prayer by asking, **give me understanding**. In thinking of God as Creator, the psalmist prayed for wisdom. He recognized that this was something often misunderstood, and one should ask for and expect help in understanding both God as Creator and our responsibilities to our Maker.

He explained the reason for the understanding: **That I may learn Your commandments**. Understanding God as Creator and man as creature should lead to this humble relationship where man admits his need to learn, learn God's Word (**commandments**), and receive His Word as commands from a wise, loving, and righteous Creator. Because God made us, He has the right to command us.

Today, remind yourself that you have a wonderful Creator – and you are the work of His hands.

August 9

Why God Allowed Evil

You are worthy, O Lord, to receive glory and honor and power; for You created all things, and by Your will they exist and were created. (Revelation 4:11)

The elders around God's throne sang those words, and later they sang again, taking God's praise to an even higher level: **And they sang a new song, saying: "You are worthy...for You were slain, and have redeemed us to God by Your blood out of every tribe and tongue and people and nation, and have made us kings and priests to our God; and we shall reign on the earth."** (Revelation 5:9-10)

We believe in a God who is all-wise, and all-powerful. We trust in His eternal purpose and plan, but we don't always understand it. Why did God find it necessary or good to allow Satan's evil to happen, and once it happened, why did He allow it to continue?

Following the course of God's entire plan of the ages, we see that God's work of *redemption* is greater than His work of *creation*. If the innocence of original creation was most important to God, He could have made worshipping robots which would declare His praise. But for God to have the allegiance of creatures that are more than robots, sin and rebellion must be allowed. The greatest work of God is in redeeming those creatures of His who have rebelled, but by His grace, have turned their hearts to Him.

Part of our problem is we don't understand what the best possible world would be. We think it would be a world where sin and evil never happened. We want to go back before Satan fell and brought sin into the universe, or before Adam sinned and brought sin into humanity. We think the ultimate world is the world of innocence, the world that never knew sin.

However, in God's eyes, it seems that the best possible world is the world that has been redeemed from sin and evil. Here in Revelation, we have a unique insight into the worship that surrounds God's throne. The elders praise God for creating all things (Revelation 4:11), but their new and greater song praises God for redemption (Revelation 5:9-10).

We look at a fallen world and ache over the magnitude of sin and evil. We admit this is not the best possible world – but we absolutely believe God has made the best way to the best possible world. The best possible world is the world of redemption, where all things are resolved, where all true righteousness is rewarded, and all true evil is properly judged; it is the resolution of all things in Jesus.

The next time you wonder why a particular sin or evil has been allowed to bring pain to your life, remember God's greatest purpose is found in triumphing over that evil and He invites us to be a part of that work.

Understanding some of God's eternal purpose can help you make it through today.

August 10

Affliction and Revival

**Consider my affliction and deliver me,
For I do not forget Your law.
Plead my cause and redeem me;
Revive me according to Your word.** (Psalm 119:153-154)

We do not precisely know who wrote Psalm 119, the longest chapter or psalm in the Bible. Many suppose that it was King David, the sweet psalmist of Israel – but the Bible itself does not tell us that. Perhaps we will never know the author's name, but we know this: he lived a difficult life. The man who wrote, **consider my affliction and deliver me**, did not live in constant comfort and the peaceful environment of a library. He lived a real life, interacting with people, and some of those people became his enemies or opponents. The author of this psalm lived a life that experienced affliction.

Yet he also knew what to do in those seasons of affliction – he knew to cry out to God. In this short passage, he did not even ask for deliverance but asked for God's attention to his affliction. He knew that if God considered his problem, God Himself would see if it was best to deliver him in or out of the situation.

Amid it all, he could say to God. **for I do not forget Your law**. In the lives of some people, affliction drives them *away* from God and His Word. For the author of Psalm 119, such troubled times moved him *closer* to God and His Word.

Then he asked God, **plead my cause, and redeem me**. The psalmist looked for help and salvation outside of himself. He knew that he needed God to plead his case, and he knew that he needed God to redeem him. The phrase plead my cause uses language from the courtroom. The psalmist asked God to defend him as a lawyer would defend his client.

The brief section concludes with the plea, **revive me according to Your word**. This thought is repeated from previous passages in this psalm (verses 25 and 107). The psalmist wanted to be made alive and to have that life brought to him according to God's Word.

- This tells us that the Word of God is a *source of revival*. If we will read the Word of God and do what it tells us to do – in prayer, in repentance, in dedication, and in pursuing God with the whole heart – it is a source of personal and corporate revival.

- This tells us that revival is *according to God's Word*. The concept of revival (both personal and corporate) is biblical. A genuine revival will honor and promote God's Word.

- This tells us that there is *maybe a false or pseudo revival*, which is not **according to Your word**. It is fair to assess purported words of revival according to the measure, "Is this according to God's Word?"

This is a prayer for you to pray today: "Lord, **revive me according to Your word**."

August 11

Enlighten My Eyes

How long, O Lord? Will You forget me forever? How long will You hide Your face from me? I will sing to the Lord, because He has dealt bountifully with me. (Psalm 13:1 and 13:6)

Almost every follower of God has felt neglected or that they have waited a long time for God to answer prayer. David knew the feeling well – he repeated the question **How long**? four times in Psalm 13. David was a man after God's own heart, yet he asked this question again and again.

The good news is that God will never forget us. When Israel thought God forgot them, the Lord assured them that He would never forget and promised, *See, I have inscribed you on the palms of My hands.* (Isaiah 49:16)

Of course, God did not forget David nor hide His face from him – but David felt like it. When we have such strong feelings, those feelings can create their own reality. David felt God had forgotten him and was hiding. So, in a sense, it was true for David, but true according to feelings, not fact.

Some people ignore feelings and think that feelings should have nothing to do with our relationship with God. This is out of balance because God gave us feelings as an expression of His image in us. We can feel anger, love, sorrow, and many other feelings because God feels those same things.

Others live ruled by feelings. They believe whatever reality their feelings present. The problem with this is that our feelings are affected by our fallenness, meaning we can't fully trust our feelings. It was all right for David to feel these feelings, and good to take them to God, but he should never accept the genuineness of feelings as "true" reality.

Psalm 13:6 shows David singing praises. How did he come from despair and arrive at singing? The key is in Psalm 13:3, when David prayed, **enlighten my eyes**. David had the wisdom to know that though he had powerful feelings, he didn't see reality clearly. He cried out to God, **enlighten my eyes**. No matter what problem we are in, we should cry out with all our heart, **enlighten my eyes**.

At the end of the psalm David declared, **He has dealt bountifully with me**. David had good reason to rejoice and sing because God was good to him. Every person on this earth has reason to rejoice because in some way God has been good to every one of us (Matthew 5:45).

Before God can enlighten our eyes, we must agree that we don't see everything clearly. Our feelings do not give us full and accurate information. If we cry out to the Lord, He will enlighten our eyes and bring us from a place of despair to a place of trust, joy, confidence, and praise. He loves us too much to leave us drowning in feelings of despair without throwing us a lifeline.

Will you take hold of it today?

August 12

It's So Embarrassing

But the woman, fearing and trembling, knowing what had happened to her, came and fell down before Him and told Him the whole truth. (Mark 5:33)

Humiliated by her affliction, she didn't dare ask Jesus for healing. She knew that He was the Messiah and had power over every disease. So, her hand reached out for a secret touch, trusting He would heal her secret ailment. At the point of contact, she knew she was healed, and Jesus knew that someone had touched Him with genuine faith.

Healing in hand, she hoped to sneak away through the crowd. But Jesus stopped the crowd with a strange question: "Who touched Me?" As the disciples questioned Jesus' sanity for asking such a question while the crowd pressed against Him, Jesus looked right at the woman. She knew she was caught, and she meekly submitted to Jesus' request to come forward, falling at His feet.

Why did Jesus make her go through this? He knew who she was, so it might seem that His only purpose was to embarrass her. But that wasn't His purpose at all.

Jesus "called her out" so she would absolutely know that she was healed. She felt in her body that she was healed, but she might begin to doubt that it was real. But Jesus told her "Go in peace, and be healed of your affliction." (Mark 5:34)

Jesus did it so others would know she was healed. This woman had a hidden ailment that made her a public outcast. It would sound suspicious to many if she just announced that she was healed. They would think that she made it up. Jesus "called her out" so others would absolutely know that she was healed.

Jesus did it so that she would know why she was healed. When Jesus said, "Daughter, your faith has made you well" it showed the woman that it wasn't touching the clothing of Jesus that healed her. Instead, it was her faith in Jesus and what He could do for her.

Jesus did it because He didn't want her to think that she stole a blessing, that she could never look Jesus in the eye again. She didn't steal anything, she received her healing by faith, confirmed by Jesus.

Jesus did it because He wanted to bless her in a special way. He called her "Daughter." Jesus never called any other person by this name. Jesus wanted her to come forth and hear this special name of tenderness. When Jesus calls us forward, it is because He has something special to give us.

Jesus may ask us to do things that seem embarrassing. He doesn't ask us to do them because they embarrass us. There is a higher purpose even if we can't see it. But if avoiding embarrassment is the most important thing in our lives, then pride is our god.

Today, choose to love Jesus more than yourself or your self-image.

August 13

The Greatest Motivation for Purity

Blessed are the pure in heart, for they shall see God. (Matthew 5:8)

In this famous beginning to the most famous sermon ever preached, Jesus explained the way to a blessed life. Up through Matthew 5:8, He pronounced blessings on the poor in spirit, those who mourn, the meek, those who hunger and thirst after righteousness, and on the merciful. Now in this sixth Beatitude, Jesus spoke to the **pure in heart**, announcing a great blessing: **for they shall see God**.

In ancient Greek, the phrase **pure of heart** has the idea of straightness, honesty, and clarity. There can be two ideas connected to this. One is of genuine inner moral purity as opposed to the mere image of purity, or ceremonial purity. The other idea is of a single, undivided heart – speaking of those who are utterly sincere and not divided in their devotion and commitment to God.

Charles Spurgeon observed: "Christ was dealing with men's spirits, with their inner and spiritual nature. He did this more or less in all the Beatitudes, and this one strikes the very center of the target as he says, not 'Blessed are the pure in language, or the pure in action,' much less 'Blessed are the pure in ceremonies, or in raiment, or in food;' but 'Blessed are the pure in heart.'"

What is their reward? Jesus said: **For they shall see God**. In this, the pure of heart receive the most wonderful reward. They shall enjoy greater relationship with God than before. The polluting sins of covetousness, oppression, lust, and chosen deceptions have a definite blinding effect on a person, and the one who is **pure of heart** is freer from these pollutions. It isn't so much that God changes and becomes more visible; their reward is that they see better.

On this side of eternity, no human eye can see and take in the essence and core of God's glory. Yet the **pure of heart** can, by the eye of faith, see and enjoy God in this life in a greater way than those who are not pure of heart. It is as Paul wrote in 1 Corinthians 13:12 – now we see God in His glory dimly, yet the **pure of heart** see Him better than others.

- The heart-pure person can see God in nature.
- The heart-pure person can see God in the Scriptures.
- The heart-pure person can see God in his church family.
- The heart-pure person can see something of God's true character.

There are some people who can go their whole lives without seeing anything of God. They are totally unconscious to spiritual things and Divine reality.

This close relationship with God must become our greatest motivation for purity. Understood rightly, it is much greater than a fear of getting caught or of consequences. We say, "I want purity of heart because I want to see God better than ever before."

Today, this is a great reward and a great blessing.

August 14

The Importance of a Good Example

In all things showing yourself *to be* a pattern of good works; in doctrine *showing* integrity, reverence, incorruptibility, sound speech that cannot be condemned, that one who is an opponent may be ashamed, having nothing evil to say of you. (Titus 2:7-8)

Paul told Titus how to speak to the different groups of people in the church, and he instructed Timothy to tell the young men to be sober-minded (Titus 2:6). Then Paul explained to Titus the importance of being a good example himself.

This is what Paul wrote: **In all things showing yourself to be a pattern of good works**. Titus had to be more than a teacher, he also had to be an example, a **pattern**. His guidance to others could not be taken seriously if he himself was not walking after God's truth. This is a powerful, basic principle that is often neglected. If the preacher or teacher does not live what he teaches, why should anyone else?

This doesn't mean that leaders in the church must be perfect. Like anyone else, they will have their weaknesses and failings. Leaders can't be examples of perfection, but they certainly can be examples of humility and repentance.

There's a specific way that Titus had to be an example, leading with **integrity** in **doctrine**. Titus must be an example in doctrinal stability and integrity. If he wasn't comfortably settled in his understanding of the Scriptures, he wasn't ready to lead.

Titus also had to be an example of **reverence**, of **incorruptibility**, and of **sound speech**. Titus had to teach the older men (Titus 2:2) and the older women (Titus 2:3) to be reverent, but he had to be an example of **reverence** first. Titus had to teach the older men to be sound in faith (Titus 2:2), but his faith had to be incorruptible.

When God's leaders live this way, it gives those who oppose God's work no excuse to accuse and reject the truth. Paul put it this way: **That one who is an opponent may be ashamed**. Of course, Jesus lived this better than anyone. Jesus could say to an angry mob, *which of you convicts Me of sin?* (John 8:46) and no one could say anything.

I'm sure there are people that you really want to see come to faith and a real relationship with Jesus Christ. There are probably many others you know who already love Jesus but need to be taught in some important areas of the Christian life. With both groups, remember that your example means so much.

- If we fail to be good examples of the Christian life, what we teach others is of little effect.
- If we fail to be good examples of the Christian life, we give others the opportunity to excuse their unbelief.

We can humbly ask Jesus to forgive us for all the times we have failed in being good examples, and then ask Him for the ongoing strength to represent God and His people by our good example.

August 15

Why We Need God to Speak

And God spoke all these words, saying: "I am the Lord your God, who brought you out of the land of Egypt, out of the house of bondage. You shall have no other gods before Me." (Exodus 20:1-3)

Having come out of Egypt and on the way to the Promised Land, God commanded Israel to stay a year at a mountain named Sinai. God did some important things during that time, and one of the most important things was giving Israel His law. When God gave the law, He started with Ten Commandments, and He began the Ten Commandments by noting, **God spoke all these words**.

It was important for Israel to hear God speak these words from heaven. This God-based moral code established that this people, this nation of Israel, belonged to God and not to Moses. This was not Moses' law (though we often casually refer to it as such). Rather, **God spoke all these words**, and Moses nor any other man was ever to think of himself or allow others to think of him as above the law. God was above all, and His law was and is the expression of His will.

We need God to instruct and guide us morally. We need to know that there is a God in heaven who expects certain moral behavior and that there are consequences from obeying or disobeying these commands.

The Ten Commandments (and all the Law of Moses that follows) is a God-based moral code. It does not just say that certain behavior is unwise or unhelpful; it says that God commands us to do or not to do certain things, and it either states or implies that:

- God sees our obedience or disobedience.
- God measures our obedience or disobedience.
- God, in some way, rewards our obedience and punishes our disobedience.

Without a God-based moral code, it is difficult or even impossible to answer the question "Why?" in response to any moral demand.

You say, "Do not steal." I ask, "Why not?"

You say, "It does not belong to you." I say, "He has much, and I have little."

You say, "It belongs to him." I say, "I want what he has."

You say, "You might get caught." I say, "I probably will not."

You say, "It is not nice." I say, "It seems nice to me."

You say, "It is not fair." I say, "It seems fair to me."

But when we can answer, "Do not steal because God commands you not to, and there will be consequences from God if you do," we live on a completely different moral basis. The more individuals and the culture reject this God-based moral code, the worse it will be for those individuals and the culture.

Think of how wonderful it would be if we all obeyed the Ten Commandments.

August 16

A Better Mountain

For you have not come to the mountain that may be touched and that burned with fire, and to blackness and darkness and tempest... But you have come to Mount Zion and to the city of the living God, the heavenly Jerusalem, to an innumerable company of angels. (Hebrews 12:18, 22)

In the days of Moses, Israel came to a burning mountain. Exodus 19:10-25 explains what it was like when Israel came to Mount Sinai. The mountain was blocked off and there was no access on the penalty of death. The people were commanded to wash their clothes and abstain from sexual relations. There was thunder, lightning, and a thick cloud. Soon came the sound of a trumpet, calling forth the nation to meet with God. Then more smoke (like a furnace), and earthquakes. The trumpet sound continued until Moses spoke, and God Himself answered. God spoke to Israel from Sinai, but He warned them in every way possible to stay away from the mountain.

In Exodus 19 Israel got the message. Hebrews 12 explains that they begged Moses to keep a distance between them and God. They wanted the experience to stop, not to continue. They were genuinely afraid, but this fear failed to promote holiness among the people of Israel. 40 days later they worshipped a gold calf and said that *it* was the god that brought them out of Egypt.

Hebrews 12 has good news. Our relationship with God does not have to be like coming to Mount Sinai. We can come to God at a different mountain – Mount Zion, the name of the hill on which Jerusalem sits.

Consider the contrasts between Mount Sinai and Mount Zion.

- Mount Sinai was marked by fear and terror – Mount Zion is a place of love and forgiveness.
- Mount Sinai spoke of earthly things – Zion speaks of heavenly things.
- At Mount Sinai, only Moses was allowed to draw near to God – at Mount Zion, an innumerable company is invited to draw near.
- Mount Sinai was characterized by guilty men in fear – Mount Zion features just men who are made perfect before God.
- At Mount Sinai Moses was the mediator – at Zion Jesus is the mediator.
- Mount Sinai brings an old covenant, ratified by the blood of animals – Zion brings a new covenant, ratified by the blood of God's precious Son.
- Mount Sinai is all about Law – Mount Zion is all about grace.

Be thankful that as God met Moses at Mount Sinai, Jesus stands ready to meet all mankind on Mount Zion. After all, Calvary stands on Mount Zion. Put away your hesitation and get bold in coming to God. By a relationship of love and faith, the work of Jesus opens privileged access to God. Are you using that access?

Anointed

Then Samuel took a flask of oil and poured it on his head, and kissed him and said: "Is it not because the Lord has anointed you commander over His inheritance?" (1 Samuel 10:1)

The people of Israel demanded a king, and God gave them one – even though their desire for a king showed that Israel had rejected God's leadership. God led a man named Saul to the prophet Samuel, and then God told Samuel that this was the man to become the first king of Israel.

The prophet did something memorable to declare Saul as king: Samuel took a flask of oil and poured it on his head. This was a literal anointing of Saul. The word "anoint" means "to rub or sprinkle on; to apply an ointment or oily liquid to." When Samuel poured it on his head, Saul was anointed with oil.

But in the Bible, the idea of anointing is much more significant. The oil poured out on Saul's head and running down to his body was a picture of what God did in him spiritually. The Holy Spirit was poured out on him, equipping him for the job of ruling as king over Israel.

As Christians under the new covenant, we also have an anointing: *But you have an anointing from the Holy One* (1 John 2:20). In the New Testament sense, anointing has the idea of being filled with and blessed by the Holy Spirit. In the New Testament, anointing is not just for a few special believers. This is something that is the common property of all Christians, but something we can and should become more submitted to and responsive to.

After the anointing, Samuel **kissed him**. This was not only a greeting; it was also a sign of Samuel's support of Saul. It was important for the king of Israel to feel the support of the man of God.

The prophet explained it all to the new king: **Is it not because the Lord has anointed you?** God anointed Saul, and there were many aspects to this anointing that were especially memorable to Saul.

It was a secret anointing because it was not yet time to reveal Saul as king to the nation. As Christians, our anointing often comes in a private way, not in a public ceremony for show.

It was a memorable and evident anointing, because Saul's head was drenched with oil. Psalm 133:2, describes how messy an anointing could be: *It is like the precious oil upon the head, running down the beard and running down on the edge of his garments.* As Christians, our filling and empowering of the Holy Spirit should be memorable and evident. Saul could look back on this event and know that God called him to something special as Israel's king.

Saul had his anointing; as a follower of Jesus, you also have your anointing for what God calls you to be and to do.

Receive it from Him today; live in it always.

August 18

Discernment and How to Get It

Now it happened when…our enemies heard that I had rebuilt the wall, and that there were no breaks left in it (though at that time I had not hung the doors in the gates).… [They] sent to me, saying, 'Come, let us meet together.… But they thought to do me harm. So I sent messengers to them, saying, 'I am doing a great work, so that I cannot come down. Why should the work cease while I leave it and go down to you?' But they sent me this message four times, and I answered them in the same manner. (Nehemiah 6:1-4)

For Nehemiah, the attacks and challenges didn't stop. In the first four verses of Chapter 6, he faced the snare of the enemy's false friendship. But Nehemiah was equipped with discernment and could see the truth.

Discernment is the ability to judge matters according to God's view and not their outward appearance. *For the LORD does not see as man sees; for man looks at the outward appearance, but the LORD looks at the heart* (1 Samuel 16:7). Many people confuse being discerning with being negative or cynical, but discernment is also able to see the good where others might miss it.

Christians often suffer because they lack discernment, following leaders and teachers who give a good appearance but don't walk in the character of Jesus. They accept things blindly because it looks or sounds good, without carefully judging it against the whole counsel of God's Word.

The Bible is our key to discernment – and not an isolated verse here and there, but an understanding of God's whole counsel. Perhaps Nehemiah read Proverbs 27:6: *Faithful are the wounds of a friend, but the kisses of an enemy are deceitful.*

First, if you want to see things as God does, know His Word! Second, discernment comes through spiritual maturity; Hebrews 5:12-14 says discernment is something spiritual babies don't have. Third, discernment can be a gift from the Holy Spirit (1 Corinthians 12:10). Seek Him for it!

Without discernment, we can think a dangerous invitation from an enemy is really an offer of reconciliation; we can think presumption is faith; we can think our own noble desires are God's promises; we can think God is saying "now" when He is saying "later," or "later" when He is really saying "now"; we can think someone is a great man or a spiritual leader when they are actually doing damage to God's people.

Discernment gave Nehemiah focus; he knew what God wanted him to be doing and he did it. Things that sounded good but weren't of the LORD for him didn't sidetrack him. Anyone doing work for God must contend with a hundred different noble causes that might look and be good, but they are not what they are called to do at that time. Discernment gives us focus!

Make it your prayer today: "Lord, give me discernment, and help me seek it Your way."

August 19

Fading Glory

And when Moses had finished speaking with them, he put a veil on his face. But whenever Moses went in before the LORD to speak with Him, he would take the veil off until he came out; and he would come out and speak to the children of Israel whatever he had been commanded. And whenever the children of Israel saw the face of Moses, that the skin of Moses' face shone, then Moses would put the veil on his face again, until he went in to speak with Him. (Exodus 34:33-34)

When Moses came down Mount Sinai, fresh from his extraordinary encounter with God, the impact on his life was more than spiritual. There was also a physical impact; his **face shone** with an intense radiance. When the people of Israel saw Moses and his shining face, fresh from the radiance of God, they were afraid, and they didn't want to come near him.

In the last part of our passage, the Hebrew verb for **shone** literally means, "shot forth beams." The word is also related to a Hebrew noun for a *horn*. Because of this, the Latin Vulgate mistranslated this verb as "having horns," and so in most medieval works of art, Moses wears a small pair of horns on his head.

With a shining face and no horns, Moses reported to the people everything the LORD told him. Then Moses did something curious. He put a veil over his radiant face. We could assume that Moses wore the veil so the people wouldn't be afraid to come near him. Paul explained the real purpose of the veil wasn't to hide the glowing face of Moses but to hide his *fading* glory. Moses wore the veil because his glory faded.

In 2 Corinthians 3:13, Paul wrote: *Moses, who put a veil over his face, so that the children of Israel could not look steadily at the end of what was passing away.* The old covenant had a glory, but it was a fading glory. God didn't want people to lose confidence in Moses. So, under God's leading, Moses put the veil over his face. This is consistent with Exodus 34. Moses came down with a shining face and didn't put the veil on until he had spoken to the people, reporting all that the LORD had told him on Mount Sinai.

The old covenant was great and glorious – but it looks pretty pale compared to the new covenant (Jeremiah 31:31-34, Ezekiel 36:24-28, Luke 22:14-20, Hebrews 7-8). A bright autumn moon may look beautiful and light up the night, but it is nothing compared to the noonday sun.

As good as the old covenant was, it is nothing compared to the brightness of the new covenant. When we try to make our way before God, we trust the same principle at work in the old covenant. When we trust in who Jesus is for us and what He did for us, then we live under the new covenant.

Today, make sure that you do not settle for fading glory.

August 20

When the Music Stops

Hell from beneath is excited about you, to meet you at your coming; it stirs up the dead for you, all the chief ones of the earth; it has raised up from their thrones all the kings of the nations. They all shall speak and say to you: "Have you also become as weak as we? Have you become like us? Your pomp is brought down to Sheol, and the sound of your stringed instruments; the maggot is spread under you, and worms cover you." (Isaiah 14:9-11)

When Satan ends up in hell, those already there will comment on his arrival: **Have you also become as weak as we? Have you become like us?** When he went to hell, the king of literal Babylon was exposed as a mere man, though he thought of himself as greater than that. As well, when Satan – the king of spiritual Babylon – goes to hell, all will be amazed to see that he was only a creature.

We often – to the devil's great delight – inflate Satan's status and importance. We think of him as the opposite of God, as if God was light and Satan was darkness or as if God was hot and Satan was cold. Satan *wishes* he was the opposite of God, but God wants us to know now what everyone will know someday – that Satan is a mere creature and is in no way the opposite of God. If Satan has an opposite, it is not God the Father or God the Son; it would be a high-ranking angelic being such as Michael. Everyone will see this on the day Satan is sent to hell. Knowing this now, why would any of us serve him or work for his cause, even for a moment?

God also told Satan that the **sound of** his **stringed instruments** would cease. Before his fall, Satan was associated with music in heaven. Ezekiel 28:13 speaks of Satan before his fall: *the workmanship of your timbrels and pipes was prepared for you on the day you were created.* The musical career of Satan did not end with his fall – the sound of his stringed instruments will only be brought down when he is imprisoned in hell.

We can see today how the devil wants to use music as a destructive and seductive force. We're grateful that the Lord and His people haven't abandoned the field to Satan, and use music to glorify God, to build up His people, and to bring beauty and goodness into the world. The difference is this – in hell, the music stops; in heaven, it goes on forever and ever. The sound of instruments will never be heard in hell, but God will be forever glorified by the best music anyone can imagine in heaven.

It's just one more reason to put your trust in Jesus and what He did for you on the cross to make sure we get to heaven – and that the music never ends for you. Satan and all His agents were disarmed and defeated by what Jesus did at the cross (Colossians 2:15), and the glory of God's symphony never ends.

August 21

The Man Who Walked with God

After he begot Methuselah, Enoch walked with God three hundred years, and had sons and daughters.... And Enoch walked with God; and he was not, for God took him. (Genesis 5:22, 24)

These verses from Genesis 5 introduce two remarkable men. **Methuselah** was noted as the man in the Bible with the longest recorded life: 969 years (Genesis 5:27). **Enoch** was the man who walked with God in such a special way that God took him – presumably, to God's immediate presence in heaven.

We wouldn't believe it unless the Bible said it, but it is clear. Enoch, the son of Jared, was carried away to God in a miraculous way. These verses emphasize that Enoch walked with God, repeating the phrase to make sure we understand the idea. Walking with God, in this sense, speaks of a true, deep relationship.

It is impossible to walk with a person unless you know they exist and have a vital sense of their presence. Walking next to someone, you may not see their face, but you can sense and hear their steps. When friends walk together, they communicate, enjoying a bond that goes beyond words. This was the kind of deep relationship Enoch enjoyed with God, and God enjoyed with Enoch.

Enoch walked with God, and walking with God means walking by faith (2 Corinthians 5:7), walking in the light (1 John 1:5-7), and walking in agreement with God (Amos 3:3). Hebrews 11:5 tells us the foundation of Enoch's walk with God: *By faith Enoch was taken away so that he did not see death, "and was not found, because God had taken him"; for before he was taken he had this testimony, that he pleased God.* You can't walk with God or please God apart from faith.

After walking like this with God, it was as if one day God told Enoch, "You don't need to walk home. Why don't you just come home with Me?" The text simply says, **God took him**. Charles Spurgeon wondered if perhaps some of the great patriarchs saw Enoch rising through the sky even as Jesus, many years later, ascended to heaven.

It seems Enoch began to walk with God in a special way **after he begot Methuselah**. The name Methuselah may mean, *when he is dead, it shall come*. At the birth of Methuselah, Enoch had a special awareness from God that judgment was coming, and this was one of the things that got him closer in his walk with God.

Jude v. 14 also tells us Enoch was a prophet; even from his vantage point long ago, he could see the second coming of Jesus (*...the Lord comes with ten thousands of His saints, to execute judgment on all*).

I don't know which comes first: a close walk with God, or a deep anticipation of the return of Jesus. Whichever comes first, they are linked. Walk with God closely and look for the return of Jesus. One day God may take you away!

August 22

Left Alone

Ephraim is joined to idols, let him alone. (Hosea 4:17)

After the people of God split into two nations – Judah and Israel – the largest, most influential tribe in the northern kingdom was Ephraim. It isn't unusual to find the prophets addressing the nation of Israel as "Ephraim." In Hosea 4:17, we have a vivid and tragic example: **Ephraim is joined to idols, let him alone**.

When the people of God went after idols, it wasn't because they got a thrill out of bowing down to statues. It was because they wanted things those idols represented. Baal was the weather god, and in an agricultural community, farmers felt they needed to appease the weather god. Ashtoreth was the goddess of sex and fertility. People "worshipped" her for the sake of illicit pleasure or appease her for fertility in the family, flocks, or fields.

When the people of God went after idols, there was rarely conscious rejection of the LORD. They believed they were "adding" the worship of a local deity to their worship of Yahweh. In their minds, they said, "We still love the LORD, it's just that we also want to honor these other gods." But the LORD God of Israel would have none of it. When He saw that Ephraim was joined to idols, He pronounced His judgment: **Let him alone**.

It seems like a pretty mild judgment: **Let him alone**. Most criminals would be happy if the police and courts would just leave them alone. Any debtor would be thrilled if their creditors left them alone. But when God leaves us alone, it is a form of His judgment.

In the case of ancient Israel, it was a judgment because God knew what was coming. When the mighty Assyrian army came against them, they could fight for themselves – God will **let him alone**. In a crisis like that, suddenly we don't want God to leave us alone. But sometimes God says, "You didn't want Me, so I will respect your wishes. You're on your own."

We need God with us because we need His protection against our spiritual enemies. Satan wanted to sift Peter like wheat, but Jesus did not leave Peter alone to face the attack. Jesus prayed for Peter, and he emerged victorious (Luke 22:31-32).

We don't want God to leave us alone because we need His protection against ourselves. Left alone with our own sinful hearts, we will surely drift away from the LORD. All God must do to make certain a man goes to hell is simply leave him alone. Our prayer should always be, "LORD, don't leave me alone. Keep working on me."

He never really leaves us. It's just that sometimes He will respect our desire to be left alone. At the end of it all, if you don't want God to leave you alone, then don't leave Him alone.

Today, be like the widow who wouldn't quit (Luke 18:3-5) and you'll never have to worry about being left alone.

God's Enduring Word

August 23

The voice said, "Cry out!" And he said, "What shall I cry?" "All flesh is grass, and all its loveliness is like the flower of the field. The grass withers, the flower fades, because the breath of the LORD blows upon it; surely the people are grass. The grass withers, the flower fades, but the word of our God stands forever." (Isaiah 40:6-8)

This message was about the frailty of man: **All flesh is grass**. Isaiah thought of the beautiful green grass covering the hills of Judah after the winter rains, and how quickly that grass died, and the hills were left brown and barren. Even the beauty of man is fleeting and passes as quickly as spring wildflowers (**all its loveliness is like the flower of the field**). Why is man so frail? It is **because the breath of the LORD blows upon it**. It is to God's glory and according to His plan that man is this frail, and the glory of man is so fleeting.

This message was about the permanence of God and His Word: **The word of our God stands forever**. In contrast to the frailty and fleeting glory of man, the **word of our God** endures. God's Word certainly has endured, surviving centuries of manual transcription, of persecution, of ever-changing philosophies, of all kinds of critics, of neglect both in the pulpit and in the pew, of doubt and disbelief – and still, **the word of our God stands forever**.

This message, cried out by the voice in the wilderness, was meant to prepare hearts for the coming of the LORD by leading them into repentance. The understanding of our frailty and fleeting glory, contrasted with the eternal enduring of God and His Word, should humble us in repentance before the LORD. It certainly worked in the ministry of John the Baptist (Luke 3:7-18).

In 1 Peter 1:22-25 there is a stirring call for love among believers. Then, using the passage from Isaiah 40:8, Peter explained why we should love one another this way: *having been born again, not of corruptible seed but incorruptible, through the Word of God, which lives and abides forever, because "All flesh is as grass, and all the glory of man as the flower of the grass. The grass withers, and its flower falls away, but the word of the Lord endures forever." Now, this is the word, which by the gospel was preached to you.*

Peter made a beautiful connection, showing that the enduring word Isaiah spoke of is the same word of the gospel that is preached and believed, bringing salvation. Peter also made a beautiful application. Since this eternal, always potentially fruit-bearing seed is in us, we have both the obligation and the ability to have a sincere love of the brethren.

Perhaps we could say that if we need more love for others, it will begin with having more of the incorruptible seed set in our hearts and allowing it to grow. Let God's Word grow in you today!

August 24

Eating Good Things

Ho! Everyone who thirsts, come to the waters; and you who have no money, come, buy and eat. Yes, come, buy wine and milk without money and without price. Why do you spend money for what is not bread, and your wages for what does not satisfy? Listen carefully to Me, and eat what is good, and let your soul delight itself in abundance. (Isaiah 55:1-2)

With the opening word, **Ho!** the prophet spoke to all that can hear. It is as if God bends down to plead with His people, "Please listen to Me!"

The invitation is to **everyone who thirsts**, but only those who thirst will **come to the waters**. If we aren't thirsty for what God can give us, then we will never come to His waters. Maybe Jesus had this passage from Isaiah in mind when He cried out, *If anyone thirsts, let him come to Me and drink.* (John 7:37)

Those who do thirst, and answer the LORD's invitation, don't need to bring **money**. They can simply bring their trust and faith and receive what God will give them. It is all free: water, **wine**, and **milk** – everything that sustains us in our life with God is freely given. It isn't that the entrance into the Christian life is free and then we must pay something to advance in the Christian life. It's all free; our growth is just as much a gift of grace as our salvation. It is all a gift from His goodness.

In this invitation through the prophet, God asked His people to ask themselves, "Why do I **spend money** for what can't **satisfy**?" This is a remarkably relevant question considering all the things we pour our time, money, and effort into – things, which will never satisfy the way God can.

Asking for the attention of His people, God made a clear invitation for the, to **eat what is good** and find abundant **delight** for their **soul**. The offer is made, the provision is given, and everything is available – but the one who receives must still do some things.

First, we must **listen diligently**. The satisfaction God promises doesn't come to those who don't listen and listen diligently. It takes time, attention, and effort to listen diligently, and some aren't willing to do this.

Second, we must **eat what is good**. This requires some discernment. We must choose what is good, and then eat that. Many just simply eat whatever spiritual meal is set before them without taking care to see that it is good.

Third, we must **let** our **soul delight itself in abundance**. Even when we listen, even when we eat what is good, we still must let our soul delight itself in abundance.

It is possible to sit down at a great spiritual meal but by your stubborn or bad attitude, simply not **let your soul delight itself in abundance**. Today, God has abundant life for you – let your soul delight in it!

August 25

Do You Remember?

Moreover He said, "I am the God of your father; the God of Abraham, the God of Isaac, and the God of Jacob." And Moses hid his face, for he was afraid to look upon God. (Exodus 3:6)

In his first 40 years, Moses was raised in a royal family and made ready for national leadership. In the second 40 years of his life, he watched over someone else's sheep out in a dry wilderness. Between those two periods was a futile attempt to fulfill God's destiny for his life his way, instead of letting God do it His way.

God captured this 80-year-old man's attention, standing in front of a bush that was on fire yet not burning up. God spoke to Moses out of this burning bush, and after calling his name and telling him to take off his sandals, the Lord told Moses precisely who He was.

Who was this God who spoke to Moses out of the burning bush? God revealed Himself as **the God of your father; the God of Abraham, the God of Isaac, and the God of Jacob**. Abraham, Isaac, and Jacob were the ancestors of the Jewish people, known as the patriarchs. They lived some 400 years before Moses, and their stories are told in the book of Genesis. In Genesis, we read that God made many promises to Abraham, Isaac, and Jacob and their descendants. God promised them a land (the Promised Land of Israel), a nation, and a blessing that would come through them to the whole world.

God identified Himself to Moses in connection with **Abraham**, **Isaac**, and **Jacob** because He wanted Moses to know that He remembered those 400-year-old promises to the patriarchs. Moses probably felt that God had neglected His covenant for 400 years. Yet God had been at work, preserving and multiplying the nation.

Moses responded by hiding his face in fear. He **was afraid to look upon God** because he knew himself to be not only a creature but also a sinful creature. In his 40 years of watching sheep, Moses must have spent many lonely days and nights troubled in his conscience about the murder of an Egyptian, of his pride in thinking that he could deliver Israel himself, and of a thousand sins both real and imagined. Yet God was ready to forgive, and He wanted Moses to put all that away and get on with knowing and serving Him.

Moses' humility before God was a good thing. But a crippled, guilty conscience was a bad thing. Hebrews 9:14 makes this challenge: *How much more shall the blood of Christ, who through the eternal Spirit offered Himself without spot to God, cleanse your conscience from dead works to serve the living God?* God is the God of the covenant, a promise to forgive and restore.

Afraid as Moses was, God wasn't done with him yet – and God isn't done with you.

August 26

Giving More Grace

But He gives more grace. Therefore He says: "God resists the proud, but gives grace to the humble." (James 4:6)

In the previous verses, James warned us of the great danger of compromise, and how the Spirit of God within will warn us of this, with the good kind of jealousy that God has for His people. It was a strong passage that warned us of the danger of friendship with the passing vanities of this world.

Knowing that, it is wonderful to see how he continued to comfort the people of God, assuring them that God **gives more grace**. The same Holy Spirit convicting us of our compromise will grant us the grace to trust God and serve God as we should.

We could say that this beautiful statement **He gives more grace** completes the thought from the previous sentences. James did not want to leave us with only a strong finger pointing at our sin and compromise (though he wanted to start there). He wanted to point at our weakness and failure, and then point upward to God in heaven, and the richness of the grace He gives.

To paraphrase Charles Spurgeon: "We see how weak we are, and how strong He is: We see how proud we are, and how low God reaches to meet us. How often we err and how God never errs. How much we provoke God and how much He forgives us. Truly, **He gives more grace**."

We also see that if we suffer from not having what we need from God, it is not His fault. After all, **He gives more grace**. If we do not have the spiritual resource we need, it isn't because God hasn't given it – it because we have not received it.

Think about it – **more grace**. More is a word that implies a measure; whatever the measure is, we have more grace than that. More than what?

- God gives more grace than our sin.
- God gives more grace than our giving to Him.
- God gives more grace than we deserve.
- God gives more grace than others give.
- God gives more grace than our needs of the past, present, and future.

Are you living with **more grace** or less? This is an aspect of life where more is better. **More grace** is better than less grace. Maybe your reaction is, "I don't deserve it." It is true that no one deserves more grace. But the wonderful thing is that God's grace is given apart from what we deserve, and we don't receive because we deserve it, but because we believe God and receive it by faith.

James has a lot more to tell us about grace, even in this single verse. But for today, think about this one truth: **He gives more grace**.

Then believe God for it.

August 27

According to Love, According to Justice

**My eyes are awake through the night watches,
That I may meditate on Your word.
Hear my voice according to Your lovingkindness;
O Lord, revive me according to Your justice.** (Psalm 119:148-149)

In the previous verse (Psalm 119:147), the psalmist spoke of how he rose early in the morning to seek God and His Word. Now he adds another thought: that he also stayed **awake through the night** to think about God and His Word: **My eyes are awake through the night watches, that I may meditate on Your word**.

If someone will both wake up early and stay awake late into the night to seek God, it shows a great love for God and the word that reveals God to us. As you might expect, Jesus Christ was the ultimate fulfillment of this man who loves God and His Word. Jesus sometimes prayed early in the morning (Mark 1:35), and on some occasions, Jesus prayed all night (Luke 6:12).

The psalmist stayed up in the night to meditate on God's Words. We might define this meditation as taking the Bible's teaching so purposefully into our mind and heart that the truth of God's Word becomes a part of how we think. Proper meditation on God's Word makes us think differently and behave differently.

This determined seeking after God brought forth a desire: **Hear my voice according to Your lovingkindness; O Lord, revive me according to Your justice**. The psalmist asked for God to hear him according to the goodness and mercy (**lovingkindness**) of God; he also asked God to revive him according to the **justice** of God. Both of these are important reasons to pray and to have confidence as we bring our prayers before God.

God's people are invited to pray **according** to His **lovingkindness**. This is how an **according to Your lovingkindness** prayer sounds: "Lord, I know that I don't deserve to be heard by You. Yet I believe that You are rich in grace and mercy. Please, according to Your generous and kind love, hear my prayer."

God's people are also invited to pray **according** to His **justice**. "Lord, I know that my sins are righteously forgiven because of what Jesus did on the cross. I know that You have forgiven me according to Your justice, and as one so forgiven I pray. I also know that You, according to Your justice, see the righteousness of my cause with those who are against me. Because of these things, please bring me new life."

Those are great prayers to pray, especially with the thought, **revive me according to Your justice**. Though revival from God is never deserved, it can still be confidently asked for according to God's justice. It can be prayed for based on the justice-satisfying work of Jesus Christ. It can also be prayed for to honor God's justice on earth, especially when wickedness abounds.

It is a great time to pray for true revival and to ask that it begin in me.

August 28

No Fear?

There is no fear in love; but perfect love casts out fear, because fear involves torment. But he who fears has not been made perfect in love. (1 John 4:18)

What are you afraid of? There are not many people who seem to be afraid of God. There are a few here and there, but many people think God only owes them a big reward. Some even say that when they get to heaven, they will have a few questions for God, and He will have some explaining to do.

It wasn't always that way. At one time, people were much more aware of the sin problem. People believed in sin and hell and judgment. Martin Luther – probably the most influential man of the last thousand years – believed it. As a young man, Luther was rising as one of the great legal minds of Europe. But it was the great legal mind of Martin Luther that led to his decision to renounce the world and become an Augustinian monk. Luther was troubled because he knew that God was the great judge and a righteous enforcer of His holy law. How then, could anybody find acquittal in the courts of the Almighty? Luther was almost obsessed with his sense of guilt. His legal training made him aware of the difference between guilt and innocence, and he knew beyond a doubt that he was guilty, completely guilty, of breaking the pure and holy law of God.

Luther came to know peace in the love of God, which provided a way for him to be righteous before God's court. The Father's love sent God the Son, Jesus Christ, to pay the price our sin deserved, and to give us His perfect righteousness.

It is a beautiful declaration: **There is no fear in love**. The complete work of God's love means we do not cower in fear before God, dreading His judgment, either now or in the day of judgment. We know that all the judgment we ever deserved – past, present, and future – was placed on Jesus Christ on the cross.

But what about scriptures such as Ecclesiastes 12:13 and 1 Peter 2:17, which tell us we should fear God? The fear John wrote about here is not the appropriate reverence we all should have of God, but the kind of fear which **involves torment** – that agonizing kind of fear which robs our soul of all joy and confidence before God. It is the fear that is the opposite of boldness in the day of judgment (1 John 4:17).

If this tormenting fear marks our relationship with God, it shows that we have not been **made perfect** – complete and mature – in His love. If you do not stand before God in the righteousness of Jesus of Nazareth, you have reason to fear. Your goodness will never be enough.

Today, if you have trusted in Who Jesus is and what He did for you, then you really can have no fear – knowing the perfect love of God.

August 29

So Blind

Woe to those who seek deep to hide their counsel far from the LORD, and their works are in the dark; they say, "Who sees us?" and, "Who knows us?" Surely you have things turned around! Shall the potter be esteemed as the clay; for shall the thing made say of him who made it, "He did not make me"? Or shall the thing formed say of him who formed it, "He has no understanding"? (Isaiah 29:15-16)

In Isaiah 29, the prophet confronted his people over their sad condition of spiritual blindness. They were like silly children who try to hide by simply covering their own head with a blanket, thinking that if they can't see others then others can't see them. This is why Isaiah could say that they **seek deep to hide their counsel far from the LORD, and their works are in the dark; they say, "Who sees us?"** In their false wisdom, the proud people of Jerusalem thought they could hide their thoughts (**hide their counsel**) and their deeds (**their works are in the dark**) from the LORD.

No wonder Isaiah said, **surely you have things turned around!** They thought they could hide from the LORD, and that they had Him all figured out. The truth is turned around. The LORD had them all figured out, and they really don't know God at all.

Isaiah confronted their lack of knowing God by asking them, **shall the potter be esteemed as the clay?** The people of Jerusalem made the terrible mistake of raising themselves up and lowering God at the same time. For them, the clay was just as worthy, just as intelligent, just as powerful, as the potter was.

The prophet pressed the point further: **For shall the thing made say of him who made it, "He did not make me"?** Indeed, man says exactly this today. Man looks at God our Creator, and says, "He did not make me." For the LORD and His prophet, this was absurd, but today it can pass for high science.

Many today say exactly what Isaiah confronted Israel about thousands of years ago: **Shall the thing formed say of him who formed it, "He has no understanding"?** Instead of seeing the absolute need for an intelligent designer who created all things, many believe that chance – absolute blind, random, purposeless chance, having no understanding at all – has brought all things into being.

People who are otherwise intelligent often fall into this delusion. But assigning such power to "chance" is crazy. Chance has no power. Chance doesn't "do" anything but describe a probability.

When someone says the universe or anything else came about by chance, they are ignorant, superstitious, or just repeating a line they have heard before and have unthinkingly accepted. We can never look to the Creator and say, "He did not make me."

That Isaiah's ancient audience could say this demonstrated their severe spiritual blindness; what does it say of us today?

August 30
Burned Clean

Then one of the seraphim flew to me, having in his hand a live coal which he had taken with the tongs from the altar. And he touched my mouth with it, and said: "Behold, this has touched your lips; your iniquity is taken away, and your sin purged." (Isaiah 6:6-7)

The angel flew to Isaiah with a **live coal** – which means the coal was still hot and burning. It was so hot that even an angel had to use the tongs from the altar. The mention of the altar itself catches our attention; this must be heaven's version of the altar of incense that was set before the holy of holies in the tabernacle of God (Exodus 30:1-10). We know that the earthly tabernacle God instructed Moses to build was made after the pattern of a heavenly reality (Exodus 25:9).

In Isaiah's heavenly vision, he mentions two pieces of "furniture." The first is the throne, and the second is the altar. The throne is for God; that is where He rules and reigns. The altar is for us; that is where we find cleansing and purging from sin. We should never confuse the two – and what each one is for.

The angel had a surprising purpose for the burning coal from the altar. Isaiah says, **He touched my mouth with it**. Isaiah knew he did not serve the Lord like these seraphim, whose name means "the burning ones." In a sense, God said, "I will light a fire in you, also!" That is one reason burning coal was used to purify the prophet.

Isaiah had just cried out, *Woe is me, for I am undone!* (Isaiah 6:5) We might think that burning coal to the lips would be more painful than a vision of the holy God. Nevertheless, for Isaiah, it was more disturbing to see the holiness of God and compare it to his lack of holiness, than it was to have a lump of burning coal applied to his lips. This was an essential step of brokenness for Isaiah in preparation for ministry. Abraham experienced some 13 years of "burning" in his life, and Moses had 40 years. It seems Isaiah only had a few moments, but they were enough. God's work is different in every person.

The result was good for Isaiah: **Your iniquity is taken away, and your sin purged**. Isaiah's sin had to be burned away; the fire of judgment was applied to his place of sin. This was obviously a *spiritual* transaction. The same principle works on our behalf regarding Jesus' work on Calvary. Our sin was placed on Him, and He was burned with the fire of God's judgment. Yet because Jesus was holy and righteous, the fire of God's judgment did not harm Him; it only burned away the sin – our sin.

Once Isaiah had met with the Lord, been convicted of his sin, and cleansed from its guilt, then he was ready to serve God. In Jesus, God can make us ready the same way.

August 31

Give Him No Rest

I have set watchmen on your walls, O Jerusalem; they shall never hold their peace day or night. You who make mention of the Lord, do not keep silent, and give Him no rest till He establishes and till He makes Jerusalem a praise in the earth. (Isaiah 62:6-7)

In the earlier portions of Isaiah, the prophet warned Judah of the coming invasion and devastation at the hands of the Babylonians. Yet Isaiah, a true prophet of the Lord, could not give such bad news without also giving the good news: God would restore Israel, and bring His people back from captivity.

God made rich promises to defend Jerusalem for His people. It was as if God said, "Yes, I will allow Jerusalem to be conquered by the Babylonians. Yet I will bring you back, restore you, and give you safety and security again one day." Isaiah 62:1 says: *For Zion's sake I will not hold My peace, and for Jerusalem's sake I will not rest, until her righteousness goes forth as brightness.*

Because God loves and rejoices over Zion, He will protect them, explaining that He will **set watchmen on** Jerusalem's **walls**. Though the Babylonians conquered them before, the day will come when **He makes Jerusalem a praise in the earth**.

The duty of these **watchmen** is especially wonderful. Here in Isaiah 62, they aren't watchmen who look for threats and warn the people. They aren't watchdogs that look for error and expose it. That is a duty God does give to a few, and we pray that those who take such duty also receive the grace to do such a difficult job in truth and love.

The watchmen Isaiah spoke of here have a different duty they perform **day or night**. They are to **make mention of the Lord**, and to never **keep silent**, to give God **no rest** from hearing their prayers **until He makes Jerusalem a praise in the earth**. The watchmen are prayer warriors, who constantly pray until God's people and His city are restored.

God does not rest regarding His concern for Jerusalem and for His people. It shows us that God does not want these watchmen of prayer to stop their prayers for Israel. Finally, it shows us that God wants His people to bother Him – to **give Him no rest** when they pray for the deliverance of Israel.

When it comes to prayer, we are to give God no rest. Can you imagine such an invitation from God to His people? He invites us – virtually commands us – to bother Him in prayer all the time. This applies to all of us, yet especially to those who consider themselves watchmen. Their greatest work should be done in prayer.

God tells us to keep asking Him, to keep pressing Him, to lay hold of His strength with all our strength. All of this and more are included in that great invitation, **give Him no rest**. Boldly come to God today – you won't "bother" Him!

September 1

A Warning...and What Happened Later

For I know this, that after my departure savage wolves will come in among you, not sparing the flock. Also from among yourselves men will rise up, speaking perverse things, to draw away the disciples after themselves. (Acts 20:29-30)

Nevertheless I have this against you, that you have left your first love. (Rev. 2:4)

In Acts 20, Paul warned his dear friends – the leaders among the Ephesian Christians – that dangerous times were ahead. Paul warned them that threats would come from the outside (**savage wolves**) and the inside (**from among yourselves**). Therefore, they had to be on guard against these threats. They had to take heed to how they lived as leaders and carefully watch over God's people.

Someone can give a warning, but it doesn't mean that the warning is taken seriously. How did the leaders of the Ephesian church do with the warnings Paul gave them?

Looking at the New Testament, their response was a mixture of good and bad. This was true even though the church in Ephesus had a New Testament all-star team of gifted Christians who led and served that church. Think of the notable people who gave their gifts and talents to the Ephesian Christians:

- The apostle Paul (who served there for three years, Acts 20:31).
- Aquilla and Priscilla (Acts 18:24-28).
- Apollos (Acts 18:24-28).
- Timothy (1 Timothy 1:3).
- The apostle John (according to strong church tradition).

Nevertheless, some 30 or 40 years after Paul's warning, Jesus sent a letter to this church in Ephesus. That letter is found in Revelation 2:1-7. Jesus complimented the church in Ephesus on many things. Jesus noted their hard work for the kingdom of God and their endurance through difficult times. Jesus saw their dealing with those who are evil, and with false apostles and that they didn't give up when weary.

Yet despite it all, Jesus gave them a severe warning: they had **left** their **first love**. They didn't love Jesus the way they once did, and they didn't love each other the way they once did. It was so bad among the Christians in Ephesus that unless things changed in a hurry, Jesus would remove His presence among them.

There might very well be a connection between Paul's warning in Acts 20 and their later leaving of love (though they did a good job of holding to the right doctrines). Perhaps in their zeal to fight against false doctrines, they somehow left behind their love for Jesus and their love for one another. If this were the case with the Ephesians, it would not be the last time this happened among God's people.

It's a great illustration of the principle that the devil doesn't care which side of the boat we fall out of, if he gets us in the water and out of the boat. Our soul's enemy is equally pleased if we miss the truth (wrong doctrine) or miss love.

God helping us, we will walk in both truth and love.

September 2
Handling Success – Pit to the Pinnacle

Then Pharaoh said to his servants, "Can we find such a one as this, a man in whom is the Spirit of God?" Then Pharaoh said to Joseph, "Inasmuch as God has shown you all this, there is no one as discerning and wise as you." (Genesis 41:38-39)

It's been said that the successful executive is the one who can delegate all the responsibility, shift all the blame, and take all the credit. That's the strategy many adopt in their search for success, but that strategy is like a house of cards. It rarely builds lasting accomplishments. Joseph's example in Genesis 41 shows us how to achieve and handle success in God's way.

Note that timing is important to the success that God gives. Here, in Genesis 41, Joseph had just arrived at the pinnacle of his success; but it took him a long time to get there. Joseph spent the previous years in prison, but that wasn't wasted time. God had a purpose for that time, and He arranged everything for Joseph's future success. From his youth, Joseph had the idea God had destined him for great things. But Joseph didn't know the fulfillment would take so long.

In Psalm 31:14-15 David said, *but as for me, I trust in You, O LORD; I say, "You are my God." My times are in Your hand*. Can you say this also? It is easy to feel as though we are completely ready for what God has for us in the future. Yet, it is easy to overestimate our readiness. It is important to rest in the LORD and say to Him, *my times are in Your hand*.

Genesis 41 describes how Pharaoh promoted Joseph. He had risen from the pit to the pinnacle. But Pharaoh wasn't the one responsible for Joseph's promotion – God was. Joseph wasn't waiting on Pharaoh to get out of jail; he was waiting on God. In Psalm 75, Asaph reminds us: *For exaltation comes neither from the east, nor from the west nor from the south. But God is the Judge: he puts down one and exalts another* (Psalm 75:6). The credit for Joseph's amazing rise to power did not belong to Pharaoh, or to Joseph, and certainly not to blind fate or circumstance. It was the fulfillment of God's divine plan.

Genesis 41:50-52 explains that Joseph had two sons whom he named Manasseh and Ephraim. Joseph, though he lived in Egypt, married an Egyptian woman, and worked for the Egyptian Pharaoh, gave his two sons Hebrew names. This shows us that Joseph did not forget about God, even in his success. Many people, when they have been promoted the way Joseph was, feel they no longer need God. They think that God is only good for the prison, not the palace. We should be like Joseph, who was devoted to God no matter what – good times or bad.

Here's a good prayer for today: "God, give me a heart that will wait on You and serve You faithfully even when I am successful in the eyes of the world."

September 3

God's Building Materials

And the king commanded them to quarry large stones, costly stones, and hewn stones, to lay the foundation of the temple. (1 Kings 5:17)

It was one of the most amazing building projects in the ancient world. Thousands of men worked together to make the temple God inspired David and his son Solomon to build. There were seventy thousand men who carried burdens and who quarried stones on this job site.

Solomon the **king** gave a command regarding the building materials for the temple. His orders were to **quarry large stones**, **costly stones** and **hewn stones** all to be used for the **foundation of the temple**. When it says, **costly stones** this is literally "quality stones," showing that Solomon used high-quality materials even in the foundation where the stones could not be seen.

God's people are being built up like a temple, with Jesus Christ as the chief cornerstone and God's apostles and prophets as the rest of the foundation. God builds on that foundation with the rest of His people, *in whom the whole building, being joined together, grows into a holy temple in the Lord* (Ephesians 2:19-21).

1 Peter 2:5 addresses God's people and says, *you also, as living stones, are being built up a spiritual house.* The picture is of God constructing a building, and we are the "bricks" or the "stones" that He uses to construct it.

So, Solomon using only **costly stones** in building the temple illustrates the way we should work for God. We don't work for appearance only, but also to excel in the deep and hidden things. All our work for God should be done excellently – perhaps especially the work that is like a foundation in that it is essential, yet it lays low and hidden, and is not commonly seen by others.

This speaks to the way God works in us. He works in the deep and hidden things when others are concerned with appearances. You probably know this from your own life – how God has done a lot of unseen, underground work in your life. He usually spends a lot of time on the secret and hidden things of a life, making a broad and strong foundation. Then God builds on that hidden work that others can see.

This is the way God builds the church. He wants to make a deep, strong foundation instead of a work a mile wide but an inch deep. If we want to see a solid work of God in our churches, it will be built on solid people. Therefore, we must aim at genuine godliness. Twenty thousand churchgoers may not have the same spiritual vitality and strength as 20 solid believers. Yet it is on those solid believers that God will build His work because He uses costly stones in His temple.

Best of all, never forget who paid the price for every one of those costly stones: Jesus our Redeemer. It is His temple and all the materials in it are His purchased possession.

Today, thank Jesus for buying, building, and living in His temple.

September 4

The Effect of His Message

And so it was, when Jesus had ended these sayings, that the people were astonished at His teaching, for He taught them as one having authority, and not as the scribes. (Matthew 7:28-29)

Through the Sermon on the Mount, Jesus dealt with many themes, speaking with astonishing authority about:

- The character of the citizens of His kingdom and their responsibility to live as lights to the world.
- The way the citizens of His kingdom should understand the law of God.
- The manner and heart in which the citizens of His kingdom should do spiritual works and regard money and material things.
- The way the citizens of His kingdom should treat one another.
- The way the citizens of His kingdom should pray and trust God.

Jesus gave all His listeners a better understanding of who He was, and what kind of kingdom He brought to this earth. Many people in those days were confused by wrong expectations about the kingdom. One purpose of the Sermon on the Mount was to correct those misunderstandings and for Jesus to say, "I come to you as a King; and this is what My kingdom is like; this is how it is experienced in the life of the citizens of this kingdom."

In these last few verses of Matthew 7, we learn what the reaction of the people was. The people were astonished at His teaching. They were amazed and felt that what they heard from Jesus was not like anything else they had heard before.

The next line tells us what they thought was different about the teaching of Jesus: **For He taught them as one having authority, and not as the scribes**. His audience could not but notice that Jesus taught with authority lacking in the other teachers in His day. It was common for a teacher to quote other rabbis when they discussed the Scriptures in those days. "Rabbi so-and-so says this; scribe this-and-that says something else."

Jesus was different. He spoke with authority all His own, and the authority of God's revealed Word.

But that was not the only thing that impressed the people who heard Jesus. The people were also **astonished at His teachings**. They were mostly surprised by the way Jesus taught (as one having authority), but they were also astonished at the content. What Jesus taught them about the Kingdom of the Messiah was radically different than what they previously thought. Jesus corrected their wrong ideas.

When we understand Jesus in this Sermon on the Mount, we should also be astonished. If we are not, then we probably have not understood what Jesus said. Until we are corrected, His kingdom is different than what we think. Let Jesus tell you what He and His kingdom are like. Let Him astonish you today.

September 5

The Foolish Wise Man

And he had seven hundred wives, princesses, and three hundred concubines; and his wives turned away his heart. (1 Kings 11:3)

Solomon was one of the wisest men to ever live, but the end of his life shows us just how foolish a wise man can be.

We can say that Solomon had so many marriage partners because he followed the bad example of his father David, who had many wives and concubines himself (2 Samuel 5:13-16).

We can say that Solomon had so many marriage partners because of his sexual lust. Solomon shows us that 1,000 women cannot satisfy the lust of man. He should have listened to his own words in Proverbs 27:20: *Hell and destruction are never full; so the eyes of man are never satisfied.*

We can say that Solomon had so many ungodly marriage partners because of his lust for power and prestige. In those days, a large harem was a status symbol. It said to the world, "Look how many wives and children I can support. Look how many women I have authority over."

Sadly, **his wives turned away his heart**. Of course they did. Based on the Song of Solomon, we can say that in his early days Solomon seemed to know what true love was with one woman. Yet his later life shows us that it is possible to be in that place and later depart from it.

After Solomon had added his second wife, it was easy for him to rationalize it. Once he followed his father David into this departure from what was God's plan from the beginning (Matthew 19:4-6 and Genesis 2:23-24), he apparently found it easy to keep adding wives.

As he added wives, he broke the specific commandment God gave to the future kings of Israel in Deuteronomy 17:17: *Neither shall he multiply wives for himself, lest his heart turn away.* Solomon knew that command, but probably did what many of us do. He somehow thought that he would be the exception, that he would escape the consequences of this sin, despite seeing how it affected others. Solomon learned (or should have learned) that he was not the exception to this rule.

One could never lead this wise man astray through the mind. He was too smart for that. In a debate, Solomon could always win. Yet through his heart – and through his sensual lusts – he was led to a place he never dreamed he would end. Satan knew where to tempt one of the wisest men who ever lived.

The last look at the life of Solomon in 1 Kings leads us to believe that he died in apostasy. There is no hopeful or cheerful end to the story in this account. We hope he repented, but have no firm record of it. If he did repent, God wanted to conceal it from us as a warning.

Today, you have the opportunity to live more wisely than Solomon – if you learn from this foolish wise man.

September 6

A Big Use for Small Things

For who has despised the day of small things? For these seven rejoice to see the plumb line in the hand of Zerubbabel. They are the eyes of the Lord, which scan to and fro throughout the whole earth. (Zechariah 4:10)

Zechariah's question rings true to us today. Many of us could answer, "I am the one who has despised the day of small things." Of course, the question itself reveals our heart because none of us should despise the day of small things. After all, God has a wonderful, though perhaps difficult, purpose for those days.

These words were first directed to **Zerubbabel**, who led the city government of Jerusalem and oversaw the project to rebuild the temple. The work had stalled for many years, yet the Lord calls it only a **day of small things** for Zerubbabel. It must have seemed like a very long "day" because the work of the temple was paused for almost 20 years. He probably would say to God, "What do you mean **day of small things**? I've lived with 20 years of small things." Even so, God tells Zerubbabel to not despise the season of small things and to consider it is all as just a day.

In many of God's choice workers He trains them with an important season of **small things**. Those days are not a mistake nor are they punishment; they are days of priceless shaping and preparation. They are not days to **despise**. Satan fears the day of small things in our life because he sees what great things God does in them and brings out of them.

Zechariah 4:10 says, **these seven rejoice to see the plumb line in the hand of Zerubbabel**. The **seven** are the eyes of the Lord mentioned previously in the same context. God's eyes were happy when they saw Zerubbabel busy with the building work, with the **plumb line** in his hand. The eyes of the Lord see it all, and they are happy to see God's people at work. This is an important lesson for us. Though the work was empowered by the Spirit of God, Zerubbabel still needed his **plumb line**. He still needed to get to work. God could have given Zerubbabel a shortcut and with an instant miracle finished the work. That isn't God's normal way of doing things because His work *in* the life of Zerubbabel was as important to Him as His work *through* him.

Does this explain, at least in part, a season of **small things** in your life? Sometimes we think that the work is more important to God than the worker, but God is truly interested in loving, growing, and maturing the worker right along with the work. God has a lot to do in our life by the **day of small things**, and we should never despise it.

Instead, we should thank God for His love and care, and trust His wisdom when it comes to small things or great things.

September 7

Finally

Finally, my brethren, be strong in the Lord and in the power of His might. (Ephesians 6:10)

This verse begins the well-known and often quoted passage from the apostle Paul dealing with spiritual warfare and the whole armor of God. It is a theme that has fascinated Christians for a long time, probably because it touches the life experience of most every follower of Jesus Christ.

One pastor captivated by the themes of this Ephesians 6 passage was named William Gurnall. Starting in 1655, he published his book *The Christian in Complete Armour*, an explanation of Ephesians 6:10-20. In his dedication, he described his book as a "mite" and a "little present," but it takes up three volumes, 261 chapters, and 1,472 pages – all on these eleven verses.

I am impressed by how William Gurnall subtitled his book: *The saint's war against the Devil, wherein a discovery is made of that grand enemy of God and his people, in his policies, power, the seat of his empire, wickedness, and chief design he hath against the saints; a magazine opened, from whence the Christian is furnished with spiritual arms for the battle, helped on with his armor, and taught the use of his weapon; together with the happy issue of the whole war.*

That was just the long subtitle to the book – not the book itself!

We don't have to look at this passage with the same depth as William Gurnall, but we can start by noting that Paul began this section with the word **finally**. This comes at the end of the letter of Ephesians – a letter in which Paul carefully established our privileges and our place in Jesus Christ, and then explained the basics of the Christian walk. This is Paul's last section dealing with that walk.

Therefore, the foundations for success in spiritual warfare (and the entire Christian life) are the truths and principles in the previous sections of Ephesians. Everything about our spiritual battle comes "finally," considering all those things.

- Considering all that God has done for you.
- Considering the glorious standing, you have as a child of God.
- Considering His great plan of the ages that God has made you part of.
- Considering the plan for Christian maturity and growth, He gives to you.
- Considering the conduct, God calls every believer to live.
- Considering the filling of the Spirit and our walk in the Spirit.
- Considering all this, there is a battle to fight in the Christian life.

Some Christians get excited about spiritual warfare and want to rush into it. But before you launch out into spiritual battle, give attention to the basics, the foundations of Christian living – who Jesus is and what He has done for you.

Building on those foundations explained from Ephesians 1:1 to 6:9, we come to the critical subject of spiritual battle – but not before.

September 8
Relenting, Repenting, and Contradictions

So the LORD **relented from the harm which He said He would do to His people.** (Exodus 32:14)

As Moses was up on Mount Sinai receiving special instructions from God, Israel was in rebellion against the LORD. Moses went into intense prayer, and he begged for God's mercy towards the people. God relented, and Israel was saved.

This verse from Exodus 32 is an excellent example of what some consider a problem passage in the Bible. This is especially true when we read the King James Version, where this verse is translated "The LORD repented of the evil which he thought to do unto his people." So, this is the problem. Does God need to repent of evil? Did God change His mind?

This devotional uses the New King James Version. But there are other good translations available. Here is this passage in a few other well-known translations:

"Then the LORD relented." (New International Version)

"So the LORD changed His mind about the harm which He said He would do to His people." (New American Standard Bible)

"The LORD turned from the evil which He had thought to do." (The Amplified Bible)

Moses wrote in Numbers 23:19, *God is not a man, that He should lie, nor a son of man, that He should repent.* How could Moses say that God changed His mind?

Moses described the actions of God as they appeared to him. Moses' prayer did not change God, but it changed the standing of the people in God's sight – the people were now in a place of mercy, when before they were in a position of judgment. God's promises of judgment are designed to call men to repentance and prayer, and therefore turn away God's judgment. Ezekiel 33:13-16 is a passage that beautifully describes this dynamic of God's judgment.

To speak of God after the manner of God is reserved for God himself. Even if Moses could write it, we couldn't understand it. In this sense, the LORD often speaks, not according to the literal fact, but according to the way things appear to us, so that we may understand as much as humans can understand the divine. We take the Bible literally – that is, according to its literary context. When it uses figures of speech and human-centered word pictures, we understand it that way.

When we read a passage like this, it should bring forth at least three reactions:

First, we should thank God that there are no true contradictions in His Word.

Second, we should thank God that He has given us His Word using terms we can understand.

Finally, thank God that He has relented from the harm we deserved from Him, and He relents when we receive by faith what Jesus did to make us right before God.

September 9

Appreciation in Affliction

**It is good for me that I have been afflicted,
That I may learn Your statutes.
The law of Your mouth is better to me
Than thousands of coins of gold and silver.** (Psalm 119:71-72)

They are remarkable words: **It is good for me that I have been afflicted**. The psalmist spoke here of lessons learned the hard way. There was a time when he was far more likely to go astray from God's Word, and the wise life revealed there. Yet, under a season of affliction, he was now devoted to the Word of God.

Our trials sometimes act as guardrails on the side of a dangerous road, keeping us safely on the path. Prosperity and ease can be like gaps in the guardrail, where we can easily go astray. This principle has worked its way in the life of virtually everyone who has pursued God. This is one reason why God appoints affliction for His people (1 Thessalonians 3:3). Yet, as Adam Clarke noted, affliction set apart for God is a great blessing; it is an additional curse if it is not set apart.

Affliction, brought under the wisdom and guidance of God's Word, did genuine good in the psalmist's life. Yet we must guard against the wrong idea that seasons of affliction automatically make us better or godlier. Sadly, many are worse from their affliction – because they fail to turn to God's Word for wisdom and life-guidance at such times. We could say that the worst afflictions are those lost for any good purpose because they were never surrendered to God.

This also shows how valuable the learning of God's Word was to the psalmist. It was entirely worth it for him to endure affliction if only he could learn God's statutes in the process. This made a time of painful affliction worthwhile.

Therefore, he could say that the **law of Your mouth is better to me than thousands of coins of gold and silver**. This is a logical extension of the thought in the previous verse. If the psalmist understood that even trouble could be good if it taught him God's truth – if it was more valuable than his comfort – then it is also possible to say that it is more valuable than riches. Today, Bibles are inexpensive to purchase – but do we value God's Word?

This great estimation of the Word of God came from a life that had known affliction. It was love and appreciation from the field of battle, not the palaces of ease and comfort.

Unfortunately, it seems that there are too few with the spirit of the psalmist, and too many with the spirit of Judas – who betrayed his Lord for 30 pieces of silver.

To paraphrase a quote from Spurgeon's work on this psalm: The Word of God must be nearer to us than our friends, dearer to us than our lives, sweeter to us than our liberty, and more pleasant than any earthly comfort.

Today, let the wisdom of God's Word bring some good out of your season of affliction.

September 10

The Patience of a Farmer

Therefore be patient, brethren, until the coming of the Lord. See how the farmer waits for the precious fruit of the earth, waiting patiently for it until it receives the early and latter rain. You also be patient. Establish your hearts, for the coming of the Lord is at hand. (James 5:7-8)

James wrote about the problem of the rich oppressing the poor, and he spoke in strong terms about the judgment of God on those oppressors. The people of God needed to **be patient** regarding God's work of judgment. James brought the issue of the ultimate judgment before us in his remarks about the ungodly rich and their destiny. He calls Christians (especially those enduring hardship) to endure with patience **until the coming of the Lord**.

James gave an example of patience: **See how the farmer waits for the precious fruit of the earth, waiting patiently**. A farmer does not give up when his crop does not come to harvest immediately. He keeps on working even when the crop cannot be seen at all. Also, Christians must work hard and exercise patient endurance, even when the harvest day seems far away.

We are to wait on God and not lose heart, just like the farmer doesn't expect a harvest the day after he plants. The waiting and need for endurance in the Christian life are like the farmer's waiting:

- The farmer waits with a reasonable hope and expectation of reward.
- The farmer waits a long time but works all the while.
- The farmer waits as he depends on things out of his power, with his eye on the heavens and its rain.
- The farmer waits despite changing circumstances and many uncertainties.
- The farmer waits encouraged by the value of the coming harvest.
- The farmer waits inspired by the work and harvest of other farmers.
- The farmer waits having no other option – it does no good to give up.
- The farmer waits aware of how the seasons work.

James noticed that the farmer waits for the land **until it receives the early and latter rain**. The pictures of the **early and latter rain** should be taken literally. James referred to the **early** rain (coming in late October or early November), which were essential to soften the ground for plowing, and to the **latter rain** (coming in late April or May), which were crucial to the maturing of the crops shortly before harvest. There is no allegorical picture here of an early and a latter outpouring of the Holy Spirit on the church.

Expecting the soon **coming** of Jesus, God's people should **establish** their **hearts**, rooting them in Jesus and His eternal resolution of all things.

Today, wait for the coming of Jesus – with the wise patience of the farmer.

September 11

Two Kinds of Power

Now when he [Herod] had arrested him, he put him in prison and delivered him to four squads of soldiers to keep him.... Peter was therefore kept in prison, but constant prayer was offered to God for him by the church.... [Peter was] sleeping, bound with two chains between two soldiers. (Acts 12:4-6)

The first of the apostles had just been martyred – James, who was one of the closest companions of Jesus; one of the three: Peter, James, and John. Yet Herod, after killing James, was not satisfied. He saw his approval ratings going up in the opinion polls and thought they might go up even more if he killed Peter. So, Peter was **kept in prison**.

Herod was not a fool – he knew that the apostles were famous for mysterious jail escapes. Acts 5:17-21 is a good example of one: *Then the high priest rose up, and all those who were with him.... and they were filled with indignation, and laid their hands on the apostles and put them in the common prison. But at night an angel of the Lord opened the prison doors and brought them out...*). So, Herod took no chances – he gave four squads of soldiers the job to guard Peter. Herod also chained Peter between two soldiers. Normally, a maximum-security prisoner would be chained to one solider.

So, Herod had his soldiers and his prisons; but the church had the power of prayer. The outcome would be decided easily. The prison was shut up securely. But when every other gate is shut and locked, the gate to heaven is wide open. The church took advantage of that open gate through their earnest prayers.

Most remarkably, Peter showed no signs of anxiety; he was able to sleep soundly on what seemed to be the last night before his execution. Peter could do this because he had something stronger than the best gates, guards, and chains – Peter had the promise of God. In John 21:18, Jesus had told Peter about his death: *When you are old, you will stretch out your hands, and another will gird you and carry you where you do not wish.*

Peter could reason like this: "Jesus promised me that I would not die for Him until I am old. It has only been a few years since He said that, and I am not old yet. So, this is not my time. I may as well get a good night's sleep." The power of the God he trusted was greater than all of Herod's power.

When we have a genuine trust in God's promises, it brings a peace that passes understanding in our lives. Are you stressed? Worried? Filled with anxiety about things?

Then get your eyes off your circumstances and fix your eyes on the promises God has made. Then you can be peaceful enough to sleep in even the most desperate times!

Remember, God gives His beloved sleep (Psalm 127:2).

September 12

The Ultimate Shepherd

He will feed His flock like a shepherd; He will gather the lambs with His arm, and carry them in His bosom, and gently lead those who are with young. (Isaiah 40:11)

The prophet Isaiah announced something wonderful: **He will feed His flock like a shepherd**. One aspect of our God to behold is His loving care as a **shepherd**. The first thing a shepherd must do for his sheep is feed them, and the LORD feeds us like a shepherd feeds his flock.

Sheep must be directed to the good pasture and must be moved on to new pasture when they have stripped the grass bare. We need as much carefully directed feeding as sheep! Some say that there are few creatures that have less power to take care of themselves than sheep have.

God loves to call Himself a **shepherd**. Many of the greatest men of the Bible were shepherds and their character points to Jesus Christ. Abel is a picture of Jesus, the sacrificed shepherd. Jacob is a picture of Jesus, the working shepherd. Joseph is a picture of Jesus, the persecuted and exalted shepherd. Moses is a picture of Jesus, the calling-out-from-Egypt shepherd. David is a picture of Jesus, the shepherd king.

Our LORD shows special care for the **lambs**, who are gathered in **His arm**. The youngest, the weakest, are not despised – they are given special care by the LORD who first gathers them and then will **carry them in His bosom** close to His heart. He does not cast the weak lambs over his shoulder, as a shepherd might carry a sheep; He carries them in a safe and tender place. The shoulders are for power, and the back is for carrying burdens, but the bosom is a place of love.

It is the LORD Himself who does this. He does not delegate this work to an angel, or even to His ministers or preachers. He promised that He, working through His Spirit, does the work of carrying His lambs. The shepherd carries a rod and staff and knows how to use them; He also knows how to **gently lead those who are with young**.

Jesus is given three wonderful titles regarding His work as a shepherd.

- Jesus is the Good Shepherd (John 10:11-15). He is good in His care and sacrifice for the flock.
- Jesus is the Great Shepherd (Hebrews 13:20). He is great in His glorious triumph over every enemy.
- Jesus is the Chief Shepherd (1 Peter 5:4).

Jesus is the ultimate Shepherd. Is He your Shepherd? Are you responding to Him as a sheep should respond to its Shepherd? Let Him feed you; let Him comfort and care for you; let Him lead you.

September 13

From the Inside Out

Moreover you shall make the tabernacle with ten curtains of fine woven linen and blue, purple, and scarlet thread; with artistic designs of cherubim you shall weave them. (Exodus 26:1)

After Moses met God on Mount Sinai, he descended with the tablets of the Law. He also came down with a pattern for a special tent God told him to build. It was called the "tent of meeting" or the **tabernacle of God**. A "tabernacle" is simply a tent, but this was no ordinary tent – it was the traveling house of God.

In Exodus 25, God told Moses to build three essential pieces of furniture inside the tent. The first was the ark of the covenant, the second was the table of showbread, and the third was the golden menorah that gave light to the tent. After describing these three pieces for the inside of the tent, God gave Moses the pattern for building the tent itself – the outside part of the structure.

There were to be four layers of material covering the tent. The first was of fine woven linen, with the artistic design of cherubim. This was the inside layer, which the priests saw inside the tabernacle, reminding them that this represented God's throne room in heaven. The second layer was a large blanket made of goat's hair, the third a covering made of ram's skin dyed red, and the fourth and outside layer was of badger skins sewn together in a large leather tarp. These large coverings lay over a system of boards, set on silver bases, covered with gold, and connected by gold-covered wood rods.

When these four layers of curtains were laid on one another, the result was a very dry and dark tent – the only light came from the golden menorah described in the previous chapter. It was here that the priests performed their duties before the Lord.

Much could be said about each aspect of the tent. The colors, the fabrics, the metals, and the way the structure joined together – each had an important significance. But there is also value in looking at the broader picture, noticing just how the plans for the tabernacle were revealed to Moses. God started from the inside, telling Moses what to put in the tent. Then God worked out from there and told Moses how to build the outside. Even in His description of the four coverings, God started from the inside and worked out.

This is how the work of God is always done in us: from the inside out. First, He makes us new men and women in Jesus Christ and lifts us up to sit in heavenly places with Him. With that inner work done, He then works on the outside.

Today, spend some time recognizing the work God has already done inside you, making you a new person in Jesus Christ; then let that make the difference on the outside, in how you live your life.

He works from the inside out.

September 14

Feast or Famine?

"Behold, the days are coming," says the Lord GOD,
"That I will send a famine on the land,
Not a famine of bread,
Nor a thirst for water, but of hearing the words of the LORD.
They shall wander from sea to sea,
And from north to east;
They shall run to and fro, seeking the word of the LORD,
But shall not find it. (Amos 8:11-12)

The prophet Amos reminds us that there is another kind of famine: **a famine on the land, not a famine of bread, nor a thirst for water, but of hearing the words of the LORD.** It is not a *lack* of God's Word, but a famine of *hearing* God's Word. It is not a case of God withholding His revelation but of people being in such a state that they do not take heed to the words.

1 Thessalonians 2:13 describes the right way to hear the Word of God: *When you received the word of God which you heard from us, you welcomed it not as the word of men, but as it is in truth, the word of God, which also effectively works in you who believe.* They received the word, they welcomed the word, they regarded it as the Word of God, and they allowed it to work effectively in their life. That is effective hearing.

Amos continued his warning: **They shall wander...seeking the word of the LORD, but they shall not find it.** When we push away God's Word for a long time, we may find ourselves in the place where we could not find it even if we wanted to. This makes us remember that the ability to hear God's Word and to benefit by it is a gift from God, and it is a gift that should not be despised.

Jesus alluded to this principle in the Parable of the Soils and the Sower: *Take heed what you hear. With the same measure you use, it will be measured to you; and to you who hear, more will be given. For whoever has, to him more will be given; but whoever does not have, even what he has will be taken away from him* (Mark 4:24-25). When we seek God, it generally becomes easier to find Him. When we push away God, it generally becomes more difficult to hear and to receive His Word.

Is there famine in your life right now? Perhaps the famine in your life is a famine of hearing, and the problem is with you. You owe it to yourself to seek God on the matter.

Since it is true that man doesn't live by bread alone, but by every word that proceeds from the mouth of God (Matthew 4:4), then it is true that a famine of hearing God's Word can be as catastrophic as a famine of bread.

The bread is out there – today, get your hearing right and enjoy the feast.

September 15

Worthless Things

Incline my heart to Your testimonies, and not to covetousness. Turn away my eyes from looking at worthless things, and revive me in Your way. (Psalm 119:36-37)

The composer of the great Psalm 119 knew something specifically about himself, and in general about human nature. He knew that **covetousness** is a threat to walking in God's way. Therefore, he prayed, **Incline my heart to Your testimonies, and not to covetousness**. A heart inclined towards God's Word would help him be satisfied with whatever God provides.

The psalmist also knew that one way to fight against covetousness is to keep one's eyes on the LORD and away from worthless things. So, he prayed, **turn away my eyes from looking at worthless things**. It is true that some things, comparatively speaking, are **worthless things**. They are of no value for eternity and of little value for the present age. He prayed that God would empower and enable him to turn away his eyes and attention from such things.

Many lives are wasted because people find themselves unwilling or unable to **turn away** their **eyes from worthless things**. The media and entertainment technology of the modern world brings before us an endless river of **worthless things** to occupy not only our eyes and time, but also our heart and minds.

Some things are obviously worthless; other things are thought by many to be worthy but are worthless. They are worthless because they do no good. They are worthless because they do not last. They are worthless because they do not build faith, hope, or love. They are worthless because they distract from truly worthy things and worthless because they have nothing to do with Jesus.

Like many of us, the psalmist understood that he had a natural tendency towards worthless things, so he prayed for that natural tendency to be counter-acted. Yet the eyes are so powerful that the psalmist had to pray – to pray for power outside of himself to turn his eyes from worthless things. Did he have no eyelids? No muscles in his neck to turn the head? Yet we all sympathize with this prayer; the eyes are so small – yet they can lead the whole person, and often lead to utter destruction. This is because the eyes lead the heart, lead the mind, and can lead the entire person.

He did not gouge out his own eyes, or pray for God to do that; instead, he wanted to look another way, a better way. The best way to look away from sin is to look at something else.

He then prayed another prayer for revival: **And revive me in Your way**. He wanted to be made alive again in God's pathway. The psalmist wanted to walk in God's way and to do it with a revived heart. He prayed for deadness in one direction – towards **worthless things** and prayed for life in another direction – towards God's way.

September 16

When God Stops Speaking

And when Saul inquired of the LORD**, the L**ORD **did not answer him, either by dreams or by Urim or by the prophets.** (1 Samuel 28:6)

God is a God of revelation – He loves to reveal Himself. He reveals Himself in creation, in conscience, and especially in His Word. There are many amazing promises in the Bible to those who seek God:

- *And you will seek Me and find Me, when you search for Me with all your heart.* (Jeremiah 29:13)
- *Ask, and it will be given to you; seek, and you will find; knock, and it will be opened to you.* (Matthew 7:7)

Knowing these passages, it's a little strange to read 1 Samuel 28:6 – that Saul inquired of the LORD, but God did not answer him. Someone can feel like that today. I don't mean just for a day or so, but an extended season. They read the Bible but have no sense God is speaking. They hear good preaching, with no sense God is speaking. They seek God in prayer and have no sense God is speaking. This verse teaches us something about such an extended season.

First, we can feel sorry for Saul. The king of Israel was in a terrible place. The Philistines threatened, Saul's courage failed, and God was silent when Saul sought Him. Saul hoped God would speak to him through dreams. He hoped God would talk to him through the **Urim**. He wanted to hear from God through the prophets, but God wouldn't speak to Saul.

Then, we can learn from Saul. The **L**ORD **did not answer him**, and this silence shows that God does not always answer everyone who seeks Him. Sometimes the reason for God's silence is the person seeking Him has a false and insincere heart.

Sometimes people sincerely seek, and God doesn't answer. I think that was Saul's situation. Saul was in a place of judgment. Saul continually rejected what God already said to him. Since Saul didn't obey God, the LORD wouldn't give him more. Saul knew that God did not want him hunting David to kill him (1 Samuel 24:16-20 and 26:21). Yet Saul disregarded God's will. If we want God to guide us, we must follow what guidance we already have from Him.

There are three principles to take away from this:

- If you are going to seek God, do it sincerely and with your whole heart.
- If you want to hear from God, obey what He has already told you.
- If God speaks to you through His Word, good preaching, in prayer – find comfort in that.

God would have spoken to Saul if he had come with a humble heart and sincere repentance (Psalm 51:17). Even if you're in a place as bad as King Saul was, you can once again hear God speak.

No one is beyond hope.

September 17

The Right Kind of Wisdom

Therefore the L<small>ORD</small> said: "Inasmuch as these people draw near with their mouths and honor Me with their lips, but have removed their hearts far from Me, and their fear toward Me is taught by the commandment of men, therefore, behold, I will again do a marvelous work among this people, a marvelous work and a wonder; for the wisdom of their wise men shall perish, and the understanding of their prudent men shall be hidden." (Isaiah 29:13-14)

Isaiah 29 is all about spiritual blindness – the causes of it, and the cures for it. In part, Israel was spiritually blind because they wanted it and chose it. In part, they were blind because God sent blindness on them.

Through Isaiah, the L<small>ORD</small> confronted His **people** who drew near with their words, but not their **hearts**. In Isaiah's day, those in Jerusalem knew how to talk the spiritual talk, but their hearts were **far from** God. Jesus quoted this same passage from Isaiah when He rebuked the religious leaders of His day for their hypocrisy (Matthew 15:7-9, Mark 7:6-7).

Jesus said, *for out of the abundance of the heart the mouth speaks* (Matthew 12:34). Though only God can truly know the heart, the closest we can come is by looking at the whole of one's life – not only what is said or done.

God said that His people had **removed their hearts far from** Him. God doesn't move away from His people; they removed their hearts from Him.

God also explained that the people of Jerusalem had no **fear** of or respect for God; it had to be commanded by others (**taught by the commandment of men**). Their hearts did not respond to God, but only to the threats of men.

Because Jerusalem's pride had led them into spiritual blindness, sleep, drunkenness, illiteracy, and hypocrisy, God promised to destroy the **wisdom of their wise men**.

Isaiah called this **a marvelous work and a wonder** when God decides to reject the wisdom of man and to display His own superior wisdom. Many years later, the apostle Paul was also amazed at the so-called wisdom of man, and how it compared to the so-called foolishness of God:

> *Since, in the wisdom of God, the world through wisdom did not know God, it pleased God through the foolishness of the message preached to save those who believe. For Jews request a sign, and Greeks seek after wisdom; but we preach Christ crucified, to the Jews a stumbling block and to the Greeks foolishness, but to those who are called, both Jews and Greeks, Christ the power of God and the wisdom of God. Because the foolishness of God is wiser than men, and the weakness of God is stronger than men.* (1 Corinthians 1:21-25)

Human wisdom must always take a second place to the wisdom of God. You would have to be blind to not see this.

September 18

Stronger and Stronger

Now there was a long war between the house of Saul and the house of David. But David grew stronger and stronger, and the house of Saul grew weaker and weaker. (2 Samuel 3:1)

David was the rightful king of Israel, and Ishbosheth was a pretender to the throne. Some in Israel embraced David and accepted him as king, but most of the nation gave their allegiance to the counterfeit king, Ishbosheth. War was inevitable, and when their armies clashed, David's army won the battle, losing only twenty men. Abner and Ishbosheth's army lost 360 men.

After that crucial battle, the matter was not settled. Shortly before the war was utterly lost for Abner and the forces loyal to Ishbosheth, Abner appealed for a cease-fire. Joab unwisely accepted, thinking it could make for peace. Yet there could not be peace between a legitimate king and a counterfeit king.

Despite the gesture towards peace, there was a long war between the house of Saul and the house of David. This shows how wrong it was for Joab to accept Abner's appeal for a cease-fire at the battle of The Field of Sharp Swords. They could not just get along; there could be no peace between the rightful king David and the pretender to the throne, Ishbosheth. The cease-fire seemed to make things better, but it only worsened and caused a prolonged war.

No man can serve two masters – true kings and counterfeit kings can't co-exist. When we try to make peace between King Jesus and King Self, the result is a long, bitter war. It is much better to surrender and submit to the reign of Jesus.

The great Bible teacher Alan Redpath wrote: "In the lives of many Christian people today there is raging, literally, a civil war. The flesh – the kingdom of Saul, struggles with the spirit – the kingdom of David, and the conflict is bitter. We do everything we possibly can to hold up the tottering kingdom of self, so it might exist just a bit longer. If only we could preserve some rights; if only we could have at least part of our own way; if only we could keep this or that at any cost! We feel we must bolster up this kingdom of self, that we cannot let ourselves be crucified with Christ."

David grew stronger and stronger. We can look forward to the increasing strength of the True King in our lives. The counterfeit kings will be exposed for their weakness, which can't stand before the power of the one True King. We could say that David's increasing strength and the increasing weakness started when God first chose David and withdrew His Spirit from Saul (1 Samuel 16:13-14).

We can allow the Lord's reign to grow stronger and stronger within us – just like John the Baptist said: *He must increase but, I must decrease* (John 3:30).

Make room for Jesus to grow stronger and stronger in your life.

September 19

The Way of Cain

Woe to them! For they have gone in the way of Cain. (Jude v. 11)

What do you know about these three people: Cain, Balaam, and Korah? Most people would have a vague recollection of them from the Old Testament. As Jude used these three for illustrations, he expected that Christians would see how they fit in as bad examples to learn from.

Cain is perhaps the best known of the three men mentioned in Jude v. 11. Cain's story is found in Genesis 4. There, we find each of the sons of Adam and Eve brought an offering to the Lord. Cain (being a farmer) brought an offering from his harvest. Abel (being a shepherd) brought an offering from his flocks. God accepted Abel's offering, but not Cain's.

Many people assume that because Abel brought a blood sacrifice and Cain brought a grain sacrifice, that the difference between the two offerings was sacrificial blood. But the real difference was between faith and unbelief.

Hebrews 11:4: *By faith Abel offered to God a more excellent sacrifice than Cain, through which he obtained witness that he was righteous, God testifying of his gifts; and through it he being dead still speaks.*

Cain's sacrifice was probably more pleasing to the senses than the carcass of a dead lamb. But his sacrifice was offered without faith, and therefore it was unacceptable to God. You can give to God whatever you have, or whatever you are, but you must offer it in faith.

Genesis 4:5 says that after God rejected his sacrifice, Cain was very angry, and his countenance fell. He became angry because he knew God rejected him. In a fit of anger Cain murdered Abel, and then he lied about it to God. 1 John 3:12 tells us that Cain murdered his brother because Abel's works were righteous (by faith), while Cain's own works were wicked. Cain's lack was not in works but in faith.

Notice the phrase: **the way of Cain**. Jude says that Cain typifies a way that certain men follow in. It is the way of unbelief and empty religion, which leads to jealousy, persecution of the truly godly, and eventually to murderous anger.

There is no greater curse on the earth than empty, vain religion. We must always be on guard against those having a form of godliness but denying its power. (2 Timothy 3:5) No wonder Paul added, *and from such people turn away!* We must make sure that our own faith isn't just a matter of outwardly observing a few rituals but is rooted in a real personal experience of Jesus. We can't be satisfied with the image of a Christian; we must press on to the reality.

Many Christians are deathly afraid of secular humanism or atheism or the world. But dead religion is far more dangerous and sends more people to hell than anything else. Across the centuries, Cain speaks to us of this dangerous way of false religion.

Are you listening?

September 20

Getting to the Root of the Matter

You have heard that it was said to those of old, "You shall not murder, and whoever murders will be in danger of the judgment." But I say to you that whoever is angry with his brother without a cause shall be in danger of the judgment. And whoever says to his brother, "Raca!" shall be in danger of the council. But whoever says, "You fool!" shall be in danger of hell fire. (Matthew 5:21-22)

In this part of the Sermon on the Mount, Jesus shows the true meaning of the Law of Moses, exposing some of the false and superficial interpretations of Moses of His time. Regarding the law, the two errors of the scribes and Pharisees were that they both *restricted* God's commands (as in the law of murder) and *extended* the commands of God past His intention (as in the law of divorce).

The people Jesus spoke to had not studied the Law of Moses for themselves. All they had was the teaching they had **heard** about the law from the scribes and Pharisees. In this matter, the people had heard the scribes and Pharisees teach, **you shall not murder**.

In contrast to what they had heard about the law, Jesus proclaimed, **but I say to you**. With this, Jesus showed His authority and did not rely on the words of previous teachers. He taught them the true understanding of the Law of Moses.

We learn from Jesus, **whoever is angry with his brother without a cause shall be in danger of the judgment**. The teaching of the scribes and Pharisees (**you shall not murder**) was true enough. Yet they also taught that anything short of murder might be allowed. Jesus corrected this and made it clear that it was not only those who commit the act of murder who are in danger of judgment. Those who have a murderous intention are also in danger of the judgment.

Jesus exposed the essence of the scribes' heresy. To them, the law was only a matter of outward performance, never the heart. Jesus brought the law back to a matter of the heart. Jesus warned the person who would say **Raca** to his brother. To call someone **Raca** expressed contempt for their intelligence. Calling someone a **fool** showed contempt for their character.

Jesus didn't say that anger was just as bad as murder. It is deeply wrong to think that someone who shouts at another person in anger has sinned as badly as someone who angrily murders someone. Jesus emphasized that the law condemns both, without saying the law declares that they are the same. The laws of the people could only deal with the outward act of murder.

Jesus exposed those who thought they could hide behind the law. God is concerned with both the fruit and the root, thus we come closer to truly understanding the law.

Today, let Jesus speak to the heart and motives of what you do – not only the outward action.

September 21

How Much More?

Or what man is there among you who, if his son asks for bread, will give him a stone? Or if he asks for a fish, will he give him a serpent? If you then, being evil, know how to give good gifts to your children, how much more will your Father who is in heaven give good things to those who ask Him! (Matthew 7:9-11)

In this section of the Sermon on the Mount, Jesus taught about prayer. In the previous words of this sermon, He encouraged the simple act of persistent prayer, telling us to keep asking, seeking, and knocking in prayer.

In these lines, Jesus corrects the wrong idea many people have about prayer. They think of prayer as if it is our job to convince a reluctant, stubborn God that He should give us things that He doesn't want to give us, but if we nag Him enough, He may do what we want. This is a wrong understanding of God and prayer, and Jesus here corrected it.

He said, **or what man is there among you who, if his son asks for bread, will give him a stone?** Jesus made it clear that God does not have to be persuaded or appeased in prayer. He is a loving God who is ready to give to His children. Just as a man would never give a stone to a son who asked for bread, God will provide us with the good things we ask for.

Of course, we do not always know that the good things are. There are times when we ask for something that would be like a stone or a serpent to us, and God knows better than to give us what we mistakenly ask for. Yet we do not miss the main point of Jesus here: God is a loving, giving God and should be approached that way in prayer.

The point made is clear: **If you then, being evil, know how to give good gifts to your children, how much more will your Father who is in heaven**. It is a sinful misunderstanding of the nature of God to deny that He answers the seeking heart. If we do this, we then imply that God is worse than even an evil man is.

Instead, in comparison to even the best human father, **how much more** is God a good and loving father to His children? How much more is God than even the best human father? Jesus did not tell us. He did not say "100 time more" or "1,000 times more." Jesus left it to our meditation because it is beyond calculation.

When we realize how loving and how good God is, it prompts us to prayer. The God who is there is more loving than we often think. Today, think about how much God loves you – and let that lead you to real prayer.

Believe today that He knows how to **give good things to those who ask Him**.

September 22

Sighs from the Christ

Then, looking up to heaven, He sighed, and said to him, "Ephphatha," that is, "Be opened" .... But He sighed deeply in His spirit, and said, "Why does this generation seek a sign?" (Mark 7:34 and 8:12).

Sometimes people sigh merely for dramatic effect. Other times we sigh unconsciously. We're confronted with a situation so desperate, so grieving, that we just let out a sigh. Perhaps a sigh is a way we let off pressure – our sense of injustice or offense builds up, and we must let off the pressure through a sigh.

In the Gospel of Mark, there are two notable occasions where Jesus sighed. It's remarkable that these sighs are recorded at all – they show that the source Mark had for the information in his Gospel was truly an eyewitness.

What made Jesus sigh? Two things. The first thing was the tragic condition of man. In Mark 7:34, Jesus sighed when a man deaf and mute was brought to Him for healing. The sigh was an inward groan – our Lord's compassionate response to the pain and sorrow sin brings into the world. It seems that for a moment, Jesus saw this man as a picture of every man. We are all born deaf to God's voice. We all have trouble speaking, as we should. The man's own trouble was bad enough, but as a representative of all humanity, he was even more tragic.

The second thing that made Jesus sigh was the hardness of hearts towards Him. In Mark 8:12, we read that Jesus **sighed deeply in His spirit** when the Pharisees came demanding a sign from heaven. Jesus knew that His whole life and work were more than enough to prove His credentials, and the demand from the Pharisees showed how deep their rejection of Him was. This demand for a "special" sign was an extreme example of the arrogance and pride of the religious leaders towards Jesus.

Their attack, and the unbelief it showed, distressed Jesus. He was amazed at the unbelief and audacity of these men. The sigh was physical, but its cause was spiritual. Jesus knew deep within His spirit that these religious leaders were tragically set against Him.

Jesus sighed with the deaf and mute man, and against the religious leaders who hardened themselves against Him. In the first sigh, we see the mercy and tenderness of God, sharing our hurt and tragedy – and we see the power of God to redeem that hurt and tragedy. In the second sigh, we see the mercy and tenderness of God in the face of man's hardened rejection – after all, Jesus could have destroyed these men with a word, yet He showed them mercy in a sigh.

In this, we see how great the mercy and love of God is – they are evident even in the sighs of the Son of God.

Ask God to make that mercy and love a reality in your life today.

September 23

What to Tear

"Now, therefore," says the LORD, "Turn to Me with all your heart, with fasting, with weeping, and with mourning." So rend your heart, and not your garments; return to the LORD your God, for He is gracious and merciful, slow to anger, and of great kindness; and He relents from doing harm. (Joel 2:12-13)

God told Judah, through His prophet Joel, that they must **Turn to Me with all your heart, with fasting, with weeping, and with mourning**. Earlier in the chapter, Joel warned Judah that though they were in a tough time, worse judgment would come unless they got right with God. Now he told them to respond – because they heard the warning of judgment, God's people should repent. The important thing is that God told them how to sincerely repent.

- Sincere repentance is to **turn to** God, and therefore away from our sin.
- Sincere repentance is done **with all your heart**, giving everything you can in surrender to God.
- Sincere repentance is marked by action (**with fasting**) and emotion (**with weeping… mourning**). Not every act of repentance will include fasting and weeping, but if action and emotion are absent, it isn't authentic repentance.

One thing Joel spoke against that offends God was phony repentance: **rend your heart, and not your garments**. One expression of mourning in Jewish culture is tearing the clothes. It was a way to say, "I am so overcome with grief that I don't care if my clothes are ruined, and I look bad." Joel knew that one could tear their garments without tearing their heart, and he described the kind of heart-repentance that pleased God. A ripped heart is a truer sign of true repentance than a ripped shirt.

If real repentance is such deep work, it's easy to think that it isn't worth it. Joel reminds us all that it is worth it: **Return to the LORD your God, for He is gracious and merciful, slow to anger, and of great kindness; and He relents from doing harm**. This was another encouragement to repentance. The first was a present chastisement, and the second was the threat of coming judgment. But knowing the goodness and mercy of God is another motive for true repentance. We come to Him confident that He will heal and forgive, and that He may relent from the judgment He announced.

It is an important point to understand. We don't repent with the idea "God is so mean that if I don't return to Him, He will squash me like a bug." Instead, the idea is "God is so gracious and merciful, slow to anger, and of great kindness that He will spare me from what I deserve if turn back to Him." Ultimately, it is His goodness that leads us to repentance (Romans 2:4).

Today, take God's goodness as motivation to real repentance – a repentance of the heart, not only of external things. Tear your heart and not your clothes.

September 24

Behold Your God

**O Zion, you who bring good tidings,
Get up into the high mountain;
O Jerusalem, you who bring good tidings,
Lift up your voice with strength, lift it up, be not afraid;
Say to the cities of Judah, "Behold your God!"
Behold, the Lord GOD shall come with a strong *hand*,
And His arm shall rule for Him;
Behold, His reward is with Him, and His work before Him.** (Isaiah 40:9-10)

Isaiah 40 is truly one of the most wonderful chapters in the Bible; almost every verse presents or suggests a wonderful idea, and then builds on each other in the chapter. First comes the comfort to God's people (Isaiah 40:1-2); then the preparation of a way for the Lord (Isaiah 40:3-5); then onto a description of the great and eternal Word of God (Isaiah 40:6-8).

In Isaiah 40:9-10, the prophet tells us what the word of comfort is; why the road needs to be prepared for the messenger; and where this eternal Word of God directs our attention: to **Behold your God!**

Isaiah spoke of a message so great – **tidings** so good – that they must be spread as widely as possible. From on top of the **high mountain**, the messenger can proclaim this great message to as many people as possible. It is a message that should be shouted out, so the messenger is told, **lift up your voice with strength**.

What is he to say? Say to the cities of Judah, **Behold your God!** The great message that should be shouted so loud was an invitation to **Behold your God**. There is nothing greater for a believer to do than to study and to know their God.

The message was not, "Give God a passing glance." No, God's people are invited to **Behold your God**. This speaks of a study, of a long-term mission to know the greatness and the character of our God. It also shows how important it is for the message of God's preachers to focus on God. After every sermon, a preacher should ask, "Did I help the people to **Behold your God**?"

More specifically, they are to behold the returning of the LORD. **Behold, the Lord GOD shall come with a strong hand**. One aspect of our God we should behold is the fact of His return. Our God will return to this earth, and He will come with power (**a strong hand...His arm shall rule**).

When the LORD comes back, He will come to reward His people (**His reward is with Him**). He comes to inspect His work (**and His work before Him**). This is something very important for us to know about our God!

So, look to Him. Behold Him. It will be rewarded, and it is the highest occupation of mankind. It is what you were created for – the greatest thing that separates humanity from the rest of creation. Do it today – **Behold your God!**

September 25
The Real God or the God We Make?

And Aaron said to them, "Break off the golden earrings which are in the ears of your wives, your sons, and your daughters, and bring them to me." So all the people broke off the golden earrings which were in their ears, and brought them to Aaron. And he received the gold from their hand, and he fashioned it with an engraving tool, and made a molded calf.

Then they said, "This is your god, O Israel, that brought you out of the land of Egypt!" (Exodus 32:2-4)

Moses went up on Mount Sinai to listen to the LORD and receive His law for Israel. The people of Israel decided Moses had been gone too long. They wanted to get going to the Promised Land, and if Moses didn't come down soon enough, they would fashion their own god to lead them. They came to Aaron, the high priest, asking him to make the god they wanted, and he was happy to help – if it could be called "help," because it did no good for Israel.

First, Aaron took an offering: **break off the golden earrings…and bring them to me**. Before this, God had given Moses instructions for receiving an offering to fund the building of a holy place for the LORD (Exodus 25:1-7). Aaron made an ungodly imitation of that offering – he took an offering of gold to make an idol, an image to worship. And the people were generous: **all the people broke off the golden earrings…and brought them to Aaron**. It's sad but true; that sometimes we are more generous with what we will give to idolatry than with what we give to the things of God.

Look at what Aaron did once he had the gold: **he fashioned it with an engraving tool**. Aaron thought it out, melted the gold, molded it, and fashioned it carefully with an engraving tool. It didn't just happen. Aaron put work into it. Aaron didn't initiate this idolatry, but he put a lot of energy into carrying out that impulse of worshipping an idol instead of the Living God.

Then they said, **this is your god**. Aaron did not say the statue was a god; it was the people who said it, and Aaron agreed with them. Aaron's lack of leadership supported the people's idolatry. When we leave the wisdom of following the true God, we can easily fall for the most foolish things. Someone once said, "In the beginning, God made man in His own image, and man has been returning the favor ever since." It's common to fall into that trap.

Don't fall into the trap of worshipping a god of your creation. Nothing is more important than letting the Bible tell us who God is, instead of shaping our god in our mind.

Today, you can do the opposite of Aaron and lead people to the true God – the God of the Bible – instead of a god made by man.

September 26

The God Who Created It All

Lord, You have been our dwelling place in all generations. Before the mountains were brought forth, or ever You had formed the earth and the world, even from everlasting to everlasting, You are God. (Psalms 90:1-2)

The truth of God's existence tells us about more than only God Himself; it also tells us about who man is. A philosopher named Jean-Paul Sartre said this was the essential problem of philosophy: that there is something, instead of nothing – but why? Everything else in our life flows from the answer to this question. If everything around us, including ourselves is the result of random, meaningless occurrences apart from the work of a creating God, then it says something about who I am. It also says something about my destiny and the destiny of the whole.

Of course, there was never a time when there was nothing, and the Bible tells us so. In the beginning, there was God – and there was a time before time began when there was only God. When we think about such things, a common question that arises is "who created God?" The answer is simple: God wasn't created; God has always been.

For some people, this isn't an adequate explanation. But really, we are only left with one of two alternatives: either God is eternal, or matter is eternal. The fact that there is something instead of nothing means that there must have always been something – or more exactly, some One. Something was the first cause of everything; some One set the universe in motion. We understand God, by definition, to be the One who is uncreated, who has always been.

At the same time, the Bible tells us that God has the power of "self-existence" – He does not depend on anything for His existence, as we depend on air, water, and even the good pleasure of God. In other words, no one "grants" life to God, as He grants it to us – He has life within Himself, and always has had life within Himself. This helps us to understand that big question "who created God?" The answer is simply that no one created God; by definition, God is uncreated – He is self-existent, He is eternal, without beginning and without end.

By going back to God's eternal existence, the psalmist understood that Yahweh's help to His people did not begin with the exodus from Egypt. From their pilgrim beginnings under their patriarch Abraham to the days of Moses, God had been their **dwelling place**, their refuge and protection.

God can be your **dwelling place**. No one really wants to be *homeless*. Spiritually speaking, that never needs to be the state of the believer. We have our home in our Creator God. His **dwelling place** is a place where we rest, where we can be ourselves, and where love and happiness dominate.

Today, the God who created everything wants to be your **dwelling place**. Answer His invitation!

September 27

Know Now What We Will See Then

How you are fallen from heaven, O Lucifer, son of the morning! How you are cut down to the ground, you who weakened the nations! For you have said in your heart: "I will ascend into heaven, I will exalt my throne above the stars of God; I will also sit on the mount of the congregation on the farthest sides of the north; I will ascend above the heights of the clouds, I will be like the Most High." Yet you shall be brought down to Sheol, to the lowest depths of the Pit. (Isaiah 14:12-15)

Isaiah 14 combines a prophecy against the literal king of Babylon (of Isaiah's day) with a prophecy against the power behind that king's throne – the dark being commonly known as Satan or the Devil.

God allows us to know now what we will see then – knowing the fate of the world system and Satan – and allow it to affect our thinking and actions.

Isaiah identified the "real" king of Babylon: **How you are fallen from heaven, O Lucifer, son of the morning!** There are four falls of Satan, and this refers to his final, fourth fall.

First, Satan *fell from glorified to profane* (Ezekiel 28:14-16). This is what Jesus spoke of in Luke 10:18 when He says He saw Satan fall like lightning from heaven. This is the only fall of Satan that has already happened.

Second, Satan will *fall from having access to heaven* (Job 1:12, 1 Kings 22:21, Zechariah 3:1) to restriction on the earth (Revelation 12:9).

Third, Satan will *fall from his place on the earth* to bondage in the bottomless pit for 1,000 years (Revelation 20:1-3).

Finally, as mentioned here in Isaiah 14:12, Satan will *fall from the bottomless pit to the lake of fire*, which we commonly know as hell (Revelation 20:10).

Before his fall he was called the **Son of the morning**. This is a title of glory, beauty, and honor. Lucifer was characterized by the glory of the morning.

Jesus Himself is called the *Bright and Morning Star* (Revelation 22:16). Satan, though only a created being, had some of these glorious qualities. But *Satan himself transforms himself into an angel of light* (2 Corinthians 11:14), deceiving many.

Look at the contrast in the phrase, **how you are cut down to the ground**. God wants us to know now that Satan is destined for hell. He isn't the lord of hell. Satan will go to hell as a victim, as the ultimate prisoner in the dungeon of darkness, and hell will be happy to receive him this way (Isaiah 14:9-11). His end will be disgusting and degrading.

We often forget Satan's destiny and inflate his status and importance. We can wrongly think of him as the opposite of God – as if God were light and Satan was darkness. Satan wishes he was the opposite of God, but Satan is a mere creature.

Know today what everyone will know on that day to come.

September 28
The Sin and the Heart Behind the Sin

You have heard that it was said to those of old, "You shall not commit adultery." But I say to you that whoever looks at a woman to lust for her has already committed adultery with her in his heart. (Matthew 5:27-28)

In this section of the Sermon on the Mount, Jesus said several times, **you have heard that it was said**. In this, Jesus contrasted what the people had heard about the law of God with what God had actually said and meant. Of course, the teachers of the day taught that adultery itself was wrong. But they applied the law only to the very act of adultery, not to the heart that motivated it.

Therefore, Jesus said: **Whoever looks at a woman to lust for her has already committed adultery with her in his heart.** Jesus explained that it is possible to commit adultery in our heart or mind, and this also is sin and forbidden by the command against adultery.

Jesus went deeper than just the act itself. Some people only keep from adultery because they are afraid to get caught, and in their hearts, they commit adultery every day. Jesus was not saying that the act of adultery and adultery in the heart are the same thing. The act of adultery is far worse than adultery in the heart. Jesus' point was to say they are both sins and forbidden by the command against adultery.

We can also say that this principle applies to just about anything we can covet with the eye or mind. Since Jesus considered adultery in the heart a sin, we know that what we think about and allow our heart to rest on is based on choice. Many believe they have no choice – and therefore no responsibility – for what they think about, but this contradicts the clear teaching of Jesus. We may not be able to control passing thoughts or feelings, but we certainly do decide if our heart and mind will rest on them.

There is an important distinction between the temptation to sin and the sin itself. Jesus, though tempted in all ways (Hebrews 4:15), endured such temptations never yielding to sin. As a man, Jesus would be tempted to see women in this way; yet He resisted the temptation and instead was moved by the power of a pure love to look on every woman as a daughter, a sister, or a mother. We need to see beyond what might allure and tempt us to regard others as mere objects and see them as they truly are before God.

We pause and thank God that though, by His Spirit, we do our best to keep these challenging commands, our hope is set in Jesus Himself – the only One to ever completely live out the truth of the Sermon on the Mount.

Today our prayer is, "Jesus, live in me; save me and move me to do Your will – in both my actions and my heart."

September 29

Dreamers

Likewise also these dreamers defile the flesh, reject authority, and speak evil of dignitaries. (Jude v. 8)

In warning early Christians about dangerous men among them Jude used three Old Testament examples: Israel in the Exodus, rebellious angels, and Sodom and Gomorrah. Then Jude described the character of these dangerous deceivers.

With the words **likewise also**, Jude connected these "certain men" with the people of Sodom and Gomorrah in their sensuality (**defile the flesh**) and in their rejection of God's authority (**reject authority**).

God gives every human an aspect of their being known as the flesh. The flesh includes the will, the mind, and the emotions. The flesh is something that can be surrendered to God and be used to glorify Him. But we can also **defile the flesh**, by stubbornly using it in the service of sin and self. They did more than **defile the flesh** – these certain men also rejected authority. They wanted to be in charge, so they rejected the authority of God, and rejected those God put in authority.

Our culture encourages us to reject authority and to recognize ourselves as the only real authority in our lives. Some do it with the Bible, only choosing to believe certain passages. Some do it with their beliefs, by choosing at the "salad bar" of religion. Some do it with their lifestyle, by making their own rules and not recognizing the proper authorities God has established.

In the darkest days of Israel, society was characterized by a term: *every man did what was right in his own eyes* (Judges 21:25). It's just how many people think. We think it is good to set our own rules, to know no boundaries, to just do it.

The third characteristic mentioned in Jude v. 8 is that these men were those who **speak evil of dignitaries**. The dignitaries were probably the apostles or other leaders in the church. Their rejection of authority related to their speaking evil of dignitaries.

We live in an age when many in and out of the church think nothing of speaking evil against dignitaries. This character description of dangerous men in the early church should remind us that Christians must not speak evil of those in authority – even if they seem to deserve it. Our critical words against leaders in politics, business, faith, or other areas of authority must always be respectful and carefully chosen.

Notice Jude called these dangerous men **these dreamers**. It is possible that Jude means they claimed to have "prophetic dreams" which were really deceptions. But it is also possible that Jude meant that these certain men were out of touch with reality. Certainly, that's the case when anyone defiles the flesh, rejects authority, and speaks evil of dignitaries.

Today, ask God to search your character regarding these things.

September 30
Remain in Ephesus

As I urged you when I went into Macedonia – remain in Ephesus that you may charge some that they teach no other doctrine. (1 Timothy 1:3)

Timothy was the young partner of Paul the apostle; Paul was a mentor to Timothy. Their warm relationship is seen throughout the two letters Paul wrote to his young associate. From this statement in 1 Timothy 1:3, we can see that Paul left Timothy in the city of Ephesus, where they had been serving together.

It was not easy to serve the Lord and lead the church in Ephesus. It was one of the great cities of the ancient world, and it was famous as both a religious and economic center. Ephesus had the well-known temple to the goddess Diana, and it was home to a thriving banking industry. There were many things, both spiritual and material, that would make it difficult for Timothy to stand strong for the true message of God as expressed in the gospel.

Even though Timothy had a tough job to do, Paul wanted him to **remain in Ephesus** and not to give up. Paul would not have said this to Timothy if there were no pressure for him to leave. Something or many things pulled on Timothy to give up, resign, or back off from the calling of spiritual leadership God gave him. Paul had to tell Timothy in a direct way not to give in to that pull, and to pursue what God had for him instead.

The way God worked in and through Timothy is an example to us. It shows us that God will allow us to be in difficult situations. We should never expect that if we were really in God's will, everything would be easy. It is possible to be in great difficulty and under intense pressure and still be entirely in the will of God. Therefore, we must set our minds to meet the challenge, or we will surely give up.

Many years ago, this advertisement appeared in a London newspaper: "Men wanted for hazardous journey, small wages, bitter cold, long months of complete darkness, constant danger, safe return doubtful. Honor and recognition in case of success." A famous Arctic explorer signed the ad, and thousands of men responded to such a big challenge. They were willing to give their lives for a huge, difficult mission if a great leader had called them to do it.

Timothy had a tough job, as do we – but who has called us? Who is our Leader? The Bible tells us: *the people who know their God shall be strong, and carry out great exploits* (Daniel 11:32). Perhaps God has called you to stay faithful through a difficult situation when you would prefer to escape.

Maybe today has been one of "those" days for you.

Today, you can find the strength to remain where God wants you to remain if you look for that strength, not in yourself, but in your God.

October 1

No Guarantee

As Sodom and Gomorrah, and the cities around them in a similar manner to these, having given themselves over to sexual immorality and gone after strange flesh, are set forth as an example, suffering the vengeance of eternal fire. (Jude v. 7)

Jude warned early Christians about the presence of dangerous men among them – men with bad doctrine and compromised lives. These words speak to us about the dangers in our midst. Jude used three bad examples to stress one principle. They are Israel in the Exodus (Jude v. 5), sinning angels (Jude v. 6), and Sodom and Gomorrah (Jude v. 7). The principle is that a good start is no guarantee of a good finish.

The cities of **Sodom and Gomorrah** (and cities around them) stand as examples of God's judgment. Their sexual sin was well known, but their sins included far more than the notorious ones – and these brought forth God's judgment.

Sodom and Gomorrah were blessed, privileged places (Genesis 13:10). Yet as Jude tells us, they gave **themselves over to sexual immorality** and went **after strange flesh**. Jude refers to the account in Genesis 19, where the sexually immoral conduct of the men of Sodom was described. Sodom and Gomorrah were guilty of their well-known sexual sins.

Ezekiel 16:49 reveals some other sins of Sodom: *Look, this was the iniquity of your sister Sodom: She and her daughter had pride, fullness of food, and abundance of idleness; neither did she strengthen the hand of the poor and needy*. Sodom and Gomorrah were indeed prosperous, blessed areas. Despite this, they were judged for their sin.

Jude described the fierce judgment of these ancient cities: **suffering the vengeance of eternal fire**. In Genesis 19, Sodom and Gomorrah were destroyed with fire from heaven. But far worse than what happened in Genesis 19, they suffered **the vengeance of eternal fire**. This example gives two lessons.

First, it assures us that those who cause trouble for the church will be judged, no matter how much they were blessed in the past. Just as Sodom and Gomorrah were once wonderfully blessed, but eventually suffered the vengeance of eternal fire.

Second, it warns us that we also must continue to walk with Jesus. If the blessings of the past did not guarantee their future spiritual state, then neither do our blessings.

As you look at your life you probably see great blessings. We thank God for them, and we gratefully receive them – but we also understand they are no guarantee of our continued faithfulness. Someone can be blessed and still end up in trouble.

Understanding this, make sure to pray about it today – "God, You have blessed me and I thank You for it. But I ask you to work mightily in me and make me faithful to the end."

That is the kind of prayer God loves to answer.

October 2
A Small Thing Guiding a Bigger Thing

Indeed, we put bits in horses' mouths that they may obey us, and we turn their whole body. Look also at ships: although they are so large and are driven by fierce winds, they are turned by a very small rudder wherever the pilot desires. Even so the tongue is a little member and boasts great things. (James 3:3-5a)

In this part of his letter to Christians, James wrote about the power of the words we speak – power to do good, and power to destroy. Before addressing the power of our words, James wrote about the importance of our words, focusing on the little part of our body that shapes our speech: **the tongue**.

The word pictures are simple enough to understand: the horse and the ship. First, the horse: **we put bits in horses' mouths that they may obey us**. A strong horse can be controlled by a small bit in its mouth. Then, the ship: **Look also at ships: although they are so large and are driven by fierce winds, they are turned by a very small rudder wherever the pilot desires**. A small rudder can turn a large ship.

Even as with the examples of the bit for the horse and the rudder for the ship, if we have control over our tongue, it is an indication that we have true self-control. Whoever can control the tongue can bridle the whole body (James 3:2).

The horse's bit and the ship's rudder are small but extremely important. If they are not adequately controlled, then the whole horse is out of control, or the entire ship is out of control. Similarly, it is possible for something as small as the tongue is to have tremendous power for either good or evil.

But you don't solve the problem of a wild horse by keeping it in the barn. You don't fix the problem of a hard-to-steer ship by keeping it tied to the dock. In the same way, even a vow of silence is not the ultimate answer for the misuse of our tongue.

If the tongue is like a bit in the mouth of a horse or the rudder on a ship, it leaves us with the question: who or what holds the reins, or who or what directs the rudder? Some people have *no hand* on the reins or rudder, and therefore say whatever comes into mind. Others run their tongue *from their emotions* and say whatever they feel at the moment. Some let the tongue do *whatever* their base, lower nature wants it to do, and they continuously speak curses and profanity.

James points us towards having the Spirit of God, working through the new man, to set His directing hands on the reins and rudder that is our tongue. With that guidance for the little tongue, it will guide the larger thing – the power and potential of our words – to do good and to bring glory to God in this world.

Choose to yield to the Spirit of God and His guiding hand today.

October 3

Mocked, Yet Comforted

The proud have me in great derision, yet I do not turn aside from Your law. I remembered Your judgments of old, O Lord, and have comforted myself. (Psalm 119:51-52)

Sometimes those who choose to follow God, who love His Word, and who love to Him in His Word, are mocked by this world's high and mighty. The poet of the great Psalm 119 knew this personally. He wrote from his own experience, **the proud have me in great derision**. The idea is that the psalmist was mocked and criticized for his love and trust in God's Word. These proud mockers looked at him and his dedication to God's Word and they held him in great disdain.

Those who love and trust God's Word – especially with the depth and passion reflected by the psalmist – these are mocked by the proud who want nothing to do with God or His Word.

None of this shook the confidence of the psalmist. There's almost a note of defiance when he writes, **Yet I do not turn aside from Your law**. No matter how great the derision that comes from the proud, he would hold faithful to God and His Word.

Great harm has been done to God's cause when believers find themselves unable to endure this **great derision**, and they begin to downgrade their view of God's Word and its inerrant character. Hoping to appease or impress the proud, they lead themselves and others to trust and love God's Word less. Such ones should find their strength and comfort in these very passages and declare, **Yet I do not turn aside from Your law**.

Isn't it enough that God accepts us? Isn't it enough that He has adopted us into His family and sealed us for His kingdom? Must we run after the praise of every proud person who criticizes or mocks the faith? What God gives us in Jesus Christ more than outweighs the sting of the mocking of the proud.

When challenged to lessen his confidence and trust in God's Word by the proud mockers, the psalmist wisely responded by *increasing* his confidence in God's Word. So, he said, **I have remembered Your judgments of old, O Lord, and have comforted myself**. By remembering these things, he comforted himself.

There was comfort in remembering **Your judgments of old, O Lord**. We are comforted and hopeful as we remember how God dealt with men and circumstances in the past. We think of His righteous judgment at the flood, Babel, the Red Sea, and against all His enemies. It reminds us that if we are on His side, we are really on the winning side. That is a great comfort.

The proud who hold the humble believer in **great derision** might enjoy the applause and honor of some in this world, but they can never know the comfort that the psalmist wrote about.

Today, you can know it – hold on to God, His Word, and remember His great faithfulness.

October 4

When It Is Wrong to Pray

And the Lord said to Moses, "Why do you cry to Me? Tell the children of Israel to go forward." (Exodus 14:15)

The situation was desperate, with the Egyptian army charging against the defenseless people of Israel. There was nowhere to go except through the impossible – through the waters of the Red Sea right in front of them. Moses did what a spiritual man would do: he prayed. However, it was the wrong thing to do at the time. It wasn't time to pray; it was time to act.

God asked Moses, **why do you cry to Me?** The answer seemed obvious. "Lord, I cry to You because there is nothing else to do. We are going to be destroyed in a matter of hours unless You do something." But there is a time to pray and a time not to pray. Moses had his times mixed up.

Sometimes it is the wrong time to pray. The Bible does say that we should live in an attitude of constant communication with God, thus fulfilling the command to *pray without ceasing* (1 Thessalonians 5:17). Yet there is also a kind of a separated, "I'm-doing-nothing-else-but-praying-right-now" kind of prayer. For that kind of prayer, sometimes it is the wrong time. It can be against God's will to stop doing and to pray in a particular situation.

It is also wrong to pray out of wrong motives. Sometimes we pray selfishly, not just asking things for ourselves (which isn't necessarily wrong) but asking things to meet our selfish desires and ambitions. That is the wrong kind of prayer.

It is also wrong to pray with others, intending to inform those who listen. Some people who think they never gossip do so in prayer meetings. Instead of talking to God in prayer, they use prayer as a time to tell others gossipy things in a "holy" setting. That is the wrong kind of prayer.

It is wrong to pray to control a situation. With just the right touch of holy tone in their voice, some know how to say, "Let's pray." Then they pray, talking to people more than to God, hoping to influence others instead of crying out to God. That is the wrong kind of prayer.

It is wrong to pray to avoid action. When asked to do something, many say, "Let me pray about it," and they never pray about it at all. They may think about it, or talk to others about it, but they don't pray about it at all. Or, if they do, they don't seek God about it. For them, prayer is more of a delaying tactic than seeking the face of God. That is the wrong kind of prayer.

It's a testimony to our fallen humanity that we can take something as good and holy as prayer and use it in the wrong ways.

May God help you to pray more in the right ways, and less in the wrong ways!

October 5

After God's Own Heart

But now your kingdom shall not continue. The LORD has sought for Himself a man after His own heart, and the LORD has commanded him to be commander over His people, because you have not kept what the LORD commanded you. (1 Samuel 13:13-14)

King Saul foolishly sinned against the LORD. He failed to keep God's commandment, and Saul made excuses instead of getting right with God. It wasn't only that Saul sinned; the sin came from a heart far from God.

Therefore, God promised to take the kingdom away from Saul and his family. Through the prophet Samuel, God told Saul: **But now your kingdom shall not continue**. From these words, we might expect Saul to be removed as king right at that moment, but he would reign another 15 to 20 years. He was still on the throne as king, but the end of his kingdom was inevitable.

The kingdom was taken from Saul because he sinned, but it was more than that. The man who replaced Saul (David) also sinned, yet God never took David and his descendants' kingdom. The issue was more significant than an incident of sin; it was to be a man after God's own heart.

What does it mean to be a man after God's own heart? We can compare a man who was not a man after His own heart (Saul) with the man who was (David).

Saul was more concerned with his will than God's will. David knew God's will was most important. Even when David didn't do God's will, he still knew God's will was more important. All sin is a disregard of God, but David sinned more out of weakness, and Saul sinned more out of a disregard for God.

A man after God's heart enthrones God as king. For Saul, he was king. For David, the Lord God was king. Both David and Saul knew sacrifice before a battle was necessary. Saul thought it was important because it might help him win the battle and believed God would help him achieve his goals. But David thought it was important because it pleased and honored God, and that was the goal.

A man after God's heart has a soft, repentant heart. When Saul was confronted with his sin, he offered excuses. When David was confronted with his sin, he confessed his sin and repented (2 Samuel 12:13).

A man after God's heart loves others. Saul became increasingly bitter against people and lived more and more to himself, but David loved people. When David was down and out, he still loved and served those who were even more down and out (1 Samuel 22:1-2).

The LORD has sought for Himself a man after His own heart. God was looking for this kind of man, and God found this man in an unlikely place. In fact, at this time, he wasn't a man at all – just a boy!

God is still looking for men and women after His own heart.

October 6

Looking Upward

Now to Him who is able to keep you from stumbling, and to present you faultless before the presence of His glory with exceeding joy, to God our Savior, who alone is wise, be glory and majesty, dominion and power, both now and forever. Amen. (Jude v. 24-25)

First, the focus is on God's care for us: **Who is able to keep you from stumbling, and to present faultless.** Perhaps Jude understood that his message of warning and doom might have depressed and discouraged his readers. With so much false teaching and immorality around, how can Christians ever reach heaven? The answer lies only in the power of God. He can keep you, even though you aren't able to keep yourself.

Jude began the letter by addressing those who are preserved in Jesus (Jude 1). Then he exhorted Christians to avoid dangerous men and to keep themselves in the love of God (Jude 21). At the end he concluded with the recognition that it was ultimately God who keeps us from stumbling and falling. Paul wrote the same concept in Philippians 2:12-13: *Work out your own salvation with fear and trembling; for it is God who works in you both to will and to do for His good pleasure.*

It is God's work. But you can always tell the people He is working in because they are working also. God doesn't call us to simply let the Christian life happen to us, and He doesn't command us to save ourselves. He calls us to a partnership with Him, as He works His salvation in us. Therefore, we are confident in our destiny – that one day we will stand **before the presence of His glory with exceeding joy**. As God is faithful, we won't have to come with shame into the presence of God. We come before Him with exceeding joy.

Most of all, we are confident in God Himself. We declare who He is: **Who alone is wise, be glory and majesty, dominion and power, both now and forever**. This reminds us of God's wisdom, glory, and power. When we acknowledge and declare the truth about God, it glorifies Him. We aren't giving God more majesty or power than He had before; we just recognize it and declare it.

Because of who God is and the faithfulness of His promises, Jude knew that this is all **both now and forever**. This could also be translated "unto all the ages." Our victory, our triumph in God, is **forever**.

We recognize that there is serious deception out there. There are enemies of the gospel who infiltrate the church. But despite the greatness of the threat, God is greater still. He wins, and if we stay with Him, we are guaranteed victory also. Jude is a book full of warning, but it closes with supreme confidence in God.

You can trust God, even in dangerous times. He is more than worthy of our trust.

October 7

Lions of Judgment

Then the king of Assyria brought *people* **from Babylon, Cuthah, Ava, Hamath, and from Sepharvaim, and placed** *them* **in the cities of Samaria instead of the children of Israel; and they took possession of Samaria and dwelt in its cities. And it was so, at the beginning of their dwelling there,** *that* **they did not fear the Lord; therefore the Lord sent lions among them, which killed** *some* **of them.** (2 Kings 17:24-25)

The kingdom of Israel, the ten northern tribes, were conquered as a nation. The brutal Assyrians defeated them and then forced the people of Israel to relocate to different areas of the Assyrian empire. After that, **the king of Assyria brought people** into the land. The policy of the Assyrians was to *remove* rebellious, resistant people and to *resettle* their former lands with people from other parts of the empire.

In doing this, the kings of Assyria hoped to re-populate their conquered lands, bringing in people who had no previous attachment to the area. They wanted the people of the empire to be attached to and loyal to the king of Assyria, and no one else.

But our Bible passage tells us something of these new people brought into the land: **they did not fear the Lord; therefore the Lord sent lions among them**. When the Israelites were conquered and could not defend the land, God supernaturally defended it – and **the Lord sent lions among them** to do it!

This shows that there was not only something special about the *kingdom* of Israel, but also something special about the *land* of Israel. God demanded to be feared among the people of the land, even if they came from other nations.

Zechariah 2:12 tells us that the land of Israel is the *Holy Land*. God regards it as something special, and He will hold accountable those who live there and who do not fear Him.

2 Kings 17 goes on to explain that the Assyrians figured out that the lions were sent because they did not honor the God of Israel. It's amazing that the Assyrian officials seemed to know what the people of the recently-conquered kingdom of Israel *did not know* – that they had to honor the God of Israel. They even had a priest from Israel come and teach them to fear the Lord (2 Kings 17:28).

You could say, as Charles Spurgeon did, that they were "converted by lions." But, 2 Kings 17:29-33 explains, it wasn't much of a conversion. They still honored the corrupt, pagan gods along with the Lord God of Israel.

Coming to God only because you are afraid of judgment – afraid of the lions – is never enough. It might be a good start, but it can't stop there. We need to come to God and put our trust in Him based on His love for us in Jesus Christ.

Today, thank God for His kindness and goodness that leads us to true repentance (Romans 2:4).

October 8

The Prophet's Call

Also I heard the voice of the LORD**, saying: "Whom shall I send, and who will go for Us?" Then I said, "Here am I! Send me."** (Isaiah 6:8)

Everyone experiences the call of God in his own way, but Isaiah's experience was both striking and instructive. During his heavenly vision, Isaiah met with God, was convicted of his sin, and was cleansed by a burning work. Isaiah was drawn in by the glory of God's throne, but then he heard words from the throne of God that would change his life forever: **Whom shall I send, and who will go for Us?** God asked for a person because God wants to reach the world and He wants to reach it through willing people.

This God of majesty, sovereignty, and power asked for volunteers. He could easily create robots to do His work, or command angels to carry out His will – but God wants willing, surrendered servants. This means we should never wait for God to *force* us to serve Him. He looks for willing hearts to step forward.

The question **Whom shall I send?** tells us that the missionary, the Christian worker, the witness of Jesus Christ, is *sent*. This is a divine commission. The question **Who will go for Us?** means that the missionary, the Christian worker, the witness of Jesus Christ, has *decided* to go. Here we see a cooperation of the divine "sent" and the human "will go."

We also can't miss the wonderful reply of the prophet: **Here am I! Send me**. Isaiah emphatically answered God's call. He did not hesitate. Isaiah wanted to be the answer to God's question. We can see the things that created this responsive heart in Isaiah.

- He had a heart that had been in the presence of God.
- He had a heart that knew its own sinfulness.
- He had a heart that knew the need among the people, the need for God's Word.
- He had a heart that had been touched by God's cleansing fire.
- He had a heart that heard God's heart to reach the nations.

Send me meant Isaiah was submitted to the LORD in all his service. He didn't say, "Here I am, I will go." Isaiah would not go at all unless he knew the LORD sent him. Many are quick to say, "Here I am, I will go" but never wait for the LORD to send them.

More than anything, remember that Isaiah did not go to heaven looking for a call. Isaiah came to draw near to God. God didn't give a specific call to Isaiah, as if He said, "Isaiah this is what I want you to do." Isaiah spent time with God, heard His heart, and responded accordingly – and that was the prophet's call.

Seek God's call for your life in the same way – draw near to Him and as you learn His heart, you will know what He wants for you.

October 9

Redeemed and Adopted

But when the fullness of the time had come, God sent forth His Son, born of a woman, born under the law, to redeem those who were under the law, that we might receive the adoption as sons. (Galatians 4:4-5)

The idea behind the phrase the **fullness of time** is "when the time was right." Jesus came at just the right time in God's redemptive plan when the world was perfectly prepared for God's work.

At just the right time, **God sent forth His Son, born of a woman**. Jesus came not only as God's Son, but also as one **born of a woman, born under law**. The eternal Son of God in heaven added humanity to His deity and became a man, **born of a woman, born under law**.

God's great purpose in doing this was to **redeem those who were under the law**. Because Jesus is God, He has the power and the resources to **redeem** those who believe. Because Jesus is man, He has the right and the ability to **redeem** His people. He came to purchase believers out of the slave market, from their bondage to sin and death.

The famous hymn *Amazing Grace* was written by John Newton, a man who knew how to remember his redemption. He was an only child whose mother died when he was only seven years old. He became a sailor and went out to sea at eleven years old. As he grew up, he worked on a slave ship and had an active hand in the horrible degradation and inhumanity of the slave trade. But in 1748, when he was twenty-three, and his ship was in immediate danger of sinking off the coast of Newfoundland, John Newton cried to God for mercy, and he found it.

John Newton never forgot how amazing it was that God had received him, as bad as he was. To keep it fresh in his memory, he fastened across the wall over the fireplace mantel of his study the words of Deuteronomy 15:15: *You shall remember that you were a slave in the land of Egypt, and the* L<small>ORD</small> *your God redeemed you.* If we keep fresh in our mind what we once were, and what we are now in Jesus Christ, we will do well.

But God's work for the believer doesn't end with redemption; it goes on to **adoption**. It would be enough that believers are purchased out of the slave market. But God's work for His people doesn't end there; they are then elevated to the place of sons and daughters of God by **adoption**.

Notice we receive the adoption of sons; we do not recover it. In this sense, we gain something in Jesus that is greater than what Adam ever had. Adam was never adopted as believers are. God doesn't merely restore what was lost with Adam. Believers are granted more in Jesus than Adam ever had.

Cherish the glory of the standing God gives to His people: In Jesus Christ, you are redeemed and adopted.

October 10

Prove It to Me, God

And he (Abraham) said, "Lord GOD, how shall I know that I will inherit it?" (Genesis 15:8)

Jesus spoke of a faith that could move mountains (Matthew 21:21), but we're all too familiar with the doubt that creates those mountains. Trusting God and His plan for our lives is a constant challenge and it is faced by everyone who has ever tried to chase away doubt.

Sometimes doubt springs from unbelief – the sort of attitude that doubts if God will or can keep His Word to us. Other times doubt is a by-product of a faith that is growing and maturing – this is the kind of doubt that recognizes that there is no weakness or wavering in God but knows that we are often weak in our ability to trust.

Abraham had waited ten years for the son God promised to him. Abraham couldn't forget the promise and he wondered when God would keep His promise. Abraham was successful in business and every other enterprise, but he must have thought "what good is all this without the fulfillment of God's promise?" This was the ache of Abraham's heart, and it prompted his doubt-filled question to God.

Abraham did what we all should do with our doubts. He brought his doubts to God, and he let God speak to them. We must understand this was not a doubt, which denied God's promise, but a doubt that desired God's promise. God is always willing to help that kind of doubt.

What did God do to help Abraham? God, in effect, said: "Abraham, do you want to know for certain? Then let's make a contract." One way to make a contract in Abraham's day was to have both parties walk together through the carcasses of sacrificed animals, while they repeated the terms of the contract. It seems barbaric to us today, but to them, it represented two things:

First, it showed plainly this was a blood covenant, and therefore it was a serious agreement.

Second, it was a dramatic warning: if one of the parties failed to live up to the contract, he could expect that all his animals, and perhaps even himself, would end up cut in two.

God wants to help our doubts with a contract. But our contract is not Abraham's; it is the contract that Jesus called *the new covenant* (Matthew 26:28). This covenant was also sealed by sacrifice. When we want to believe, but still seem to doubt, we don't have to think God is angry and irritated with us. We can even ask God to prove Himself to us. But when we ask for proof, God will speak to us the same way He did to Abraham. He will point us to a new covenant, made with a sacrifice, that proves God's love and concern for us is real.

Today, ask God to help you with your doubts and to remember He has proven His love for you at Calvary.

October 11

Free Indeed

They answered Him, "We are Abraham's descendants, and have never been in bondage to anyone. How can you say, 'You will be made free'?" Jesus answered them, "Most assuredly, I say to you, whoever commits sin is a slave of sin. And a slave does not abide in the house forever, but a son abides forever. Therefore if the Son makes you free, you shall be free indeed." (John 8:33-36)

Some people are good at lying to others, but often the most damaging lies are the ones we tell ourselves. The ability to lie to ourselves is real – and has a frightening power. Here, Jesus offered real freedom to the Jewish religious leaders, freedom found in Jesus Himself. But the religious leaders answered back to Jesus and insisted that they had **never been in bondage**. They claimed to be free and had always been free but apparently, they forgot about their bondage under the Egyptians, Persians, Syrians, and the Romans. This shows us that people can be in bondage and lie to themselves about it.

But far worse than their slavery to foreign governments in their past was their present slavery to sin. Slavery to sin is the worst kind of bondage, because there is no escape from ourselves. You can't go to a new place and escape slavery to sin, because wherever you go, you take yourself with you! The only escape is to be set free by the Son of God, Jesus Christ.

Here Jesus made a contrast between freedom in name only and the real freedom He offers in Himself. Some people talk about freedom and know something about freedom as an idea, but for them freedom is only a word – not a fact.

An 82-year-old Christian woman from Hong Kong told of her life in mainland China, but still used much of the vocabulary of the Communists. The Communists called their oppressive revolution "the liberation." Once she was asked, "When you lived in China, were you free to gather together with other Christians to worship?" "Oh no," she answered. "Since the liberation no one is permitted to gather together for Christian services." "But surely you were able to get together in small groups and discuss the Christian faith?" "No, we were not," the woman replied. "Since the liberation all such meetings are forbidden." "Were you free to read the Bible?" "Since the liberation, no one is free to read the Bible." Some liberation!

The point is clear: freedom does not consist in the word "freedom," or in words, but a relationship to Jesus Christ, through abiding in His Word. When the Son sets you free, you will be free indeed.

Is freedom from sin real in your life? Or are you in bondage? Today, draw close to Jesus because He is the One who can set you free. You can't set yourself free. A government can't set you free from sin. A program can't set you free.

But Jesus makes His people free indeed.

October 12

God's Way of Escape

No temptation has overtaken you except such as is common to man; but God *is* faithful, who will not allow you to be tempted beyond what you are able, but with the temptation will also make the way of escape, that you may be able to bear *it*. (1 Corinthians 10:13)

I don't know if this saying is used elsewhere, but in the United States people sometimes say, "Nothing in life is certain except for death and taxes." It's supposed to be a slightly humorous observation on the uncertainties of life, but I think at least one more thing could be added to the certain things of life: **temptation**.

We're all tempted, and none of our temptations are truly unique; what we go through is **common to man**. Others before you have found strength in Jesus Christ to overcome the same temptation you experience, or even worse. Therefore, you can be victorious, but in the strength of Jesus, not in your own strength. We fight temptation with Jesus' power, like the girl who explained what she did when Satan came at the door of her heart with temptation: "I send Jesus to answer the door. When Satan sees Jesus, he says, 'Oops, sorry, I must have the wrong house.'"

The truth is **God is faithful** and has promised to supervise all temptation, whether it comes at us through the world, the flesh, or the devil. God promises to limit temptation according to our capability to endure it, or at least according to our capability as we rely on Him, not our capability as we rely only on ourselves.

Satan would destroy us in a moment if God would allow him, even as he wanted to destroy Job (Job 1:6-12) and Peter (Luke 22:31), but God will not let him. God faithfully supervises what comes to His children and though we may face grievous hardship, in Him we have the power to endure.

God has promised to not only *limit* our temptation, but also to provide a **way of escape** in tempting times. He will never force His children to use **the way of escape**, but He will **make the way of escape** available. It's up to us to take God's **way of escape**.

One commentator noted that in the original language, the word for **a way of escape** has the idea of *a mountain pass*, with the idea of an army being surrounded by the enemy, and then suddenly seeing an escape route to safety. Like a mountain pass, the **way of escape** isn't necessarily an easy way—but it is available.

At a market, a little boy stood by a candy display, looking as if he was going to take some without paying. A clerk watched the boy, and finally said, "Looks like you're trying to take some candy." The boy answered, "Mister. I'm trying to *not* take any."

For the time, that boy was **able to bear it**. In Christ, you can also bear temptation.

October 13

Not So Certain

Come now, you who say, "Today or tomorrow we will go to such and such a city, spend a year there, buy and sell, and make a profit"; whereas you do not know what will happen tomorrow. For what is your life? It is even a vapor that appears for a little time and then vanishes away. Instead you ought to say, "If the Lord wills, we shall live and do this or that." But now you boast in your arrogance. All such boasting is evil. (James 4:13-16)

As a child grows, it becomes more and more independent of the parent. A baby in the womb is entirely dependent on the mother, and a newborn, virtually so. Yet as time goes on, so does the progress to independence. Our Christian life is not like this at all; as we progress in the Christian life, we become more dependent on God, not less.

That is what James had in mind when he wrote of those who say, **Today or tomorrow we will go to such and such a city, spend a year there, buy and sell, and make a profit**. James rebuked the kind of heart that lives and makes its plans apart from a constant awareness of God's hand, and with an underestimation of our limitations (**you do not know what will happen tomorrow**).

James counsels us to take a humbler attitude: **For what is your life? It is even a vapor that appears for a little time and then vanishes away.** James asked us to consider the fragility of human life and the fact that we live and move only at God's permission. James does not discourage us from planning and doing, only from planning and doing apart from a reliance on God.

In our easy-going pride, many think their life is secure. Yet people pass from this life to eternity because of all sorts of small things. They slip on a grape; they choke on a bone; a microbe brings a fatal disease. This should not make us paranoid, marking every step with fear; but it should make us humbler, always relying on God and His goodness.

Living in the humility God commands will lead us to put our trust in Him, not in our plans. The humble believer says, **If the Lord wills, we shall live and do this or that**. It is nothing but sheer arrogance that makes us think that we can live and move and have our being independent of God. Paul knew and lived out this principle: *I will return again to you, God willing* (Acts 18:21); *But I will come to you shortly, if the Lord wills* (1 Corinthians 4:19); *I hope to stay a while with you, if the Lord permits* (1 Corinthians 16:7).

We know two things for sure about the future: that God knows it, and that we do not. The key to all this isn't fear or worry; it is a humble dependence on God.

Live this way today and make every day of this life count – and you will also prepare for eternity.

October 14

Keys to Prayer from the Heart

Now, O LORD God, the word which You have spoken concerning Your servant and concerning his house, establish it forever and do as You have said. So let Your name be magnified forever, saying, "The LORD of hosts is the God over Israel." And let the house of Your servant David be established before You. For You, O LORD of hosts, God of Israel, have revealed this to Your servant, saying, "I will build you a house." Therefore Your servant has found it in his heart to pray this prayer to You. (2 Samuel 7:25-27)

Was it selfish for David to ask God to establish his dynasty, his house? This started when David wanted to build God a temple. God was honored, but He had a different plan – He would build a house for David and through him establish a ruling dynasty over Israel that would never end. David simply brought God's promise back to Him. David said, "Lord, You promised this – now do all that You promised."

This wasn't *passive* prayer saying, "Well God, do whatever You want to do – I just don't care one way or another." This wasn't *arrogant* prayer saying, "Well God, let me tell You what to do." This was *bold* prayer saying, "God, here is Your promise – now I trust You to fulfill it and to be faithful to Your word."

The phrase **therefore Your servant has found it in his heart to pray this prayer to You** emphasizes this idea. This kind of prayer *appropriates* God's promises. If we don't appropriate in faith, many of God's promises are left unclaimed.

We may claim His promises:

- For forgiveness: *If we confess our sins, He is faithful and just to forgive us our sins and to cleanse us from all unrighteousness* (1 John 1:9).
- For peace: *Peace I leave with you, My peace I give to you: not as the world gives do I give to you. Let not your heart be troubled, neither let it be afraid* (John 14:27)
- For guidance: *I will instruct you and teach you in the way you should go: I will guide you with My eye* (Psalm 32:8).
- For growth: *He who has begun a good work in you will complete it until the day of Jesus Christ* (Philippians 1:6).
- For help: *Let us therefore come boldly to the throne of grace, that we may obtain mercy and find grace to help in time of need* (Hebrews 4:16).

David's prayer was powerful and glorious because it depended on God's own promise – yet there is another element to this great prayer. Notice that David said, **Your servant has found it in his heart to pray this prayer to You**. This means that David prayed from the heart. Some people pray from a book; others pray from their heads. The right place to pray from is the heart.

Today, pray from the heart and plead God's own promises to you – and enjoy great power in prayer.

October 15

God and His Word

Righteous are You, O Lord, and upright are Your judgments. Your testimonies, which You have commanded, are righteous and very faithful. (Psalm 119:137-138)

Sometimes people say, "God is greater than His Word." In one sense, that is a true statement, but it is also commonly misunderstood. The way some people mean this is to say that there is some *difference* between God and His Word, and if you must choose between God and His Word, you should always choose God. One problem with this is that it is a false choice.

The great penman of Psalm 119 gives us some insight on this idea when he wrote, **righteous are You, O Lord, and upright are Your judgments**. The psalmist understood that the righteous character of God was displayed in His Word (**Your judgments**). In this, the Word of God is an accurate revelation of God, not only of His thoughts but also of His very character.

We might say that God's written word is an incomplete display of His character and nature; that is, there is more to God than what we can receive from His Word. But what we do have in His Word is accurate, and properly displays who He is.

We might say that the God who actually exists is not any different than how His written revelation presents Him. He is greater than what can be comprehended through His written word, but He is not different than what is revealed to us through that word.

Continuing the thought, he wrote: **Your testimonies, which You commanded, are righteous and very faithful**. For emphasis, the psalmist repeated the idea from the previous verse. The written Word of God reflects both His righteous character and the fact that He is very faithful.

According to some (such as John Stephen, cited in Spurgeon's *Treasury of David*), **Your testimonies, which You commanded, are righteous and very faithful** is a relatively tame translation of a rather strong phrase in the original Hebrew. Stephen wrote that the idea is more like, "You have commanded righteousness, your testimonies" – the idea that God's Word is one with His righteousness.

God's words are especially helpful for knowing He is **very faithful**. We often judge a person's faithfulness by looking at what they say and do and seeing if their words and actions match. Along with countless other believers through the centuries, the author of Psalm 119 could say that the words of God and the actions of God were completely consistent, and that consistency shows that God is **very faithful**.

We can say it like this: the Bible displays the character of God. If you want to know what is righteous and if you are going to act righteously, you should study the Bible. The greatness and glory of God are on display in His Word given to us.

Today, follow the God whose actions match His words, and then you will become more like Him.

October 16

Great Joy from Seeds Already Sown

Then Philip went down to the city of Samaria and preached Christ to them. And the multitudes with one accord heeded the things spoken by Philip, hearing and seeing the miracles which he did.... And there was great joy in that city. (Acts 8:5-8)

At the very end of Jesus' earthly ministry, He had commanded the disciples to preach the gospel to all the earth – first in Jerusalem, then in Judea, then to the uttermost parts of the earth. But before you got far out of Judea, you were in Samaria. And most Jews – or most Christians from a Jewish background – were not interested in bringing the good news of Jesus Christ to the Samaritans.

Curiously, none of the apostles spearheaded this mission. It was up to one of the deacons of the early church – a man named Philip. When the Christians were scattered because of the persecution following Stephen's death, Philip went to Samaria. So, who were the Samaritans?

Six hundred years before this, the Assyrians conquered this area of northern Israel, and they deported all the wealthy and middle-class Jews. They then moved in a pagan population from afar. These pagans intermarried with the lowest classes of the remaining Jews in northern Israel, and from these people came the Samaritans. One commentator says, "There was deep-seated prejudice, amounting almost to hatred, standing between the Jews and the Samaritans."

James and John (and other disciples with them) once thought that the Samaritans were only good for being burned up by God's judgment (Luke 9:51-56).

Most Jews considered Samaritans compromisers, half-breeds, and idolators, and they didn't want to have anything to do with them. But Jesus didn't feel that way about the Samaritans. He was never prejudiced against people just because of their nationality or ethnic background. Because Jesus had touched Philip's heart, there was no room for this kind of prejudice in him. He wasn't a racist towards the Samaritans.

Philip came to the Samaritans presenting the gospel, with signs and wonders following as an impressive confirmation. And when the people found Jesus, **there was great joy in that city**! There were spectacular results from Philip's ministry. But undoubtedly, one reason there was such fruit was that Jesus had sown the seed in Samaria during His ministry and *both he who sows and he who reaps may rejoice together* (John 4:1-36).

Maybe you don't see as much success as you would like in the things you do to honor God. Perhaps you are sowing seed for a later harvest. Maybe someone else will reap that harvest. Is that all right with your heart before the Lord? Can you serve Him, in whatever way He has led you to, knowing that you might plant the seeds but someone else will reap the fruit? Jesus served His Father and we should ask God for the same heart.

By the way – is there **great joy in that city** for you?

October 17
The Story of the Vineyard

And now, O inhabitants of Jerusalem and men of Judah, judge, please, between Me and My vineyard. What more could have been done to My vineyard that I have not done in it? Why then, when I expected it to bring forth good grapes, did it bring forth wild grapes? (Isaiah 5:3-4)

Isaiah 5 begins with a story about a vineyard that had many advantages. It belonged to a loving person. It was planted on a fruitful hill. The ground was carefully prepared. It was planted with good stock. It was protected. Provision was made for the fruit to be processed.

With all these advantages, it's not surprising that God – who is represented in the story as the owner of the vineyard – expected it to bring forth good grapes. Instead, it brought forth **wild grapes**. Isaiah didn't mean "bad grapes," he meant "wild grapes." This plant is known as the wolfsbane or the wild vine and is said to bear beautiful berries, but they are bitter, bad-smelling, and poisonous.

One could never "blame" a vineyard for its lack of production. But in the LORD's vineyard, the will of man is a factor. In response God, through His prophet, asked: **What more could have been done to My vineyard?** There was nothing left undone by the owner of the vineyard. He did all he could do. In the same way, God could not be blamed at all for the bitter, bad-smelling, and poisonous wild grapes that Israel brought forth.

Therefore, the fault lays with man, not God. God can do a work in His people, yet His people receive that work in vain. The apostle Paul warned, *we then, as workers together with Him also plead with you not to receive the grace of God in vain.* (2 Corinthians 6:1)

As God's vineyard, we are called to work with the grace of God so that grace is not received in vain. Grace is not given because of any works, past, present, or promised; yet it is given to encourage our work. God does not want us to receive His grace and become passive.

Why then, when I expected it to bring forth good grapes, did it bring forth wild grapes? God's question through the prophet Isaiah comes to us again today. Does this reflect our current condition? Has it been this way with us? Have we rewarded God ungratefully for all He has done for us? Have we given him hardness of heart, instead of repentance? Have we given Him unbelief, instead of faith? Have we returned indifference, instead of love; idleness, instead of holy effort; impurity, instead of righteousness?

Isaiah speaks to us across the centuries in the story of the vineyard and tells us to return good to God for all the good He has done for us.

We do not do it to earn or deserve the good He does for us, but in gratitude for the good we receive from Him.

October 18

Examples of Patient Endurance

Do not grumble against one another, brethren, lest you be condemned. Behold, the Judge is standing at the door! My brethren, take the prophets, who spoke in the name of the Lord, as an example of suffering and patience. Indeed we count them blessed who endure. You have heard of the perseverance of Job and seen the end intended by the Lord; that the Lord is very compassionate and merciful. (James 5:9-11)

James wrote to Christians living through hard times, warning them to **not grumble against one another**. Times of hardship can cause us to be less than loving with our Christian brothers and sisters. James reminds us that we cannot become grumblers and complainers in our hardship – lest we are condemned.

James reminds us that the prophets of the Old Testament endured hardship yet practiced patient endurance. They are an **example of suffering and patience**. Among these prophets, Jeremiah is an example of someone who endured mistreatment with patience. He was put in the stocks (Jeremiah 20:2), thrown into prison (Jeremiah 32:2), and lowered into a miry dungeon (Jeremiah 28:6), yet he faithfully persisted in his ministry.

James also told us three things about **Job** and why he is a significant example to the suffering Christian. First, we see the **perseverance** of Job. Passages such as Job 1:20-22 show us the tremendous perseverance of this afflicted man, who refused to curse God despite his severe and mysterious suffering.

We also see the ultimate goal and purpose of God in allowing Job's suffering. Perhaps the most significant end intended by the Lord was to use Job as a lesson to angelic beings, even as God promises to use the church (Ephesians 3:10-11).

We see further through Job that the **Lord is very compassionate and merciful**. This is not immediately apparent in the story of Job; we can quickly think that God was cruel to Job.

We can see that God was indeed **very compassionate and merciful** to Job:

- Because He only allowed Job's suffering for a very good reason.
- Because He restricted what Satan could do against Job.
- Because He sustained Job with His unseen hand through all his suffering.

At the end of it all, God had accomplished something wonderful: To make Job a better and more blessed man than ever. Remember that as good as Job was at the beginning of the book, he was a better man at the end. He was better in character, humbler, and more blessed than before.

In all this, we see an excellent example of the kind of patient endurance that God works in His people.

Today, invite Him to work that in you and through you.

October 19

Running the Red Lights

So David sent and inquired about the woman. And someone said, "Is this not Bathsheba, the daughter of Eliam, the wife of Uriah the Hittite?" (2 Samuel 11:3)

King David was the greatest monarch ancient Israel had. David backslid more than once in his life, but 2 Samuel 11 describes what most believe to be his worst season of shame. One day David was on his rooftop balcony when he saw the alluring image of a beautiful woman bathing.

It should have stopped right there. It might have been that David's worst sin was entertaining a lustful image and impure thoughts. Yet David went further and in 2 Samuel 11:3 we see him take deliberate steps in the wrong direction.

King David could have ended the temptation on his balcony. Instead, David put himself into a more tempting situation by following up on this attractive woman – he **sent and inquired** about her. Many an adulterer has looked with regret on the moment they decided to pursue temptation instead of denying it.

Nevertheless, God did not give up on David. Amid this downward spiral, He gave David a red light – a warning to "stop" immediately. The warning came in the form of the response to David's inquiry. Someone told him, **Is this not Bathsheba, the daughter of Eliam?** David learned her father was Eliam, one of David's Mighty Men (2 Samuel 23:34). Her grandfather was Ahithophel – one of David's chief counselors (2 Samuel 23:34, 2 Samuel 15:12).

Then God gave David another red light, and this one was brighter. David was told that she was **the wife of Uriah the Hittite**. David learned that the woman was married, the wife of another of his Mighty Men (2 Samuel 23:8, 23:39). David should have received this news as a warning. In taking Bathsheba David sinned against Uriah, Eliam, Ahithophel – and of course, against Bathsheba.

Tragically, David ignored God's warning signs. He didn't "stop" when God gave him a way of escape. But even worse, David used God's warnings as an occasion to sin. He pressed the gas pedal and sped through the red lights. When David heard the beautiful woman's husband, Uriah, was away in battle it made the situation far more tempting.

David committed adultery in his heart up on the roof. Now he knew that he had an opportunity to commit adultery in practice. Adultery in the heart and mind is bad; adultery in practice is far worse.

In His great love and mercy, God gave King David many warning signs and opportunities to stop his sinful course. That same love would sustain David after the sin, restoring him after confession and repentance. We can be sure that David wished he listened to God's loving warnings before the sin.

God's great love warns us and provides a way of escape in temptation. Are you running red lights?

October 20

Training to Trust

So Moses returned to the Lord and said, "Lord, why have You brought trouble on this people? Why is it You have sent me? For since I came to Pharaoh to speak in Your name, he has done evil to this people; neither have You delivered Your people at all." (Exodus 5:22-23)

Things weren't going well for Moses. After God dramatically called him to deliver the people of Israel. Moses confronted Pharaoh and hoped God would open the doors. But Pharaoh slammed the door shut. When Moses said, "Let my people go," Pharaoh said, "I will make them even more miserable." All this made the people of Israel angry, and it confused and discouraged Moses. So, Moses poured out His heart to God, blaming the Lord who **brought trouble** to Israel, and who **sent** Moses to stir up the trouble. For Moses, God didn't make sense, and nothing was going according to plan.

When you are confused and discouraged, it is good to pour out your feelings to God, but it is terrible to forget God's promise. Back at the burning bush, God said: *But I am sure that the king of Egypt will not let you go, no, not even by a mighty hand. So I will stretch out My hand and strike Egypt with all My wonders which I will do in its midst; and after that he will let you go* (Exodus 3:19-20). As far as God was concerned, everything was working according to plan.

Even though God warned Moses, it seems that Moses hoped it would all happen quickly. He hoped that he would ask, then Pharaoh would say, "Yes," and God would be glorified. But it didn't work the way Moses thought it might work. In this challenging time, the same old fears came back to Moses: "I'm not the man God should send." "God won't come through." "Pharaoh and the Egyptians are too strong." Moses still had unbelief and a lack of focus on God, which had to change or improve.

F.B. Meyer wrote of this time in Moses' life: "The agony of soul through which Moses passed must have been as death to him. He died to his self-esteem, to his castle building, to pride in his miracles, to the enthusiasm of his people, to everything that a popular leader loves. As he lay there on the ground alone before God, wishing himself back in Midian, and thinking himself hardly used, he was falling as a grain of wheat into the ground to die, no longer to abide alone, but to bear much fruit."

Perhaps Moses thought that all the dying to himself was finished after forty years of watching his father-in-law's flocks in Midian. But for Moses, the process of dying to self wasn't finished. It never is. God will still use adversity to train us to trust Him until the day we go to be with Him in heaven.

If that's discouraging to you, come back to a trust in a loving God who knows you better than you know yourself.

October 21

Having, Taking

Above all, taking the shield of faith with which you will be able to quench all the fiery darts of the wicked one. And take the helmet of salvation, and the sword of the Spirit, which is the word of God. (Ephesians 6:16-18)

Paul introduced the idea of "the whole armor of God" back in Ephesians 6:11. In the verses following, he detailed the specific items related to the armor of God. In verses 14 and 15, Paul described three aspects of this armor to have: truth represented by a belt, righteousness represented by a breastplate, and the gospel represented by sandals or boots. He wrote using spiritual analogies, relating these parts of the Roman soldier's equipment to these spiritual truths and principles.

At this point, after putting forth the idea of armor to have, Paul now wrote, **above all**, as he introduced three additional parts of God's armor for the believer in Jesus Christ. In this sense, **above all** has the idea of "in addition to the previous," and it applies to each of the three pieces of armor that follow. In this context, **above all**, doesn't have the idea, "these parts of armor are more important than any of the other." They are all important.

Yet notice the phrasing Paul used with these following aspects: **taking the shield of faith…. And take the helmet of salvation**. Ephesians 6:14-15 tells of armor to *have*, armor we must wear all the time, and that we possess as a standing foundation. If you want to put an order to it, *having* comes before *taking*. In the spiritual battles that we face, we begin with being rooted in the belt of truth, the breastplate of righteousness, and the "combat boots" of the gospel.

After that, we come to the armor that we must *take* when the battle is being fought. These aspects of the armor we take up from situation to situation, as the moment demands. We can consider these kinds of "demanding moments" in spiritual warfare.

- A flood of depression or discouragement comes over us, feeling like a black cloud.
- A relatively insignificant thing becomes exaggerated far out of proportion.
- We have an opportunity to speak with someone about what Jesus did for us.
- We face opposition against the sense that God wants us to do something or follow through on something.
- We have a strong sense of panic and helplessness.

It is in just those critical moments that it is so important to take the shield of faith, to take the helmet of salvation, and to take the sword of God's word. Exactly how we are to do that is something to learn. But before we understand this, we must first recognize this important distinction between the armor to have and the armor to take – and be ready to take up what is needed at the moment.

God knows how to supply what we need at the critical moment; we need to take it.

October 22

Hunger and Thirst Satisfied, But Still There

Blessed are those who hunger and thirst for righteousness, for they shall be filled. (Matthew 5:6)

The Sermon on the Mount was not primarily evangelistic; more so it confronted people with the true character of the kingdom of God and what it meant to live as a citizen of that Kingdom. We can imagine Jesus preaching these themes not only once, but many times in His preaching ministry, proclaiming to disciples and potential disciples what it truly means to follow Him.

Jesus opened this greatest of sermons by pronouncing blessing on some unexpected people. First, He described how the poor in spirit are blessed, those who mourn are blessed, and how the meek are blessed. Now in its progression of thought, Jesus marked out **those who hunger and thirst for righteousness** for special blessing. He told us that those who have poverty of spirit, who mourn for sin, and who are meek desire righteousness like a hungry man desires food and a thirsty man desires water.

It is good to remember that Jesus said this in a day and to a culture that actually knew what it was to be hungry and thirsty. Modern man – at least in the western world – is often so distant from the basic needs of hunger and thirst that they find it difficult to relate to the ideas of hungering and thirsting after righteousness.

When Jesus said, **blessed are those who hunger**, He described a profound hunger that cannot be satisfied by a snack. This is a longing that endures and is never completely satisfied on this side of eternity. This is a passion for God's order, for God's way.

This is a person transformed for the kingdom of God and transformed by the King. They started out aware of sin, both in their poverty of spirit and mourning over sin and its effects. Then they meekly approach both God and man. Now things get expressed in a positive desire; a transformed nature that makes someone really want what God wants and wants it so deeply that it could only be described as **hunger** and **thirst**.

This isn't a desire for partisan power or promotion, but a longing for God's agenda. This person isn't thirsty for the advancement of their own opinions but for God's truth. They are hungrier for the expansion of God's Kingdom than for their own personal success.

Notice the promise: **For they shall be filled**. Jesus promised to fill these hungry ones; to fill them with as much as they could eat. This is a strange filling that both satisfies us and keeps us longing for more.

Today we see Christians hungering for many things: power, authority, success, comfort, happiness – but how many **hunger and thirst for righteousness**?

Today, be among those who do and find the blessing that Jesus promised.

October 23

What No Man Can Do

For every kind of beast and bird, of reptile and creature of the sea, is tamed and has been tamed by mankind. But no man can tame the tongue. It is an unruly evil, full of deadly poison. (James 3:7-8)

In this section, where James warns us about the destructive power of the words we speak, we repeatedly see the power of the tongue. James makes the point that the tongue can't be tamed. No one, it seems, has perfect control over the words that they say.

James makes his point using the idea of the animal kingdom: **For every kind of beast and bird, of reptile and creature of the sea, is tamed and has been tamed by mankind**. A wild animal can be more easily tamed than the tongue. In fact, James tells us, **no man can tame the tongue**.

The human spirit has an amazing capacity for sacrifice and self-control. Sometimes we hear a desperate survival story of someone who cuts off their own arm or leg to get free from a tree or a rock that has fallen on them and pinned their limb. With incredible courage and will, they will self-amputate and drag themselves to help and medical treatment. Yet that same person who showed such amazing courage can't tame the tongue perfectly.

Yet notice what James wrote: **No man can tame the tongue**. Man can't tame the tongue, but God working in a man, or a woman can. The tongue can indeed be brought under the power and the control of the Holy Spirit. We might say that only God Himself is mightier than the human tongue!

Then James reminded us of the importance of taming the tongue. He tells us again of the damage that uncontrolled words can do: **It is an unruly evil, full of deadly poison**. The untamable tongue is even more dangerous when we consider the deadly poison it can deliver.

These brief sentences from James suggest at least a few points of application.

First, knowing how hard it is to tame my own tongue, I must then be gracious and merciful towards others who say mean or hurtful things to me or against me. I remember that many times I have said words I did not really mean and that I wish others would forget. May I not choose to forget an unwise thing someone has said to me simply? Of course, I may, and often this is an essential and beautiful display of Christian love.

Second, if no man can tame the tongue, it reminds me of my great need to be ruled by the Spirit of God. Have I consciously yielded to His presence and work in my life today? Have I invited Him to be the Lord over my words? This is my only hope in taming the tongue.

You can't do it on your own, but the Spirit of God may do it in and through you.

October 24

The Meekness of Wisdom

Who is wise and understanding among you? Let him show by good conduct that his works are done in the meekness of wisdom. (James 3:13)

At the beginning of James 3, he reminded teachers that they would be judged on a stricter standard, and then told such teachers how they should talk. What James wrote about the importance of the spoken word, he didn't write *only* to teachers, but *especially* to teachers.

Starting at James 3:13, now God begins to speak about how we should all live – we should live a life full of wisdom.

He begins by speaking to the one, **who is wise and understanding among you**. According to some commentators, the word translated **wise** (*sophos*) was a Jewish way of referring to a rabbi, a scribe, or a teacher. Here and in the following verses, James especially had in mind teachers and leaders, yet again – not *only* them.

James explains that the **wise** believer will be revealed **by good conduct**. Your wisdom (or lack of it) will show in your life. Wisdom is not merely head knowledge. Real wisdom and understanding will show in our lives, by our **good conduct**.

In this sense, wisdom and understanding are like faith; they are invisible, inner qualities. If a person considers himself or herself to be wise or understanding, it is fair to expect that this invisible internal quality would show itself in regular life. Here James told us how to judge if a person is truly **wise and understanding**.

One way to see it is that in a life of wisdom, **his works are done in the meekness of wisdom**. True wisdom will be known for its meek manner.

What is **meekness**, in the sense James meant it here? In part, **meekness** is gentleness and the willingness not to push oneself forward. Meekness is willing to hold back from honors and privileges that might be aggressively taken. At the same time, it is essential to note that biblical meekness does not come from *weakness* or from just being *passive*. Biblical meekness is an active attitude that chooses to accept its place deliberately instead of forcefully demanding its way.

The **meekness of wisdom** trusts in God. To be meek means to show a willingness to submit and work under proper authority. It also shows a willingness to disregard one's rights and privileges. For this reason, the ancient understanding of meekness was connected to strength, not weakness. The idea behind the concept of meekness was strength under control, like a strong horse that was trained to do the job instead of running wild.

When the world thinks of wisdom, it often thinks of the man or woman who is so clever they can control others through their great insight and knowledge. Biblical wisdom, God's wisdom, isn't like that at all.

Whether you are a teacher among God's people or not, you need the **meekness of wisdom**. Ask God for it today.

October 25
A Better Way to Pray

And when you pray, you shall not be like the hypocrites. For they love to pray standing in the synagogues and on the corners of the streets, that they may be seen by men. Assuredly, I say to you, they have their reward. But you, when you pray, go into your room, and when you have shut your door, pray to your Father who is in the secret place; and your Father who sees in secret will reward you openly. (Matthew 6:5-6)

Jesus assumed that His disciples would give, so He told them the right way to give (Matthew 6:1-4). He also assumed that His disciples would pray, and it was important that they not pray in the same manner as the **hypocrites**.

Jesus did not say, "If you decide to pray." Jesus knew that the people of God would talk to their God. In this section of the Sermon on the Mount, Jesus will tell us how to pray – and to avoid praying like hypocrites.

There were two main places where a Jew in Jesus' day might pray in a hypocritical manner. They might pray in the **synagogues** at the time of public prayer, or **on the corners of the streets** at the appointed times of prayer.

In the synagogue, often someone from the congregation was asked to offer a public prayer. They would stand in front of the others and pray on their behalf. The hypocrites loved to pray with this kind of audience.

These hypocrites prayed not to be heard by God, but to **be seen by men**. This is a common fault in public prayer today when people pray to impress or teach others instead of genuinely pouring out their hearts before God.

This kind of prayer is an insult to God. When we mouth words towards God, while really trying to impress others, we then use God merely as our tool to impress others.

Those praying to be seen of men have their reward, and they should enjoy it in full – because that is all they will receive. **They have their reward**. There is no reward in heaven for such prayers.

Instead of praying to be seen by men, we should meet with God in our **room**. The idea is of a private place where we can impress no one except God. The ancient Greek word translated **room** was used for a storeroom where treasures were kept. This reminds us that there are treasures waiting for us in our private place of prayer.

Jesus certainly did not prohibit public prayer, but our prayers should always be directed to God and not towards man.

Today, seek the treasure of prayer – it is found with sincerity before God and not performance before people.

October 26

Haven't You Heard?

Why do you say, O Jacob, and speak, O Israel: "My way is hidden from the LORD, and my just claim is passed over by my God"? Have you not known? Have you not heard? The everlasting God, the LORD, the Creator of the ends of the earth, neither faints nor is weary. His understanding is unsearchable. (Isaiah 40:27-28)

Looking at the glory of God's creation, Isaiah asked: **Have you not known? Have you not heard?** The prophet couldn't believe that anyone would doubt the greatness of God when they saw the majesty of the universe He made. Isaiah's amazement was well placed. How can anyone look at the glory and design evident in creation, and fail to understand that there must be a glorious Designer behind such a glorious design?

God's power and glory are not only exalted above His creation, but also over men of power on the earth. Isaiah 40:23 says, *He brings the princes to nothing; He makes the judges of the earth useless.* When people have political power or legal power it is easy for them to think of themselves as gods! Yet there is a God in heaven who reigns over the universe, over the stars, and over the great men of this earth.

Isaiah shows us how understanding this makes a difference in our life – beyond our obvious need to honor and worship this great God.

Isaiah asked: **Why do you say, O Jacob... "My way is hidden from the LORD, and my just claim is passed over by my God?"** Understanding the greatness and glory of God persuades us that there is nothing in our life hidden from God, and there is nothing neglected by God. He is there, He is real, and He is not silent.

Isaiah asked, **have you not known? Have you not heard?** This question was addressed to both real atheists who doubt the existence of God, and to practical atheists, who may believe in God; yet they don't seem to understand that the fact there is a God of all creation Who makes a difference in everyday life.

It's easy to believe that God exists, but then to doubt His care or concern over our life. We can intellectually understand that there is a great God who created the heavens and the earth, but we forget – or doubt – that He is able or willing to meet our personal needs.

We can ask the same question Isaiah asked: **Have you not heard?** These practical atheists need to hear what they already know: that the LORD God is **the Creator of the ends of the earth**. Then they need to hear about the Creator: that He **neither faints nor is weary. His understanding is unsearchable**. Those who really believe these truths about God should live as if God is really there. He is there; and He really cares.

The God that is big enough to create the universe is personal enough to care about you.

October 27

The Throne in Heaven

In the year that King Uzziah died, I saw the LORD sitting on a throne, high and lifted up, and the train of His robe filled the temple. (Isaiah 6:1)

King Uzziah of Judah had a long and distinguished reign, described in 2 Chronicles 26 and 2 Kings 15:1-7 (Uzziah is called Azariah in 2 Kings 15). Uzziah reigned 52 years. Overall, he was a good king, and 2 Kings 15:3 says, *he did what was right in the sight of the LORD, according to all that his father Amaziah had done.* 2 Chronicles 28:5 says, *He sought God in the days of Zechariah, who had understanding in the visions of God; and as long as he sought the LORD, God made him prosper.*

Uzziah also led Israel in military victories over the Philistines and other neighboring nations, and he was a strong king. Uzziah was an energetic builder, planner, and general. 2 Chronicles 26:8 says, *His fame spread as far as the entrance of Egypt, for he strengthened himself exceedingly.*

Yet, Uzziah's life ended tragically. 2 Chronicles 26:16 says, *But when he was strong his heart was lifted up, to his destruction, for he transgressed against the LORD his God by entering the temple of the LORD to burn incense on the altar of incense.* In response, God struck Uzziah with leprosy, and he was an isolated leper until his death.

Isaiah had great reason to be discouraged and disillusioned at the death of King Uzziah, because a great king had passed away, and because his life ended tragically. Where was the LORD in all of this?

Isaiah answered powerfully: **I saw the LORD sitting on a throne**. God was still enthroned in heaven, and He was in charge of all creation as the sovereign ruler of the universe. This is a central fact of heaven; that there is an occupied throne in heaven.

Almost everyone in the Bible who had a vision of heaven, was taken to heaven, or wrote about heaven spoke of God's throne. This was true of the prophet Michaiah (1 Kings 22:19), of Job (Job 26:9), and of David (Psalm 9:4 and 9:7, 11:4). The Sons of Korah mentioned God's throne (Psalm 45:6, 47:8), as did Ethan the Ezrahite (Psalm 89:14), and Jeremiah (Lamentations 5:19), Ezekiel had a great vision of the throne (Ezekiel 1:26, 10:1), so did Daniel (Daniel 7:9). Especially, the apostle John saw God's throne (Revelation 4:1-11). The book of Revelation may as well be called "the book of God's throne," because God's throne is specifically mentioned more than 35 times.

The main idea of atheism or materialism is that they believe there is no throne; there is no seat of authority or power that all the universes must answer to. The main idea of humanism is that there is a throne – but man himself sits on it.

But the Bible makes it clear that there is a throne in heaven, and no fallen man sits on the throne, but the LORD God is enthroned in heaven.

Take comfort today – God is still on His throne!

October 28

The Greatest of These Is Love

And now abide faith, hope, love, these three; but the greatest of these *is* love. (1 Corinthians 13:13)

For many people, 1 Corinthians 13 is their favorite chapter in the Bible. Because it describes the character and nature of love so well, it is sometimes called "The Love Chapter." These words conclude the chapter and tell of the never-ending nature of love.

The three great pursuits of the Christian life are not miracles, power, and gifts; they are **faith**, **hope**, and **love**. Though the gifts are precious, and given by the Holy Spirit today, they were never meant to be the focus or goal of the Christian life. Instead, the believer's main pursuit is **faith**, **hope**, and **love**.

What is your Christian life focused on? What do you really want more of? It should all come back to **faith**, **hope**, and **love**. If it doesn't, we need to receive God's sense of priorities, and put our focus where it belongs.

Because **faith**, **hope**, and **love** are so important, we should expect to see them emphasized throughout the New Testament. Think of these passages:

*Remembering without ceasing your work of **faith**, labor of **love**, and patience of **hope** in our Lord Jesus Christ in the sight of our God and Father.* (1 Thessalonians 1:3)

*But let us who are of the day be sober, putting on the breastplate of **faith** and **love**, and as a helmet the **hope** of salvation.* (1 Thessalonians 5:8)

*For we through the Spirit eagerly wait for the **hope** of righteousness by **faith**. For in Christ Jesus neither circumcision nor uncircumcision avails anything, but **faith** working through **love**.* (Galatians 5:5-6)

You could add to these 1 Peter 1:21-22, Colossians 1:4-5, and 2 Timothy 1:12-13.

Faith, hope, and love are all important, **but the greatest of these is love**. Love is greatest because it will continue and even grow in the eternal state. When we are in heaven, **faith** and **hope** will have fulfilled their purpose. We won't need faith when we see God face to face. We won't need to hope in the coming of Jesus once He returns. But we will always love the Lord and each other and grow in that love through eternity.

Love is also the greatest because it is an attribute of God (1 John 4:8), and faith and hope are not part of God's character and personality. God does not have faith in the way we have faith, because He never has to "trust" outside of Himself. God does not have hope the way we have hope, because He knows all things and is in complete control. But God is love and will always be love.

The point isn't to get us to choose between **faith**, **hope**, and **love**. The point is that without **love** as the motive and goal, the gifts of the Holy Spirit are meaningless distractions. If you lose love, everything is lost.

Let the greatness of God's love fill your life today.

October 29

You Have an Anointing

But you have an anointing from the Holy One, and you know all things. (1 John 2:20)

All too often, when Christians hear the word **anointing**, they hear it said in an unusual, overly spiritual, strange tone of voice that lets everyone know something really "holy" is being spoken of. Sometimes as the word anointing is spoken, the word is dramatically drawn out and said with a certain tremor in the voice. More than anything, **anointing** is spoken of as something some Christians have, and other Christians don't.

The New Testament doesn't teach anything about that kind of anointing. 1 John 2:20 was written to all Christians, not to just a select few, and it tells them **you have an anointing**. In this, John spoke of a common anointing, something that belongs to all believers. This is an anointing that makes discernment possible for those who seek it in the Lord. As John said, the believer can have discernment (**you know all things**) because of this anointing.

When the New Testament speaks of anointing, it speaks of it as the common possession of all believers, though some Christians may not appreciate or use the anointing God gave them. Among some Christians today, there is a rather magical or superstitious approach to this idea of anointing. In their mind, "the anointing" is like a virus or a germ, something that can be spread by casual contact or can even infect a whole group. Usually, these folks think that when one "catches" the anointing, you can tell because they start talking and acting in a strange way. This is not the Bible's idea of anointing.

Anointing has the idea of being filled with and blessed by the Holy Spirit. This is the common possession of all Christians, but this filling and blessing is something that each believer can and should become more and more submitted and responsive to. God has blessed you with the Holy Spirit, but are you submitted and responsive to Him? God has given you resources of spiritual discernment and wisdom – you can **know all things**. Certainly, this is not in the sense of knowing everything as God knows everything; but you can learn everything you need to know to live the life God sets before you. If you need to know it, the Spirit who has anointed you will reveal it as you seek Him.

This idea of anointing – literally, to be blessed with oil, an emblem of the Holy Spirit – was behind one of the punishments given to the apostle John in persecution. Old accounts say that a Roman emperor ordered that John be cast into a boiling vat of oil as if to say, "Here is your anointing." John came out from the vat of oil unharmed because he genuinely had an anointing from God, and God had more for him to do.

Today, submit and respond to God's anointing in your life, and God's Spirit will also protect and guide you.

October 30

The Letter That Didn't Want to Be Written

Beloved, while I was very diligent to write to you concerning our common salvation, I found it necessary to write to you exhorting you to contend earnestly for the faith which was once for all delivered to the saints. (Jude v. 3)

Jude intended to write a letter to early Christians about **our common salvation**. But something happened, and Jude found it necessary to write a letter that didn't want to be written. He was willing to change his plan because the Holy Spirit prompted him to do something different.

It concerned **our common salvation**. Salvation is not "common" in the sense that it is cheap or that everyone has it. It is "common" in the sense that we are saved in *community*. God doesn't have one way for the rich and another way for the poor, or one way for the good and another way for the bad. We all come to God the same way – in common.

We join with an invisible, mighty army going back through generations, standing shoulder to shoulder with millions of Christians who have gone before. Being in Christ means we are part of a big family, one that crosses denominational lines.

We **contend earnestly for the faith** because it is valuable. If you walk into an art gallery and there are no guards and no security system, you must draw one conclusion: there is nothing very valuable in that art gallery. Valuables are protected; worthless things are not.

We must each **contend earnestly for the faith**. This is something that Jude wanted you – the individual Christian – to do. But how can an everyday Christian **contend earnestly for the faith**?

We contend for the faith in a *positive* sense when we give an unflinching witness, distribute tracts, make possible the training of faithful ambassadors for Jesus, or when we strengthen the hands of faithful pastors who are honoring the Word of God in their pulpits. These are a few among the many ways that we can contend earnestly for the faith in a positive sense.

We contend for the faith in a *negative* way when we withhold support and encouragement from those who compromise the faith, when we speak out against the preaching of another gospel or speak out against a manner of living that contradicts the message of the gospel.

We contend for the faith in a practical sense when we live uncompromising Christian lives and give credit to the Lord who changed us.

Who contends for the faith? Missionaries and evangelists do. But so does the Sunday school teacher who is faithful to the Scriptures. So does the woman who gives a godly witness at her workplace. People like this fight for the faith just as much as a front-line missionary, and each one of us should contend for the gospel wherever God has put us.

Hopefully, you contend for the faith. Ask God for the opportunity to do so today.

October 31

When Enough Is Enough

But he himself went a day's journey into the wilderness, and came and sat down under a broom tree. And he prayed that he might die, and said, "It is enough! Now, LORD, take my life, for I am no better than my fathers!" (1 Kings 19:4)

Elijah must be ranked among the greatest men or women of prayer in the entire Bible. He was mighty enough in prayer to make the heavens hold back rain for three and a half years, and then he had enough power in prayer to bring the rain back at the appointed time. Elijah had enjoyed an amazing period of spiritual success with the defeat of the prophets of Baal on Mount Carmel and the sincere (if brief) restoration of a belief in the true God among the people of Israel.

Yet at the end of that high season a crashing depression came on him. Here we find Elijah alone in the wilderness. In that solitary place he began to pray. This prayer was now personal: **and he prayed that he might die**.

Thankfully, this was a prayer that was not answered for Elijah. In fact, Elijah was one of the few men in the Bible to never actually die! We can imagine that many years later as he was caught up into heaven, he smiled and thought of this prayer – and the blessed "no" that answered his prayer. To receive a no answer from God can be better than receiving a yes answer – it certainly was true in Elijah's case.

Look at what Elijah said in his prayer: **It is enough**. We sense that Elijah meant, "I can't do this anymore, LORD." The work was stressful, exhausting, and seemed to accomplish nothing. The great work on Mount Carmel did not result in a lasting national revival or return to the LORD.

God had a great revelation of Himself to give to Elijah. Though he was worn out and discouraged by all the battles he had to fight, it seems that peace and calm communion with God marked the later period of Elijah's life.

Look at the rest of Elijah's unanswered prayer: **Now, LORD, take my life, for I am no better than my fathers**. When Elijah examined the apparent failure of his work, he instinctively set the blame on his own unworthiness.

It is easy to wonder how a great man of God could have such gloomy thoughts. Yet we see that all of his spiritual accomplishments did not prevent Elijah from feeling greatly depressed and discouraged. Perhaps Elijah had especially hoped that the events on Mount Carmel would turn around Ahab and Jezebel and the leadership of Israel. If so, Elijah forgot that people reject God *despite* the evidence, not *because* of the evidence.

Have you recently said, "That's enough?" The lesson from Elijah is clear: God knows when enough is enough.

Today, comfort yourself in that knowledge and thank God for the prayers that He, in His wisdom and grace, answered with "No."

November 1

Undone

So I said: "Woe is me, for I am undone! Because I am a man of unclean lips, and I dwell in the midst of a people of unclean lips; for my eyes have seen the King, the LORD of hosts." (Isaiah 6:5)

When Isaiah saw the angels (Isaiah 6:3-4) in their holy humility, obedience, and praise to God, he realized that he was not like the God of all majesty. He also realized that he was not like the angels. They cry out holy, holy, holy, and praise God beautifully – Isaiah could not because he was a man of unclean lips.

When Isaiah saw the LORD, he knew what kind of man he was. As poorly as he compared to the seraphim, that was relatively nothing to how he compared to the LORD. This vision (or perhaps the actual experience) of the throne of God did not immediately make Isaiah feel good. The more clearly he saw the LORD, the more clearly he saw how bad he was. Isaiah's deep sense of depravity is consistent with the experiences of other godly men in the presence of the LORD. Job (Job 42:5-6), Daniel (Daniel 10:15-17), Peter (Luke 5:8), and John (Revelation 1:7), each had similar experiences. Isaiah knew his broken state before God when he despaired, **for my eyes have seen the King, the LORD of hosts**.

Isaiah was a righteous and godly man by all outward appearances. Yet when he saw the enthroned King, the LORD of hosts, he saw how sinful he was in comparison. When you lay a diamond on a black background and shine light on it, you can see every flaw and imperfection.

What made Isaiah feel **undone**? Isaiah saw his sinfulness, and the sins of his people, mainly in terms of sinful speech. He said, **I am a man of unclean lips, and I dwell in the midst of a people of unclean lips**.

- By nature, our lips are full of flattery and false intent: *With flattering lips and a double heart they speak* (Psalm 12:2).
- By nature, our lips lie and are proud: *Let the lying lips be put to silence, which speak insolent things proudly and contemptuously against the righteous* (Psalm 31:18).
- By nature, our lips deceive: *Keep your tongue from evil, and your lips from speaking deceit* (Psalm 34:13).
- By nature, our lips are violent: *Swords are in their lips* (Psalm 59:7).
- By nature, our lips bring death to others: *The poison of asps is under their lips* (Psalm 140:3).

Isaiah did not think for a moment that this was his only sin, but he saw that this was an example of the great and incurable disease of sin in him and his people. No one likes to feel **undone**, but to genuinely say, **I am undone** is not a bad place to be.

Today, recognize your need before a glorious God, and receive what He gives you in Jesus Christ.

November 2

The Know-It-All

He spoke three thousand proverbs, and his songs were one thousand and five. Also he spoke of trees, from the cedar tree of Lebanon even to the hyssop that springs out of the wall; he spoke also of animals, of birds, of creeping things, and of fish. And men of all nations, from all the kings of the earth who had heard of his wisdom, came to hear the wisdom of Solomon. (1 Kings 4:32-34)

Sometimes when someone is boasting about their wisdom, we call them a "know-it-all." It can be annoying to be around these people, but every so often we meet someone who deserves the title. Solomon deserved the title, "know-it-all."

In 1 Kings 3, God answered Solomon's prayer for wisdom to lead the people and God blessed him with great wisdom. In Chapter 4, Solomon used that wisdom to organize his government, to lead the people, and exercise justice.

Solomon's wisdom makes up a portion of the book of Proverbs. He was also a singer and songwriter, composing many songs but few compared to David – the sweet psalmist of Israel.

Solomon had a divinely gifted intellect and ability to understand. His wisdom was applied to understanding life and human problems.

The old rabbis said that even animals brought their disputes to Solomon. According to an old legend, a man walked in a field on a hot day with a jug of cool milk when he came on a serpent dying of thirst. The serpent asked the man for some milk, but he refused. Finally, the serpent promised to show the man some hidden treasure if he gave him some milk, and the man agreed. When they went to the place of hidden treasure, the man moved a rock and was about to take the treasure when the serpent pounced on him and coiled around his neck. The man protested that this was unfair, but the serpent insisted the man would never take his treasure. The man said, "Let's take our case to Solomon" and the serpent agreed.

When they went to Solomon the serpent was still coiled around the man's neck. Solomon asked the serpent what he wanted, and the serpent said, "I want to kill this man because the Scriptures command it when they say that I will 'bruise the heel of man.'" Solomon told him to first let go of the man because the two parties in a trial must have equal standing. When the serpent went to the floor, Solomon asked him again what he wanted, and the serpent again said that he wanted to kill the man based on the verse "You shall bruise the heel of the man." Then Solomon turned to the man and said, "To you, God's command was to crush the head of the serpent – do it!" And the man crushed the serpent's head.

That never happened, but it is a fun story. Yet, Solomon's wisdom was real, and a gift from the LORD. God has not stopped giving the gift of His wisdom to those who ask for it and seek it. Apart from charming legends about talking snakes, you need God's wisdom for daily living.

Today, ask God for His wisdom in your life.

November 3

Looking Inward

But you, beloved, building yourselves up on your most holy faith, praying in the Holy Spirit, keep yourselves in the love of God, looking for the mercy of our Lord Jesus Christ unto eternal life. (Jude v. 20-21)

Jude did not tell us to go out and crush the certain men who were a danger to the church. Instead, he told us to focus on our walk with the Lord, to help others affected by the certain men, and to focus on God. We simply are to pay such dangerous men no attention, except for what is necessary for our warning. God will take care of them.

In these verses, Jude emphasized for us each to **keep yourselves in the love of God**. We know that God loves even the ungodly (Romans 5:6). The idea is that you must keep yourself in harmony with God's ever-present love.

God's love extends everywhere, and nothing can separate us from it. But we can deny ourselves the benefits of God's love. An example of this is the Prodigal Son of Luke 15. He was always loved by the father, but for a time he did not benefit from it.

We keep ourselves **in the love of God** by building ourselves up on our most holy faith. This means to keep growing spiritually and to keep building up. We are responsible for our own spiritual growth.

Jude showed us the frailty of men and how deceivers infiltrated the church. If you give your spiritual growth to someone else, not only will you not grow, but you may also be led astray. Others can help provide an environment helpful for spiritual growth. But no one can make another person grow in the Lord. We grow on the foundation of the truth.

We also keep ourselves **in the love of God** by **praying in the Holy Spirit**. The battle against wrong living and teaching is a spiritual battle, requiring **prayer in the Holy Spirit**. Many of our prayers are directed by our own needs, by our own intellect, or by our own wishes and desires. But there is a higher level of prayer: *Likewise, the Spirit also helps in our weaknesses. For we do not know what we should pray for as we ought, but the Spirit Himself makes intercession for us.* (Romans 8:26)

We keep ourselves **in the love of God** by **looking for the mercy of Lord Jesus Christ unto eternal life**. As we keep the blessed hope of Jesus' soon return alive in our hearts, this effectively keeps us **in the love of God** and helps us to not give away our faith.

See the three ways Jude gives us to keep ourselves in the love of God:

- Building up on the most holy faith.
- Praying the in the Holy Spirit.
- Looking for the merciful return of Jesus Christ.

If you do these things today, you can start enjoying the love of God He freely gives.

November 4

A Bad Sense

These are sensual persons, who cause divisions, not having the Spirit. (Jude v. 19)

Concerned about dangerous people among the early church, Jude wrote his letter of warning. This verse comes at the end of an extended description of these dangerous men. It's as if Jude wanted to leave us with a few final identifying marks of these men so that we could identify them when necessary.

First, he says **they are sensual persons**. When he called these dangerous men **sensual**, he meant it in the sense that they were *not spiritual*. They were carnal and insensitive to the Holy Spirit. It describes the person who lives only by and for what they can get through their physical senses and live this way selfishly.

God has a higher life for us than merely living by what we feel. He intends for us to enjoy life in the Spirit – not set apart from feelings, but putting the things we can sense in their proper order. These dangerous men Jude wrote about didn't keep the proper priorities when it came to the sensual and the spiritual, so they lived as if the material was more important than the spiritual. It is wrong – and a historical error – to believe that the material is unimportant. God has a purpose and a plan for our material bodies and this material world. Yet we dare not promote the material over the spiritual, and we keep each in their proper order – something the dangerous men did not do.

Second, these men were those **who cause divisions**. This particular word for **divisions** is only found here in the New Testament. It has the idea of people who think themselves superior and therefore keep themselves separate from the common people. It speaks of a spiritual elitism more like the Pharisees who opposed Jesus and His humble disciples. It's always a danger sign when we think ourselves better than other Christians and keep ourselves separate. As you grow deeper in the Lord beware of the corruption of elitism.

Jude mentioned one final characteristic in this verse, describing these men as those **not having the Spirit**. This sad epitaph could be written over many churches, church projects, evangelism campaigns, home groups, or even individual Christian lives. Just as in Jude's day, today the church needs truly spiritual men and women.

Could the phrase **not having the Spirit** describe your life? It can be the attitude that first looks to self for solutions and strength, only depending on the Holy Spirit when every other option finally fails. You may thankfully remember many precious *past* experiences with the Holy Spirit, but what difference has the Holy Spirit made in your life this last week?

Remember the promise of Jesus, and simply ask in faith: *If you then, being evil, know how to give good gifts to your children, how much more will your heavenly Father give the Holy Spirit to those who ask Him!* (Luke 11:13)

November 5

The Gift of Friendship

Paul valued the Philippians as his special friends; I thank my God upon every remembrance of you, always in every prayer of mine making request for you all with joy, for your fellowship in the gospel from the first day until now. (Philippians 1:3-5)

Paul was thankful for the gift of friendship. Often, we take our friendships for granted. We assume that this is just another wonderful part of the Christian life. But Paul knew what it was like to be alone and friendless. Paul directed his thanksgiving to God because he saw that this gift of friendship was from Him – God deserved the credit.

Prayer sustained Paul's friendship with the Philippians. Paul didn't get to spend much time with them; his first visit there was cut short after he was thrown in jail and miraculously rescued. Afterward, he only came to Philippi as he was passing through; it was never for many months or years. Paul probably wrote this letter some ten years after his first visit to Philippi, yet his affection towards them was still alive.

What kept it going? Prayer. It wasn't long telephone calls, text messages, or frequent letters; it wasn't simply thinking about them – it was praying for them. We often say, "out of sight, out of mind"; but it is more accurate to say, "out of prayer, out of heart" when it comes to our friendships in Jesus. We often think that we must resort to prayer to maintain a friendship only when we're out of contact, but prayer is what keeps the friendship of next-door-neighbors together. When we stop praying for our friends, our friendship will start becoming less than what it can be.

Let those words **with all joy** sink deeply into your heart. Paul could not pray for the Philippians without a sense of joy filling his heart. What a great way to judge our friendships – do we have joy when we pray for our friends?

Paul's friendship with the Philippians was centered in the gospel. We gain friends through all sorts of common interests, but the best kind also has the gospel of Jesus Christ in common. Friends in Jesus are not called to just enjoy themselves, but also to be used together for purposes of the gospel. For many friendships, this is a missing element. You may enjoy each other, yet something is lacking because there is no real **fellowship in the gospel**. What those friends need is to pray together about what God would have them do together to further the work of God's kingdom.

Some may sense a lack of friendship in their lives. The best advice is that old saying: "If you want a friend, be a friend." There is no person less likely to develop friendships than the person who is self-focused and just waiting around for someone to be their friend.

Today, let God guide you as you reach out in prayer and friendship to those around you.

November 6
Only Sounding Spiritual

Moreover the L**ORD**** spoke again to Ahaz, saying, "Ask a sign for yourself from the L****ORD**** your God; ask it either in the depth or in the height above." But Ahaz said, "I will not ask, nor will I test the L****ORD****!"** (Isaiah 7:10-12)

A dangerous army approached the land of Judah, and King Ahaz had every reason to be concerned. He made every human preparation a king could think of and worried about the arrangements when the armies of the northern kingdom of Israel and Syria came together to attack Judah. Ahaz expressed almost no trust in God and sacrificed his son to the pagan god Molech. About the only good thing Ahaz seemed to do was bring forth another son named Hezekiah, who became a great and godly ruler of Judah.

When the invading army threatened, Ahaz panicked – and the prophet Isaiah came to encourage the king and strengthen his faith. God assured King Ahaz that though the armies would attack and damage the kingdom of Judah, they would survive by the gracious hand of God. Isaiah offered the king the opportunity to find assurance in God's promise. Isaiah told Ahaz, **ask a sign for yourself**.

Instead of taking God up on His invitation, Ahaz said, **I will not ask, nor will I test the L****ORD****!** This sounded very spiritual from Ahaz. He almost seemed to say what Jesus later said in Matthew 4:7: *You shall not tempt the Lord your God.* Ahaz refused to ask for a sign because when God fulfilled the sign, he would be obligated to believe.

This was not tempting or testing God in the wrong way. It is never testing God to do as He says, and if the LORD invites us to test Him, we should. For example, in Malachi 3:10, the LORD invited Israel to give as He commanded, and thereby to *prove Me now in this* – in the matter of giving proportionally to God and His work from our resources.

Again, perhaps Ahaz was bitter against the LORD because of all the disasters Judah had already been through at the hands of their enemies. Perhaps he thought, "I want nothing to do with the God who allowed it to get this bad." Whatever the reason, he rejected God's invitation and found himself in a worse place because of it.

What has God offered that you refused? Perhaps there was a very spiritual sounding reason for refusing; we can be pretty good at thinking up reasons for going our own way. It is humbling to realize that God sees through our spiritual sounding reasons and sees the secret place of our hearts. There is no hiding from His searching gaze, and when He offers us something we can trust that a loving hand is extended to us.

We should each examine ourselves; perhaps we have been just as strange and foolish as Ahaz by refusing some good thing God wants to give to us.

November 7

All Sons and Daughters

For you are all sons of God through faith in Christ Jesus. For as many of you as were baptized into Christ have put on Christ. (Galatians 3:26-27)

The false teachers among the Galatian Christians taught one could only come to Jesus through Judaism. This went against the Gospel of Jesus Christ, the gospel that Paul preached. God's true good news says we are made right before God because of who Jesus is and what He did for us, especially what He did for us in His sacrifice at the cross and His victory in resurrection.

Therefore, compared to what some taught among the Galatians, this was a revolutionary statement: **you are all sons of God through faith in Christ Jesus**. In some traditional Jewish thinking, standing before God was measured by obedience to the law. To truly be close to God – as His **sons** – one had to be *extremely observant* of the law, just as the Scribes and Pharisees attempted (Matthew 23). Believers are considered **sons of God** in a completely different way: **through faith in Christ Jesus**.

The *standing* is impressive. To be among the **sons** (and daughters) **of God** means we have a special relationship with God as a loving and caring Father. It is a place of closeness, affection, special care, and attention.

The *method* is impressive. To become a son (or daughter) of God **through faith in Christ Jesus** means much more than believing that He existed or did certain things. It is to put *trust* in Him, both for now and eternity.

Using the picture of baptism, Paul illustrated what it means to have **faith in Christ**. He didn't say believers were **baptized** into water but **baptized into Christ**. In water baptism one is *immersed* in water, so when we place our **faith in Christ Jesus**, we are *immersed* in Jesus.

Some Christians seem content with just dipping a bit into Jesus. God wants us to be *fully immersed* in Jesus; not sprinkled, not just moistened. When one is immersed in water, you don't even see much of the person anymore – you mostly see the water. When we live as **baptized into Christ**, you don't see much of "me" anymore; you mostly see Jesus.

Another way of expressing our *immersion* in Jesus is to say that we have **put on Christ**. This phrase has the idea of putting on a suit of clothes. So, we "clothe ourselves" with Jesus as our identity.

Some might wonder if this is only play-acting, like a child playing dress-up. The answer is simple. It is only an illusion if there is no *spiritual reality* behind it. In this verse, Paul really speaks of the *spiritual reality* – those who **were baptized into Christ** really have **put on Christ**. Now they are called to live each day consistent with the spiritual reality.

If you by faith are in Jesus, then you are a child of God. You are immersed in the Savior. You have put on Christ. Now live it!

November 8
Strangely, Not Far Enough

If your right eye causes you to sin, pluck it out and cast it from you; for it is more profitable for you that one of your members perish, than for your whole body to be cast into hell. And if your right hand causes you to sin, cut it off and cast it from you; for it is more profitable for you that one of your members perish, than for your whole body to be cast into hell. (Matthew 5:29-30)

I once heard an outstanding Bible teacher speak on this text, and I will never forget what he said: "I wish Jesus had never said this." That might sound irreverent, but as he explained, I understood him completely. The preacher had once dealt with someone who had disfigured himself based on a misunderstanding of this passage.

The words that were so misunderstood were, **if your right eye causes you to sin, pluck it out**. Understood correctly, we see that Jesus used a figure of speech. Sadly, some have not taken it so and have mutilated themselves in mistaken efforts to pursue holiness. A famous early Christian named Origen castrated himself on the principle of this passage.

The trouble with a literal interpretation is that it does not go far enough. Even if you cut off your hand or pluck out your eye, you could still sin with your other hand or eye. When all those are gone, you can always sin with your mind.

Like most Bible passages, it is best to keep reading to get the real sense of the meaning. **It is more profitable for you that one of your members perish, than for your whole body to be cast into hell.** Jesus stressed the point that we must be willing to sacrifice to obey God. If part of our life is given over to sin, we must be convinced that it is better for that part of our life to "die" rather than to condemn our whole life.

Many are unwilling to do this, and that is why they remain trapped in sin or never come to Jesus. They never get beyond a vague wish to be better. With this dramatic figure of speech, Jesus reminded us that vague wishes aren't enough.

You have heard the dramatic stories of a man or woman trapped with an arm pinned under a massive rock or tree. Faced with the choice between losing an arm and losing their life, the man or woman gains the courage to make the terrible decision to do the necessary thing – to trade their arm for their life.

Without performing the act – which, as we have seen before, doesn't go far enough – Jesus told us to have the same attitude of sacrifice for the sake of obedience and following Him. Something this great can only begin to happen as Jesus works His work in us.

Today, a good prayer is "Jesus, work in me the willingness to sacrifice in the struggle against sin."

November 9

Gambling on God

Because for the work of Christ he came close to death, not regarding his own life, to supply what was lacking in your service toward me. (Philippians 2:30)

The Christians in the ancient city of Philippi had a close relationship with the apostle Paul. They even sent a special messenger to Paul, a man who carried encouragement and support from the Philippian church to Paul when he was still in prison. This messenger, named Epaphroditus, became sick while on his mission to visit and help Paul.

Epaphroditus' noble heart was evident because he put the work of Jesus first, and his personal safety and concern second. He was willing to do something extreme for God. Paul even wrote that Epaphroditus didn't regard his own life – but when he wrote that, he used a particular phrase worthy of our notice.

The phrase **not regarding his life** was used in Paul's day as a gambler's phrase. It meant to risk everything on the rolling of the dice. Can you picture a gambler ready to roll the dice, having wagered everything he had on the outcome? That is a gambler who is considered "all in."

In using this phrase, Paul meant that for the sake of Jesus Christ, Epaphroditus was willing to gamble everything – he was **not regarding his life**. What are we willing to risk for Jesus? People today will take big risks for fame, fortune, or just for an adrenaline rush. We see this and must ask ourselves: are we willing to risk *anything* for God? Perhaps that is an excellent way to find out just what our God is: our God is whatever we will take the biggest risk for. With that in mind, what is your God? What will you take a risk for?

In the days of the Early Church, there was an association of men and women who called themselves *The Gamblers*, a term taken from this same Greek word used in Philippians 2:30. Their goal was to visit prisoners and the sick, especially those who were ill with dangerous and infectious diseases. Often, when a plague struck a city, the heathen threw the dead bodies into the streets and fled in terror. But *The Gamblers* – these Christians who risked everything for Jesus – buried the dead and helped the sick the best they could, and they risked their lives to show the love of Jesus.

When a gambler takes a risk, there is always a probability that he will lose. The odds are always in favor of the house. But when we are God's "gamblers" – as Epaphroditus was – we can never lose. What is God calling you to do that seems risky? For some of us, obedience in a particular area seems too dangerous – it seems to be too big of a gamble. But the only sure way to win is to put your wager on God and risk it all.

We can never lose when we bet on God.

November 10

Remembering and Forgetting

Now the mixed multitude who were among them yielded to intense craving; so the children of Israel also wept again and said: "Who will give us meat to eat? We remember the fish which we ate freely in Egypt, the cucumbers, the melons, the leeks, the onions, and the garlic; but now our whole being is dried up; there is nothing at all except this manna before our eyes!" (Numbers 11:4-6)

Exodus 12:38 tells us that a mixed multitude went out of Egypt – not all of those who came out of Egypt with Moses were ethnically Israelites. Some Egyptians went with them because they were fellow slaves in Egypt and the God of Israel proved Himself more powerful than the gods of the Egyptians. Israel was a mixed multitude spiritually – not all had a genuine relationship with God. This is true of the visible church as well, which Jesus said would contain good and bad until the final harvest.

The complainers **yielded to intense craving**; their desire would not be fulfilled unless they **yielded** to it. James 1:14 says *but each one is tempted when he is drawn away by his own desires and enticed*; the attraction to sin is present within us, yet we must still yield to it in choosing to sin.

Look at their question: **Who will give us meat to eat?** How could they forget the God in heaven who met their every need? It seems Israel looked for another provider because they were not satisfied with what came to them from God – and were so distraught over this they wept! Tears of repentance or sorrow over sin or joy in the Lord can be beautiful before God; but many tears shed, even by believers, are over childish disappointments.

By the way they described life in Egypt, one would think their slavery was heaven on earth! Israel here engaged in "creative memory," choosing to remember certain things about Egypt and exaggerating them, while choosing to forget other things.

Memory, both in recording and recalling, is a creative process – and "memories" can be created of events that never happened. Memory often romanticizes the past. One may long for a return to the spiritual environment of one's youth when everyone seemed more right with God and more on fire. Yet, this is often confused with a simple longing for our youth – when things seemed simpler, responsibilities fewer, and everything newer.

Israel fell in love with an illusion from the past instead of looking for what God had for them in the future – the Promised Land, which was truly a land of milk and honey. Canaan had all the food they could ever want! God's best for us is always ahead, never behind us. Are you stuck in the trap of the romanticized past?

Today, ask God to give you an appropriate sense of excitement for what He will do in the future – even in the future that starts today.

November 11

Keep Your Boots On

Stand therefore, having girded your waist with truth, having put on the breastplate of righteousness, and having shod your feet with the preparation of the gospel of peace. (Ephesians 6:14-15)

With one powerful word, Ephesians 6:14 expresses one of the great goals of our spiritual warfare: to **stand**. The idea is to be courageous and steadfast in the critical and crazy moments. Our footing is sure, and in God, we are immovable.

To **stand** in the Christian life – to stand amidst the conflicts and struggles that comes and goes as we live for God – God gives us essential help. This help is represented to us with the picture of the equipment of a Roman soldier.

In this last part of Ephesians 6:14-15, Paul explains the help God gives to His people using the example of a particular part of the Roman soldier's equipment – the unique sandals on the feet of the Roman Legions. As it connects to the Christian experience, those sandals are like having **shod your feet with the preparation of the gospel of peace**.

Notice, the **preparation of the gospel** is represented as these protective boots (or sandals) that were worn by Roman soldiers. It was almost impossible for a Roman soldier to fight effectively or adequately go about their business without these well-known sandals.

The ancient Jewish historian Josephus described these sandals as being "shoes thickly studded with sharp nails." Many historians believe that one reason for the great success of Roman armies was that they could march long distances over rough ground, which made them much more mobile than other armies. And when it came to the time of battle, the Roman soldier could fight with a better footing than their enemies.

The word **preparation** here has the sense of "a prepared foundation." The gospel provides the footing for everything we do. However powerful the rest of your body is, if you are wounded in your feet, you can't do much against the enemy.

Paul probably had Isaiah 52:7 in mind when he referred to **having shod your feet**: *How beautiful upon the mountains are the feet of him who brings good news, who proclaims peace, who brings glad tidings of good things, who proclaims salvation, who says to Zion, "Your God reigns!"* It is all vitally connected to the good news of who Jesus is and what He did for us at the cross. This was announced by prophets like Isaiah and reported by Paul.

If we are prepared with the gospel of peace, it means that we are ready – we are mobile, flexible, and ready with the gospel. This is something to have in the Christian life, living in constant readiness and firm standing.

Don't miss the point – the gospel must be your constant foundation, as much as a soldier always has his boots. Otherwise, you aren't prepared and are an easy target.

Today, don't let go of the preparation of the gospel of peace.

November 12

Like Our King

Blessed are the peacemakers, for they shall be called sons of God. (Matthew 5:9)

The Beatitudes begin the famous Sermon on the Mount recorded in the Gospel of Matthew. These eight statements of blessing describe the character of true citizens of the Kingdom Jesus preached – the Kingdom of His reign. Thus far we have seen that when Jesus is King in our life there will be:

- Poverty of spirit, recognizing our need for God (Matthew 5:3).
- Mourning over our sinful state and that of this lost world (Matthew 5:4).
- A meek, gentle attitude that trusts God more than self (Matthew 5:5).
- Hunger and thirst after righteousness, both received from God and seen in our life (Matthew 5:6).
- Mercy to others, remembering mercy received (Matthew 5:7).
- Purity of heart, leading to a greater relationship with God (Matthew 5:8).

Now, **blessed are the peacemakers**. This does not describe those who live in peace, but those who bring about peace, overcoming evil with good. One way is through spreading the good news of what Jesus did for mankind at the cross, because God has given us the ministry of reconciliation (2 Corinthians 5:18). In evangelism, we make peace between people and the God whom they have rejected and offended.

This blessing for making peace comes after the blessing for purity. This is the order of spiritual life: first purity, then peace. It isn't making peace with sin or evil; the citizen of Jesus' kingdom sets their face against all that goes against God and His purity. Once this is received through faith, then peace comes forth.

God loves reconciliation and longs to make peace. The reward for the peacemakers: **For they shall be called sons of God**. Their reward is that they are recognized as true children of God. They share His passion for peace and reconciliation, the breaking down of walls between people.

God blesses the peacemakers. Though people may treat them badly, God blesses them. Being a peacemaker can be a thankless job, at least among men. To take the initiative to bring together two parties in conflict may be unappreciated. In Jesus' kingdom, we do this for God's glory, not for the applause of man. Perhaps unappreciated by man, God welcomes peacemakers as sons and daughters.

If anyone knew the blessedness of the peacemaker, it was Jesus Himself. Jesus set Himself between two irreconcilable parties, and in doing so was afflicted by both sides. Think of Jesus on the cross: afflicted by man, who beat Him, nailed Him, and mocked Him; and afflicted by God the Father Himself, who put on Him the guilt and judgment our sin deserved. Yet in enduring this suffering from both sides, Jesus made peace between man and God. The citizens of His kingdom who also make peace shall **be called sons of God**.

Where does God want you to make peace today? There is a blessing in it for you.

November 13

Forgetfulness and Fruitfulness

Joseph called the name of the firstborn Manasseh: "For God has made me forget all my toil and all my father's house." And the name of the second he called Ephraim: "For God has caused me to be fruitful in the land of my affliction." (Genesis 41:51-52)

Today, we carefully choose the names of our children, often looking up baby names to see what the meaning of each name is. We want to give our children names that mean something special, both to us and to them in the future. Certainly, this is nothing new. Many thousands of years ago, Joseph gave names to his two sons to reflect what God had done in his heart. When we see what the names meant, we see what a great work God had done.

First, notice that Joseph gave his sons Jewish names: **Manasseh** and **Ephraim**. Joseph had lived in Egypt for many years now, and he had married an Egyptian woman. Joseph was in Egypt because the other sons of Israel had rejected him, selling him as a slave. Yet Joseph knew who he was: a covenant son of Israel. He was in Egypt, but not an Egyptian. In the same way, Jesus wants us to be in the world, but not of the world (John 17:14-16).

Second, notice the name of the first son: **Manasseh**, which means "forgetfulness." He named his firstborn Manasseh because God made Joseph forget all the previous pain and affliction in his life. Joseph had been spoiled by his father, rejected by his brothers, then attacked and sold into slavery by them. He had been thrown in jail for honoring God and those he had helped forgot about him. Despite years of this kind of treatment, Joseph could say, "I choose to forget it all."

Thirdly, the name of the second-born son is **Ephraim**, which means "fruitfulness." Joseph gave him this name because God had made him fruitful in Egypt. He was raised from the pit up to the pinnacle and was second in power only to the Pharaoh. God had blessed Joseph and given him peace and blessing.

Do you see the connection? We can't be **Ephraim** until we are first **Manasseh**. In other words, we can't be truly fruitful until we are also forgetting.

In his book *The Great Divorce*, C.S. Lewis described hell as a place where no one forgets anything. It was his idea that in hell each person would remember every offense, every slight, every cruel exchange of words, every wrong ever done to them; and everyone would be utterly unforgiving. But in heaven, all these things are put away, because all things have become new.

What type of fruitfulness is being held back in your life because you will not forget?

May we be more like Paul, who said: "forgetting those things which are behind and reaching forward to those things which are ahead, I press toward the upward call of God in Christ Jesus." (Philippians 3:13-14)

November 14

Our Light Affliction

For our light affliction, which is but for a moment, is working for us a far more exceeding and eternal weight of glory. (2 Corinthians 4:17)

Jun Sato, 25, could not find work in downtown Tokyo, Japan, so he made up his own job. Dressed in protective padding, he let people on the street out on boxing gloves and beat him for three minutes for the equivalent of about $10. Sato said, "I enjoy being used as a punching bag, it is another way to experience life. I want to continue as long as my body holds up."

Most people don't feel that way. Most of us don't knowingly seek out suffering, and when we're in it, we want to get out of it as soon as possible. This makes the apostle Paul's description of **our light affliction** hard to accept. Paul might feel all his afflictions have been **light**, but our afflictions don't seem that way!

Looking at the kind of life Paul lived and the kind of afflictions he suffered, it changes our perspective. 2 Corinthians 6:4-5 gives us a start in understanding what Paul went through personally: *in much patience, in tribulations, in needs, in distresses, in stripes, in imprisonments, in tumults, in labors, in sleeplessness.* Paul certainly did not have an easy life, yet he could still say **our light affliction**.

Our affliction is light compared to what others are suffering. No matter how bad we have it, you don't have to look far to find others who are suffering worse. Are we really better people than they are?

Our affliction is light compared to what we deserve. We often don't like to think about it, but haven't we sinned against God again and again? If you believe God is teaching you through your affliction, don't you have far more to learn than He could confront in you right now?

Our affliction is light compared to what Jesus suffered for us. There is simply no comparison between what we are going through, and all Jesus suffered spiritually, emotionally, and physically – and for us, not for Himself.

Our affliction is light compared to the blessings we enjoy. In a time of affliction, we may ask God, "Why do I deserve this?" Instead, we should be asking that question in our times of blessing, which are far greater than our afflictions.

Our affliction is light compared to the sustaining power of God's grace. He can and does strengthen us if we will only come to Him humbly – and anticipate that His help may come through another servant of His.

Our affliction is light compared to the glory it leads to. God has eternal glories to work in us through our present affliction. Olympic athletes are willing to afflict themselves, knowing the glory it can lead to.

Our affliction may seem greater than athletic training, but the glory is infinitely more certain, and ultimately more wonderful, than any prize this world can give.

November 15

Going with the Glory

So they departed from the mountain of the LORD on a journey of three days; and the ark of the covenant of the LORD went before them for the three days' journey, to search out a resting place for them. And the cloud of the LORD was above them by day when they went out from the camp. So it was, whenever the ark set out, that Moses said: "Rise up, O LORD! Let Your enemies be scattered, and let those who hate You flee before You." And when it rested, he said: "Return, O LORD, to the many thousands of Israel." (Numbers 10:33-36)

It took over a year, but now Israel was progressing towards the Promised Land again. As the cloud moved, imagine the excitement flowing through the people. Their journey had been from Egypt and slavery; now it was on to Canaan and liberty.

They were prepared to walk as Promised Land people – they were ordered and organized; cleansed and purified; set apart and blessed; taught how to give and how to function as priests; to remember judgment spared and deliverance brought; given God's presence as a guide, and the tools needed to lead the people. It was all focused on bringing them into the Promised Land.

One would think that after such extensive preparation that the actual entering the Promised Land would be easy. But ahead were the greatest challenges, challenges that could only be met by faith. A soldier might think boot camp finishes something – but it only prepares him for greater challenges: The actual battle itself.

As they journeyed toward the Promised Land, they were guided by God's presence. They followed the cloud no matter where God led them. If they were to camp in a rough place, or told to leave a comfortable place, they obeyed. They allowed themselves to be guided by God, not their own desire for comfort.

When God's presence led them, Moses prayed: **Rise up, O LORD! Let Your enemies be scattered, and let those who hate You flee before You!** The idea is simple: "God, go before us and take care of our enemies. It's too dangerous ahead unless You do so!"

Today, God has things before you, places to lead you. Shouldn't you pray this same prayer? We know we can face anything when the LORD is with us.

Remember the glory and strength of our resurrected LORD. When Jesus rose up, weren't all His enemies scattered? Who dared oppose Him?

Is not all our victory found in His risen glory?

When God's presence stopped, Moses prayed: **Return, O LORD, to the many thousands of Israel**. The idea is, "here we camp, LORD. Stay with us!" God sometimes tells us to move on or to "camp out" – either is fine when we are guided by His presence. Do you sense His presence today? If you don't, ask God to give you a special sensitivity to His presence.

November 16

What Is It?

In the morning the dew lay all around the camp. And when the layer of dew lifted, there, on the surface of the wilderness, was a small round substance, as fine as frost on the ground. So when the children of Israel saw it, they said to one another, "What is it?" For they did not know what it was. And Moses said to them, "This is the bread which the Lord has given you to eat." (Exodus 16:13-15)

The people of Israel came to call it "manna" (Exodus 16:31), but at first, they just wondered what it was. A huge nation traveled through a vast wilderness, and they needed food. They couldn't just buy it; they had to trust God to provide it, and He sent it every morning from heaven.

The bread from heaven came each day as something left behind from the morning dew. It was small, round, and fine as frost on the ground. Thus, it was not easy to gather. It had to be swept from the ground. Exodus 16:31 further describes the bread from heaven as like coriander seed (about the size of a sesame seed), and sweet like honey. Numbers 11:7 says it was the color of bdellium (a pearl-like color). They prepared manna by either baking or boiling (Exodus 16:23).

Some researchers identify manna with what some Arabs today call *mann*, which is naturally formed as an extract from insects that take in the sap of the tamarisk tree. It is a small, sugary drop that quickly melts in the sun. Though this bread from heaven may have been like the modern-day *mann* in the Sinai Peninsula, it wasn't the same thing.

Why did God feed them with manna? His purpose in sending them bread from heaven was not only to provide for the material needs of Israel, but to teach them eternal lessons of dependence on God: *So He humbled you, allowed you to hunger, and fed you with manna which you did not know nor did your fathers know, that He might make you know that man shall not live by bread alone; but man lives by every word that proceeds from the mouth of the Lord* (Deuteronomy 8:3).

When God puts us in a place of need, He wants to do more than meet the need. He wants to teach eternal lessons. Sometimes God must teach us this way because we are too thickheaded to learn any other way.

The sending of manna also taught Israel how to work with God. They couldn't just lay back and have God set it into their mouths. Feeding Israel through the bread from heaven was an example of God's way of cooperating with man. Israel could not bring the manna, and God would not gather it for them. Each had to do their part.

When the manna came, Israel did not know what it was. The name "manna" (given later in Exodus 16:31) means, "What's that?" and it comes from the question asked in Exodus 16:15. When God provides, we often do not recognize it. God has promised to meet all our needs, not all our expectations.

Will you let God do the unexpected for you today?

November 17

Getting the Blessing

Speak to Aaron and his sons, saying, "This is the way you shall bless the children of Israel. Say to them: The LORD bless you and keep you; the LORD make His face shine upon you, and be gracious to you; the LORD lift up His countenance upon you, and give you peace." So they shall put My name on the children of Israel, and I will bless them. (Numbers 6:23-27)

Phrase by phrase, consider this great blessing on the people of God.

The LORD bless you: This simple desire prefaces everything. God loves to bless His people, and He loves to have leaders long that the people be blessed. We remember also that God's blessing has always in mind our greatest and highest good; we often expect God's blessing in our life to mean a world of comfort and ease – but that certainly isn't for our greatest and highest good. God knows how you need to be blessed, even if you don't!

And keep you: To be kept by the LORD is a true blessing. Some people are kept by their sin and desire, some are kept by idolatry and greed, others are kept by their bitterness and anger. But to be kept by the LORD ensures life, peace, and success.

The LORD make His face to shine upon you: To have the glorious, happy face of God shining on man is the greatest gift one could have. To know that as God looks on you, He is well pleased – not because of who you are, or what you have done, but because you are in Jesus Christ – there is no greater source of peace and power in life.

And be gracious to you: The idea is that God shows tender mercy and care for His people.

The LORD lift up His countenance upon you: The priest prayed God would look on His people; when God blesses, keeps, shines, and is gracious towards His people, any look He casts towards His people is filled with nothing but blessing. His loving attention is on the believer!

And give you peace: The Hebrew word is *shalom*, which is more than the cessation of hostility – it is God's Word for wholeness and goodness and total satisfaction in life. This is the abundant life Jesus promised (John 10:10).

Through the blessing, the three-fold repetition of LORD does not prove the Trinity, but it certainly illustrates it. God the Father blesses and keeps His children. God the Son makes God's face to shine on us and brings us grace. God the Holy Spirit communicates God's attention to us and gives us peace.

Notice God's promise at the end: **and I will bless them**. God promises to bless in response to this blessing. How important for every believer to remember that we have a High Priest in heaven who ever lives to intercede for us and to bless us. Do you sense this blessing in your life?

Receive the blessing of Jesus –who is your High Priest – in your life today.

November 18

Has God Let You Down?

And there was a certain nobleman whose son was sick at Capernaum. When he heard that Jesus had come out of Judea into Galilee, he went to Him and implored Him to come down and heal his son, for he was at the point of death. Then Jesus said to him, "Unless you people see signs and wonders, you will by no means believe…." (John 4:46b-48)

Sometimes a crisis draws a person closer to God. Other times, it makes one feel that God has let them down. Many years ago, a reporter was a hostage in the Middle East for many years. When he was finally released, he said: "I prayed so many times and prayed so hard – so hard! And nothing happened. After thinking about it deeply, I'm not so sure there is a God." The man felt that God had let him down.

Almost everyone, no matter what the depth of their relationship with God, have felt disappointed by Him. We've prayed a prayer, wished a wish, or projected a need towards God that was not met the way we had hoped. How should we react in times when we feel God has let us down?

John chapter 4 gives us some guidance. This man came to Jesus saying his son was dying. He begged Jesus to come some twenty miles to his home and help. At first, Jesus seemed to put off his request, saying that people often won't believe unless they see something miraculous. The man had probably hoped that Jesus would say, "Of course I'll come to help your son!" But the man would not stop, even though Jesus didn't say what he wanted Him to say.

Jesus didn't do what the man wanted him to do. The man figured that Jesus had to be with his son to heal him, so he was disappointed when Jesus wouldn't come. Instead, Jesus told the man to go home, because his son had been healed from a distance.

This man had reason to feel Jesus had let him down. Jesus didn't say what the man wanted Him to say and did not do what the man wanted Him to do. Yet, when Jesus told the man that his son was healed, he believed Him. When he came home, he saw his son was completely better from the exact time that Jesus had said he was healed.

Jesus did not let him down. His son was healed! The man had a plan for Jesus, but Jesus didn't respond as he had expected. We often set up our own expectations of how God should work. If you feel God has let you down, maybe you feel that way because God didn't follow your plan.

The nobleman heard what Jesus wanted to say to him, he took Jesus at His Word, and he didn't let his own idea of how God should work get in the way of what God wanted to do.

It's good to see that God will never disappoint us.

November 19

No More Tears

And God will wipe away every tear from their eyes. (Revelation 7:17)

In its context, this promise is made to a specific group that had especially suffered for Jesus in their earthly lives. By extension, we take it as a promise to every believer, even those who have not suffered in a remarkable way. Heaven is a place where there are no more tears. God Himself permanently wipes them from our eyes.

Consider first what this does not mean. It does not mean that in heaven some will weep as they think over their wasted life or unconfessed sin, but God will still wipe those tears away. That idea may be a powerful, guilt-inducing motivator, but it has nothing to do with the meaning of this verse. John Walvoord put it like this: "The point is that the grief and tears of the past, speaking of their trials in the tribulation, will be over when they get to heaven…God will wipe away all tears resulting from their suffering on earth."

Instead, this precious promise means that **God will wipe away every tear from our eyes**. In heaven, the redeemed will know no more sorrow or pain. The hurt and the struggle of this earthly life are gone, and tears are a thing of the past, because God will wipe away every tear. What tender love! We picture a mother's loving hand, brushing away the tears from her child's face. God loves us with that kind of nurturing care.

We also understand from this that every tear will be wiped away *only* in heaven. On this earth, we have our share of pain and tears to endure and bring to God. King David knew what it was like to have God take notice of his tears. He prayed in Psalm 56:8, *You number my wanderings; put my tears into Your bottle*. David understood that God shows His love to us in the here and now with sweet consolation and strength, even when our struggles drive us to tears. We appreciate God's tender care for us now; but one day those tears will be gone. God will wipe them away forever.

Many wonder, "How can there be no sorrow in heaven if we have relatives or loved ones who perish in hell? Won't we be sorry for them?" Apparently, we won't be sorry in the way we think of sorrow now. How can this be? I hope you know because I don't. In heaven we certainly won't be less loving, less tender, or less caring. At the same time, in heaven our acceptance and understanding of God's plan will also come to perfection. I like the answer of Charles Spurgeon: "I do not know what handkerchief the Lord will use, but I know that he will wipe all tears away from their faces, and these tears among them."

This beautiful work of God will be perfected in heaven, but He loves to "preview" His work on earth.

Are there some tears you can let God wipe away today?

November 20

Just Perfect

And there shall be no more curse, but the throne of God and of the Lamb shall be in it, and His servants shall serve Him. They shall see His face, and His name shall be on their foreheads. There shall be no night there: They need no lamp nor light of the sun, for the Lord God gives them light. And they shall reign forever and ever. (Revelation 22:3-5)

The greatness of heaven is found in what it doesn't have and in what it does have. Think of all the things that won't be in heaven.

In heaven, the curse is gone. Since the fall, man and creation have lived with the effect of the curse described in Genesis 3:16-19: sorrow and pain in childbirth for women, friction between the sexes, the necessity of hard, often futile work for man's survival, and most of all the curse of death. These aspects of the curse will be present during the millennium, though they will be greatly lessened by the perfect rule of Jesus. Isaiah 65:20 shows us that it is still possible for a sinner to be cursed in the millennial earth. But in the new heaven and new earth, they are done away with forever for **the throne of God and of the Lamb shall be in it**.

In heaven, there is no more night. Heaven will be a place where the darkness of this age is forever gone. The light of heaven is not artificial, or from the sun – God Himself is the light.

Now, for what is present in heaven:

First, **His servants shall serve Him**. Heaven will be a place of work and service for God's people. However, this is a picture of the pure blessedness of service rather than difficult, curse-stained labor.

Second, heaven is a place where God's people **see His face**, a place of close fellowship with God. Moses was denied the privilege of seeing God face to face (Exodus 33:20-23), but everyone in heaven **shall see His face**. This means that they will literally and physically, with their risen bodies, look into the face of Jesus. We will investigate the very heart, soul, and character of Jesus, and understand Him, His work, and His love. We will see Jesus clearly because sin is done away with. There will be nothing to cloud our vision of Jesus. The greatest glory of heaven is to know God, to know Jesus, more intimately and wonderfully than we ever could on earth.

Third, in heaven, **His name shall be on their foreheads**. Heaven is a place where God's people will forever be identified with their God, and there will never be any doubt that they belong to Him.

Fourth, we **shall reign forever and ever** in heaven. Heaven is a place where God's people enjoy an eternal reign, in contrast to the limited duration of the millennium. It will never end.

Today, look forward to heaven – the perfect answer to paradise lost, perfect in every way.

November 21

His Days Are Numbered

It shall come to pass in the day the Lord gives you rest from your sorrow, and from your fear and the hard bondage in which you were made to serve, that you will take up this proverb against the king of Babylon, and say: "How the oppressor has ceased, the golden city ceased!" (Isaiah 14:3-4)

Little nations always live in the shadow of their stronger neighbors, and ancient Israel was no exception. This little kingdom was surrounded by superpowers and was often caught in the struggle between Ancient Egypt and the empires of Babylon, Assyria, or Persia.

In Isaiah's day, the most threatening superpower was Babylon. Their strength was a source of constant insecurity for Judah. Nothing drains your strength like the constant tension of a permanent threat. No wonder God's people needed rest, and no wonder the promise through the prophet was precious: **In the day the Lord gives you rest from your sorrow, and from your fear and the hard bondage in which you were made to serve**. The Babylonians would indeed conquer Judah, yet the Lord announced a day when He would give rest to believing Israel. They will have rest from **sorrow**, from **fear**, and from their **hard bondage**.

God also promised that in the day of restoration, the defeat and weakness of the king of Babylon would be exposed and God's people would rejoice. Isaiah had two aspects of prophetic fulfillment in mind. First, there is the immediate and partial fulfillment regarding the empire of Babylon and its king. Second, there is the distant and ultimate fulfillment regarding the spiritual empire of Babylon – the world system – and its king, Satan. So, this proverb against the king of Babylon was, in a partial sense, in the mouth of the returning exiles when Babylon was finally conquered, and the people of Judah returned to the Promised Land. But in an ultimate sense, this proverb against the king of Babylon will be in the mouth of God's people when the world system and her king – Satan – are each conquered and destroyed.

God is allowing us the opportunity to know what we will see then, and to allow it to affect our thinking and our actions. There will come a day when his oppression has ceased, and when the Lord will break Satan's power and every emblem of his authority. Sometimes, when we get so weary and discouraged from Satan's attacks, it is almost as if we think his day will last forever. It is an encouragement to remember that one reason Satan works so hard is that even he knows his time is short.

This promised rest is the birthright of every believer in Jesus Christ. Jesus said, *Come to Me, all you who labor and are heavy laden, and I will give you rest.* (Matthew 11:28).

Today, receive it in Jesus Christ: rest from sorrow, rest from fear, and rest from the hard bondage of trying to make yourself right before God.

November 22

Wings in the Right Places

In the year that King Uzziah died, I saw the Lord sitting on a throne, high and lifted up, and the train of His robe filled the temple. Above it stood seraphim; each one had six wings: with two he covered his face, with two he covered his feet, and with two he flew. (Isaiah 6:1-2)

Isaiah – like others in the Bible who had a vision of heaven – saw God's throne. They saw the Lord God high and lifted up. The throne was exalted and majestic. The throne set its Occupant in a superior position. He saw that **the train of His robe filled the temple**. Kings of that time sometimes wore robes with long trains following behind them, because that made it difficult to maneuver and work in. Wearing a long train meant, "I am important enough that I don't have to work. I am a person of honor and dignity. Others must serve me and wait on me." This tells us that God is honored, important, and dignified.

Surrounding the throne were majestic angelic beings: **above it stood seraphim**. In many other passages, these angels are known as *cherubim* (Psalm 80:1; Isaiah 37:16; Ezekiel 10:3) or as the *living creatures* of Revelation 4:6-11. This is the only chapter in the Bible where these creatures are named **seraphim**.

When we compare some passages in Ezekiel (such as Ezekiel 1:4-14 and 10:20-22, with Ezekiel 28:14) we learn that Satan was once one of these high angelic beings, according to Ezekiel 28:14. Cherubim were also prominent in design of the tabernacle, particularly in the Most Holy Place (Exodus 25:17-22 and 26:1, 31). The Scriptures show us that the tabernacle was, in some manner, a model of the throne of God (Exodus 25:8-9). Way back in the days of Moses, God gave His people a glimpse of this normally invisible heavenly reality.

Isaiah also saw that each of the **seraphim** had **six wings**. In Revelation 4:8, John also mentioned their six wings. They need the six wings, so each could:

- Cover his **face** (to show they were too lowly to look on the Lord).
- Cover his **feet** (to hide this "humble" area of the body, so nothing even possibly deficient is seen in the Lord's presence).
- Fly and be constantly ready to serve God.

The Lord said to Moses, *you cannot see My face; for no man shall see Me, and live* (Exodus 33:20). Apparently, the same is true even for angels, so the seraphim cover their faces.

When you think about the seraphim, think about the proportion in which they use their wings. They used four of their wings to express their humility, and two of their wings to express their willingness and ability to serve God. This is the proper balance.

Perhaps our prayer should be "Lord, give me wings to worship – and give me those wings in the proper proportion, with proper humility and reverence before You."

Why not pray that today?

November 23

Consider What Great Things He Has Done

For the LORD **will not forsake His people, for His great name's sake, because it has pleased the L**ORD **to make you His people. Moreover, as for me, far be it from me that I should sin against the L**ORD **in ceasing to pray for you; but I will teach you the good and the right way. Only fear the L**ORD**, and serve Him in truth with all your heart; for consider what great things He has done for you.** (1 Samuel 12:22-24)

This section from 1 Samuel 12 concludes a speech by the prophet Samuel to the people of Israel at King Saul's coronation. He reminded them of how many times Israel had forsaken God and how ungrateful they had been. God confirmed Samuel's words by sending thunder and rain in an unusual season.

Samuel reminded the people of God's faithfulness and love, even though they had failed many times. Samuel told them, **For the L**ORD **will not forsake His people… it has pleased the L**ORD **to make you His people**. Samuel wanted Israel to know that God loved them. Despite the sin of their past, they could continue serving the LORD and still see His blessing. His favor towards Israel was not prompted by the good they did, were doing, or promised to do. It was for His great name's sake because it pleased the LORD to do it.

Samuel said, **far be it for me that I should sin against the L**ORD **in ceasing to pray for you**. Samuel knew the best thing he could do for Israel was to pray for them. His words would make no difference if the LORD did not work in their hearts, and the best way to promote the work of the Lord in their hearts was through prayer.

Samuel's statement makes it plain: it is a sin for a leader of God's people to stop praying for them. And if it is a sin to *stop* praying, how much worse must it be to fail to *start* praying!

Samuel continued: **I will teach you the good and the right way**. So, he taught them: **Only fear the L**ORD **…for consider what great things He has done for you**. All our service, all our obedience, all our love for God should be put in this context. We do it because of the **great things He has done for** us. We do not serve God to persuade Him to do great things for us. He has done great things and asks us to receive them by faith. Then we serve Him because of the great things He has done for us.

We can only keep perspective in our Christian life if we stay focused on what great things He has done for you. If we lose perspective, everything is distorted. Many people tend to magnify their problems and lose sight of what great things He has done for them.

Don't ever forget those great things.

November 24

Do It All

And whatever you do in word or deed, do all in the name of the Lord Jesus, giving thanks to God the Father through Him. (Colossians 3:17)

We are made new men (or new women) in Jesus Christ out of the free gift of His grace. The same power that raised Jesus from the dead works in the believer, bringing new life and a new heart. The changes in the new life don't happen all at once, and the change isn't complete until we are glorified in heaven.

The new man needs instruction. He is ready to learn, and instinctively wants to obey God, so he wants to be taught. That's why the Bible gives new men and new women practical instruction on how to live – what to do and what not to do.

Occasionally, we read a wonderful summary statement, something that is easily remembered as a reliable guide to how we should live as new men and women in Jesus Christ. Colossians 3:17 is an example of this.

It first speaks to **whatever you do in word or deed**. That covers just about everything – every word spoken; every deed done. God cares about them all.

Here is what God wants us to do with every word and every deed: **do them all in the name of the Lord Jesus**. Simply said, the new man (or woman) lives his life, all his life, for Jesus. They are only interested in doing the things that can be done according to the character of Jesus, consistent with the honor of Jesus and the heart of Jesus. The new man only wants to do things that Jesus could put His name on, that Jesus would endorse.

This gives a wonderful guide for the tough choices we sometimes face. We wonder if something should be permitted or denied in our life. Ask the question: "Could Jesus put His name to this? Can I do this **in the name of the Lord Jesus**?" If you apply that to every word you speak and every deed you do, you will have a useful guide.

You can only know that if you know something about Jesus. The only genuinely reliable place to learn Jesus is from God's Word, especially the four gospels. The better you know Jesus through His Word, the better you will be able to do everything in word and deed in His name.

For certain, sometimes you will get it wrong. Yet even in those times, God will see and honor your heart, if the real goal was to say and do everything **in the name of the Lord Jesus**.

The last aspect of this is that we also do everything giving thanks to God the Father through Him. We say and do all things with an attitude of gratitude to God, remembering all He has done in the past and all He promises for the future.

In the past, present, and future, we all have reasons to be thankful – give God thanks today!

November 25

Altars and Tents

And Abram moved from there to the mountain east of Bethel, and he pitched his tent with Bethel on the west and Ai on the east; there he built an altar to the Lord and called on the name of the Lord. (Genesis 12:8)

God had told Abram to get out of his country and go to the place God would show him (Genesis 12:1). God promised Abram a *land*, a *nation*, and a *blessing*. However, if Abram was to make these promises his own, he had to follow through and obey God. Though Abram's full obedience was slow, it came over time.

True faith will embrace both God's promise and His command. The great Scottish preacher Alexander Maclaren said: "Some people's faith says that it delights in God's promises, but it does not delight in His commandments. That is no faith at all. Whoever takes God at His word, will take all His words. There is no faith without obedience; there is no true obedience without faith."

Before Abram's faith could fully inherit the promise of receiving a land, it had to obey God's command to separate from his old country and his family. God still requires that those who will receive new life in Jesus separate themselves from the damaging aspects of their old life. You really can't have it both ways. Either your faith will separate you from the world, or the world will separate you from your faith and your God.

Genesis 12:8 shows there are two emblems that can always be associated with a true man or woman of faith: the **tent** and the **altar**.

The **tent** speaks of someone who lives as a traveler; a person who is a sojourner or a pilgrim. They recognize that the land they are presently in is not their home; therefore, they live in a tent, not a house. Every true man and woman of faith recognizes that this world is not their ultimate home; they are citizens of heaven (Philippians 3:20, Ephesians 2:19). They ultimately belong to a better country, a New Jerusalem that will come down from heaven (Hebrews 13:14), not one that can be built on this earth. They live, work, and do good on earth, but always with the consciousness that they are really aliens and pilgrims; they will one day travel on to their true country.

The **altar** is the other mark of the man or woman of faith. It speaks of a life of worship and sacrifice. Though this world is not our own, while we are here, we will worship our God, obey Him, and give our life to Him as a sacrifice of service. The world will see our altars of worship, and such altars testify that there are those who honor and worship God in the land, that there are those who will sacrifice to please their God.

May God grant you the power and the grace to be such an example, and to be a witness of the tent of the pilgrim and the altar of the worshipper.

November 26

Words of a Worshipper

Behold, God is my salvation, I will trust and not be afraid;
For Yah, the Lord, is my strength and song;
He also has become my salvation.
Therefore with joy you will draw water
From the wells of salvation. (Isaiah 12:2-3)

The worshipper presented in Isaiah 12 was excited about what God has done in his life and invites everyone to **behold** the work of the Lord. He says, "I am not my salvation. My good works, my good intentions, my good thoughts do not save me. **God is my salvation**."

Many don't ever feel the need for salvation. They think their lives are fine, and they come to God for a little help when they need it. But they never see themselves as drowning men in need of rescue, or as hell-destined sinners in need of salvation.

The worshipper's peace and security come from knowing that God is his **salvation**. When we try to be our own salvation, it is hard to trust and not be afraid. Paul says in Romans 5:1: *Therefore, having been justified by faith, we have peace with God through our Lord Jesus Christ.* The place of peace and trust comes only from seeing our salvation in God, and not ourselves.

The worshipper decides to trust and not be afraid. Feelings of trust are different from the decision to trust. We can say to our will, **I will trust and not be afraid**.

The Lord is not only the worshipper's salvation, God is also his **strength and song**. When the Lord is our strength, it means that He is our resource; He is our refuge. We look to Him for our needs and are never unsatisfied. The Lord isn't part of our strength; He is our complete strength. The Lord is also our song; it means that He is our joy; He is our happiness. We find our purpose and life in Him.

Jesus promised, *whoever drinks of the water that I shall give him will never thirst. But the water that I shall give him will become in him a fountain of water springing up into everlasting life* (John 4:14). We can come to Jesus and draw water from the **wells of salvation**. When water is rare, a well is life. To have a place where you can continually come and draw forth to meet your need is a precious gift.

There is not one well of salvation. There are many **wells of salvation**. This doesn't mean there are many ways to be rescued, made right with God. All the wells draw forth from the same reservoir of salvation, Jesus Christ.

When we draw from God's wells, there is something for us to do. God calls us to activity, not passivity. We reach out and draw forth what He provides.

Because it is all from God, we draw from the wells of salvation **with joy**. There should be no sad faces at the Lord's wells of salvation.

Today, draw from what God has provided, and do it with joy.

November 27

Seeing Him and Being Like Him

Beloved, now we are children of God; and it has not yet been revealed what we shall be, but we know that when He is revealed, we shall be like Him, for we shall see Him as He is. (1 John 3:2)

Many people want to be like someone else. We see the lives of social media influencers, celebrities, and famous people and we often want to be like them. We wish that we had their talent, their fame, their glory, and their wealth.

1 John 3:2 is one place in the Bible where God promises His children that they will one day become like Jesus. We can clearly see our present status: **now we are children of God**. Yet, our future destiny is not so clearly seen; **it has not yet been revealed what we shall be**.

We don't know what in detail what we will be in the world beyond. In this sense, it is beyond our imagination what we will become when we are in heaven's glory. But we are not left entirely in the dark about our future state. When Jesus is revealed to us, either by His coming for us or by our coming to Him, **we shall be like Him**.

This does not mean that we will no longer be ourselves. In heaven, we will not lose the distinct personality and character God gave us. The biblical truth of heaven is not like the concept of Nirvana found in Eastern mysticism, where all personality is dissolved into the deity like a drop of water disappears into the ocean.

When we get to glory, we will not have our personality erased and then be re-created into "clones" of Jesus. In heaven, we will still be ourselves, but our character and nature will ultimately be perfected into the image of Jesus' perfection. You will always be you, but the perfection of love, joy, and strength that Jesus had in His humanity will also be in you.

Yet, we must ask: do you want to be like Jesus? God will never force a person to become like Jesus if they don't want to. One could say that is what hell is for: people who don't want to be like Jesus. The sobering, eternal truth is this: in the end, God gives people what they want. If you want to be like Jesus, it will show in your life now, and it will become a fact in eternity. If you don't want to be like Jesus, it will also show in your life now, and it will also become a fact in eternity.

John is careful to say, **we shall be like Him**. It is true that right now, God is working in His people to make them more like Jesus. God's great goal is to conform His people into the image of the Son, Jesus Christ (Romans 8:29). Here in 1 John 3:2, the word **shall** reminds us that even though we grow somewhat into the image of Jesus now, we still have a long way to go. None of God's transforming work in us will be finished until we see Jesus, and only then we shall indeed become like Him in our full measure.

You aren't there yet. But are you on the way?

November 28

The Breaker

The one who breaks open will come up before them; they will break out, pass through the gate, and go out by it; their king will pass before them, with the LORD at their head. (Micah 2:13)

If you spend some time reading the Minor Prophets, you get a feel for a familiar pattern – God warns of coming judgment, pleading with His people to come back in repentance and wanting a relationship with Him. Then there are generous promises of restoration, to not bring His people to despair and to assure them of His final victory. That's the familiar context.

What makes this passage special is the unique title hidden in the verse. There are many wonderful titles and names for Jesus found in the Bible, such as: Apostle, Author and Finisher of our Faith, Bread of Life, Bridegroom, Captain of Our Salvation, Chief Cornerstone, Immanuel, King of Kings, Lion of the Tribe of Judah, Lord of Lords, Lamb of God, the Last Adam, Light of the Nations, Man of Sorrows, Mediator, Prince of Peace, Root of David, Son of David, Sun of Righteousness, Word of Life.

This verse contains a special and unique name for our Messiah: "The Breaker."

The Amplified Bible translates Micah 2:13: *The Breaker [the Messiah] will go up before them. They will break through, pass in through the gate and go out through it. And their King will pass on before them, the LORD at their head.*

The King James Version has this idea: *The breaker is come up before them: they have broken up, and have passed through the gate, and are gone out by it: and their king shall pass before them, and the LORD on the head of them.*

A German translation renders the name, "Der Durchbrecher" – "The Break-Through One."

No matter how you translate it, Micah's thought is not difficult to follow. He saw Jesus here as The Breaker. In this office, He is the captain and leader of His people, advancing in front of His flock.

We need a Breaker, a trailblazer in our life! Jesus goes before us like a mighty icebreaker clearing a path so that His people can follow. We could never go forward if Jesus did not break the way, but because He has, we can and will go forward. Jesus cuts the trail, He breaks the way, and His people follow. It means that He has endured the worst, and though following behind is not always easy, it is always possible because every trial or difficulty we face has first been broken through by Jesus.

Do you see a hard path in front of you? Don't despair. Ask The Breaker to go before you and trust Him to do that. Then follow behind knowing that as hard as it might be, He has broken the way before you so that you can follow.

Today, find comfort in this more obscure title of Jesus, and when you need a breakthrough, you know Jesus can do it!

November 29

His Promise, Our Vow

Then Jacob made a vow, saying, "If God will be with me, and keep me in this way that I am going, and give me bread to eat and clothing to put on, so that I come back to my father's house in peace, then the Lord shall be my God. And this stone which I have set as a pillar shall be God's house, and of all that You give me I will surely give a tenth to You." (Genesis 28:20-22)

Sometimes we make foolish vows to God. That is why the Bible warns: *When you make a vow to God, do not delay to pay it; for He has no pleasure in fools. Pay what you have vowed — better not to vow than to vow and not pay* (Ecclesiastes 5:4-5).

In Genesis 28:20-22 Jacob was on the run from his brother who had threatened to kill him. As Jacob fled, he tried to make a deal with God. Bargaining with the Lord, he demanded a condition from God when he said, **if God will be with me**. God gave Jacob a promise, yet Jacob still tried to make "deals" with God – even promising God money if the Lord kept up His part of the deal. Look at the contrast between God's promise and Jacob's vow:

In God's promise (Genesis 28:13-15), He said: *I am the Lord God…I will give to you…. I am with you…I will not leave you until I have done what I have spoken.*

In Jacob's vow, he said: **If God will be with me…and keep me…in this way that I am going…give me bread and clothing…so that I come back to my father's house.**

God promise was, "This is what I will do for you." Jacob's vow was, "It's all about me." The promise was God-centered, and the vow was man-centered.

Jacob should have prayed something like this: "Lord, because You have promised to be with me and to keep me and provide for all my needs and bring me back to the land which you swore to give to my fathers and to me, I will surrender completely to You."

Jacob tried to set the terms of his covenant with God instead of humbly receiving what God had promised. Jacob was not submitted to God, but God would use the coming years to teach him submission. God was gracious and willing to be called the God of Abraham, the God of Isaac, and the God of Jacob (Exodus 3:6). Despite the foolish vow, God kept His promise.

The way Jacob prayed it was evident God's Word was not enough for him. He had to see God do it before he could believe. Are we the same way? God says, *my God shall supply all your need according to His riches in glory by Christ Jesus* (Philippians 4:19). He says, *The Lord is good, a stronghold in the day of trouble; and He knows those who trust in Him* (Nahum 1:7).

Do you believe such things before you can see them? Today, put more trust in God's promise than in your vows.

November 30

Miraculous Power, Miraculous Love

When He had come down from the mountain, great multitudes followed Him. And behold, a leper came and worshiped Him, saying, "Lord, if You are willing, You can make me clean." (Matthew 8:1-2)

After His Sermon on the Mount (Matthew 5-7) Jesus came down from the mountain and He once again attracted a crowd. The miracles of Jesus drew attention, as did His teaching ministry.

One man came to Jesus with a terrible disease: **Behold, a leper came and worshipped Him**. In the ancient world, leprosy was a horrible, destructive disease – and it still is in some places. The leper had no hope of improvement, so he came to Jesus with a great sense of need and desperation. Over 20 or 30 years, a leper might lose hands and feet; leprosy was, as William Barclay wrote, "a kind of terrible progressive death in which a man dies by inches."

The condition of leprosy was a picture of sin and its effects. It was a contagious, debilitating disease that corrupted its victim and made him nearly dead while alive. Almost universally, society and religious people scorned lepers. Many rabbis especially despised lepers and saw them as people under God's special judgment, deserving no pity or mercy.

Nevertheless, this leper came to Jesus by himself, and despite many discouragements.

- The leper knew how terrible his problem was.
- He knew that other people gave up on him as having a hopeless condition.
- He had no one who would or could take him to Jesus.
- He had no previous example of Jesus healing a leper to give him hope.
- He had no promise that Jesus would heal him.
- He had no invitation from Jesus or the disciples.
- He must have felt ashamed and alone in the crowd.

Like this leper, we should be willing to come to Jesus through many discouragements. The leper didn't only beg to be made better, he also worshipped Jesus. When he asked, the leper said it like this: **Lord, if You are willing**. The leper had no doubt about the *ability* of Jesus to heal, and only asked if Jesus was **willing** to heal.

The leper believed in the power of Jesus. Leprosy was so hopeless in the ancient world that healing a leper was compared to raising the dead, yet this leper knew that all Jesus needed was to be willing. He believed in the power of Jesus; he wasn't so sure about the love and concern of Jesus for his problem. It is often easier for us to believe in miraculous power than in miraculous love.

The good news is that Jesus showed both miraculous power and miraculous love to this leper. This is another reason we should be willing to fight through whatever discouragements come our way to bring ourselves to Jesus.

Today, you can receive from both His miraculous power and His miraculous love.

December 1

The Glorious Branch

In that day the Branch of the LORD shall be beautiful and glorious; and the fruit of the earth shall be excellent and appealing for those of Israel who have escaped. (Isaiah 4:2)

The end of Isaiah chapter 3 spoke of the great judgment coming against a disobedient Israel; God promised devastating exile would come to Israel. Yet, as is often the case, God did not prophesy coming judgment without also promising a glorious restoration. To powerfully communicate the restoration, the prophet used the word-picture of a branch, the **Branch of the LORD**. This is a wonderful Messianic title, used prophetically of Jesus Christ.

The ideas behind the title **Branch of the LORD** are those of fruitfulness and life. Jesus used the same image when He said that He was the vine, and we are the branches (John 15:5). We are to think of a healthy, strong branch, flowing with life and sap, shooting forth smaller green branches, and bringing good fruit. Not only does the branch itself surge with life, but everything connected to it also does. If one is not connected to the branch, it is cut off from the source of life.

Isaiah 11:1 announced, *there shall come forth a Rod from the stem of Jesse, and a Branch shall grow out of his roots.* The idea is that the living Branch springs up from a dead stump; that the life and vitality of Jesus the Messiah is a life full of resurrection power.

Jeremiah 23:5 declared, *Behold, the days are coming," says the LORD, "That I will raise to David a Branch of righteousness; a King shall reign and prosper, and execute judgment and righteousness in the earth.* Jeremiah 33:15 used the same idea of the *Branch of righteousness*, emphasizing the idea that this is not a wild branch that grows in an uncontrolled, out-of-boundaries way. It grows in righteousness and order.

The idea was repeated in Zechariah 3:8: *For behold, I am bringing forth My Servant the Branch.* Zechariah said this would be a *wondrous sign*; a sign showing that God could not only bring forth a branch full of such life but also that all those connected to His branch would also receive this glorious life.

We see in Isaiah 4:2 that the **Branch of the LORD** is beautiful and glorious. He also brings forth fruit: **the fruit of the earth shall be excellent and appealing**. It makes us wonder why our life sometimes lacks this **excellent and appealing** fruit. When there is this lack, instead of condemning yourself, just check your connection to the **Branch of the LORD**. Abiding in Jesus is the sure and certain way to bring forth this wonderful fruit.

Remember those great words from the **Branch of the LORD** Himself at John 15:5: *I am the vine* [the big branch], *you are the branches* [the little branches]. *He who abides in Me, and I in him, bears much fruit; for without Me you can do nothing.* Today, abide in Jesus Christ, the **Branch of the LORD**.

December 2

Open Your Ear

The Lord God has given Me the tongue of the learned, that I should know how to speak a word in season to him who is weary. He awakens Me morning by morning, He awakens My ear to hear as the learned. The Lord God has opened My ear; and I was not rebellious, nor did I turn away. (Isaiah 50:4-5)

Isaiah 50 is a deep and wonderful chapter describing the greatness of God's Ultimate Servant, the Messiah. In presenting The Servant, Isaiah beautifully shows the steadfast obedience of the Servant of the Lord, the Messiah.

Isaiah prophetically spoke on behalf of the Messiah: **The Lord God has given Me the tongue of the learned**. He explains that the Lord God gave Him the ability to speak wisely, but for what purpose? **To speak a word in season to him who is weary.**

Our Messiah used His intelligence and eloquence to strengthen discouraged and broken people. It is worth going through the gospels and noticing all the kind words Jesus spoke to others.

In His daily, **morning by morning** fellowship with His Father, in His humanity Jesus received strength and guidance (**He awakens My ear to hear as the learned**). The Messiah could speak with the tongue of the learned because in daily time with God He learned to hear as the learned.

The Messiah continues: **The Lord God has opened My ear, and I was not rebellious**. This looks back to a custom described in Exodus 21:5-6, where a servant became a willing slave to his master. The sign of this willing servant was the ear opened by the piercing of an awl, done against the entry doorway of the master. This speaks of the total submission of the Messiah to the Lord God.

If, after the six years of servitude, a servant wished to make a life-long commitment to his master – considering the master's goodness and his blessings for the servant – he could, through this ceremony, make a life-long commitment to his master. This was a commitment not motivated by debt or obligation but only love for the master.

In the ceremony, the servant's ear would be pierced – **opened** – with an awl, in the presence of witnesses – then, *he shall serve him forever* (Exodus 21:5-6). Psalm 40:6 also speaks of this ceremony taking place between the Father and the Son, where the psalmist speaks prophetically for the Messiah: *Sacrifice and offering You did not desire; my ears You have opened.* Jesus was a perfect Servant to the Father (Philippians 2:7).

When we think of "opening our ears," we usually think of hearing better. Isaiah points us towards another meaning that is also necessary and glorious: the idea that we, like our Messiah, should offer ourselves as such willing servants of God. We are His servants, bound to Him not by debt or obligation but only out of love.

Has He opened your ear?

December 3

Time to Wake Up

And do this, knowing the time, that now it is high time to awake out of sleep; for now our salvation is nearer than when we first believed. (Romans 13:11)

Accident investigators say the car was airborne for about 150 feet (30 meters) before it crashed through the roof of Joanne and Mahlon Donovan's house in Derry, New Hampshire. It was about 3:00 in the morning, and a 20-year-old woman who was later arrested for drunk driving drove the car. Her car came crashing through the ceiling and dropped right over the Donovan's bed. "The thing was right in front of my face," Mr. Donovan, 65, said. "I could feel the heat from the exhaust system coming right through the sheets."

That car crashing into a house was scary enough. But there was an even more frightening aspect to that accident. According to the Associated Press story, the wife of the home, Joanne Donovan, didn't wake up. She slept right through it. Mr. Donovan had to shake her awake after the crash.

It's amazing what people can sleep through. God can do a fantastic work among many, but others sleep right through it, spiritually speaking. In Romans 13:11, we find out what it takes to keep us awake, or to awaken us from our spiritual slumber.

First, Paul wrote about **knowing the time**. Often, when we oversleep it is because we didn't know the time. We wake up late, and in a panic look for the time, and get a sick feeling – "I'm late! I overslept!" Spiritually speaking, if we know **the time** we are in, then we won't sleep when we shouldn't. And when we look around at the world today with open eyes and an open Bible, we see that the time is short. If we really believe Jesus is coming soon, if we know the time – then we will wake up.

Second, Paul wrote about what would happen at the right time: **now our salvation is nearer than when we first believed**. The coming of Jesus, and the completion of our salvation, is closer than ever. Every day since you first decided to follow Jesus, the time has become closer and closer, and the finishing of your salvation is nearer and nearer. When we remember how wonderful it will be to have our salvation finished – no more sin, no more death, no more of the frailty of this flesh – it will keep us awake.

Right now, are you taking a spiritual nap? Perhaps there is some spiritual activity in your life, but you might as well be sleepwalking through it. So, the right prayer for you today is, "Lord, wake me up. Help me to know it is time to awaken. Get me excited about the completion of my salvation." God loves to answer that kind of prayer.

Even if you are sleeping so soundly that if a car crashed through the roof of your house, you wouldn't know it – God can still wake you up and keep you awake for His glory.

December 4

Wandering and Returning

Brethren, if anyone among you wanders from the truth, and someone turns him back, let him know that he who turns a sinner from the error of his way will save a soul from death and cover a multitude of sins. (James 5:19-20)

In the previous verses, James introduced the topics of sin and confession. Now, in writing, **if anyone among you wanders from the truth**, James reminds us of the need to confront those who have wandered from the truth. James is dealing with those who were numbered among the Christian community (**if anyone among you**). Those who wandered in this dangerous way were professed Christians.

James presented a helpful picture with the phrase, **wanders from the truth**. Most people don't wander on purpose – it just sort of happens. Nonetheless, it still gets them off track and possibly in danger.

James knew that God could use people to help bring them back to spiritual safety and health. That is why he wrote, **and someone turns him back**. This shows us that God uses human instruments in turning sinners back from the errors of their ways.

God can work without human instruments in bringing back wanderers, but He often chooses to use willing, obedient people. One reason is that it brings Him more glory than if He were to do His work by Himself.

When we refuse to make ourselves available to God's service – weak and failing as we are – we rob God of some of His glory. He can glorify Himself through a weak vessel like you; you should let Him do it.

We should seek out those who have wandered from the faith and seek to win them back. These are beautiful miracles of grace, and those who work with God to restore those wandering in danger have done significant work. Seek them with prayers, seek them with tears, and seek them with warm, persuasive words.

The reward is great for the one who **turns a sinner from** their **error**. A soul is saved from death, and many sins are covered. There is a blessing for the one who loves his brother enough to confront him, and who turns him from the error of his way. He has saved that soul from death and covered a multitude of sins.

This speaks powerfully of the restoration possible for those who have sinned. Someone can turn from the error of his way and see his soul saved from death. When a person has been restored – especially if the time of their wandering is long past – it's sad when others still remember them as the one who had sinned instead of the one who has been restored. We should choose to remember them for the greatness of their turning from error, instead of their wandering into it.

Today, is there someone wandering that you can pray for? Perhaps God would want you to do more than pray, but certainly it begins with that. God may work powerfully through you to help another.

December 5

Blessings to Healed Backsliders

I will heal their backsliding, I will love them freely, for My anger has turned away from him. I will be like the dew to Israel; he shall grow like the lily, and lengthen his roots like Lebanon. His branches shall spread; his beauty shall be like an olive tree, and his fragrance like Lebanon. Those who dwell under his shadow shall return; they shall be revived like grain, and grow like a vine. Their scent shall be like the wine of Lebanon. (Hosea 14:4-7)

All through Hosea, God spoke to a backslidden Israel. Here, God promised to **heal** ther **backsliding**. God saw that Israel was bent on backsliding from Him (Hosea 11:7), but He promised to heal the backsliding of a repentant Israel. Not because Israel deserved it, but because it was in His nature to love them freely.

This promise is *compassionate*. God looks on our backsliding more like a disease than a crime. He did not say, "I will pardon their backsliding." It is as if God sees His poor, weak people and remembers that they are only dust, they easily fall prey to a hundred temptations and they quickly go astray.

The promise is *certain*. **I will heal their backsliding** is a definite word. God did not say, "I might heal" or "I could heal" or "I can try to heal," but **I will heal their backsliding**. If we come to God for healing of our backsliding, He will do it!

The word is *personal*. **I will heal their backsliding** speaks of specific people; God addressed them personally. We must come to the Great Physician and say, "Heal my backsliding. I want to be one of those who are healed." To get the healing, you must count yourself among the backsliders.

The word is *powerful*. When God says, **I will heal their backsliding** He does not mean a little healing or a partial healing. He intends to do a great, complete restoration. This passage shows us all that is restored when we return to the Lord from our season of backsliding:

- Growth is restored (**He shall grow**).
- Beauty is restored (**He shall grow like the lily**).
- Strength is restored (**Lengthen his roots like Lebanon**).
- Value is restored (**His beauty shall be like an olive tree**).
- Delight is restored (**His fragrance like Lebanon**).
- Abundance is restored (**Revived like grain…grow like the vine.... scent shall be like the wine of Lebanon**).

Best of all, the promise of restoration means that the formerly backslidden one will become a blessing to others. **His branches will spread** suggests a broad tree that provides fruit, shade, and shelter to others. When God restores His people, they then become a blessing to others.

Don't let the cancer of a backslidden relationship with God eat away at your strength. Take Him up on His gracious and generous promise of restoration.

December 6

Hearts Assured

And by this we know that we are of the truth, and shall assure our hearts before Him. For if our heart condemns us, God is greater than our heart, and knows all things. (1 John 3:19-20)

It is a terrible thing to lack social confidence. Sometimes when others are around, we wonder if our breath smells bad, if our hair is a mess, or if we smell like sweat. It feels terrible to lack social assurance – to wonder if we belong among a group and if they accept us.

Years ago, advertisements took advantage of the lack of assurance we often feel in social situations. In those ads, everybody noticed body odor or bad breath – but no one told the person, and the person suffered some social disgrace.

It's terrible to lack social assurance, but what about assurance before God? John's point is simple. When we see God's love flowing through our lives into the lives of others, **we know that we are of the truth, and shall assure our hearts before Him.**

Gayle Erwin (www.servant.org) tells a wonderful story about Jake, the meanest, drunkest man in town. He came to church occasionally, but only to beat up the elders. One night, Jake came to church, but not to beat anybody up. Remarkably, Jake gave his life to Jesus. He walked down the aisle and kneeled at the altar. The next night the pastor asked if anyone wanted to share what God had done in their life. Jake stood and said: "I have something to say. Last night when I came I hated you people." Heads nodded. "But something happened to me and I don't understand, but tonight I love you." Having that kind of love is a great assurance that we are born again!

But what if we walk in love, yet our hearts condemn us before God? John assures us that **God is greater than our heart**. It reminds us that we cannot base our relationship with Him purely on how we feel in His presence. Condemnation may rise inside, having nothing to do with our standing before God. It may be the work of the enemy of our souls (who, according to Revelation 12:10 accuses the brethren), or the work of an over-active conscience. At those times, we trust what God's Word says about our standing, not how we feel about it.

Yet, when we are in fellowship with God, and **our heart does not condemn us**, we know that we can have confidence toward God and our standing with Him. Confidence comes from a double dose of assurance. First, God already knows everything about you, and He loves you, He cares for you, and He desires you. Second, because God **knows all things**, He knows who we truly are in Jesus Christ. If we are born again, the real self is the self that is created in the image of Jesus.

Today, let your assurance rest in the God who is greater than your heart.

December 7

The God of All Comfort

Blessed be the God and Father of our Lord Jesus Christ, the Father of mercies and God of all comfort, who comforts us in all our tribulation, that we may be able to comfort those who are in any trouble, with the comfort with which we ourselves are comforted by God. (2 Corinthians 1:3-4)

How would Paul know about God's comfort? He was constantly in uncomfortable circumstances where if he didn't have the comfort of God, he would have no comfort at all.

Paul described some of these uncomfortable circumstances in 2 Corinthians 11:23-28. In that passage he relates how he was beaten, imprisoned, stoned, and shipwrecked for the cause of Jesus Christ. He was in peril from robbers, from his fellow Jews, from Gentiles, in cities, in the wilderness, in the sea, and among false brothers. Paul suffered from weariness and toil, sleeplessness, hunger, thirst, and exposure. If the man who went through all that says that God is the **God of all comfort**, then we should believe him.

The word for **all comfort** in this passage is the ancient Greek word *paraklesis*. The idea behind this word for **comfort** in the New Testament is always more than soothing sympathy. It has means strengthening, helping, and making strong. The idea behind this word is communicated by the Latin word for comfort (*fortis*), which also means, "brave."

When Paul said that God the Father is the **God of all comfort**, he tells us that the Father is our *Paraclete*, our comforter or helper. We also know the Holy Spirit is our *Paraclete* (Jesus said so in John 14:16, 14:26, 15:26, and 16:7) and that God the Son is our *Paraclete* (according to 1 John 2:1, Hebrews 2:18, and Luke 2:25). God in every aspect of His being is full of comfort, strength, and help for us!

God isn't just full of comfort and strength *for* us; He is also full of comfort and strength *through* us. This is what Paul meant when he wrote **that we may be able to comfort those who are in any trouble**. One great purpose of God's comfort to us is so that we can bring comfort to others.

Doesn't this explain why we sometimes go uncomforted? It's because we refuse to look for comfort or receive comfort through another person. Often, we never receive the comfort God wants to give us because He wants to give it through another person. Pride can keep us from revealing our needs to others, so we never receive the comfort God would give us through them.

With all the apostle Paul suffered, he knew the great comfort of God. Sometimes God brought the comfort to Paul directly, and sometimes He brought it through another person. With such a great God, and with all three Persons of the Trinity working to bring us comfort, there's no reason for us to go uncomforted.

Today, put away pride and receive His comfort, letting Him decide how He will give it to you. It's a comforting thought!

December 8

Beyond Casual Contact

And Jesus, immediately knowing in Himself that power had gone out of Him, turned around in the crowd and said, "Who touched My clothes?" But His disciples said to Him, "You see the multitude thronging You, and You say, 'Who touched Me?'" And He looked around to see her who had done this thing. (Mark 5:30-32)

Here at a village on the shores of the Sea of Galilee – probably Capernaum – Jesus was on His way to visit the sick daughter of the ruler of the local synagogue. She was near death and then died before Jesus reached her. Still, on the way, something unusual happened.

In the crowd with dozens pressing in on Jesus through the narrow streets, a woman secretly touched the hem of Jesus' garment and touched that hem in faith that she would be healed. Her faith was rewarded – she touched, believed, and was healed of a 12-year ailment.

Then Jesus did something unexpected and interesting. In Mark 5:30, Jesus asked: **Who touched My clothes?** The disciples were amazed that Jesus could ask this question. His disciples questioned Him, **You see the multitude thronging You, and You say, "Who touched Me?"** But the disciples did not understand the difference between *casual contact* with Jesus and reaching out to *touch Him in faith*.

Because of the pressing crowd, there were dozens and dozens of people who made some kind of physical contact with Jesus. When the woman's miracle was revealed, those people might say, "I bumped into Jesus, I touched Him, yet I was not healed."

There is a vast difference between bumping into Jesus and reaching out to touch Him in faith. You can come to the gathering of God's people week after week and "bump into" Jesus. That is not the same as reaching out to touch Him in faith. Casual contact with Jesus is better than no contact at all, but the best connection with Him is that of active, believing faith.

Some attend church services, or a gathering of Christians and they feel that others receive something, but they do not. I can't say that it applies to every situation, but in many cases, the difference is that some reach out to Jesus in faith, and others have casual contact with Him.

Not every contact with Jesus brings salvation. One can be in the presence of Jesus and "bump" into Him. It is the determined, decided, dedicated believing connection to Jesus that brings all we need from Him.

Jesus knows whenever someone reaches out to touch Him in faith, and He never disappoints.

Decide today not to be satisfied with a mere casual contact with Jesus; reach out to Him with the same heart of faith that this woman had.

December 9

Day and Night

**But his delight is in the law of the Lord,
And in His law he meditates day and night.** (Psalm 1:2)

Psalm 1 is a beautiful contrast between the way of the righteous and the way of the ungodly. It begins by telling us what the righteous man does not do. He does not walk in the counsel of the ungodly, he does not stand in the path of sinners, and he does not sit in the seat of the scornful (Psalm 1:1).

Then in verse 2, the psalmist tells us what the righteous man does, in fact, do.

First, **his delight is in the law of the Lord**. Throughout the Psalms, the **law of the Lord** is used to describe God's entire word, not only the "law" portion of the first five books of the Bible. The righteous man is delighted with the Word of God.

What makes you happy? What gets you excited? This is a good way to see what is important to you. If personal pleasure is the only thing that makes you happy, then it would seem to mean that you are a selfish, self-centered person. If being with your family or friends delights you, that is far better, but it is still not yet complete. The righteous man loves the good things God blesses us with in this world, but also finds that **his delight is in the law of the Lord**.

If a person delights in something, you don't have to beg them to do it or to like it. In the same pattern, you can measure your delight for the Word of God by how much you hunger for it.

The delight is shown in a second way: **in His law he meditates day and night**. The righteous man ponders the Word of God. He does not just hear it and forget it; he thinks about it. Christians should meditate on God's Word.

In eastern meditation, the goal is to empty the mind. This is dangerous, because an empty mind may present an open invitation to deception or a demonic spirit. But in Christian meditation, the goal is to fill your mind with the Word of God. This can be done by carefully thinking about each word and phrase, and applying it, and praying Bible-soaked prayers back to the Lord.

Many people live poor spiritual lives because they only *read* and do not *meditate* on what God says in the Bible.

Finally, we see that the righteous man has God's Word on his mind only two times a day: **day and night**. That about covers it all!

The next verse – Psalm 1:3 – tells of the wonderful blessing that God has for the one who meets Him in His Word like this. You want that kind of blessing in your life; you need it. Find it by delighting in God's Word, the Bible, and by filling your mind with the truth of the Bible and feeding on it. Blessing belongs to those who do it!

December 10

Happy People or New Men?

Happy are the people who are in such a state; happy are the people whose God is the LORD! (Psalm 144:15)

There was a time when everyone thought the most important question was, "How can I be right with God?" Now, for most people, the most important question is "How can I be happy?" The author C.S. Lewis had something to say to those searching for happiness: "I didn't go to religion to make me happy. I always knew that a bottle of Port would do that. If you want a religion to make you feel really comfortable, I certainly don't recommend Christianity."

Some professing Christians, about as much as anyone else, make an idol of the happy life. Usually, we judge how good something is based on how happy it makes us. If it makes us happy, we think it is good. If it doesn't make us happy, it is bad.

We must remove the idol of happiness and learn a new habit of thinking. It isn't that God's goal is for us to be unhappy. His goal is for our ultimate happiness and fulfillment; but idolatry of immediate happiness often gets in the way of ultimate fulfillment. God's greatest purpose in our lives is not to make us happy in the here-and-now, but to transform us into godly people – people who are becoming more and more like Jesus. Romans 8:29 explains it like this: *For whom He foreknew, He also predestinated to be conformed to the image of His Son.*

God loves us too much to allow us to worship at the altar of the "happy life" for very long. The Lord has a way of bringing circumstances to pass, forcing us to focus more on godliness than on happiness. If you find yourself in those difficult circumstances, don't resent it. Don't think that God wants you to be unhappy. It's just that He cares more about your godliness than your happiness. The happiness will settle itself as we pursue Jesus.

This is one great secret of life: that happiness is most securely achieved when we put godliness first. Happiness is like a bird that flies about, and if we set our focus on chasing it, it just flies further away. But when we set our heart on God and His kingdom, the bird of happiness will set down right on our shoulder.

David the psalmist knew this: *Surely goodness and mercy shall follow me all the days of my life* (Psalm 23:6). David wasn't concerned with following goodness and mercy – he followed God's path, and then goodness and mercy followed him. When we seek God and His kingdom first, He promises to take care of us – including our happiness.

In another psalm David explained it like this, saying to God: *You will show me the path of life; in Your presence is fullness of joy; at Your right hand are pleasures forevermore.* (Psalm 16:11)

In the likeness of Jesus, at the end of it all is ultimate satisfaction, perfect fulfillment.

December 11

What Makes God Laugh

**He who sits in the heavens shall laugh;
The LORD shall hold them in derision.** (Psalm 2:4)

We do not often think of God as laughing, though we should more than we do. The God presented on the Bible's pages is not depressed and is not filled with fear or anxiety. God has the settled confidence of the one who both knows and controls the future. Plus, when God sees man – in both his glory and foolishness – it must often make Him smile.

Psalm 2 tells us God laughs because man thinks he can plot and work against God with a hope of success. When nations, people, and even kings conspire against the LORD and His Messiah, it is laughable to think they could succeed (Psalm 2:1-3) God is not afraid, confused, or depressed about the opposition of man. Securely seated in heaven, God **shall laugh** at man's opposition.

God laughs because He **sits in the heavens**. He sits as the Great King on a glorious throne. He is not pacing back and forth in the throne room of heaven, wondering what He should do next. God sits in perfect peace and assurance on His throne of authority over all creation. What does heaven have to fear from earth?

God does not laugh at the suffering of humankind, or their suffering because of sin. God laughs at the proud man or woman who thinks so highly of themselves that they will fight against God and seek to prevent His will.

Through the centuries, many have opposed God and His Kingdom in Jesus Christ. Each one of these opponents has been and shall be frustrated and crushed; God shall **hold them in derision**.

A famous example of an opponent of Christianity was the Roman Emperor Diocletian (AD 245-313). He was such a determined enemy of Christians that he persecuted the church without mercy and wanted to believe that he had defeated Christianity. He struck a medal with this inscription: "The name of Christianity being extinguished."

Diocletian also built two monuments on the frontier of his empire with these inscriptions:

> *Diocletian Jovian Maximian Herculeus Caesares Augusti for having extended the Roman Empire in the east and the west and for having extinguished the name of Christians who brought the Republic to ruin.*

> *Diocletian Jovian Maximian Herculeus Caesares Augusti for having everywhere abolished the superstition of Christ for having extended the worship of the gods.*

Diocletian is dead and gone, a few paragraphs on the pages of history. The LORD **shall hold them in derision**!

Be happy that the fame and glory of Jesus Christ are spread over all the earth.

December 12
Holding Fast to the True Word

I am small and despised, yet I do not forget Your precepts. Your righteousness is an everlasting righteousness, and Your law is truth. (Psalm 119:141-142)

The writer of Psalm 119 was a confident man, yet even so, he knew that sometimes others had little regard for him. He wrote, **I am small and despised, yet I do not forget Your precepts**. The psalmist felt insignificant, both in his estimation (**small**) and in estimation of others (**despised**). Yet, he found comfort and strength in remembering the Word of God.

We think of others who have been small and despised – young men like David (1 Samuel 16:10-13) and older men like Paul (2 Corinthians 11). Yet they found courage in God and understood God by His Word.

It also shows us that the psalmist would not neglect God's Word when he was depressed or downcast. **Small and despised** does not feel good, yet he still remembered God's Word when he felt this way. It is common to run away from precisely what we need when we feel **small and despised**.

We're also assured that these were actual words from the psalmist and not merely projecting humility. He wasn't the type to say, "See how humble I am." He genuinely felt small and despised.

He didn't continue to look at himself; instead, he saw **Your righteousness is an everlasting righteousness, and Your law is truth**. The psalmist confidently stated the everlasting character of God's righteousness; He is righteous and will not change. What God is, He always will be. Connected to that, he proclaimed that this unchanging God had given us a word (**Your law**) that is truth.

That phrase, **Your law is truth**, makes us remember the conversation between Jesus and Pontus Pilate. Jesus said, *For this cause I was born, and for this cause I have come into the world, that I should bear witness to the truth. Everyone who is of the truth hears My voice.* Pilate's cynical reply was, *What is truth?* (John 18:37-38) For Pilate, soldiers and armies were truth; Rome was truth; Caesar was truth; political power was truth. Yet Jesus knew what truth was, while Pilate was still seeking. Jesus knew perfectly what the psalmist also knew, God's **law is truth**.

This is especially meaningful in a day when relativism has a stronghold in the everyday thinking of people. It is common for people today to think there is no such thing as "real" truth; there is only your truth and my truth and their truth. Western society used to believe that truth was that which directly related to reality; now, truth is often held to be what makes sense or is helpful to me individually.

The late Christian philosopher Francis Schaeffer used to promote the idea of "true truth." His concept was that the biblical message is valid fundamentally, apart from how one receives it or how it works in one's life. Schaeffer knew what the psalmist knew, and what you can know today: God's **law is truth**.

December 13

They Feared the LORD, Yet...

So they feared the LORD, and from every class they appointed for themselves priests of the high places, who sacrificed for them in the shrines of the high places. They feared the LORD, yet served their own gods — according to the rituals of the nations from among whom they were carried away. (2 Kings 17:32-33)

God brought His judgment against the kingdom of Israel – the ten northern tribes – through the army of Assyria. The Assyrians forced them to relocate to other parts of the empire. Then they brought in the conquered from other lands, to re-populate the now empty land of Israel.

But these foreign newcomers to the land of Israel didn't honor the God of Israel. The LORD, Yahweh, the covenant God of Israel, sent His judgment against these newcomers for their idolatry. So, the Assyrians sent a priest from among the Israelites removed from the land, sending him to teach the newcomers about the LORD. The newcomers did what the priest told them to do – in part. They didn't honor God completely.

2 Kings 17:29 says that *every nation continued to make gods of its own*. The priest-for-hire brought in by the Assyrians did not tell the new inhabitants of the land that they must *only* worship the LORD God of Israel. He did not teach it because, coming from Israel, he did not believe it.

2 Kings 17:33 says it well: **They feared the LORD, yet served their own gods**. This described the *pagan* peoples that the Assyrians brought in to populate the area of the Northern Kingdom of Israel. They gave a measure of respect to the God of Israel – after all, they did not want to be eaten by lions. Yet they also served their own gods and picked and chose among religious and spiritual beliefs as it pleased them.

This accurately described the pagan newcomers who re-populated Israel. This accurately described the *Kingdom of Israel* before they were conquered and exiled This accurately describes *common religious belief* in the modern world – today.

Don't you know many people like this? They give some respect to God, and maybe even attend church. Others might look at them and think, "that is someone who fears the Lord." Despite all that, they serve their own gods.

Charles Spurgeon said this in 1876: "Is not worldly piety, or pious worldliness, the current religion of England? They live among godly people, and God chastens them, and they therefore fear him, but not enough to give their hearts to him." What Spurgeon said of England is true of many more nations since his time. Is it true of you?

We may bow down before many of our **own gods**. Ask God to examine your heart and life for hidden idolatry.

December 14

A Good Kind of Jealousy

Adulterers and adulteresses! Do you not know that friendship with the world is enmity with God? Whoever therefore wants to be a friend of the world makes himself an enemy of God. Or do you think that the Scripture says in vain, "The Spirit who dwells in us yearns jealously"? (James 4:4-5)

James addressed the problem of conflict among those in the Christian family. He points to a root cause of these conflicts, and he does it powerfully, confronting his readers with this accusation: **Adulterers and adulteresses!** God spoke this way in the Old Testament when His people were attracted to some form of idolatry (Jeremiah 3:8-9, Ezekiel 6:9, Hosea 3:1). As James saw it here, their covetousness was **friendship with the world** and idolatry (Colossians 3:5).

According to many scholars, better ancient Greek manuscripts only say **you adulteresses**. This fits well, because according to the image, God is the "husband," and we are His "wife" (as in Isaiah 54:5, Jeremiah 3:20, and Exodus 34:15-16).

Having his readers' attention, James explained: **Do you not know that friendship with the world is enmity with God?** James recognized that we could not be friends of the world system in rebellion against God and be friends of God at the same time (Matthew 6:24). Even the *desire* to be a friend of the world (**wants to be a friend**) makes that one an enemy of God.

The strong statements James made here remind us that all was not beautiful in the early church. They had plenty of carnality and worldliness to deal with. While the New Testament church is a pattern for us, we should not over-romanticize the spiritual character of early Christians.

Despite their problems, James was confident that God was at work in his readers: **The Spirit who dwells in us yearns jealously**. The indwelling presence of the Holy Spirit has a jealous yearning for our friendship with God. The Spirit will convict the Christian who lives in compromise.

James agreed with the many passages in the Old Testament that tell us God is a jealous God (Deuteronomy 32:16, Exodus 20:5, Zechariah 8:2). When we say God is jealous, we mean that He loves us so deeply that He cannot approve of any competing love. Think of the inner pain and torture inside the person who is betrayed by an unfaithful spouse, who must reckon with the truth, "I am faithful to them, but they are not faithful to me." This is what the Spirit of God feels regarding our world-loving hearts.

Do you feel the jealousy of God in your life? The sense that God disapproves of the idols we make and cling to whatever form they may take? If so, please remember that *this is a good thing*. It shows the depth of God's love for you and points you to the kind of relationship with Him that He created you for.

Learn to appreciate His jealous love for you.

December 15

The Choice Between Two Visions

The lamp of the body is the eye. If therefore your eye is good, your whole body will be full of light. But if your eye is bad, your whole body will be full of darkness. If therefore the light that is in you is darkness, how great is that darkness! (Matthew 6:22-23)

In this section of the Sermon on the Mount, Jesus emphasized the idea that His followers must make choices – choosing between two treasures, between two visions, and between two masters. To follow Jesus means that one must decide not to follow anything or anyone contrary to Him.

Jesus used the illustration of light and the human eye, saying, **the lamp of the body is the eye**. The idea is that light comes into the body through the eye. If our eyes were blind, we would live in a dark world.

Here, having a **good** eye is understood either as being generous or as being single-minded. Some think that Jesus deliberately chose wording that had both meanings because both principles apply to the disciple's attitude towards material things.

Truly, being generous brings **light** to our lives. We are happier and more content when we have God's heart of generosity. But if we are not generous, it is as if **your whole body will be full of darkness**.

Truly, being single-minded brings **light** to our lives, and we are also happier and more content when we focus on the kingdom of God and His righteousness, knowing that all the material things will be added to us (Matthew 6:33). But when we are double-minded, it is as if **your whole body is full of darkness**. Living for two masters puts a dark shadow over everything in our life.

This choice between two visions has a similar consequence, either to be **full of light** or **full of darkness**. In any case, Jesus told us that either our eye is directed at heavenly things (and therefore **full of light**) or it is directed at earthly things (and consequently **full of darkness**).

Jesus reminded us that if we are blind in our eyes, the whole body is blind. The darkness is then significant in our entire body. Similarly, our attitude towards material treasure will either bring great light or **great** darkness to our lives.

Often a materialistic, miserly, selfish Christian justifies their sin by saying, "It's just one area of my life." But even as the darkness of the eye affects everything in the body, so a wrong attitude towards material things can bring darkness to our whole being.

The words of Jesus call us to a choice – a vision full of light or under darkness. A choice that seems rather small turns out to be very large – as big as the difference between light and darkness. The cost of choosing selfishness and double mindedness is more than we can afford.

Today, by God's grace choose to be both generous and single-minded.

December 16

The Choice Between Two Treasures

Do not lay up for yourselves treasures on earth, where moth and rust destroy and where thieves break in and steal; but lay up for yourselves treasures in heaven, where neither moth nor rust destroys and where thieves do not break in and steal. For where your treasure is, there your heart will be also. (Matthew 6:19-21)

In this great sermon – perhaps the most excellent sermon ever preached – Jesus now focused His attention on the place of material things in a disciple's life. He began by saying, **do not lay up for yourselves treasures on earth**. The ancient Greek more literally says *do not treasure for yourself treasures on earth*. The idea is that earthly treasure is temporary and fading away (**where moth and rust destroy and where thieves break in and steal**), but heavenly treasure is secure.

The problem isn't that earthly treasures are evil in themselves, but they are of no ultimate value. If this is the case, then it's wrong for the disciple of Jesus to dedicate their life to continually expanding their earthly treasures.

To **lay up for yourselves treasure on earth** is also to doom yourself to a life of frustration and emptiness. We typically think we would have to have double our income to find the good life. Regarding material things, the secret to happiness is not in having more, but in having contentment. The apostle Paul had the right idea in 1 Timothy 6:6: *Now godliness with contentment is great gain.*

Yet notice what Jesus said. He didn't say that it was wrong to have earthly treasures, but He did say that it was wrong to **lay up** such treasure **for yourself**. Whatever we have, we must hold as stewards or managers, understanding that it all belongs to God and not to ourselves.

Then Jesus set it in the positive: **But lay up for yourselves treasures in heaven**. In contrast to treasure on earth, heavenly treasures are everlasting and incorruptible. **Treasures in heaven** give enjoyment now, in the contentment and sense of well-being that comes from being a giver. But their ultimate pleasure comes on the other side of eternity.

The pharaohs of Egypt were buried with gold and treasures to take into the afterlife, but they left it all behind. Even further, though gold is a precious thing on earth, God uses it to pave the streets of heaven.

Our material treasures will not pass from this life to the next, but the good that has been done for God's kingdom by our treasures lasts for eternity, and the work God does in us through faithful giving will last for eternity.

Keeping the eternal view is essential in avoiding materialism. As Jesus added in this section, **for where your treasure is, there your heart will be also**. Mishandled earthly treasure can keep us from heaven. If handled correctly, earthly treasure is used to store up heavenly treasure.

How is your heavenly bank account?

December 17

Make a Smooth Road for the L<small>ORD</small>

The voice of one crying in the wilderness: "Prepare the way of the L<small>ORD</small>; make straight in the desert a highway for our God. Every valley shall be exalted and every mountain and hill brought low; the crooked places shall be made straight and the rough places smooth; the glory of the L<small>ORD</small> shall be revealed, and all flesh shall see it together; for the mouth of the L<small>ORD</small> has spoken." (Isaiah 40:3-5)

In this passage, Isaiah spoke for the L<small>ORD</small>'s messenger, who cried out to the barren places. The message was simple: **Prepare the way of the L<small>ORD</small>.** The idea is that the L<small>ORD</small> is coming to His people as a triumphant King, who has the road prepared before Him so He can travel in glory and ease. Every obstacle in the way must be removed: **every valley shall be exalted and every mountain and hill brought low; the crooked places shall be made straight and the rough places smooth.**

Whatever was wrong in the road had to be corrected. The problems weren't the same everywhere. Sometimes, the road in the valley needed to be lifted; other times a road had to be cut through a passage in the mountains.

The idea of preparing the way of the L<small>ORD</small> is a word picture because the real preparation must take place in our hearts. Building a road is very much like the preparation God must do in our hearts.

- They are both expensive: it will cost us something to be ready for God.
- They both must deal with many different problems and environments: being ready for God means filling every hole and leveling every hill.
- They both take an expert engineer: being ready for God means following His plans.

When the way is prepared, then **the glory of the L<small>ORD</small> shall be revealed.** His glory is revealed to the prepared hearts described in the previous verses. And it is revealed without regard to nationality; **all flesh shall see it together.** This glory of the L<small>ORD</small> is not revealed only to Jerusalem or Judah, but to every prepared heart. The certainty of this word is assured because the mouth of the L<small>ORD</small> has spoken.

This passage of Isaiah 40:3-5 has a direct fulfillment in the New Testament, in the person and ministry of John the Baptist. Zacharias, the father of John the Baptist, knew this at the birth of his son (Luke 1:76). The gospels directly relate this passage to the ministry of John (Matthew 3:3, Mark 1:3, and Luke 3:3-6).

Jesus was the coming Messiah and King, and John the Baptist's ministry was to be one crying in the wilderness, and through his message of repentance, to prepare the way of the L<small>ORD</small>. We often fail to appreciate how important the preparing work of the L<small>ORD</small> is. Any great work of God begins with great preparation.

What is God preparing in you right now?

December 18
Receiving and Giving What Isn't Deserved

Blessed are the merciful, for they shall obtain mercy. (Matthew 5:7)

No matter who you are or what your other needs are, everyone needs at least one thing from God: **mercy**. In this remarkable line from the Sermon on the Mount, Jesus tells us how we can **obtain mercy** from God.

Often in His earthly ministry, Jesus answered when people cried out to Him, "Have mercy on me!" When we ask God for mercy, He will give it – but it is important that we understand that mercy is never deserved. Sometimes we think, "God, just give me what I deserve!" Perhaps we privately think that God has something good for us that we deserve, yet He doesn't give it because He is stingy or mean. But that is never the case. God is never less than fair with anyone. We are in a dangerous place when we regard God's mercy towards us as our right; if God is obliged to show mercy, then it is not mercy – it is obligation.

The Bible also speaks of the mercy we need to show to one another. When this beatitude addresses **the merciful**, it speaks to those who have already received mercy. Those who must show mercy are those who have already received it.

The merciful person will:

- Look for those who weep and mourn.
- Be forgiving to others, and always looking to restore broken relationships.
- Be merciful to the character of other people and choose to think the best of them whenever possible.
- Not expect too much from others.
- Be compassionate to those who are outwardly sinful.
- Have a care for the souls of all men.
- Show it to those who are weaker and poorer.

Don't miss the promise: **for they shall obtain mercy**. If you want mercy from others – especially God – then you should take care to be merciful to others. Why did God show such mercy to King David, especially in the terrible ways he sinned? God gave him mercy was because he was notably merciful to King Saul. With David, the merciful obtained mercy.

There is an old story about a woman who came to the French general and emperor Napoleon, pleading for her son's life. He was about to be executed for desertion. She begged for mercy, and Napoleon answered, "Madam, your son deserves to die!" She answered, "Yes, but I am asking for mercy, not for justice."

Some argue against showing mercy to someone: "They don't deserve it!" Yet if they deserved it, it wouldn't be mercy. Since God has given the undeserving His mercy and we want to keep receiving it, we should show mercy to others. When we judge others, we should always judge with mercy (Matthew 7:1-2).

Which measure do you wish to be judged by?

December 19

Why Jesus Came

For I have come down from heaven, not to do My own will, but the will of Him who sent Me. (John 6:38)

In the Gospel of John there are five beautiful and powerful statements where Jesus explained why He came.

We know that Jesus came to humanity in a special way. Jesus said, **I have come down from heaven**. He came down from His place of complete majesty and glory. Jesus didn't lose any of His majesty and glory, but He chose to come down from that status, allowing it to be hidden and refusing to enjoy its splendors for a time.

Why did He do it? John 6:38 says: **Not to do My own will**. This means Jesus came to be a servant, to do the will of God the Father. Sent by the Father, Jesus came as God in the flesh, taking the position of a submitted servant. Jesus showed us the importance of letting God set our agenda instead of trying to get Him to support our agenda.

John 9:39 tells us that Jesus came to divide men: *For judgment I have come into this world, that those who do not see may see, and that those who see may be made blind.* Jesus came to be a dividing line between humanity; we either accept Him or reject Him. Our choice doesn't determine who Jesus is – it determines who we are and our destiny.

John 10:10 tells us Jesus came to give life: *The thief does not come except to steal, and to kill, and to destroy. I have come that they may have life, and that they may have it more abundantly.* Many people wonder about life after death, but even more people wonder about life during life. Jesus came to give us life – eternal life. Not just long life, but life that has an eternal quality that we enjoy right now in Jesus Christ. For the Christian, eternal life doesn't begin when we die but as soon as we receive Him and receive new life.

John 12:46 tells us Jesus came as a light: *I have come as a light into the world, that whoever believes in Me should not abide in darkness.* The whole world was in spiritual darkness until Jesus came. He brings light, not only to the world but also to every life that will receive Him.

John 18:37 tells us Jesus came to bring truth: *For this cause I was born, and for this cause I have come into the world, that I should bear witness to the truth. Everyone who is of the truth hears My voice.* As Jesus walked this earth, He made many people feel good. We thank Him for every good feeling, but we center our lives on something greater. His greater cause was to bear witness to God's truth.

Today, let all these five reasons why Jesus came be real in your life.

December 20

Where Christmas Began

Sacrifice and offering You did not desire; My ears You have opened; burnt offering and sin offering You did not require. Then I said, "Behold, I come; in the scroll of the Book it is written of Me. I delight to do Your will, O my God, and Your law is within My heart." (Psalm 40:6-8)

This passage tells us where Christmas began. David spoke about his willingness to submit to God and to make an offering of his heart and life before Him. Yet the Holy Spirit took these words of passionate devotion and gave them a higher purpose: to reflect the heart of God's Son as He came into the world.

The beginning of Christmas wasn't with Mary and Joseph in a stable. It wasn't with the announcement of Gabriel to Joseph and Mary that she would bear a child by the Holy Spirit. Before the foundation of the world, in the eternal counsels of the One God in three Persons, is where Christmas began. God the Father agreed to send; God the Son agreed to go; and God the Holy Spirit agreed to guide.

Christmas began because something was lacking – **sacrifice and offering** were not enough. The reason sacrifice and offering were necessary was because of sin. The sacrifices of animals in the Old Testament weren't enough – and whatever sacrifice we make is not enough to take away our sin. God knew that we needed Christmas.

Christmas began because Someone was willing. **My ears You have opened**, mean that Jesus was willing to be the servant of the Father. **I delight to do Your will, O my God, and Your law is within my heart.** Jesus was willing to be the servant we needed to gain our salvation. He was willing to feel the feelings of a servant and do the work of a servant. That is why our Bible passages says, **Behold, I come**. Those are action words, not feeling words.

Christmas began because Someone loved. Love is written all over these verses, though the word itself never appears. **My ears You have opened** – only love could make Jesus do this for us. **In the scroll of the Book it is written of Me** – only love could promise such a plan. God planned it long ago; and He delighted in this plan. He put it in a **Book** so we could read about it. **I delight to do Your will** – only love could make the suffering Jesus endured His delight.

When we think where Christmas began – in the heaven of heavens, in the secret councils of the godhead – it should fill our hearts with true worship. It should make us humbly ask forgiveness for every time we have doubted God's love. It should make us acknowledge that we are unworthy, but that His love is even greater than our unworthiness.

David the psalmist never saw baby Jesus lying in a manger in Bethlehem, but he did see where Christmas began.

Can you see it also?

December 21

He Became Poor

For you know the grace of our Lord Jesus Christ, that though He was rich, yet for your sakes He became poor, that you through His poverty might become rich. (2 Corinthians 8:9)

This verse is like a Christmas tree, full of gifts of understanding about who Jesus is and what He did for us. We have the riches of Jesus, the poverty of Jesus, the manner of His poverty, the reason for His poverty, and the result of His poverty.

First, we learn that Jesus **was rich**. When was Jesus rich? It was before He added humanity to His deity and walked this earth. Jesus, as the eternal Second Person of the Trinity, as God the Son, living in the splendor of heaven, surrounded constantly by the glory, power, and majesty of God. These make any amount of wealth on earth seem poor. **He was rich** in possessions, honor, power, love, and happiness.

Secondly, **He became poor**. Look at the whole nativity scene. The newborn King was not laid in a cradle of gold but in a humble stable in a feeding trough, wrapped in the swaddling bands of poor children. His whole life was lived humbly. At a very young age, He was banished from his own country. Raised as the son of a humble carpenter, He had no fancy clothes, no home of His own, and often relied on others for food. He never even owned his own grave.

Third, notice the manner of His poverty: **He became poor**. It does not say that Jesus was made poor. It was completely voluntary on His part. Every moment of His life on this earth, Jesus made the conscious choice to live as a poor man.

Fourthly, the reason for His poverty: **yet for your sakes He became poor**. There was a real reason why Jesus did this. It was not for His own sake at all that He did this. It was **for your sakes He became poor**.

Look at the result of His poverty: **that you through His poverty might become rich**. Because of Jesus' poverty (in all that was related to it), we can become rich. We have a share in Jesus' eternal, heavenly wealth because He came and had a share in our poverty.

- As Jesus was rich in possessions, so are we – especially contentment.
- As Jesus was rich in honor – we have the honor of being sons and daughters of God.
- As Jesus was rich in power – we can come as sons and daughters to the God of all power.
- As Jesus was rich in love – we have the love of God poured out into our hearts.
- As Jesus was rich in happiness – so are we with the peace that passes all understanding.

Jesus isn't poor any longer. If this is what Jesus did for you when He was poor, how much more do you think He will do for you now that He is rich again?

December 22

When One Name Isn't Enough

For unto us a Child is born, unto us a Son is given; and the government will be upon His shoulder. And His name will be called Wonderful, Counselor, Mighty God, Everlasting Father, Prince of Peace. (Isaiah 9:6)

The prophet Isaiah clearly says, **His name will be called**. These names are character aspects of the promised Messiah.

First, we see that the Messiah is **Wonderful**. The glory of who He is and what He has done for us should fill us with wonder. He is Wonderful and will fill your heart and mind with amazement.

The Messiah is our **Counselor**: Jesus is the One able to guide our lives and should be the Christian's immediate resource. He may use the presence and words of another Christian to do it, but Jesus is our Counselor. It was by Satan's evil counsel that humanity fell, and it will be by Jesus' sweet and wise counsel that humanity is restored. Jesus is also our Counselor in that He sits in the High Counsel of the Godhead and takes counsel with the Father and the Holy Spirit for our good.

The Messiah is **Mighty God**. He is the God of all creation and glory, the Lord who reigns in heaven, the One worthy of our worship and praise. Can there be a more straightforward declaration of the deity of the Messiah?

The Messiah is the **Everlasting Father**. The idea in these Hebrew words is that Jesus is the source or author of all eternity, that He is the Creator Himself. It does not mean that Jesus Himself is the Person of the Father in the Trinity.

The Messiah is the **Prince of Peace**. He is the One who makes peace, especially between God and man.

John Calvin said it well:

> Whenever, in short, it appears to us that everything is in a ruinous condition, let us recall to our remembrance that Christ is called Wonderful, because he has inconceivable methods of assisting us, and because his power is far beyond what we are able to conceive. When we need counsel, let us remember that he is the Counselor. When we need strength, let us remember that he is Mighty and Strong. When new terrors spring up suddenly every instant, and when many deaths threaten us from various quarters, let us rely on that eternity of which he is with good reason called the Father, and by the same comfort let us learn to soothe all temporal distresses. When we are inwardly tossed by various tempests, and when Satan attempts to disturb our consciences, let us remember that Christ is The Prince of Peace, and that it is easy for him quickly to allay all our uneasy feelings. Thus will these titles confirm us more and more in the faith of Christ, and fortify us against Satan and against hell itself.

Today, thank Jesus that He is so great that He can't be described with just one name.

December 23

A Lot in a Little Cradle

Now after Jesus was born in Bethlehem of Judea in the days of Herod the king, behold, wise men from the East came to Jerusalem, saying, "Where is the King of the Jews? For we have seen His star in the East and have come to worship Him."

And when they had come into the house, they saw the young Child with Mary His mother, and fell down and worshipped Him. And when they had opened their treasures, they presented gifts to Him: gold, frankincense, and myrrh. (Matthew 2:1-2, 11)

There are many wrong ideas about what the Bible says happened at the birth of Jesus. Many of these have to do with the wise men from the East. The Bible never says there were three **wise men**, but we sing "We Three Kings of Orient Are."

The Bible never says they were kings – they were an order of Persian wise men – "magi."

The Bible does not tell us they came on the night Jesus was born, but probably in His first year, having set out the night He was born.

This we know from the biblical record: they brought at least three fitting gifts for the Christ Child, and fitting for the Man He would grow up to be.

Gold, a fitting gift for a *king*. In ancient Persia, whenever one appeared before the king, they had to have a gift of gold. These Persian wise men honored a child as a king. Strange, isn't it? Children aren't born kings; they are born princes and later become kings. But this Child was different – He is King of Kings and Lord of Lords and will reign from the throne of David, forever and ever.

Frankincense, a fitting gift for a *priest*. Frankincense is a glittering, fragrant resin from trees. It was used as incense by the priests of Israel and is a picture of prayer and intercession in the Bible. What an appropriate gift for Jesus, our High Priest, and intercessor before God! In Scripture, a priest represents who God is to the people, and represents the people before God. Jesus did both perfectly. The Bible says He ever lives to pray for His people.

Myrrh, a fitting gift for someone who *would die*. Myrrh is a fragrant spice used primarily in embalming. This was an appropriate gift for Jesus, who came to die. Even now, the pale shadow of the cross cast its dark image over the cradle of Jesus; here was a Man born to live, to show us God, to heal, and to teach. But more than anything, He was born to die. On the cross, He bore the judgment we deserved and stood in place for all who would receive Him.

The Person who would fulfill all three roles of king, priest, and sacrifice was a lot for God to put in a cradle – but He did! We are invited to receive Jesus Christ as our King, our High Priest, and the One who paid the price for the sin we deserve to pay. Trust Him today.

December 24
From Eternity to Here

But you, Bethlehem Ephrathah, though you are little among the thousands of Judah, yet out of you shall come forth to Me the One to be Ruler in Israel, whose goings forth are from of old, from everlasting. (Micah 5:2)

Micah 5:1 was another proclamation of judgment against Israel – but it seems that God rarely announces judgment without also giving a hopeful promise. Through the prophet Micah, God promises the ultimate hope: the coming of the Messiah, the **One to be Ruler in Israel.**

The Messiah would come forth at **Bethlehem**, but He was also coming from eternity: **Whose goings forth are from of old, from everlasting.** This glorious promise was fulfilled in Jesus Christ, and Micah's prophetic voice declares that though Jesus came from Bethlehem, He did not begin there.

Jesus is the Alpha and the Omega, the Beginning, and the End (Revelation 22:13). This means before Jesus was born in Bethlehem, He existed as the Second Person of the Trinity (John 17:5, 17:24).

Knowing the **goings forth** of Jesus are from eternity past shows us some important things:

It shows us the *glory* of Jesus and that He is far more than a just man. Jesus said He was the eternal God in human form, and if He was wrong about that, then He is wrong about everything. Jesus said that He was God; and if He is not then He was a lunatic and a liar. But if Jesus is who He said He was, then He is Lord of all creation – the One from eternity.

It shows us the *love* of Jesus, that He would leave the glory of heaven for us. It's hard to move from a great place to a lesser place, and no place is greater than heaven. Yet He left the ivory palaces of heaven, giving leave to heave out of love for us.

It shows us the *nature* of Jesus, that He would add humanity to His deity. It's wrong to think that Jesus was half man and half God, or that He was God on the inside but man on the outside. Instead, the biblical way to think about the nature of Jesus was that He was truly God and truly man; that the Second Person of the Trinity added humanity to His deity. The incarnation was addition, not subtraction.

It shows us the *sympathy* of Jesus, that He remains fully man and fully God. 1 Timothy 2:5 reminds us that Jesus is still truly man and truly God. Jesus didn't give up His humanity when He ascended to heaven. This means that the Savior born in Bethlehem – just as Micah prophesied – has an enduring sympathy with us.

This blessed place of Bethlehem – **little among the thousands** – was specially chosen to bring forth the greatest gift of all: God becoming man. God can use little places and little people to bring forth great gifts.

Today, receive His gift thankfully.

December 25

What the Baby Would Become

And behold, you will conceive in your womb and bring forth a Son, and shall call His name JESUS. He will be great, and will be called the Son of the Highest; and the Lord God will give Him the throne of His father David. And He will reign over the house of Jacob forever, and of His kingdom there will be no end. (Luke 1:31-33)

At Christmas time, we are rightly amazed at God, in Jesus of Nazareth, taking on humanity – and starting His humanity like every human does, as a little, dependent baby! Yet that beautiful baby did not stay a baby; He grew up to become exactly what the angel Gabriel told Mary He would become in Luke 1.

The focus of the angel's announcement to Mary was not Mary, but on a Son, to be named Jesus, which was a common name at that time. Gabriel went on to unmistakably identify this Son, this child, as the Messiah predicted by the Old Testament.

He is the Messiah because **He will be great**. Has anyone influenced history more than Jesus Christ? In His days walking this earth, He never ruled a nation, never commanded an army, never established a family dynasty, never was materially rich, never had more than moments of popularity, and in the end, everyone turned against Him and virtually all His friends forsook Him. Yet at this moment, and through the centuries, literally millions would gladly die for Him. Has there ever been a greater man than Jesus of Nazareth?

This Messiah **will be called the Son of the Highest**. Jesus would be the son of Mary, but not only her son; He would also be, and be known as, the Son of God. He was a man, no doubt – but also more than a man. He was, and is, the unique Son of God.

He will occupy **the throne of His father David**. Jesus was the Messiah prophesied to King David of old (2 Samuel 7:12-16), who has the rightful authority to rule over Israel, **and of His kingdom there will be no end**.

All parents who have held a newborn have wondered what would become of the gift of life in their arms. Mary and Joseph had an advantage – an express word from God, delivered by an angel, to answer that question. And it all was demonstrated to be gloriously true.

He is great – the greatest One ever to walk, and all history recognizes Him as such. He lived out the claim He was the unique Son of God – God in human flesh, having left the ivory palaces of heaven to add humanity to His deity. Jesus reigns as King – now, as a spiritual King over millions who would give their lives for Him; and soon, as a temporal King who will rule and reign over the kingdoms of this earth.

Isn't it amazing to see what the baby would become?

December 26

Your Life is More

Therefore I say to you, do not worry about your life, what you will eat or what you will drink; nor about your body, what you will put on. Is not life more than food and the body more than clothing? (Matthew 6:25)

Previously in His great Sermon on the Mount, Jesus challenged His listeners to decide between two treasures, two visions, and two masters. In each of these decisions it is better to choose a heavenly treasure, a focused vision, and God as master. Through it all Jesus made us think about the superiority of God's kingdom.

Here Jesus brought it to an important application: Because the kingdom of God is so greatly superior to our earthly pursuits, it deserves our close attention. If we allow it, the everyday cares of our life will crowd out the focus we should have on God and His kingdom.

For this reason, Jesus said: **Do not worry about your life**. We should not get tangled up worrying about the things of this world, because our life is much more than those things. It is true that we can be unfaithful to God through covetousness, as Jesus described in the previous words in this sermon. Yet we can also be unfaithful to God through worry and excessive concern about the things of this world.

Notice how powerfully Jesus expressed this; He included **what you will eat or what you will drink...what you will put on**. Those three concerns – what we will eat, drink, and wear – describe what many people in this world live for.

It is important to notice what Jesus told us to avoid. He said, **do not worry**. There is a difference between a godly sense of responsibility and an ungodly, untrusting worry. However, an ungodly, untrusting sense of worry usually pretends to be responsibility.

We take notice of the example of Jesus. We never have any evidence that Jesus was ever worried about what He would eat or drink or wear. He concerned Himself with doing His Father's will, and the Father concerned Himself with taking care of Jesus.

Remember that Jesus did not tell us to never be concerned. We are to be concerned with the right things; the ultimate issues of life – and we then leave the management (and the worry) over material things with our heavenly Father.

Jesus powerfully emphasized the point when He wrote, **is not life more than food and the body more than clothing?** The worry Jesus spoke of reduced human life to the concerns of what we put in our belly and what we wear on our back. It lowers man to the level of animals who are only concerned with physical needs. The important point for us to understand is this: Your life is more, and you have eternal matters to pursue.

Today, find a way to make your Father's business your business.

December 27

Are Your Riches Coming or Going?

Let the lowly brother glory in his exaltation, but the rich in his humiliation, because as a flower of the field he will pass away. For no sooner has the sun risen with a burning heat than it withers the grass; its flower falls, and its beautiful appearance perishes. So the rich man also will fade away in his pursuits. (James 1:9-11)

James began his letter by talking about difficult times in the life of a Christian. James called them trials or tests that we face. Then, James wrote about the need to ask God for wisdom – and that it is important to ask in faith.

James added another thought: **Let the lowly brother glory in his exaltation, but the rich in his humiliation**. As much as it is appropriate for the humble believer to rejoice when God lifts them, so it is appropriate for the rich believer to rejoice when they are brought to humiliation by testing and trials. It is appropriate for the rich believer – but far more difficult.

In this, the poor brother can forget his earthly poverty; and the rich brother can forget his worldly riches. They can put more focus on heavenly things, and there they find themselves equal in Jesus Christ.

Though we can understand the relative poverty and riches as being trials or tests of a living faith that a Christian may deal with, it nonetheless seems that James has made a sudden shift in his subject, going from trials and wisdom to riches and humility. In some ways, the book of James is like the book of Proverbs, and it can jump from topic to topic and then back again to a previous topic.

So, James added this warning to the rich brother: **He will pass away like a flower of the field**. Trials serve to remind the rich and the high that though they are comfortable in this life, it is still only this life, which fades as the grass grows brown and the flowers fade away.

In the land of Israel, there are a variety of beautiful flowers that spring to life when the rains come, but they last only for a short time before withering away. On the scale of eternity, this is how quickly the rich man also will fade away in his pursuits.

The riches of this world will certainly fade away – but James said more than that. He tells us something about the rich man himself, not only about his riches – that the **rich man also will fade away**. If we put our life and our identity into things that fade away, we will also fade away. How much better to put our life and our identity into something that will never fade!

If a man is only rich in this world, when he dies, he leaves his riches. But if a man is rich before God, when he dies, he goes to his riches. Today, put your focus on true wealth: a humble, real relationship with Jesus Christ. That will never fade away.

December 28

Shining Out That All Can See

You are the light of the world. A city that is set on a hill cannot be hidden. Nor do they light a lamp and put it under a basket, but on a lampstand, and it gives light to all who are in the house. Let your light so shine before men, that they may see your good works and glorify your Father in heaven. (Matthew 5:14-16)

Jesus said, **you are the light of the world**. In this, He gave Christians a great responsibility because He claimed the title *light of the world* for Himself as He walked this earth (John 8:12 and John 9:5).

The title **light of the world** means that we are not only light-receivers, but we are also light-givers. We cannot live only to ourselves; we must have someone to shine to and do so lovingly.

Jesus never challenged us to *become* salt (Matthew 5:13) or light. He said that we are – and we are either fulfilling or failing that responsibility.

Light is needed because the world is in darkness, and if our Christianity imitates the darkness, we have nothing to show the world. To be effective we must seek and display the Christian distinctive. We can never affect the world for Jesus by becoming like the world.

Jesus said, **let your light so shine before men**. The purpose of light is to illuminate. Light must be exposed before it is of any use. If it is hidden under a basket, it is no longer useful. This picture of light also reminds us that the life marked by the God's truth is not to be lived in isolation. We often assume that those can only be developed or displayed in isolation from the world, but Jesus wants us to live inner qualities out before the world.

Jesus said that His followers should expect persecution (Matthew 5:10-12). Jesus knew that with such a threat they would be tempted to hide their light, and not draw the world's attention to themselves. Yet Jesus never encouraged the existence of secret Christians whose virtues would never be on display.

Jesus said we should be like **a city that is set on a hill** that **cannot be hidden**. If you see such a city from a distance, it is hard to take your eyes off it. Jesus wanted His people to live in a way that attracted attention to the beauty of God's work in their lives.

Jesus continued: **Nor do they light a lamp and put it under a basket, but on a lampstand**. We are to be intentional about letting this light shine. Lamps are placed higher so their light can be more effective, so we should look for ways to let our light shine in greater ways.

Jesus pointed to a scope in the impact of disciples that must have seemed ridiculous at the time. How could these humble Galileans salt the **earth**, or light the **world**? But they did.

So can we – so can you.

December 29

What the World Needs Now

You are the salt of the earth; but if the salt loses its flavor, how shall it be seasoned? It is then good for nothing but to be thrown out and trampled underfoot by men. (Matthew 5:13)

Many people think the Sermon on the Mount was the greatest sermon ever preached. Others agree but think that it is also presented as an example of the kind of preaching that Jesus often did in His extensive ministry in the Galilee region. In the opening minutes of this most famous of sermons, Jesus tells us what the citizens of His kingdom are like. This opening section is often called the Beatitudes because of the way the lines begin with the promise of a blessing.

The last beatitude (Matthew 5:10-12) showed that the wonderful people described in the previous beatitudes would often be badly received by the world. We may have thought that the world would welcome these citizens of Jesus' kingdom; yet Jesus told us to expect that they would receive criticism, hatred, and persecution instead.

Knowing this, there is an automatic tendency: to withdraw and protect oneself. The kingdom citizen may easily reason like this: "The world doesn't like the people of Jesus' kingdom and may very well persecute us; the best thing to do is to withdraw from the world and stay away from those who might hurt us."

Jesus knew this tendency, so He spoke to it almost immediately. The idea of Jesus runs something like this: "You can't withdraw from the world, even though they will hate and persecute you. You are like salt in the earth; the world needs you and your saltiness. Don't lose your spiritual saltiness."

We can say that the citizens of Jesus' kingdom are like salt in several ways.

- Disciples are like salt because they are precious. In Jesus' day, salt was a valued commodity. Roman soldiers were sometimes paid with salt, giving rise to the phrase "worth his salt."
- Disciples are like salt because they have a preserving influence. Salt was used to preserve meats and to slow decay. Christians should have a preserving influence on their culture.
- Disciples are like salt because they add flavor. Christians should be a "flavorful" people, certainly not boring ones.

Jesus warned: **If the salt loses its flavor.... it is then good for nothing**. Salt must keep its "saltiness" to be of any value. When it is no good as salt, it is trampled underfoot. This speaks of how in the ancient world they used salt that wasn't very well processed or refined, and when its salty character had drained out and diminished, they often threw it outside to be like small gravel on a path.

If the followers of Jesus are like salt, then they are important for the world. It's a mistake for them to remove themselves from the world that needs them so badly.

The world needs what you, as a follower of Jesus, have to give.

December 30

Plays Well with Others

He who says he is in the light, and hates his brother, is in darkness until now. (1 John 2:9)

It is a great compliment for a teacher to give a child in kindergarten: "This child plays well with others." It means the child can get along with other children. What about God's children, those who are in His family? How do they get along? Do we "play well with others?"

Earlier in his letter, John wrote, telling us that our relationship to sin and obedience is a measure of our fellowship with God. Here, we see that our love for God's people is also a measure of our fellowship with God. If we say we are **in the light**, yet we hate our brother or sister, our claim to fellowship with the God who is light is hollow.

Sometimes it is easy to think, "Being a Christian would be easy if it were not for all the other Christians I have to deal with." Many Christians live like the walking wounded, crippled by the scars fellow believers have inflicted on them. But no matter how badly you have been hurt, the measure still stands. If we can't love each other, we have no basis for claiming a real love for God. Our love for other Christians can measure our relationship with God.

Is God being easy or difficult when He measures us by our love for His other children? On the one hand, God is merciful in requiring this, because we are measured by how we love other Christians, not those who are not yet believers. It isn't that we are free to hate those who aren't Christians, even if they regard us as enemies. But God's focus in 1 John 2:9 is on His children getting along with each other.

On the other hand, God has given us an incredibly difficult measure, because we often – perhaps rightly – expect much more from our Christian friends and associates. No one can hurt you like someone that you love and trust. We hope – and we should expect – Christ-like treatment from those who claim to be followers of Jesus Christ. These things make it even more challenging to keep loving others as we should when we have been hurt.

Think of the pain in your life that has come from other Christians. Was God asleep or on vacation when they hurt you? Of course not. We must understand that God has allowed this conflict, this pain, to come into your life. He has something good in it that He wants you to receive.

Perhaps He has shut you off from others to draw you to Himself, and then send you back to them with love, forgiveness, and reconciliation. Whatever His purpose is, embrace it. God hasn't allowed this to cripple you, but to bring something good in your life. Start receiving it today.

God can say of you also, "This child of Mine plays well with My other children!"

December 31

New Year's Predictions

These things I have spoken to you, that in Me you may have peace. In the world you will have tribulation; but be of good cheer, I have overcome the world. (John 16:33)

At the start of a new year, people offer all sorts of predictions. Nevertheless, I believe we could take this statement from Jesus as a prediction for any year. See what Jesus predicts for the coming year.

First, **In the world you will have tribulation**. You can count on it – you will face tribulation this year. Jesus promised it would be so. The ancient Greek word translated **tribulation** has the idea of stress or pressing. Someday, you will have a time of rest and unending happiness – but that is for heaven, not for earth.

Understanding this removes a false hope. Struggling Christians often hope for the day when they will laugh at temptation and life will be one effortless victory after another. We are promised struggle if we are in this world, yet there is peace in Jesus. Your current area of struggle may one day pass away, but after that, there will be new areas to conquer.

We are promised something greater than tribulation: **Be of good cheer, I have overcome the world**. In this Jesus shouted out the truth of His victory. It is an amazing statement from a man about to be arrested, forsaken, rejected, mocked, tortured, and executed. The glory of the resurrection made it clear that Jesus could truly say, **I have overcome the world**.

Knowing all this, Jesus made a sincere offer: the gift of courage (**good cheer**) for the tribulation we must face. Knowing – not just as a fact in a history book – that Jesus has **overcome the world** brings us courage. There is no reason to be downcast or discouraged. Your look of gloom is a witness to your unbelief. If you really believed His victory, and by faith shared in His overcoming, you would have good cheer. You would also have what He offered at the beginning of the verse: **peace**.

Remember the circumstances surrounding this opening statement to the verse: **These things I have spoken to you, that in Me you may have peace**. At that very moment, Judas met with Jesus' enemies to plot His arrest. Jesus knew that He would be arrested, forsaken, rejected, mocked, humiliated, tortured, and executed before the next day was over.

Finally, notice that Jesus did not promise peace, but He offered it. He said, **you may have peace**. People can follow Jesus yet deny themselves that peace. Jesus said, **that in Me you may have peace**. We will not find real peace anywhere else other than in Jesus.

We can predict tribulation. We can look back on Jesus overcoming the world. When we really receive His victory as our own, we can have peace. That is one prediction we are assured will come true.

This is your year.

Scripture Index

Genesis 1:1	Jul 5	1 Samuel 6:20	Mar 9
Genesis 5:22, 24	Aug 21	1 Samuel 7:3-4	Feb 15
Genesis 12:8	Nov 25	1 Samuel 10:1	Aug 17
Genesis 15:8	Oct 10	1 Samuel 10:25-27	Jan 12
Genesis 28:20-22	Nov 29	1 Samuel 12:22-24	Nov 23
Genesis 41:38-39	Sep 2	1 Samuel 13:10-12	May 15
Genesis 41:51-52	Nov 13	1 Samuel 13:13-14	Oct 5
		1 Samuel 15:7-9	Feb 2
Exodus 3:6	Aug 25	1 Samuel 15:22-23	Jan 8
Exodus 4:8-9	Jul 21	1 Samuel 25:10-12	Jul 29
Exodus 4:21	Jan 24	1 Samuel 28:6	Sep 16
Exodus 5:6-9	Feb 3	1 Samuel 30:1-2	Jan 16
Exodus 5:22-23	Oct 20		
Exodus 12:13	Mar 28	2 Samuel 1:11-12	Jan 19
Exodus 14:15	Oct 4	2 Samuel 3:1	Sep 18
Exodus 14:21	Aug 3	2 Samuel 7:8, 11	Jul 28
Exodus 15:22-25	Jul 13	2 Samuel 7:25-27	Oct 14
Exodus 16:13-15	Nov 16	2 Samuel 11:3	Oct 19
Exodus 17:11-13	May 23	2 Samuel 12:5-6	Jun 8
Exodus 19:4	Mar 27	2 Samuel 12:13	Jun 26
Exodus 20:1-3	Aug 15		
Exodus 23:20-21	Aug 1	1 Kings 4:32-34	Nov 2
Exodus 24:4-8	Apr 1	1 Kings 5:17	Sep 3
Exodus 26:1	Sep 13	1 Kings 6:7	Aug 4
Ezekiel 28:15-17	May 28	1 Kings 8:33-34	May 20
Exodus 32:2-4	Sep 25	1 Kings 11:3	Sep 5
Exodus 32:14	Sep 8	1 Kings 15:1-3	Jun 29
Exodus 34:33-35	Aug 19	1 Kings 17:1	Jul 9
		1 Kings 19:4	Oct 31
Leviticus 2:13	Apr 12		
		2 Kings 17:24-25	Oct 7
Numbers 6:23-27	Nov 17	2 Kings 17:32-33	Dec 13
Numbers 10:33-36	Nov 15		
Numbers 11:4-6	Nov 10	Nehemiah 3:10	Jan 17
Numbers 14:15-20	Jul 14	Nehemiah 6:1-4	Aug 18
Numbers 14:20	Mar 26	Nehemiah 8:4-6	Jul 20
Numbers 15:27-28	Feb 6		
Numbers 20:10-11	Jun 21	Psalm 1:2	Dec 9
Numbers 35:11-12	Mar 13	Psalm 2:4	Dec 11
		Psalm 5:11-12	Jan 20
Judges 6:14	Apr 24	Psalm 11:1, 3-4	May 19
		Psalm 13:1, 6	Aug 11

Psalm 40:6-8	Dec 20	Isaiah 7:10-12	Nov 6
Psalm 90:1-2	Sep 26	Isaiah 9:6	Dec 22
Psalm 119:9	Feb 17	Isaiah 10:4	Apr 23
Psalm 119:9	Feb 22	Isaiah 12:2	Jun 10
Psalm 119:13-16	Jan 3	Isaiah 12:2-3	Nov 26
Psalm 119:18	Apr 30	Isaiah 14:1	Apr 11
Psalm 119:36-37	Sep 15	Isaiah 14:3-4	Nov 21
Psalm 119:51-52	Oct 3	Isaiah 14:9-11	Aug 20
Psalm 119:59-60	Feb 24	Isaiah 14:12-15	Sep 27
Psalm 119:65-66	May 7	Isaiah 17:10-11	Apr 15
Psalm 119:71-72	Sep 9	Isaiah 23:9	Mar 25
Psalm 119:73	Aug 8	Isaiah 24:4-6	Jan 15
Psalm 119:81-82	May 22	Isaiah 25:1, 4-5	Feb 18
Psalm 119:87-88	May 27	Isaiah 26:3-4	Feb 9
Psalm 119:89	Apr 8	Isaiah 28:16-17	Feb 16
Psalm 119:89-91	Jul 8	Isaiah 29:13-14	Sep 17
Psalm 119:92-93	Feb 8	Isaiah 29:15-16	Aug 29
Psalm 119:105	Mar 4	Isaiah 30:15-17	Feb 26
Psalm 119:115	Jun 19	Isaiah 35:8	Jan 25
Psalm 119:116-117	Mar 12	Isaiah 40:1-2	Jul 15
Psalm 119:118-120	Jun 14	Isaiah 40:3-5	Dec 17
Psalm 119:121-122	May 30	Isaiah 40:6-8	Aug 23
Psalm 119:123-125	Jul 17	Isaiah 40:9-10	Sep 24
Psalm 119:127-128	May 16	Isaiah 40:11	Sep 12
Psalm 119:130-131	Jul 10	Isaiah 40:27-28	Oct 26
Psalm 119:132-133	Mar 24	Isaiah 44:1-4	May 11
Psalm 119:137-138	Oct 15	Isaiah 45:22	Mar 1
Psalm 119:139-140	Aug 6	Isaiah 49:15-18	Jul 25
Psalm 119:141-142	Dec 12	Isaiah 50:4-5	Dec 2
Psalm 119:143-144	Mar 18	Isaiah 53:4-6	Apr 3
Psalm 119:145-147	Jan 23	Isaiah 55:1-2	Aug 24
Psalm 119:148-149	Aug 27	Isaiah 55:10-11	Jun 5
Psalm 119:153-154	Aug 10	Isaiah 57: 15-16	Apr 6
Psalm 144:15	Dec 10	Isaiah 60:1-3	Mar 20
		Isaiah 62:6-7	Aug 31
Isaiah 3:8-9	Feb 21	Isaiah 63:7, 14	Apr 28
Isaiah 4:2	Dec 1	Isaiah 64:8-9	Jul 6
Isaiah 5:3-4	Oct 17	Isaiah 66:12-14	May 9
Isaiah 6:1	Oct 27		
Isaiah 6:1-2	Nov 22	Hosea 2:8	Mar 10
Isaiah 6:3-4	Apr 18	Hosea 3:1	Feb 14
Isaiah 6:5	Nov 1	Hosea 4:17	Aug 22
Isaiah 6:6-7	Aug 30	Hosea 5:6	Apr 10
Isaiah 6:8	Oct 8	Hosea 6:6	Apr 16
Isaiah 6:9-10	Jan 9	Hosea 14:4-7	Dec 5

Joel 2:12-13	Sep 23	Matthew 6:9-13	Apr 25
		Matthew 6:9-13	Aug 7
Amos 3:13-15	Jun 11	Matthew 6:14-15	May 10
Amos 8:11-12	Sep 14	Matthew 6:19-21	Dec 16
		Matthew 6:22-23	Dec 15
Jonah 1:3	Jan 11	Matthew 6:24	Jan 7
Jonah 1:5-6	Jul 12	Matthew 6:25	Dec 26
Jonah 1:14-16	May 31	Matthew 6:26-30	Jun 23
Jonah 2:8-9	Feb 28	Matthew 7:6	Jan 13
Jonah 3:1-2	Jun 9	Matthew 7:7-8	Jun 25
Jonah 4:4	Jul 23	Matthew 7:9-11	Sep 21
		Matthew 7:12	Jul 1
Micah 2:13	Nov 28	Matthew 7:24-27	Jun 20
Micah 5:2	Dec 24	Matthew 7:28-29	Sep 4
Micah 6:8	Mar 29	Matthew 8:1-2	Nov 30
		Matthew 16:18	May 21
Habakkuk 2:4	Jun 27	Matthew 27:62-66	Apr 9
Zechariah 4:6	Jan 26	Mark 2:17	Jun 12
Zechariah 4:10	Sep 6	Mark 4:36	Jul 19
Zechariah 7:5	May 14	Mark 5:27-28	May 2
		Mark 5:30-32	Dec 8
Matthew 1:21	Jan 29	Mark 5:33	Aug 12
Matthew 2:1-2, 11	Dec 23	Mark 7:2-3	Jul 30
Matthew 5:3	Apr 29	Mark 7:34/8:12	Sep 22
Matthew 5:4	Jan 27	Mark 8:34	Apr 21
Matthew 5:5	Jun 7		
Matthew 5:6	Oct 22	Luke 1:31-33	Dec 25
Matthew 5:7	Dec 18	Luke 6:45	Apr 19
Matthew 5:8	Aug 13	Luke 13:3, 5	Mar 14
Matthew 5:9	Nov 12	Luke 18:1	May 6
Matthew 5:10-12	May 17	Luke 18:39	May 1
Matthew 5:13	Dec 29		
Matthew 5:14-16	Dec 28	John 4:46b-48	Nov 18
Matthew 5:19-20	May 26	John 6:38	Dec 19
Matthew 5:21-22	Sep 20	John 8:33-36	Oct 11
Matthew 5:23-26	Jan 5	John 15:5	Jan 1
Matthew 5:27-28	Sep 28	John 16:33	Dec 31
Matthew 5:29-30	Nov 8		
Matthew 5:33-37	Feb 13	Acts 1:4-5	Jun 13
Matthew 5:38-42	Feb 12	Acts 1:9-11	Jul 7
Matthew 5:48	Apr 27	Acts 2:24	Mar 31
Matthew 6:1	Jul 24	Acts 5:19-20	Jul 4
Matthew 6:5-6	Oct 25	Acts 8:5-8	Oct 16
Matthew 6:7-8	Jun 6	Acts 12:4-6	Sep 11

Acts 12:5	Feb 25	Philippians 4:13	Jan 1
Acts 20:24	Apr 7		
Acts 20:29-30	Sep 1	Colossians 3:17	Nov 24
Acts 21:15	Aug 2	Colossians 4:2-4	May 13
Romans 1:17	Jun 24	1 Timothy 1:3	Sep 30
Romans 5:14	Feb 20		
Romans 10:17	Mar 5	Titus 1:1	Jul 27
Romans 12:2	Jul 16	Titus 2:7-8	Aug 14
Romans 13:11	Dec 3		
		Hebrews 1:14	Feb 5
1 Corinthians 2:8-9	Mar 6	Hebrews 7:25	Apr 26
1 Corinthians 10:13	Oct 12	Hebrews 12:18, 22	Aug 16
1 Corinthians 13:13	Oct 28		
1 Corinthians 15:5-8	Apr 4	James 1:2-4	Feb 10
1 Corinthians 15:35-38	Apr 17	James 1:2-4	May 8
		James 1:5-8	Mar 19
2 Corinthians 1:3-4	Dec 7	James 1:5-8	Jun 4
2 Corinthians 4:17	Nov 14	James 1:9-11	Dec 27
2 Corinthians 8:9	Dec 21	James 1:13-16	Mar 22
2 Corinthians 12:9	Mar 3	James 1:17-18	Jun 30
		James 1:19-21	Feb 27
Galatians 3:26-27	Nov 7	James 1:26-27	Feb 1
Galatians 4:4-5	Oct 9	James 2:2-4	Apr 14
Galatians 5:1	Jan 18	James 2:5-7	Jun 22
		James 2:10-13	Jul 3
Ephesians 2:8-9	Feb 4	James 2:14	Apr 22
Ephesians 6:10	Jun 28	James 2:15-17	Mar 23
Ephesians 6:10	Sep 7	James 2:20-24	Jan 22
Ephesians 6:11	Jul 2	James 3:1-2	Aug 5
Ephesians 6:12	Jan 30	James 3:3-5a	Oct 2
Ephesians 6:13	Jan 31	James 3:5-6	May 4
Ephesians 6:14-15	Jan 4	James 3:7-8	Oct 23
Ephesians 6:14-15	Jun 1	James 3:9-12	Jun 18
Ephesians 6:14-15	Nov 11	James 3:13	Oct 24
Ephesians 6:16-18	Feb 7	James 3:17-18	Jun 16
Ephesians 6:16-18	Mar 2	James 4:1-3	Jul 18
Ephesians 6:16-18	Jun 2	James 4:4-5	Dec 14
Ephesians 6:16-18	Oct 21	James 4:6	Mar 17
Ephesians 6:18-20	Jan 6	James 4:6	May 5
		James 4:6	Aug 26
Philippians 1:3-5	Nov 5	James 4:8-10	May 24
Philippians 1:12-14	May 18	James 4:13-16	Oct 13
Philippians 2:1	Jun 17	James 5:7-8	Sep 10
Philippians 2:30	Nov 9	James 5:9-11	Oct 18

James 5:15-16	Jan 14	Revelation 12:11	Mar 16
James 5:19-20	Dec 4	Revelation 21:5	Jan 2
		Revelation 22:3-5	Nov 20
1 Peter 1:1	Mar 8		
		Apostles' Creed	Apr 5
1 John 1:3	May 25		
1 John 1:7	Feb 11		
1 John 1:9	Feb 23		
1 John 2:1	Mar 11		
1 John 2:9	Dec 30		
1 John 2:15	Apr 13		
1 John 2:18	May 3		
1 John 2:20	Oct 29		
1 John 2:24	Jan 21		
1 John 2:28	May 12		
1 John 3:2	Mar 7		
1 John 3:2	Nov 27		
1 John 3:16	Jan 10		
1 John 3:16	Apr 2		
1 John 3:19-20	Dec 6		
1 John 4:2	Mar 30		
1 John 4:6	Mar 15		
1 John 4:17	Jun 3		
1 John 4:18	Aug 28		
1 John 4:19	Jul 22		
1 John 5:4-5	Jun 15		
1 John 5:10	Apr 20		
1 John 5:14	Jan 28		
Jude 1:1	Jul 31		
Jude 1:3	Oct 30		
Jude 1:5	Mar 21		
Jude 1:6	May 29		
Jude 1:7	Oct 1		
Jude 1:8	Sep 29		
Jude 1:11	Sep 19		
Jude 1:16-18	Jul 26		
Jude 1:19	Nov 4		
Jude 1:20-21	Nov 3		
Jude 1:22-23	Oct 6		
Jude 1:24-25	Jul 11		
Revelation 4:11	Aug 9		
Revelation 7:17	Nov 19		
Revelation 12:11	Feb 19		

Topic Index

Adam
Feb 20, Sep 19, October 9

Affliction, Trials
Feb 3, Feb 8, Mar 19, Aug 10, Sep 9, Oct 18, Nov 14, Dec 27, Dec 31

Angels
Feb 5, May 28, May 29, Aug 1, Nov 22

Anger
Jul 23, Sep 20

Anointing
Aug 17, Oct 29

Assurance
May 12, Oct 10, Dec 6

Backsliding
Oct 19, Dec 5

Blessing
May 11, Oct 9, Nov 17, Dec 5, Dec 9

Comfort, Encouragement
Jan 27, Apr 26, May 9, May 22, Jul 15, Oct 3, Oct 9, Nov 7, Nov 19, Dec 7

Confession
Feb 23, May 15, May 20, Jun 26

Covenant
Apr 1, Aug 16, Aug 19, Jul 15, Oct 10

Creation
Jul 8, Aug 8, Aug 29, Sep 26, Oct 26

The Cross
Mar 28, Apr 2, Apr 3, Apr 21

Danger, Warnings
Feb 6, Mar 15, Mar 21, Apr 23, Jul 11, Aug 18, Aug 22, Sep 29, Oct 1, Nov 3

Direction
Feb 24, Mar 24, Nov 15

Discernment
Jan 13, Aug 18, Sep 29

Discouragement
Oct 20, Oct 31, Nov 18

Endurance
Feb 10, Apr 26, May 6, Oct 18

Examples
Aug 14

Faith
Jan 14, Jan 22, Feb 4, Feb 7, Mar 5, Mar 23, Apr 10, Apr 20, Apr 22, May 1, May 2, May 8, May 19, Jun 4, Jun 23, Jun 27, Oct 21, Oct 30, Nov 3, Nov 9, Nov 29, Dec 8

Faithfulness
Jan 12, Sep 30, Oct 1

Fasting
May 14

Fear
May 18, Aug 28, Sep 5

Forgiveness
Jan 19, Feb 4, Feb 11, Feb 20, Feb 23, May 10, Aug 25, Nov 13

Freedom
Jan 18, Jul 3, Jul 4, Oct 11

Glory
Mar 20, Aug 19, Dec 17

God
Jan 11, Feb 14, Feb 18, Mar 9, Apr 9, Jun 30, Aug 1, Aug 9, Sep 16, Sep 25, Sep 26, Dec 11

God's Word
Jan 3, Jan 23, Feb 8, Feb 17, Mar 4, Mar 18, Apr 6, Apr 8, Apr 30, May 7, May 16, Jun 2, Jun 5, Jul 10, Jul 17, Jul 25, Jul 30, Aug 6, Aug 23, Sep 14, Sep 24, Oct 15, Dec 9

Gospel
Mar 6, Apr 7, Nov 11

Grace
Mar 3, Mar 17, Jun 9, Aug 26

The Heart
Jan 24, Apr 19, Jun 6, Jul 28, Aug 13, Sep 10, Sep 23, Sep 28, Oct 5, Oct 8

Heaven
Jan 2, Mar 7, Mar 8, Apr 8, Apr 18, Jun 16, Jul 7, Oct 27, Nov 19, Nov 20, Nov 27

Holiness
Jan 25, Mar 9, Apr 18, Jul 16, Nov 8

The Holy Spirit
Jan 26, Jun 13, Jul 20, Aug 17, Nov 4

Hope
Jan 23, Mar 2, May 22

Humility
Mar 29, Apr 23, May 5, May 24, Jun 17, Aug 12, Oct 13, Nov 22

Idolatry
Mar 10, Aug 22, Dec 13, Dec 21

Israel in the Exodus
Feb 3, Mar 27, May 23, Jul 13, Aug 1, Aug 3, Aug 15, Sep 13, Nov 15

Nature of Jesus
Jan 29, Mar 11, Mar 30, Apr 3, May 3, Jul 7, Jul 19, Jul 22, Sep 12, Sep 22, Nov 27, Nov 28, Dec 1, Dec 2, Dec 19, Dec 22, Dec 23, Dec 24, Dec 25

Joy
Jan 20, Aug 24, Dec 10

Judgment
Jan 15, Feb 21, Jun 3, Jul 21, Oct 1, Oct 7

Light
Dec 15, Dec 28

Love
Feb 12, Apr 2, Apr 13, Jun 3, Jul 22, Aug 27, Aug 28, Sep 1, Sep 22, Oct 28, Dec 30

Meekness
Jun 7, Oct 24

Mercy
Jan 16, Mar 29, Sep 8, Sep 22, Dec 18

Ministry
Jan 9, Jan 26, Apr 7, Aug 5, Oct 16

Miracles
May 1, Jul 13, Aug 3, Nov 30, May 2

Obedience
Jan 8, Jan 9, Feb 1, Feb 2, Feb 24, Apr 27, Aug 15, Aug 21, Nov 25

Patience
Feb 10, May 8, Jun 13, Sep 10

Peace
Feb 9, Nov 12

Persecution
Jan 10, May 17, Oct 3

The Power of Words
May 4, Jun 18, Jul 26, Aug 5, Oct 2, Oct 23, Nov 1, Dec 29

Praise, Worship
Feb 18, Jun 10, Sep 24, Nov 26

Prayer
Jan 6, Jan 14, Jan 28, Feb 25, Mar 12, Mar 26, Apr 25, May 6, May 13, May 23, Jun 6, Jun 25, Jul 6, Jul 14, Jul 18, Aug 7, Aug 11, Aug 31, Sep 11, Sep 21, Oct 4, Oct 14, Oct 25

Pride
Mar 25, May 5, Oct 13

Priorities
Jan 5, Apr 16, Jun 20

Promises
Feb 26, Mar 18, Mar 19, Apr 29, Jun 5, Jul 14, Jun 25, Aug 24, Oct 14, Nov 29, Dec 31

Protection
Mar 13, Mar 27

Purity
May 24, Jun 14, Aug 13, Aug 30, Nov 8

Religion
Feb 1, Sep 19

Repentance
Feb 15, Feb 28, Mar 14, May 15, Jun 8, Jun 26, Jul 16, Sep 8, Sep 23, Oct 5, Dec 4, Dec 5

Restoration, Revival
Feb 15, Apr 11, Apr 28, May 27, Aug 10, Dec 5

Resurrection
Mar 31, Apr 4, Apr 9, Apr 17

Righteousness
Apr 27, May 26, Oct 22

Sacrifice
Apr 12

Salvation
Jan 29, Feb 11, Feb 22, Feb 28, Mar 1, Mar 2, Mar 13, Mar 23, Apr 3, Apr 26, May 26, Jun 10, Jul 21, Oct 30, Dec 6

Satan
Mar 22, Mar 25, May 28, Aug 20, Sep 27, Nov 21

Sermon on the Mount
Jan 5, Jan 7, Jan 13, Jan 27, Feb 12, Feb 13, Apr 25, Apr 27, Apr 29, May 10, May 17, May 26, Jun 6, Jun 7, Jun 20, Jun 23, Jun 25, Jul 1, Jul 24, Aug 7, Aug 13, Sep 4, Sep 20, Sep 21, Sep 28, Oct 22, Oct 25, Nov 8, Nov 12, Dec 15, Dec 16, Dec 18, Dec 26, Dec 28, Dec 29

Sin
Feb 6, Feb 20, Feb 21, Feb 23, Jun 12, Jun 14, Jul 15, Sep 28, Oct 19, Dec 4

Spiritual Sleep
Dec 3, Jul 12

Spiritual Warfare
Jan 4, Jan 6, Jan 30, Jan 31, Feb 7, Mar 2, Jun 1, Jun 2, Jun 28, Jul 2, Sep 7, Oct 21, Nov 11

Strength
Jan 1, Feb 9, Apr 24, Jun 28, Sep 18, Sep 30, Jun 21, Jun 29, Jul 9, Sep 2

Truth
Jan 4, Mar 4, Aug 10, Mar 15, Jul 27, Sep 1, Dec 12

Unbelief
Jan 18, Apr 20

Victory, Overcoming
Feb 19, Mar 16, Jun 15, Oct 12

Wealth, Riches
Apr 14, Jun 11, Jun 22, Jul 29, Dec 21, Dec 27

Wisdom
Jan 13, Mar 19, May 4, May 7, Jun 4, Jun 16, Jun 22, Jul 29, Sep 17, Oct 2, Oct 24, Nov 2

Worldliness
Mar 8, Apr 13, Jun 19, Dec 14

Worship
Feb 18, Apr 23, Jun 10, Sep 25, Nov 22, Nov 25, Nov 26, Nov 30

Title Index

Title	Date
A Bad Sense	Nov 4
A Better Measure Than Success	Jun 21
A Better Mountain	Aug 16
A Better Refuge	Mar 13
A Better Way to Pray	Oct 25
A Big Use for Small Things	Sep 6
A Different Kind of Righteousness	May 26
A Fool and His Money	Jul 29
A Good Kind of Jealousy	Dec 14
A Good Mourning	Jan 27
A Good Reminder	Mar 21
A Gospel Worth Dying For	Apr 7
A Lamp and a Light	Mar 4
A Lot In a Little Cradle	Dec 23
A Prepared Place	Aug 1
A Real Relationship	May 25
A Refuge From the Storm	Feb 18
A Small Thing Guiding a Bigger Thing	Oct 2
A Song of Salvation	Jun 10
A Spiritual Sword	Jun 2
A Three-Way Work	Jul 31
A Tongue On Fire	May 4
A True Miracle	Aug 3
A Warning to Bible Teachers	Aug 5
A Warning, and What Happened Later	Sep 1
Able to Save	Apr 26
According to Love, According to Justice	Aug 27
According to Your Word	Mar 26
Adam's Fall and Our Fall	Feb 20
Affliction and Revival	Aug 10
Afraid and More Afraid	May 31
After God's Own Heart	Oct 5
Against the Pride of Success	Mar 25
All I Know	Mar 6
All Sons and Daughters	Nov 7
All the Armor	Jul 2
All Things New	Jan 2
Almost an End	May 27
Altars and Tents	Nov 25
Always Praying, Never Losing Heart	May 6
Angels Watching Over You	Feb 5
Angry - But Is It Right?	Jul 23
Anointed	Aug 17
Appreciation In Affliction	Sep 9
Are Your Riches Going or Coming?	Dec 27
As Secure As You Know How	Apr 9
As the Rain Comes Down	Jun 5
Asking Without Doubting	Mar 19
Asking, Seeking, Knocking	Jun 25
Asleep In the Storm	Jul 12
Bearing Our Sorrows	Apr 3
Beginning with Truth	Jan 4
Behold Your God	Sep 24
Being an Overcomer	Mar 16
Being Fair to All	Apr 14
Believe the Creed	Apr 5
Believing What God Tells You	Feb 4
Beyond Casual Contact	Dec 8
Bitter Made Sweet	Jul 13
Blessed Trouble	May 17
Blessings to Healed Backsliders	Dec 5
Boldness in the Day of Judgment	Jun 3
Building a House	Jul 28
Burned Clean	Aug 30
Choosing a Difficult Kind of Love	Feb 14
Choosing the Poor of This World	Jun 22
Combining Love With Discernment	Jan 13
Commitment Declared and Enjoyed	Jan 3
Consider What Great Things He Has Done	Nov 23
Continually Cleansed	Feb 11
Crying Out and Hoping In His Word	Jan 23
Day and Night	Dec 9
Dead Faith or Living Faith?	Mar 23
Dealing Well, According to His Word	May 7

Title	Date
Discernment and How to Get It	Aug 18
Do It All	Nov 24
Don't Conform, Transform	Jul 16
Do the Work Right at Our House	Jan 17
Do You Remember?	Aug 25
Doing Good For the Right Motives	Jul 24
Draw Near to God	May 24
Dreamers	Sep 29
Earnest Prayer	Feb 25
Eating Good Things	Aug 24
Enlighten My Eyes	Aug 11
Example of a Living Faith	Jan 22
Examples of Patient Endurance	Oct 18
Excuses	May 15
Eyes Tired For a Good Reason	Jul 17
Fading Glory	Aug 19
Fainting, Hoping	May 22
Faith That Won't Quit	May 1
Falling Down	Apr 23
Favor Like a Shield	Jan 20
Feast or Famine?	Sep 14
Finally	Sep 7
For Me or For You?	May 14
Forget-Him-Not	Apr 15
Forgetfulness and Fruitfulness	Nov 13
Free From Bitterness	Jan 19
Free Indeed	Oct 11
From Defeat to Victory	May 20
From Eternity to Here	Dec 24
From the Inside Out	Sep 13
Gambling On God	Nov 9
Getting the Blessing	Nov 17
Getting to the Root of the Matter	Sep 20
Give Him No Rest	Aug 31
Giving More Grace	Aug 26
Go	Jan 9
God and His Word	Oct 15
God Of the Second Chance	Jun 9
God's Answer to the Prayer of Faith	Jan 14
God's Building Materials	Sep 3
God's Enduring Word	Aug 23
God's Righteousness, Our Friend	Jun 24
God's Way of Escape	Oct 12
God's Wonderful Custom	Mar 24
Going With the Glory	Nov 15
Gold for the Golden Rule	Jul 1
Good Start, Bad Finish	Jan 12
Grace Sufficient for You	Mar 3
Grace to the Humble	Mar 17
Great Joy from Seeds Already Sown	Oct 16
Handling Success - Pit to the Pinnacle	Sep 2
Hands Stretched Out	May 23
Happy People or New Men	Dec 10
Hard Hearts Made Soft	Jan 24
Has God Let You Down?	Nov 18
Haven't You Heard?	Oct 26
Having Nothing, Having Everything	Apr 29
Having, Taking	Oct 21
He Became Poor	Dec 21
He Has Shown You	Mar 29
Hearts Assured	Dec 6
His Days are Numbered	Nov 21
His Promise, Our Vow	Nov 29
Hold Me Up	Mar 12
Holding Fast to the True Word	Dec 12
Honor Him With What He Gives	Mar 10
Hope and Salvation On Your Head	Mar 2
How Much More?	Sep 21
How Temptation Comes	Mar 22
How to Ask God for Help	Jul 6
How to Be a Doer of the Word	Feb 1
How to Be Perfect	Apr 27
How to Give Away Your Life	Jan 10
How to Trust God's Promises	Feb 26
Hunger and Thirst Satisfied, But Still There	Oct 22
I Can See Clearly Now	Mar 7
I Confess	Jun 26
I Touched Him	May 2
If Water Is Wet and Rocks Are Hard	Jun 17
Imprisoned Angels	May 29

Impulse, Circumstances, or God?	Jan 11	Never Ending Faithfulness	Jul 8
In But Not Of	Jun 19	Never Forgotten	Jul 25
Instead of Jesus	May 3	New Year Predictions	Dec 31
Inward and Outward Repentance	Feb 15	No Fear?	Aug 28
It Had to Happen	Mar 31	No Guarantee	Oct 1
It's Not Enough to Be Smart	Mar 15	No Hammer Was Heard	Aug 4
It's So Embarrassing	Aug 12	No More Tears	Nov 19
		No Prayer, Selfish Prayer, and Real Prayer	Jul 18
Just Passing Through	Mar 8	Not Against Flesh and Blood	Jan 30
Just Perfect	Nov 20	Not Ashamed at His Coming	May 12
Justice and Mercy	Jan 16	Not By Might	Jan 26
		Not So Certain	Oct 13
Keep Your Boots On	Nov 11	On Eagles' Wings	Mar 27
Keys to Becoming an Overcomer	Feb 19	Only Sounding Spiritual	Nov 6
Keys to Prayer from the Heart	Oct 14	Open Your Ear	Dec 2
Know Now What We Will See Then	Sep 27	Our Light Affliction	Nov 14
Knowing But Not Knowing	Jun 8	Partial Obedience	Feb 2
Knowing What Love Is	Apr 2	Patient Endurance	Feb 10
		People Who Love Too Much	Apr 13
		Planting Seeds	Apr 17
Lavishing Love on All	Feb 12	Plays Well With Others	Dec 30
Learning from Others	Jun 11	Pray In This Manner	Aug 7
Left Alone	Aug 22	Prayer, Earnest and Awake	May 13
Life Without Meaning	Jul 5	Pride and Grace	May 5
Like a Horse in Open Country	Apr 28	Protection From the Proud	May 30
Like a Meteor on a Dark Night	Jul 9	Prove It To Me, God	Oct 10
Like a River	May 9	Putting It Into Action	Jan 6
Like Dross	Jun 14		
Like Our King	Nov 12	Real Reasons for Comfort	Jul 15
Lions of Judgment	Oct 7	Receiving and Giving What Isn't Deserved	Dec 18
Listen to Me	Aug 14	Receiving Wisdom from God	Jun 4
Living In the Freedom	Jan 18	Redeemed and Adopted	Oct 9
Look to Me	Mar 1	Relenting, Repenting, and Contradictions	Sep 8
Looking Inward	Nov 3	Remain in Ephesus	Sep 30
Looking Outward	Oct 6	Remembering and Forgetting	Nov 10
Looking Upward	Jul 11	Repented - and Still Repenting	Feb 28
Make a Smooth Road for the LORD	Dec 17	Resisting and Receiving	Feb 27
Make Your Confession	Feb 23	Right In All Things	May 16
Miraculous Power, Miraculous Love	Nov 30	Rise and Shine	Mar 20
Mocked, Yet Comforted	Oct 3	Running the Red Lights	Oct 19
Moses' Kind of Prayer	Jul 14	Say What You Mean, Mean What You Say	Feb 13
		Seasoned With Salt	Apr 12

Seeing God's Good When It Looks Bad	May 18	The Kind of Prayer God Hears	Jan 28
Seeing Him & Being Like Him	Nov 27	The Know-It-All	Nov 2
Set Free for a Purpose	Jul 4	The Law That Brings Liberty	Jul 3
Setting the Right Track	Feb 22	The Letter That Didn't Want to Be Written	Oct 30
Settled In Heaven	Apr 8	The Light-Giving Word	Jul 10
Shining Out That All Can See	Dec 28	The Main Message	Apr 6
Showers of Blessing	May 11	The Man Who Walked with God	Aug 21
Sighs From the Christ	Sep 22	The Meekness of Wisdom	Oct 24
Sinning Without Shame	Feb 21	The Model Prayer	Apr 25
So Blind	Aug 29	The Need to Forgive	May 10
Stand	Jan 31	The Patience of a Farmer	Sep 10
Still Chosen	Apr 11	The Perfect Work of Patience	May 8
Stopping Flaming Arrows	Feb 7	The Prophet's Call	Oct 8
Strangely, Not Far Enough	Nov 8	The Real God or the God We Make?	Sep 25
Strong in the Lord	Jun 28	The Real Jesus	Mar 30
Stronger and Stronger	Sep 18	The Reasons for Judgment	Jan 15
Sustained by His Word	Feb 8	The Right Foundation	Feb 16
Take Him As He Was	Jul 19	The Right Kind of Wisdom	Sep 17
Taking Care of First Things First	Jan 5	The Sacrifice That Pleases God	Jan 8
Taking Heed	Feb 17	The Sin and the Heart Behind the Sin	Sep 28
Terms of the Contract	Apr 1	The Source of Strength	Feb 9
The Answer of Faith to the Advice of Fear	May 19	The Spirit and the Word	Jul 20
The Breaker	Nov 28	The Story of the Vineyard	Oct 17
The Character of Heavenly Wisdom	Jun 16	The Successful Failure	Jun 29
The Choice Between Two Masters	Jan 7	The Throne in Heaven	Oct 27
		The Ultimate Shepherd	Sep 12
The Choice Between Two Treasures	Dec 16	The Unappreciated Virtue	Jun 7
The Choice Between Two Visions	Dec 15	The Very Pure Word	Aug 6
		The Way of Cain	Sep 19
The Decision Between Two Builders and Two Destinies	Jun 20	The Wrong Way to Pray	Jun 6
		Themes for a New Year	Jan 1
The Doctor Is In	Jun 12	They Feared the LORD, Yet…	Dec 13
The Effect of His Message	Sep 4	They Will Not Find Him	Apr 10
The Foolish Wise Man	Sep 5	Think About Your Ways	Feb 24
The Gates of Hell	May 21	This Might of Yours	Apr 24
The Gift of Friendship	Nov 5	This Same Jesus	Jul 7
The Glorious Branch	Dec 1	Three Signs	Jul 21
The God of All Comfort	Dec 7	Time to Wake Up	Dec 3
The God Who Created It All	Sep 26	Total Winners	Jun 15
The Greatest Motivation for Purity	Aug 13	Training to Trust	Oct 20
		Tried and Proven	Mar 18
The Greatest of These Is Love	Oct 28	Truth and Godliness, In One Accord	Jul 27
The Highway of Holiness	Jan 25	Two Kinds of Power	Sep 11
		Two Ways to Repent	Mar 14

Understanding the Creator	Aug 8	You Can't Save Yourself	Jan 29
Undone	Nov 1	You Have an Anointing	Oct 29
Unintentional Danger	Feb 6	Your Cross to Bear	Apr 21
		Your Life Is More	Dec 26

Waiting for a Promise	Jun 13
Wandering and Returning	Dec 4
We Packed and Went	Aug 2
What Comes from God	Jun 30
What God Wants	Apr 16
What He Heard in Heaven	Apr 18
What Is It?	Nov 16
What Makes God Laugh	Dec 11
What No Man Can Do	Oct 23
What the Baby Would Become	Dec 25
What the World Needs Now	Dec 29
What to Live By	Jun 27
What to Put On	Jun 1
What to Tear	Sep 23
What We Are, What We Do	Jun 18
What We Say and Who We Are	Apr 19
What You Say	Jul 26
What's the Use?	Apr 22
When a Rite Is Wrong	Jul 30
When Enough Is Enough	Oct 31
When God Stops Speaking	Sep 16
When I See the Blood	Mar 28
When It is Wrong to Pray	Oct 4
When One Name Isn't Enough	Dec 22
When the Music Stops	Aug 20
When You Need a Good Lawyer	Mar 11
Where Christmas Began	Dec 20
Where Faith Comes From	Mar 5
Where to Live	Jan 21
Which Side Are You On?	May 28
Who Are You Calling a Liar?	Apr 20
Who Can Stand Before the Holy God?	Mar 9
Why God Allowed Evil	Aug 9
Why Jesus Came	Dec 19
Why To Not Worry	Jun 23
Why We Love Jesus	Jul 22
Why We Need God to Speak	Aug 15
Wings in the Right Places	Nov 22
Witnesses to the Resurrection	Apr 4
Wondrous Things	Apr 30
Words of a Worshipper	Nov 26
Worse Before Better	Feb 3
Worthless Things	Sep 15

In 1996, when most people still didn't have email, I started sending a weekly devotional that I named "Inspiration by EMail." I'm still doing that today, and at the suggestion and great help of Ruth Gordon, 365 of those devotionals have been compiled, prepared, and here published. Ruth, I'm so grateful for all your heart, help, and hard work on this project.

One person in paticular has walked with me before, through, and after those 25 years: my wife Inga-Lill, who is my loved and valued partner in life and in service to God and His people. Without that loving partnership, none of this would be possible. Inga-Lill, thank you so much!

If you are interested in any of my other books or Bible resources, you can find them at **enduringword.com**

David Guzik

David Guzik is the author of the widely trusted and popular Enduring Word Bible Commentary, a verse-by-verse study through the entire Bible used by everyday Christians and pastors, preachers, and Bible teachers. This commentary is available at no cost at the website **enduringword.com** and the Blue Letter Bible (blb.org).

David lives in Santa Barbara with Inga-Lill, his wife of 38 years. They have three adult children and two grandchildren.

You can email David at david@enduringword.com

For more resources by David Guzik, go to **enduringword.com** or visit the Enduring Word YouTube channel.

www.ingramcontent.com/pod-product-compliance
Lightning Source LLC
LaVergne TN
LVHW041206250326
834689LV00016BA/150/J